AVIATION LAW

AN INTRODUCTION

V. FOSTER ROLLO, C.F.I., B.A., M.A.

University of Maryland

1979

MARYLAND HISTORICAL PRESS

9205 Tuckerman Street., Lanham, Maryland 20801

Library of Congress Catalog Card No. 79-64803

ISBN 0-917882-08-3.

Maryland Historical Press
9205 Tuckerman Street
Lanham, Maryland 20801

Printed in the United States of America

To Sally, Mike and Cathy

Illustration courtesy Lockheed-California (a division of Lockheed Corporation).

An artist's conception of a RECAT (Reduced Energy Commercial Air Transport). A recently completed study by Lockheed-California, funded by NASA, shows that such a plane would burn about 17 percent less fuel than comparable aircraft. The design features advanced turboprop engines and unique, eight-bladed propellers.

CONTENTS

PART IV STATE REGULATION

PART V U.S. LAW AS APPLIED TO THE COMPONENTS OF AVIATION

PART VI INTERNATIONAL AVIATION LAW

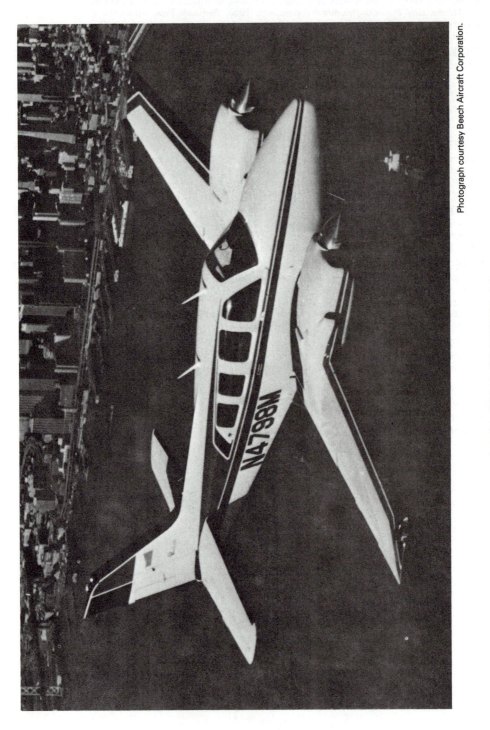

Beechcraft Baron (1979) 58P Model.

PREFACE

Aviation law is still so new, and those involved in it so occupied with day-to-day case loads, teaching, and administrative work, no text has yet been written to give an introductory overview of its many aspects. There are excellent casebooks and treatments of certain parts of aviation law but no one volume has been written up to now to introduce the subject.

In air law there is a need for specialized information from two highly complex disciplines — law and aviation. It is important that we understand the essentials of each of these in order to work in aviation management, teaching, air transport, training, executive decisions related to air transportation, personal use of aircraft and even personal travel by air.

The writer while teaching aviation management and law at the college level perceived a need for this book. Having a background in both aviation and law, degrees in history and sociology, and experience in aviation writing, the writer began work on this survey of aviation law. The reader's comments will be welcome in order that future editions may be even more helpful and up-to-date.

It is hoped that the student of aviation, law, or transportation, will find this book an important aid in understanding today's air law. In helping attorneys and airmen in explaining "what everyone knows," the book should also be valuable.

Please see the bibliography for detailed information on particular subjects and to locate sources of specific case law. Detailed treatments of all the subjects mentioned and legal cases related to them do not fall within the scope of this volume. This book should not be used as a legal advisor. For specific situations seek the advice of an attorney since many general statements are made and many exceptions exist.

The writer has found from classroom experience that documents placed in Appendix sections are often overlooked by students, therefore, extensive quotations from regulations, statements, and other documents have been inserted into the text of *Aviation Law: An Introduction.*

The laws of aviation are based on an ancient legal system yet, of course, much that is new has been added. Legal systems to be viable must be flexible. The legal systems of the United States and of the world are flexing to meet the new demands imposed upon them by the facts of flight. There is, in both aviation and in space flight, the need to acknowledge that the requirements for human rights, national security, and ecological safety must be met in an equitable manner.

You will find this text a history of the development of aviation law as well as a statement of its present status. This book is designed to introduce students, and administrators concerned with aviation, to the special considerations of air law. It is intended, as well, to assist those actively engaged in aviation to understand that there is more to aviation law than the Federal Air Regulations. Users of air transport will find the book helpful in learning how aviation can assist them in both their business and personal transport needs. Those persons interested in space technology, too, will find the book useful in the background it offers upon which space law is being formulated.

While accepting full responsibility for the use of the information and advice given to the writer, thanks are due to the many persons who offered kind assistance. Appreciation is tendered to the director of the information office of the National Transportation Safety Board, "Ed" Slattery; to the knowledgeable and helpful Jean Ross Howard of the Aerospace Industries Association; and to attorney Ronald S. Goldberg and his staff of Silver Spring, Maryland.

Thanks are due to the directors of state aviation commissions in the 50 states and Puerto Rico for filling out questionnaires and for answering questions about state law. The Aircraft

Owners and Pilots Association generously assisted the writer with particular thanks tendered attorneys John S. Yodice and Alfred L. Wolf. For essential information on general aviation the writer expresses thanks to the General Aviation Manufacturer's Association. Thanks, too, to Braniff International, British Airways, Air France and the British Aircraft Corporation for information relating to supersonic transport aircraft. On the subject of supersonic aircraft history, design, and possible future SST developments, National Aeronautics and Space Administration personnel offered valuable data and explanations.

The writer expresses appreciation to the many persons who gave expert and timely data and background material. With gratitude the author remembers those persons reviewing completed chapters to screen out out-of-date matter and to assess the correct expression of information. Agency policy in most cases does not permit the mention of these persons by name. The writer therefore here expresses sincere appreciation for assistance rendered by various government agencies. The Federal Aviation Administration bore the brunt of the author's search for data and factual checking with courtesy and patience. Invaluable assistance was received relating to material on FAA history; airports; airmen; flight theory; international treaties; aircraft regulation; and aviation law in general. Particular thanks are due to the attorneys of the FAA office of the General Counsel and FAA's information specialists in the FAA office of information. At FAA's Washington headquarters and at several General Aviation District Offices the writer met with unfailing courtesy and able assistance.

The Civil Aeronautics Board also was given many opportunities to exhibit great forbearance and to render assistance as the writer delved into CAB history, air carrier deregulation, and other recent and important events. To the office of information at CAB and persons from various CAB divisions who gave information and reviewed manuscript sections, thanks are definitely due. Again, the responsibility for the way the information and advice was used is completely assumed by the author.

The National Weather Service and the National Oceanic and Atmospheric Administration were most helpful. In particular NOAA's office of Scientific and Academic Affairs was generous with data and guidance relating to the subject of weather modification.

The U.S. Department of State, Aviation Division, rendered assistance in the field of international negotiations relating to world air commerce. The attorneys of the Department of State explained many factors relating to international aviation as did FAA's expert on international treaties.

To all of the above persons who most generously contributed material and encouragement, the writer's thanks and recognition of our mutual fascination with aviation.

Finally, appreciation is expressed to copy editor Mrs. Irene House and to GRAPHICA's director, Mrs. Sue Isaacs and her valiant staff, and to Mrs. Gayle Suddith, expert typist.

We in aviation have ever more to do as aerospace technology grows and changes, yet today the development of a very practical air and space law is quite remarkably far along, as demonstrated in the pages of this text.

V. Foster Rollo
Lanham, 1979

ABBREVIATIONS

A&P	Airplane and Powerplant Mechanic
ACs	Advisory Circular (FAA)
ADs	Airworthiness Directives (FAA)
ADAP	Airport Development Aid Program
ADIZ	Air Defense Identification Zone
AIA	Aerospace Industries Association
AOPA	Aircraft Owners and Pilots Association
ASRS	Aviation Safety Reporting System
AST	Advanced Supersonic Transport
ATA	Air Transport Association of America
ATC	Air Traffic Control
ATP	Airline Transport Pilot
BAC	British Airways Corporation
CAA	Civil Aeronautics Authority
	Civil Aeronautics Administration
CAB	Civil Aeronautics Board
CAP	Civil Air Patrol
CIDPA	Conference Internationales de Droit Prive Aeriens
CITEJA	Comite International Technique d'Experts Juridiques Aeriens
CRAF	Civil Reserve Air Fleet
DHSA	Death on High Seas Act
DOT	Department of Transportation
ELT	Emergency Locator Transmitter
EPA	Environmental Protection Agency
ETA	Estimated Time of Arrival
FAA	Federal Aviation Agency
	Federal Aviation Administration
FAR	Federal Aviation Regulation
FBO	Fixed Base Operator
FCC	Federal Communications Commission
FDR	President Franklin D. Roosevelt
GAMA	General Aviation Manufacturers Association
GPO	Government Printing Office
IATA	International Air Transport Association
ICAO	International Civil Aviation Organization
ICC	Interstate Commerce Commission
IFALPA	International Federation of Airline Pilots
ILS	Instrument Landing System
MLS	Microwave Landing System

NACA	National Advisory Committee for Aeronautics
NASA	National Aeronautics and Space Administration
NMB	National Mediation Board
NOAA	National Oceanic and Atmospheric Administration
NOTAMS	Notices to Airmen
NWRMB	National Weather Resources Management Board
OEA	Office of Economic Analysis
PGP	Planning Grant Program
PICAO	Provisional International Civil Aviation Organization
RPM	Revenue Passenger Miles
SCAR	Supersonic Cruise Aircraft Research
SCAT	Supersonic Commercial Air Transport
SST	Supersonic Transport
STOL	Short Takeoff and Landing
TIAS	Treaties and Other International Acts Series issued singly in pamphlets by the Department of State
UATP	Universal Air Travel Plan
UNICOM	Uniform Communication System
UNTS	United Nations Treaty Series
UST	United States Treaties and Other International Agreements (volumes published on a calendar-year basis by Department of State beginning as of 1 January 1950)
VCE	Variable-cycle Engine
VFR	Visual Flight Rules
WMAB	Weather Modification Advisory Board

PART I

THIS IS AVIATION

CHAPTER 1

THE PHYSICAL FACTS OF FLIGHT

Perhaps the most difficult set of ideas for persons who must cope with aviation cases yet do not have flight training is that there are unusual things that *can* be done by aircraft and space vehicles, but on the other hand, these machines have limitations, things that they cannot do. Also, even pilots find explanations to nonpilots a task requiring patience and thought.

Air law has evolved from basic legal systems to accommodate the needs of both the groundling, the air traveler, and aircraft operators.

An aircraft can make its way, sans road, sans river, through the air. It can climb thousands of feet, vault mountain ranges and oceans. Its speed is unbelievable when compared with past forms of transport. Planes, even small ones, normally operate at over one hundred miles per hour. Transport aircraft operate in a range from about two hundred up to six hundred miles per hour. Supersonic transports and supersonic military aircraft are blazing across our world at over Mach 3, i.e. over two thousand miles per hour!! Such power and such scope were never ours before this century. These are the amazing "can dos."

Yet—we must consider the limits of aircraft. Why, for example, must a plane be allowed to fly so low over homes and businesses in order to land reasonably close to the metropolitan area it serves? Because "flying speed" needs a certain length of runway to be dissipated. A plane that normally cruises at just below the speed of sound, around six hundred miles per hour, needs a certain amount of speed to stay in the air during its landing approach. It can slow down to about one hundred forty miles per hour without losing the lift needed to sustain it in the air. This depends on the kind of aircraft and its weight. Even this reduced speed is a fast one and requires quite a long runway to be dissipated and let the vehicle come to a safe and comfortable stop. Wing flaps help slow the plane, as do engines that can reverse their thrust to become a braking component. Brakes, curiously enough, help only a little toward the end of the roll out. The pilot plans his approach, coming in as low and as slowly as possible up to the runway; hence, the need to approach the airport at a low level.

Landing is, however, not the largest problem in bringing aircraft in and out of a populated area.

Takeoffs

The takeoff is an even greater problem—requiring more runway length than did the landing—for a safe and assured takeoff run and a reasonably fast (flat, low-grade, low-angle) climb away from the airport.

Just when the plane leaves the ground it needs all its power to maintain a safe flying speed (required, remember, to keep the plane flying). Here, to avoid annoyance due to sound levels, pilots are asked to reduce the engine power and to climb at a steep angle. To be done safely, both actions need careful flying. Further, some noise abatement programs also ask that a turn away from populated areas be made. A plane in a turn has less lift, so again the pilot must take extra care that this does not place his aircraft in an unsafe attitude. His is not an easy task.

If persons without flight training knew of his problems, they would find it easier to understand that he (or she) is not stubbornly sticking to old flying precepts but is simply trying to work within the limitations of his (or her) machine and to fly safely. Steep takeoff angles, power reductions and turns near the ground can be hazardous.

Via a series of compromises, both the reduction of noise and the safety of flight are being achieved today. Flight patterns favor riverways, areas of low population density, and over-water approaches whenever possible. Pilots do reduce thrust as soon as safety allows after takeoff and turn gently away from built-up locations. They try to approach, and leave, the airport at the steepest feasible angles to reduce noise reaching citizens on the ground.

Lift

To understand our statements about "lift" and the need for speed let us examine the aircraft design.

As most of us know, most aircraft cannot stop, pull over to the side of the road, or even slow down very much safely. To stay up, an aircraft needs enough air flowing over its wings to drop the air pressure there. The plane is supported by this "lift." It exists at a speed called "flying speed" attained on takeoff and, happily, maintained throughout the aircraft's takeoff, climb, cruise, descent and approach to land.

In the air, speed is safety. Likewise, height or altitude is safety. Both statements given here are contrary to personal safety at ground level.

2

Approaches and Stalls

To land the plane the pilot approaches the airport at the lowest possible speed which still allows the plane to fly. Also, this approach speed includes a few extra miles per hour to allow for momentary pilot inattention, gusts, and to give the pilot some extra maneuvering speed on approach should he need to "go around" and not land. Approaching the surface of the runway, the pilot flares the flight path, nosing the plane up to dissipate more speed. At this point the plane's wings are nearing their "stall speed." That is, the speed which is so slow that now the smoothly rushing air over the top surface no longer has a lower pressure than that on the lower wing surface — the lift decreases, the air burbles and the plane has stalled — but by now is firmly on the ground. Obviously then, at no other time in the flight would a plane be flown too near, or at, the stalling speed of that aircraft. No flying speed, no lift!

The "stall" concerns the wings of the plane and does not indicate stalling engines, as non-pilots may assume. When a plane stalls, the engines can be inoperative, idling, at cruise power, or at maximum power. It is the wing that "stalls out."

Landing Surface Needs

Planes need a long enough runway to lose this approach and landing speed. The larger and heavier planes need longer runways than light aircraft.

"Light aircraft", by the way, designates those planes weighing less than 12,500 pounds.

Planes *can* use sod, roads, or firm sand to land upon, but a reasonably smooth surface is necessary to prevent snubbing the gear with the subsequent noseover if the speed is still considerable. The larger the plane, the more it needs a long, smooth, and strong surface. The jumbo jets need very strong runways, for example. This is discussed in the chapter on airports.

Flight without Power?

Can a plane fly without power from its engines? Yes, to the extent that its pilot can trade his height above the ground for forward speed, flying speed. All planes have gliding capacity — light planes can trade off one foot of height for eight to ten feet of forward travel. Transport aircraft, much heavier and having less wing area per pound of weight, still can glide. Emergency landings have been made without power. Aircraft manufacturers, maintenance crews and pilots are making this power loss even a more distant possibility.

Total power failure is much less of a possibility today than in the early days of flight. One can fly for years without power failure.

Lift Factors

If the lift of the aircraft were affected only by the indicated speed of the plane, flying would be a simpler art. As it is, the pilot must consider several other factors. A certain mass of air must cross the wing to provide lift. Pilots know that cold air has greater mass or density than warm air. Humid air is less dense than dry air. High altitude air is less dense. (At sea level the air pressure is greatest.)

This boils down to careful calculation required of the aircraft commander regarding airport elevation, temperature, and other weather factors.

Load

Further complicating a pilot's task of taking the plane into the air is his load. A heavily loaded airplane will need a longer takeoff run and will climb at a slower rate. A pilot may even have to unload fuel to accommodate a full load if combined with high temperatures and/or a high airport elevation.

These same factors, incidentally, affect the plane upon landing. A higher approach speed and longer landing roll result when a plane lands with a heavy load, in high temperatures, and/or at a high elevation.

Nor can the plane carry its load just anywhere. Carefully the crew plots the load placed in a plane to maintain its center of gravity (CG) limits. A plane, to handle well and resist nose-up flight configurations which might contribute to a stalled condition, must carry its load inside certain limits. Foot pounds and arm moments are figured before a transport aircraft leaves the ramp. Where are passengers seated, what fuel tanks are filled, and where are mail, freight and baggage placed? All are load considerations.

The pilot in command often has an exacting question to work out. Shall he take off low on fuel and high on safety on a hot day and then face possible

4

fuel shortages later in his flight?

Load can be imposed, too, in quite another way, by certain maneuvers of the aircraft. Centrifugal force comes into play when a plane is diverted from its path — in a turn, in a pull up, or in a push over maneuver. The more quickly the maneuver is made, the more load is imposed on the aircraft. A steep turn, in a 60° banked configuration, doubles the weight of the plane and its contents. Stall speed naturally is then higher, for a heavily loaded wing stalls out sooner (at a higher-than-normal stall speed). Hence, transport aircraft generally limit such maneuvers for this reason and for passenger comfort.

Airplanes are very strong, however, and can take many times their own weight, or one force of gravity (one G), safely. They need this safety margin in order to fly through storms and turbulence.

Steep turns or abrupt pullups are not desirable when a plane is near the ground at a fairly low speed. Approaches to land and takeoff climbs have the greatest safety factor when the wings are level or only gently banked. Pilots are well aware of these factors.

Finally, a load can be placed on the plane if it passes through moisture at near-freezing temperatures and ice builds up on the structure. Deicing and anti-icing (preventative) devices are generally effective, yet pilots penetrate icing levels warily and avoid them whenever possible. Just the extra weight of the ice is not the only problem. There is also the loss of lift due to disruption of air flow over lifting surfaces.

Weather

Well trained pilots take off for cross country flights only after calling one of many convenient aviation weather stations. Radio calls enroute are possible. Pilots, too, continually re-evaluate weather changes as they proceed along their planned route. This is a legal responsibility of all pilots.

The non-pilot may not understand the weather factors involved in air travel. For example, winds aloft can speed or slow the plane's ground speed (speed made good over the ground). Winds can affect the navigation of the plane and must be plotted.

Gusty winds and turbulence may affect an approach and landing pattern. Higher than normal approach speeds will be required to avoid a possible stall.

Each airplane has what is known as a "crosswind limit". Design limits of landing gear strength and, even more to the point, control limits may cause a landing or takeoff to be cancelled. True, today's light aircraft with their sturdy tricycle gear can generally take up to a 20 mile-per-hour crosswind if necessary; past that point pilot's discression prevails. Transport aircraft can take quite severe crosswinds on takeoff and landing, but even these planes do have crosswind limits.

If runway surfaces are wet or icy or coated with light sand, the pilot must consider the consequent loss of traction. Aircraft tend to "weathercock" and swing nose into the wind — this could affect steering if crosswind limits are ignored.

Winds burble and tumble over obstructions, hence a knowledge of local conditions is helpful on windy days.

Manufacturers are aware of their legal responsibilities in building a federally set safety factor of strength into aircraft. Turbulence due to thermals, storm conditions, gusty winds can cause loads to be imposed upon aircraft. Adequate extra strength is built into all United States aircraft.

Airlines must consider also, to avoid passenger suits, all sorts of turbulence with respect to safety. The pilot and crew must try to anticipate the need for seat belts, for example.

One of the most difficult concepts for a non-pilot to grasp is the fact that a pilot cannot fly safely, or even remain level, without seeing either the horizon, the ground or his flight instruments. The reasons are complex to describe. Suffice it to say — one cannot hold a plane level long sans instruments or outside references or, of course, automatic pilot use.

While holding his plane level, on course, and at a designated altitude, the pilot further must navigate the aircraft and maintain set contact with FAA radio services. This takes, as might very well be expected, special training.

Instrument Flying

Any licensed pilot may be trained for instrument flying, pass written and flight checks, and then be awarded an Instrument Rating. All commercial pilots, flight instructors and of course airline transport pilots hold instrument ratings.

Pilots who do not hold instrument ratings are student pilots, most private pilots and some holders of commercial pilot ratings obtained when Instrument ratings were not required (due to a grandfather clause written into the Federal

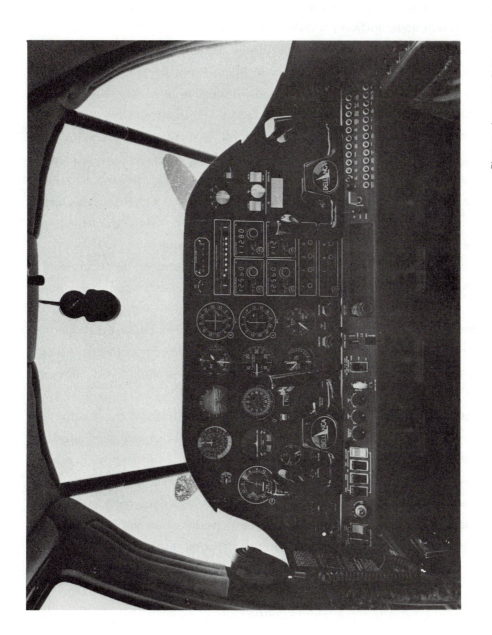

The instrument panel of a single engine Bellanca.

Aviation Regulations (FARs) when the instrument rating requirement was added. The point being that, quite legally, not all pilots hold instrument flying ratings. Most pilots do have enough training, however, to control their planes to some extent under instrument flying conditions.

Instrument flying conditions are specifically defined in the Federal Aviation Regulation (FARs). In general, Instrument Flight Rules (IFR) conditions indicate very low cloud ceilings and very poor forward visiblity. The more skilled and well-trained the pilot and the more efficient his instruments and radio equipment, the lower the weather "minimums" that pilot can use. Even the airlines, however, require some visibility and ceiling space in order that the pilot approaching to land, can see the runway, check his descent, and land. Military planes have a "zero-zero" (zero ceiling, zero visibility) capability and airlines are approaching it. There are still days, however, when heavy fog precludes a "legal" landing with the exception of certain emergencies.

Zero-zero landings are not accepted civil aircraft practice today. Instrument takeoffs, of flights with destinations at which better weather conditions prevail, are thought to be a little more acceptable.

Although planes cannot stop in the air to await good landing conditions, they can "hold" at an assigned altitude, flying a circling pattern which keeps them in a designated area. Planes can thus be "stacked" near airports and allowed into the airport approach path one by one.

Pilots have the option to, or not to, file IFR flight plans if the weather is above certain minimums. Therefore, when the weather is marginal, light aircraft and transport planes tend to mill about under low clouds in an attempt to avoid the delays possible in being held in a stack on IFR, controlled, flight.

Planes on Visual Flight Rules (VFR) flights simply call approach and tower controllers and enter the airport traffic pattern, avoiding one another by visual reference. The area radar controllers can upon request, assist the VFR aircraft as well as those being flown under an IFR flight plan.

Navigation

Suffice it to say here, that planes are generally navigated via a combination of visual observation, compass headings and radio aids. Aircraft can, of course, be navigated solely by instruments and radio.

Night Flight

Night flying away from lighted areas on a dark, overcast night is in effect an instrument flight. Without ground reference, it is essential that pilots have instrument training in order to complete the flight without incident.

Propeller Hazards

Lethal is the word for propeller accidents. Even the smallest of aircraft engines and even a propeller made of wood can carve off an arm, slice down through a body, at idling speeds! A set of rules and cautions exist to reduce propeller incidents. Pilot responsibility is great.

Runaway light aircraft are not as uncommon as one could wish. Starting an engine by "propping" it (pulling the propeller briskly down) is not considered good practice if no competent operator is at the controls inside the plane.

Aircraft can move forward and slash the person propping the engine and/or other persons, planes or other obstacles in its path. It can even run straight ahead, achieve takeoff speed, and fly away. The pistons suck air through the carburetor throat; this tends to open up the throttle valve located there. The higher the revolutions per minute (rpm), the more the throttle is pulled open until it is wide open. This might be prevented by operation of the throttle lock inside the plane. Propeller accidents offer great potential for suits to be filed against pilots and/or operators.

Over-Water, Arctic

Over-water and Arctic flying, too, have certain periods in which a pilot must fly with reference to instruments.

Engines

Briefly let us note that a reciprocating engine performs best when it has cool, dry, dense air to use. A cool, dry day at sea level will give maximum engine performance.

Engine icing is a factor of many aircraft engines in which ice forms inside the throat of the carburetor and cuts down, or off, the air supply to the engine.

Carburetor air screens, too, can ice over when flying in icing conditions. The cure for both problems is to use the carburetor heater early and to seek a flight level less conducive to icing if possible.

Manufacturers of aircraft engines have tremendous responsibilities. They seek great reliability in a device which must operate at great temperature extremes, varying flight levels, under conditions of continued vibration and turbulence, and under extremes in humidity. Their achievements have resulted in the fact that most aircraft in the world use American-built engines.

Pilot Factors

We have seen that pilots have an ascending scale of certificates with more training and experience needed for each. These are: student, private pilot, commercial pilot, airline transport pilot. From the private pilot certificate up, one can add instrument ratings and civilian flight instructor ratings.

Research has shown a correlation between prolonged anxiety and impaired judgment. Long stress reduces pilot ability, varying with individuals.

A similar loss of ability is noted with over exposure to altitudes over ten thousand feet. Lack of oxygen impairs pilot performance.

Vertigo is occasioned by sudden moves of the head after long concentration on instruments, or sometimes by the sweep of the plane's rotating beacon on cloud surfaces.

Smoking decreases tolerance of altitude. Antihistamines and altitude, also, do not mix well. Alcohol use, of course, is never indicated for safe flight.

Finally, research has shown that pilots flying persons who have been scuba diving or deep sea diving must keep to low flight levels or high cabin pressures. A better course would be to delay air transport of such persons for twenty-four hours after dives to prevent "the bends."

Summary

The above factors regarding aircraft and pilots have been discussed because these are some of the items peculiar to aviation which are often not understood by non-flying persons. This discussion may aid you, as a flyer, to realize what laymen may not understand. We hope this chapter will assist you in explaining aviation to non-air minded clients.[1]

NOTES

[1] In his book, *Cleared for the Approach*, attorney-pilot-manufacturer F. Lee Bailey gives many explanations of aviation that will assist the non-pilot to understand our air traffic control system and the manufacture and operation of the aircraft we use today. (Published by Prentice-Hall, Inc., Englewood Cliffs, N.J., 1977.)

Photograph courtesy Piper Aircraft Corporation.

Flight over water being made by a 1979 Piper Seminole.

CHAPTER 2

AN AVIATION/LEGAL CHRONOLOGY

The following chronology is a sketch, a brief time line list, of the development of aviation and aviation law. The author regrets the omission of many important and fascinating items for lack of space. The listing will serve to suggest in an orderly way how aviation has grown and how legislation and international treaties have responded to the need for national and world cooperation.

When we look back over the past century, we see that the speed of personal travel, business (freight), and war transport has moved from about five miles per hour to over two thousand miles per hour! Prior to the nineteenth century, using horses and ships, people seldom moved over fifteen to twenty-five miles per hour. The last 150 years have witnessed an astonishing transition in transport.

The following chronology of aviation reveals the progress of aircraft design and flying techniques. It shows the increase in use of aviation. With each step aviation law evolved as well. Existing legal systems provided a basis upon which aviation cases were drafted. The results were sometimes rather bizarre; yet over-all, laws in the United States and around the world are workable and ingenious.

Pre-1600s	Legends, speculations based on observing the flight of birds.
1670	Beginning of practical theorizing. Italy.
1783	Balloon flight began. Montgolfier brothers (France).
1800-1900	Some of the many experimenters attempting to fly heavier-than-air devices are listed below:
1804-1808	Sir George Cayley (England) attempted to fly gliders.
1840s	William Henson (England) attempted to fly gliders.
1848	John Stringfellow (England) flew a steam-powered model plane.
1865	Louis Pierre Mouillard (French Algeria) successfully flew a glider; wrote *The Empire of the Air.*
1880s-1911	John J. Montgomery (U.S.) and his brother James successfully flew gliders. John Montgomery died in a glider crash 31 October 1911.

1890s	Otto Lilienthal (Germany) built and flew a dozen or more gliders. After more than 2,000 successful flights, he was fatally injured in a glider crash 9 August 1896.

In this time period other glider pioneers, among them Percy Pilcher (England) and Octave Chanute (U.S.), also flew. Their major problems were control and lack of knowledge of flying techniques. Powered flight was delayed by the lack of a light weight engine. |
1899	First Hague Peace Conference prohibited the discharge of projectiles from balloons.
1902-11	Institute of International Air Law discussed air law governing international aeronautical commerce. Institute held that air space was free to all but that nations in or over which flights were made had the right to set such rules as were needed for national security.
1903	Professor Samuel P. Langley of the Smithsonian Institution, after working with Charles Manly on successfully flown powered model aircraft, made two attempts to fly a full-sized piloted machine. Very near success, he was forced to cease experimentation due to lack of funds.
17 December 1903	The Wright brothers, Wilbur and Orville, made the first piloted, powered flight of a heavier-than-air aircraft at Kitty Hawk, N.C. The Wrights studied, improved on flight theory available, built a successful light-weight engine, designed propellers, a control system and an aircraft. They taught themselves to fly and flew.[1]
1907	Second Hague Peace Conference again as in the First Hague Conference 1899 prohibited discharge of projectiles from balloons.
1908	Glenn L. Martin built his first Curtiss-type airplane and taught himself to fly it.
1911	First transcontinental flight made by Calbraith P. Rodgers.
1912	Lawrence Sperry founded Sperry Gyroscope Co. He invented and developed the first automatic pilot and made flight instruments.
1913	Igor Sikorsky, who later designed helicopters in the U.S., built and flew a four-engined aircraft in Russia.
1915	The National Advisory Committee for Aeronautics (NACA) was established by an act of Congress to guide the scientific study of the problems of flight.

NACA became a part of the National Aeronautics and Space Administration (NASA) in 1958.

1916   The Pan American Aeronautics Federation, at Santiago, Chile, noted that aircraft have nationalities and should be prominently marked to show this.

15 May   Air mail flight inaugurated between New York and
1918   Washington, D.C. using War Department planes and pilots.

12 August   Post Office Department took over the air mail service
1918   with its own planes and pilots.

World War I Impetus given to development of aircraft and equip-
1914-18   ment. Aviation came out of World War I much im-
(U.S. entry, proved but as yet unable to cope very well with night
6 April 1917) flying, instrument flight or icing conditions.[2]

1919   Versailles meeting near Paris of the International Convention for Air Navigation, the "Paris Convention" gave nations complete sovereignty over their airspace. The right of innocent passage was granted if certain conditions met.

1919-39   International Air Traffic Association originated at the Hague, and operated to help promote international aviation and to resolve technical difficulties.

1920   Death on the High Seas Act passed by Congress of the United States to allow suits to be filed for losses of life or goods. Originally intended for sea losses but came to apply to aircraft after planes began to fly over the high seas.

8 September Transcontinental airmail service began. (New York
1920   City to San Francisco). Used trains for night movement of mail.

1921   General William (Billy) Mitchell successfully demonstrated aerial bombing of a warship.

1 July 1924 Night and day transcontinental mail service began.

1925   The Air Mail Act gave the Post Office right to contract with air carriers for airmail service. Aided development of United States airlines.

1925   Curtiss (P-1) "Hawk" pursuit plane was delivered to the U.S. Army. Maximum speed: 163 miles per hour; 435 horsepower engine. Biplane.

1926   Airlines begin to carry mail on a number of routes under Post Office contracts.

1926	First Ford-Stout Trimotor transport went into airline service.
1926	Boeing XP-4 experimental pursuit plane was delivered to United States Army. Maximum speed: 168 miles per hour with one 510 horsepower engine. Biplane.
1926	United States Congress enacted Air Commerce Act. It instructed Secretary of Commerce to foster aviation in United States, establish airways, and operate navigational aids. (But not airports). Secretary of Commerce created a bureau titled the Civil Aeronautics Branch.
1927	Post Office ceases its airmail flying, all routes now served by United States air carriers.
1927	Pilot License No. 1 issued to William P. McCracken, Jr.
1927	May 20/21 — Lindberg flew Atlantic solo.
1927	Pan American Airways began operation.
1927	Improved Ford Trimotor, designed by William Stout and to be manufactured by Henry Ford, was built. Some of these planes are still in service in Alaska, the United States of America, and South America. Cruising speed was, and is, about 80 miles per hour.
1928-31	"Havana Conference," the Pan American Convention on Commercial Aviation, noted sovereignty of nations and gave agreement to theory of the right of innocent passage. However, states (nations) could refuse to recognize airworthiness certificates of whatever nations they wished. This in effect reserved the right to disallow flights into the nation which refuses recognition. The Treaty included a cabotage agreement. (Cabotage is the right of a state to allow only its own airline or other mode of transport to operate inside its boundaries if it so desires.) The "Havana Conference" regulated international flights in the Americas up to 1944. (No longer in effect).
1929	"Warsaw Convention" set forth a uniform code of rules regarding passenger and goods loss liability recognized by airlines.
1930	Airmail Act of 1930 created fewer, but stronger, airline companies with new ways of awarding airmail contracts.

1930	Boeing model 221 passenger-cargo plane in use. Low-wing airliner with retractable landing gear, a metal skin.
1932	Amelia Earhart became first woman to fly Atlantic solo.
1933	"Rome Convention" established further areas of international agreement pertaining to liabilities for damages caused by aircraft to third parties on the surface.
1933	Consolidated Aircraft Corp. low-wing pursuit plane delivered to United States Army. Maximum speed: 247 miles per hour; one 600 horsepower engine.
1934	Department of Commerce's Civil Aeronautics Branch renamed Bureau of Air Commerce.
1935	Douglas DC-3 airliner introduced, succeeding the DC-2.
1937	Inter-American Technical Aviation Conference at Lima, Peru, set up permanent body C.A.T.A. to publish a code of international law. Succeeded by the International Civil Aviation Organization (ICAO), 1944.
1937	Seversky low-wing, metal pursuit plane delivered to United States Army. Maximum speed: 281 miles per hour. Single engine, 950 horsepower.
1938	Civil Aeronautics Act of 1938.
1938	Civil Aeronautics Authority (CAA) began operations.
1938	Under the Civil Aeronautics Act of 1938, permanent route certificates were awarded to sixteen airlines, parent companies to many of today's airlines.
1940	The Civil Aeronautics Board (CAB) was established, 30 June 1940.
Early 1940s	A number of combat planes, fighters, encounter "sound barrier" in dives with loss of control and structural damage to the aircraft and fatalities. Among these were the P-38, P-47, and P-51. Shock waves and compressibility effects were not yet understood.
1941	Lockheed (P-38) "Lightning" pursuit plane delivered to United States military. Maximum speed: 390-410 miles per hour. Twin engines of 1150-1475 horsepower each.

1942	Republic (P-47) "Thunderbolt" delivered. Low-wing, single engine of 2000-2100 horsepower. Maximum speed: 429-450 miles per hour.
1943	Sonic shock wave, generated by researchers at the National Advisory Commission for Aeronautics (NACA) at Langley Field, Virginia, wind tunnel, were photographed at Mach 1.1.
1944	Provisional International Civil Aviation Organization (PICAO) predecessor of ICAO was established to develop principles and techniques of international civil air commerce.
1944	"Chicago Convention", the Convention on International Civil Aviation, set goals to develop international aviation, recognize national sovereignty, work out rules, and promote safety and uniformity. It was ratified by over 100 nations.
	Airworthiness certificates of all states would be recognized, if equal to that of country assenting to request for such recognition.
1944-45	International Air Transport Association was established to promote regular, safe, and reasonably priced air transport. It does a great deal to organize air carrier documentation, and sets rates.
1945	Northrup XP-79 experimental pursuit was built. Maximum speed: 500 miles per hour; 1500 horsepower.
1945	Lockheed (P-80) "Shooting Star" was delivered. Maximum speed: 550 miles per hour; powered with 4,000 pounds of thrust.
1946	Federal Airport Act of 1946 was passed to help provide the United States with comprehensive system of airports.
1946	The "Bermuda Agreement," an important bilateral agreement between Great Britain and the United States. The document became one widely copied as a model aeronautical agreement.
1947	International Civil Aviation Organization was set up by the "Chicago Convention". The ICAO works with technical details to obtain maximum uniformity in flight procedures, communications, weather data, etc.
1947	United States Air Force was formed as a separate military service.

1948	North American (F-86) "Sabre" was delivered to United States Air Force. Maximum speed: 650 miles per hour; 5200 pounds of thrust.
1948	The Geneva Convention on Recognition of Rights in Aircraft recognized rights of mortgage holders to the aircraft and associated parts.
1949	Republic (F-84) "Thunderjet" was delivered. Maximum speed: 600 miles per hour; 5,000 pounds of thrust.
1950s	Designers were learning the secrets of supersonic flight.
1950s	Sonic boom problems emerged.
1951	Northrop (F-89) "Scorpion" fighter was delivered. Maximum speed: 600 miles per hour; 1400 pounds of thrust.
1954	North American (F-100) "Super Sabre" was delivered. Maximum speed: 750 miles per hour; 16,000 pounds of thrust.
1955	McDonnell (F-101) "Voodoo" supersonic fighter was delivered. Maximum speed: 1,200 miles per hour; 30,000 pounds of thrust.
	Convair, Lockheed, Republic, and North American all brought out high-performance, supersonic military planes before the end of the 1950s.[3]
1957	Airways Modernization Act of 1957 elevated the CAB, which was responsible for economic regulation of the airlines, to the status of an independent board no longer under the control of the Department of Commerce.
1958	The National Aeronautics and Space Administration (NASA) was established, absorbing the old National Advisory Committee for Aeronautics, and assuming responsibility for carrying out U.S. space flight missions.
1958	Federal Aviation Act of 1958. CAA became the Federal Aviation Agency on independent level. Aim of the Act was to improve air traffic control and other aspects relating to air safety. FAA assumed responsibility for airways modernization, management of national airspace and continued to license airmen. The Agency took over much research and development work. Civil Aeronautics Board retained the task of setting the probable cause of aviation accidents and continued its role of economic regulation of the

airlines. In general, the Federal Aviation Act of 1958 was quite similar to the Civil Aeronautics Act of 1938.

1958   Boeing 707 jet airliner began passenger service. (Flight tests began in 1954).

1959   General Assembly of the United Nations passed Resolution on Peaceful Uses of Outer Space.

1964   The "Hague Protocol" was added to the "Warsaw Convention" of 1929.

1966   Department of Transportation Act of 1966 created a separate government department, the Department of Transportation (DOT), to centralize federal transportation agencies and to help cope with United States transportation problems.

Under the Department of Transportation Act, Federal Aviation Agency (FAA) lost its independent status, came under DOT, and was renamed Federal Aviation Administration. Also, the DOT's National Transportation Safety Board took over setting the probable cause of aviation accidents (formerly a function of CAB) as well as other transportation accidents.

1967   The General Assembly of the United Nations Treaty on Principles Governing the Activities of States in the Exploration and Uses of Outer Space was written in 1967. Ninety states including United States signed.

1970   Airport and Airway Development Act of 1970 was designed to help develop an effective airway system with an adequate number of up-to-date airports.

1970   Boeing 747 jet airliner began passenger service. Cruising speed: 600+ miles per hour; average passenger load 385.

1970   Lockheed (L-1011) "Tri Star" jet airliner came off assembly line. Cruising speed: 600+ miles per hour; average passenger load 300.

1970   "Hijacking Convention", formally titled the Convention for the Suppression of Unlawful Seizure of Aircraft, was signed at the Hague by the U.S. and 49 other nations. It was to take effect when ratified by ten signatories, and went into effect on 14 October 1971.

1971   Douglas DC-10s were delivered to airlines. Maximum speed: over 600 miles per hour. Average passenger load 270 to 380.

1971	"Guatamala City Protocol" established carrier liability for luggage losses, death or injury of passengers, and limits of liability.
1972	McDonnell Douglas (F-15) "Eagle" made its first flight. Maximum speed over Mach 2.
1973	"Montreal Convention", or the Convention for the Suppression of Unlawful Acts Against the Safety of Civil Aviation, became effective. This agreement strengthens opposition to hijacking.
1975	National Transportation Safety Board (NTSB) began operations as an independent agency 1 April 1975 under provisions of the Independent Safety Board Act of 1974.
1978	Air Carrier Deregulation Act passed by U.S. Congress.

NOTES

[1] See David C. Cook, *Who Really Invented the Airplane* (New York: G. P. Putnam's Sons, 1964) for discussion of pre-Wright brothers experimentation with various modes of flight.

[2] American Institute of Aeronautics and Astronautics, continuing feature and file "Out of the Past" a chronology of aeronautical and space flight events is published in their journal ASTRONAUTICS AND AERONAUTICS. Editorial offices: 1290 Avenue of Americas, New York, N.Y. 10019.

[3] U.S. Air Force CHRONOLOGY OF SIGNIFICANT AEROSPACE EVENTS, March 1903 — December 1971. U.S. Air Force, Press Relations Office, Pentagon, Washington, D.C.

PART II

THE DEVELOPMENT OF LAW
IN THE UNITED STATES

Lockheed TriStar, the L-1011, air transport aircraft.

CHAPTER 3

EUROPEAN BACKGROUND OF U.S. LEGAL PHILOSOPHY

What is Aviation Law?

A pilot will tell you that aviation law is the Federal Aviation Regulations. Ask an airline official for a definition of aviation law and he will cite the Civil Aeronautics Board regulations and rulings. An airport manager, airplane manufacturer, or the owner of a home will give you state laws in order to answer your question. Aviation law is all of these things and more.

Air law has grown in response to special needs. Aircraft can do new things — overfly homes, states, and nations. They are elusive and fast. They are vulnerable in special ways. They have special right-of-way needs rooted in the natural laws of physics and aerodynamics.

The Origin of Western Law

Looking at the origins of aviation law, we see that it is rooted in English law, which in turn is founded on Western European, Roman, Carolingian, Greek, and Jewish law. Quite a long history for such a modern thing as flight. Yet today we live out our lives governed by laws evolved from ancient systems governing human relations. Folkways, tradition, taboo, and custom ruled our prehistoric ancestors. About 1500 years before the birth of Christ, Israelites (Jews) a semicommunal, migratory people, were governed by the laws of Moses. These "Ten Commandments" and the five books of the Torah, which Moses presented as divine revelation, governed them. Law was embedded in religion.

In the sixth century B.C. with return of Jews to the Palestine area, after their "Babylonian captivity", to purists, the law of Moses and the study of the Torah ("the law") became a ruling passion. The eventual *Talmud* began to be worked out orally, a compilation of auxiliary law which had grown up to supplement the Torah and the Commandments. This later work was obscured somewhat by revelation, interpretation and poetry.

The law of Moses is important in the creation of our present legal system. It is a chief "root" of European and English law. (Our legal system is based on English law, with certain later modifications). The version of Mosaic law known as the Babylonian *Talmud* was the more complete, and it is this that was handed down by a system of "repeaters", teachers of the law.

Through foreign rules and expulsion from Palestine the law grew and throve. It lived. The *Talmud* was completed by about 500 A.D. in oral form. Later it was written.

To prevent our straying from aviation law into the fascinating history of our present United States of America law, let me refer you to books on the subject[1]. It is enough for us to say here that from Middle Eastern beginnings a legal and moral code evolved.

This Jewish law was modified by the teachings of Jesus and the hearthcentered legal customs of the Greeks. Again, with the Greek city states, law and and religion was closely linked. Concepts of justice and "right" were formulated.

Giants of intellect among the Greeks added to the law with their philosophies Homer, Solon, Lycurgus, Socrates, Plato and Aristotle. Today we still debate the same ideas and many of the same issues as did these brilliant men. Here were born concepts which we still acknowledge. Greek law saw land and home (hearth) ownership as vitally connected to a proper religion and, thus, legally most important. Laws of land inheritance have evolved from this focus of interest in their councils.

The Romans later evolved a most complete and extensive framework of workable law. It has often been said that the Romans had a genius for government. Never before had such municiple and national law been evolved. Procedures were drawn up treating with torts and criminal law, contracts, corporations, business law, trusts, property, and estates and wills. Skilled lawyers were trained. Judges abided by a most complete code. By the year 533 A.D. the Justinian code was published.

Roman law was built upon judicial opinion, imperial decrees, and written legal commentaries. An amazing legal structure was designed and built, one which could, with only a few changes, be used today.

The Romans were governed by an executive (emperor) and by what may loosely be known as two legislative branches — an upper and lower house (the Senate and the Assembly). Only the patricians really had any say in government although the sovereignty in theory rested in the people. The masses had virtually no voice in government. The people of Rome, unlike those of the Greek city states, took little interest in their government. Rule by elite, it seems, is a natural evolution from clan government and is found throughout the world.

Roman law was designed to maintain order, to provide momentum to national goals and projects, to decide between quarreling individuals or factions, to protect property, and to assist trade and business.

From prehistoric times, traders on the land and sea had evolved supernational laws that allowed business to be conducted. Letters of credit, certificates allowing passage of traders and goods, and certain other recognized practices allowed trade to expand from the Mediterranean into Europe and further. Wars and rival kingships often halted trade; still, a body of law grew up.

Technology was a factor in forming trade laws. Short-range, coast-hugging voyages gave way to long, ocean-spanning voyages in the fifteenth century with the advent of improved sailing techniques and equipment, improved rudders, compasses, and charts. Traders often took over posts in foreign lands and installed their rule over a limited area near trade centers. England was, by the eighteenth century, an avid collector of territory in American, India, and elsewhere.

This acquisition of land and trade was in fact "might is right". For example, Spain acquired most of South and Central America and claimed about one-third of North America! Spanish technology, ships, arms, and military organization, made this possible. Where one could go, one did go; and where one could take over, one did so.

Laws of the sea evolved to allow vessels of all nations to avoid collision and to do business in ports. Law aboard a vessel was that of its home port, its country of registry. Laws of the land visited, however, generally applied to crew members ashore. These same maritime laws of right-of-way and registry pertain today to aircraft law.

The U.S. Federal Aviation Regulations today are based, in a way, on the laws regarding the navigation of vessels on the seas: red light to starboard, green light to port; position lights on at night; give way to the right. Special additions for aerial "vessels" were tacked on as needed.

Roman law endured from about 500 B.C. to 500 A.D. — nearly one thousand years! It was a detailed, practical, and workable legal system.

As the Germanic people swept across the environs of Roman possessions and to Rome herself, Roman law persisted but was modified by the Germanic influence. Roman law, being more developed, persisted strongly. Clan rule, "law speakers", and the legal customs of the Germanic people overlay in a crude way the sophisticated Roman legal system.

Education and government lanquished. Few people now could read. For years only the churches sheltered and gave economic support to literacy and scholarship.

In 800 A.D. the Emperor Charlemagne, at the head of a collection of feudal territories, set about bringing order to the many and often conflicting laws in his Empire. It was made up of territory now comprising a good part of what came to be Austria-Hungary, France, most of present day Germany, Belgium, Holland, Switzerland, and about half of Italy.

Charles himself never managed to learn to read or write. He saw clearly, however, the uses of literacy and promoted literature, the forming of a royal library, and the ordering and structuring of a system of law.

He governed by decree and with assistance from councils of barons. A royal court headed the judicial system. Provincial courts were required to follow precedents set by the royal court. Inspectors checked on all parts of his realm to be sure that his decrees were being obeyed.

Despite the fact that his personal conduct was sybarite, his decrees were very much influenced by the teachings of the Roman Catholic Church. He supported it as a strong state church.

Generalized, we can see that Charlemagne and the German influence he made uniform across his realm affected our present legal system. It may have been one of the foundations of our "jury of ones peers" practice. His court system was one of the germinal influences on our courts today. Assent to clans and councils of nobles in clan gatherings, further, was an addition to the idea of representatives and legislatures.

Few people, in those feudal times, had the protection of the law. Justice was reserved for a small number of the gentry. Charles tied nobles to him by granting each a grant of land. The noble then owed the emperor military service. Federal law declined after the death of Charles and his heirs. Roman law again came to be the more workable system.

The Church, and there was only the Catholic Church, was the refuge of learning and trained people. Church and state were not separate; hence, the strong input from canonical law.

All of these influences mentioned here — the law of the Germans, and Roman, feudal, and canonical law — blended now over the years into Continental law.

Napoleon's reign had a lasting impact on the law, thanks to his support of a wholesale codification of the French legal system. Much of this work had been written. With this at hand, Napoleon sponsored a completion of the project.

As a result, the Civil Code was completed in 1804 and followed by *Criminal, Civil Procedure,* and *Criminal Procedure* codes.

Napoleon sought, and succeeded to a great degree, in forming a United Europe. But his empire was brief in its life span. Longer lasting and more effective was the effect of his *Code*. Most of Europe adopted a very similar code.

What is a "Code"? It is a set of laws to fit various situations as opposed to our system, (and that of Roman law) based on judicial decisions, opinions, precedent. The latter is more flexible and adaptable to changing conditions.

How then did England develop a legal system based on precedents, escaping the rigidity of a code? England, as even a cursory study of history reveals, was inhabited by a Celtic people, who were overrun by Rome around 43 A.D. Roman law overlay local custom and remnants of Celtic culture. The Romans with their genius for organization ruled much of England for nearly four centuries.

Groups of Germans came, sweeping the native Celts back into Wales, Ireland, and Scotland. Germanic law and government persisted in England and grew quite feudal in character by around 1000 A.D.

Feudal rule means rule by an armed elite. Each noble holds his land on sufferance from a monarch who really controls all the land. In return for the use of the land, the feudal lord owed his king military duties and loyalties.

In England the Roman Catholic Church held huge grants of land. Canonical law, that is, church law, held sway on lands held by the church. It also had considerable power over various aspects of secular life. Birth, marriage, and death records were church held. Tithes, fees, and fines were paid to England's powerful Catholic Church. It was the state church, the official religion. Citizens were by and large obliged to belong to the official church. Canon law had, naturally, many Jewish precepts within it.

When William the Conqueror arrived in England in 1066 A.D., he took over a land with an established system of Germanic law. Remnants of this system persisted. The strong and uniquely English claim of rights for the individual may well have come from the assembling of Germanic clans in which members had set rights. There was some Anglo-Saxon property rights law and quite a large body of criminal and tort law. County assemblies persisted in the form of county courts under William's strong government. Churchmen, the only literates, often operated these courts.

William ruled strongly and alone. Yet he did have a council of advisors, and the English Parliament no doubt evolved from this and later councils.

The Anglo-Saxon and feudal Roman (French) legal systems gradually merged. William removed the church men from the courts and put his own men in their place. Separate church courts then emerged. Naturally, this created conflict.

From England as early as the reign of Henry II, we have inherited our jury system. There are two types of juries: one is the grand jury, a group which decides if there is reason to indict for (accuse of) a crime; the second is the petit jury which is the familiar twelve persons, who sit to hear individual cases. Our jury judges the facts. The judge charges the jury to observe the law and explains the legal case being heard. The judge then decides what law applies. The jury decision must be unanimous.

England's government has long been known as a "constitutional government" but, in fact, England has no written constitution. There is no one written document. It is, rather, made up of separate sections of law, each reluctantly granted by Kings of England. Liberties were granted very slowly and were enjoyed for the most part by the upper reaches of society.

English law evolved through the centuries, pulling away from the Church only gradually until the reign of Henry VIII. That monarch abruptly drove the Catholic Church out of England, and headed its successor, the Church of England, himself.

The work of great legal minds affected the Church of England law: Edward Coke, Francis Bacon, John Selden, Thomas Hobbes and John Locke. The law became ever more powerful in itself and less an instrument to exert the will of the crown.

Following the industrial revolution in England of the mid 1700's, more and more the laws were applied to the masses. It might seem to us these gave little justice to the lower classes, but at least there was a start in making the law more classless and pervasive.

England established colonies in North America encompassing what is now Canada, the District of Columbia and fourteen of our present seaboard states of the United States of America. Immigrants thought of themselves as free men of England and demanded the protection and rights granted under English law. After the American Revolution, there were thirteen loosely united states under the Articles of Confederation. We all know that this arrangement was weak and not conducive to the development of a strong and prosperous business community.

The Constitution of 1781 was written, not in an entirely democratic way, by a small group of gifted men. It reflected concepts of John Locke and Jean

Rousseau. The people were seen as the basic source of power, yet property rights were assiduously protected. A central government was created with more power than the former "figurehead" one. The present court system was set up as one of three powerful branches of the federal government. We need not review here the checks and balances in the system, suffice it to say that it was flexible enough to be changed, but hard enough to change to be stable.

This then is how our United States law has evolved and is still evolving. Our basic United States document, our legal cornerstone, is the Constitution of the United States. The Supreme Court interprets the document. The people can amend it. Precedent decides and changes our laws via court decisions. Congress through its acts can write our public laws at the federal level. State legislatures and courts likewise determine the laws of each state.

Photograph courtesy the Boeing Company.

The Boeing 737.

NOTES

[1]Useful texts dealing with the history of law include: Rene David and John E. C. Brierley, *Major Legal Systems in the World Today*, (London: The Free Press, Collier-Macmillan Ltd., 1968); Gerhard von Glahn, *Law Among Nations*, (Toronto: The Macmillan Company, 1970); and Rene A. Wormser, *The Story of the Law* (New York: Simon & Schuster, 1962).

CHAPTER 4

STATE AND FEDERAL COURTS SYSTEMS, U.S.

It is astonishing to discover that so many American citizens do not understand the United States system of courts. Even at the college level of teaching, professors find that students, for example, do not know that courts of appeal are generally presided over by more than one judge, nor what dissenting opinions are. In this chapter a brief summary of the court systems of the United States will be given with a short description of their functions — i.e., what courts exist and what they do.

There is today very definitely such a thing as states' rights. Whatever powers not given to the federal government are reserved to the states, according to the Constitution of the United States.

As you know, there was at the beginning of our United States history quite a wrangle over this issue of states' rights. Pertinent to our discussion of aviation law is the fact that the leaders of the various state governments realized that some rights must go to the federal government or else thirteen quarreling, divided, and weakened small countries would exist. In the interest of all, certain rights had to be given up. Once aircraft began to overfly private property, this same premise was used. In the interests of all citizens and air commerce, property owners had to give up some of the rights they had previously enjoyed.

States' Rights

Government is seen as least harmful when nearest the people. At a distance it becomes monolithic and a tyrant. Many oppose the increasing centralization of government but must admit the need for it in many cases — treaties, public waterways, ocean borders, domestic and international air transport, and in matters relating to public health, education, welfare, and national defense.

Writers urge that the Federal government stick to those functions given it by the Constitution and leave the States to tend to their own affairs. As the United States began, the States claimed virtually all rights, under the Articles of Confederation. The Federal government was a figurehead designed to treat with other nations, serve as a clearing house of news and needs of the States, and when necessary to coordinate efforts toward national defense. The establishment of the Constitution welded the nation together more and allowed the Federal government (the President, Congress, and Supreme Court) more power; e.g., power to raise money via import and export levies, etc. Even so, the States held on to a great amount of power.

To this day there is a power struggle between the States and federal government. Why pay taxes to Washington, D.C., which are to be used at home? Many hands may be used, and paid, to take and return the funds; goals seen at home are lost in the federal bureaucracy; and control of funds is lost to people contributing taxes.

In aviation there remains this issue of states' rights. Shall a case be tried in a state court? Or shall a federal commission be asked to decide the matter.

Further, still on the subject of states' rights and how it affects aviation law, is the factor of venue, or place, a factor affecting which laws shall prevail in cases of liability and responsibility. In some instances, we will find that a state law may be more favorable to a plaintiff than a federal law.

Let us look at our state courts systems and our federal courts systems to refresh our memories regarding the United States system of justice.

State Court Systems

Our colonial court systems were fairly simple in nature. Most of the political power lay in the hands of the English governor and his council of advisors. These men, and they were all men, appointed judges from a tight circle of educated property owners. Even today differences in state governments persist which were generated in colonial times, as a result of varying religious and business pressures which changed the English common law and English court structures.

With an increase in the number of people in the colonies and the amount of business conducted, naturally, the courts responded by expanding to handle the increased litigation that arose.

After the American Revolution, political power now lay in the hands of the men in the state legislatures. Oddly, these were often the same men who had been powerful and active under English rule. Property rights and the rights to safeguard business debts were promptly written into early United States law. Only those rights which the landowners and educated elite could not monopolize, due to the pressures of the general population, were slowly relinquished. Many members of the gentry feared mob rule and distrusted the ability of citi-

31

zens to rule themselves. This was a natural fear, for self government had not been attempted before on this scale and with these particular aspirations toward republicanism and democracy. Early America was not democratic in reality but had democratic government as its eventual goal in many minds.

American courts did respond to popular demands. Unpopular judges were removed and unpopular decisions reviewed by state legislatures. Even so, a cry sometimes arose that the eventual decision in a case was "unconstitutional". The review of state actions by the Supreme Court to determine constitutionality is an American innovation. This tended to offer United States citizens a uniform and powerful legal system, and one less apt to be arbitrary and whimsical at the local level.

With the industrialization of the United States in the mid 1800s, the courts changed and became more specialized. Of interest to us investigating aviation law, were those interstate cases arising from the development of a national railway system. Railways to be useful on a national scale had to have a fairly uniform code of laws applicable in all states. Hence, federal regulation came into being, today evinced in the Interstate Commerce Commission (ICC), a federal commission to transcend state and minicipal variations with a uniform interstate code. Even so, the states demand taxes and certain operational concessions from interstate carriers.

To give preferred treatment to residents of a state, as a rule the carriage of intrastate goods is less regulated than goods carried interstate. Further, due to a history of a strong farm influence perceived by political figures, farm products are often exempted and may be carried without compliance with the regulations imposed on manufactured products.

Today our state courts offer part, or a combination, of the following courts:

The State Supreme Court which acts as a court of appeals for cases tried in a lower court in the state. Some states allow cases to be heard in the State Supreme Court without being heard by an intermediate court. That is, a person may appeal immediately after a lower court hears his case, skipping the next higher court entirely.

Intermediate Appellate Courts which are used for cases referred to them from a lower court of limited jurisdiction. For certain cases in some states this is in effect the highest court of appeals within the state system. There are trial courts of general jurisdiction in which cases may begin, be initiated, and heard. If this court decision is satisfactory to the party bringing the suit and to the defendant, then that decision stands. It may be that the decision is not really acceptable yet neither party can spare the time or money to pursue the matter further.

Trial Courts of limited jurisdiction are those hearing only traffic offenses, or only estate cases (for example, an Orphans' Court), and the juvenile courts.

Decisions made in the lower courts are important because most cases are heard at this level and are not appealed. Thousands of cases are heard at the lower level of the judicial system, while only scores or hundreds are heard at the highest court of appeals in a state. For this reason, then, these lower court decisions set precedent and become a part of the law. We cannot take for granted the idea that only important cases are appealed. Generally speaking, every litigant does have access to at least one court of appeal.

All of our states have three general "layers" of courts:

(1) At the lowest level are local trial courts of limited juridiction which hear minor cases; small claims, wills, traffic cases. Eight states have only one or two of these; nineteen states have four or five; and twelve states have over six kinds of trial courts of limited jurisdiction.

(2) Next are the state trial courts of general jurisdiction with broad authority to hear many kinds of cases. It would be at this level that most aeronautical trials would be heard initially. Names of trial courts of general jurisdiction vary. They may be called for example, a District Court of Common Pleas, a Circuit Court, or a Superior Court. Nine states have two; two states have three such courts, and one state has four. Most states (38), however, have only one.

(3) Above these courts are state intermediate appellate courts; and finally, the superior courts which review decisions reached in the lower courts and are courts of highest appeal in the state. All states have one supreme court. Nearly half the states (23) also have intermediate courts of appeal. Again, the names of these courts vary. Three states have separate intermediate courts of appeal for civil and criminal cases.

The most noticeable difference between states is the absence or existence of the intermediate appellate courts. Also, states vary in the kind and number of courts in which cases may be tried. Generally speaking, states with the most streamlined and simple systems are considered to be the most modern.

Maryland, for example, in the 1970s eliminated many courts of limited jurisdiction and did away with justices of the peace. New rules for the disciplining of the judiciary were formulated and voted into law by state referenda which amended the state constitution.

The American Bar Association (ABA) has worked out a model state court system. North Carolina has adopted the ABA system, for example, discarding its unwieldy, traditional court system.

One finds the lower courts presided over by a single judge. State courts of appeal, however, tend to have more than one justice "sitting" or "on the bench". These judges, generally, make up odd-numbered panels, such as three, five, or nine, in order to avoid ties. Majority decisions prevail but dissenting opinions often make important points. Both dissenting and assenting decisions are quoted by attorneys and jurists at later dates in arguing similar cases.

It is important in aviation law to understand that each of the states of the United States has a separate and often differing court system. True, all the states share the Supreme Court, a body of judges who interpret the Constitution, selecting out of the many cases referred to that court, ones that will make clear some aspect of the Constitution. That document was written in rather general terms and just how its provisions apply to modern legal matters requires constant interpretation, re-interpretation and even amendment. Without this flexibility our government would be unable to respond to the changing needs of the people governed. The framers of the Constitution, however, made amending the document an involved and time-consuming process. This was done for the good reason that the Constitution may be changed only after due consideration and with allowed time for detailed debate and discussion of the proposed changes.

Yet, despite sharing our basic governmental document, the Constitution, and sharing a nationally standardized federal court system, the fact remains that in the states there are separate court systems peculiar to that state and often quite different from the court systems of other states. Similarly, a body of state law has grown up in each state, quite often not at all like the laws of other states. State laws are alike in that they are to conform to the general provisions of the federal Constitution. This, however, allows scope for considerable differences, as we shall see.

States jealously guard their powers. Citizens wish to retain as much control over their lives and laws as possible. Each local area wishes to be able to choose its own rules. Federal control means that someone in Washington, D.C. will be telling them how to spend tax monies, how much to pay in taxes, and what rules of law are to be followed. Naturally in such a diverse nation as this one, each area has different preferences and needs; the local autonomy granted by state governments is a workable way in which to retain local power.

States differ in legal preferences for several reasons. Historically, for example, Louisiana with its French background will differ markedly in state government background from Massachusetts with its English historical orientation. California will reflect in some of its laws its Spanish origins. Further, varying ethnic groups settle various portions of our nation and this difference is reflected in the court systems and the laws of the states. Some states are rural, some urban in nature. Some have powerful special interest groups involved in oil production, fishing, aircraft manufacturing, tobacco raising, grain production, and on and on in great number. We can see, therefore, how states guard their powers and how each may differ from the other.

Aircraft owners and operators with their inherent ability to quite literally transcend state boundaries may still find in legal matters that they must recognize this variance in state legal systems.

One state need not necessarily follow precedents set via the same circumstances in another state. Hence, completely separate and differing sets of precedents may exist in the various states. Further, even the U.S. Supreme Court cannot overrule the decisions of the highest state court unless a Constitutional question is involved.[1]

Surprisingly, many United States citizens do not realize that such variety of law and of court systems do exist in their country. Most of us are familiar with our own state laws and pay little attention to others. Aircraft owners, pilots, operators of businesses involving aircraft use, *must* pay attention to the fact that the same use or liability may, in different states, place us under quite different rules and obligations. We cannot give the state aeronautical code for each state here, but we can strongly urge you to seek it out by writing to your state government for information.

The Federal Courts

The United States Supreme Court, of course, has nine judges, one of whom is named the Chief Justice. Here, too, majority decisions prevail yet dissenting opinions are not without importance. Basically, the Supreme Court adheres to certain principles of constitutional interpretation, that the powers of the federal government are those to be found in the Constitution, expressly stated or implied. Once a power has been established as belonging to the federal government by the Constitution that power can be broadly interpreted. All powers not granted the federal government by the Constitution are retained by the governments of the states.

The Supreme Court can pass on the constitutionality of state laws thus making the federal government superior to state governments and decisions. Further, the Supreme Court has the right to decide whether or not an Act of Congress is constitutional. The Supreme Court is the highest court of appeals in the United States, and its decisions become the law of the land.[2]

United States Supreme Court. At the apex of our court system is, of course, the United States Supreme Court.

The nine justices *select* certain cases to be heard. Hundreds of cases are appealed to this highest court of the land, yet few are heard. Those cases chosen are ones involving constitutional issues and interpretations needing review.

The Supreme Court can and does reverse itself as time, circumstances, and public perceptions cause changes in the national outlook. Nevertheless, the precepts of the Constitution give the Supreme Court a firm framework on which to build. Changes are hard fought, but this possibility of reversal, of even Supreme Court decisions, gives our court system the rather deliberate flexibility it needs. [3]

United States Courts of Appeals (Circuit Courts). Just below the United States Supreme Court are the regional United States courts which hear appeals referred to them from the state courts. By law only certain cases may be heard. The cases may involve certain (substantial) sums of money, involve cases of persons residing in two or more states, or involve some federal factor.

Again, many appeals are refused, not given a hearing.

Jurisdiction of U.S. District Courts. Under the National Aeronautics and Space Act as amended, the United States District Courts shall have original jurisdiction concurrent with the Court of Claims of civil actions or claims against the United States. These claims are those which are not to exceed

$10,000.00, and are founded on the Constitution, an Act of Congress, executive department order, a federal regulation, or any express or implied contract with the United States.

Subject to the provisions of Chapter 171 of the U.S. Code, District Courts have exclusive jurisdiction of civil actions or claims against the United States for money damages, injury, loss of property, or personal injury or death caused by the negligent or wrongful act or omission of employees of the United States Government. This applies under circumstances where the United States, if a private person, would be liable to the claimant in accordance with the law of the place where the act or omission occurred.[4]

Pension suits and suits involving the Internal Revenue Service, however, do not come under the jurisdiction of the United States District Court.

The United States District Court has the power to remand cases to an appropriate administrative or executive body.

Authority to release funds for the settlement of claims and judgements is given under Title 31, United States Code 7242.

United States Special Courts. Of interest to us in aviation law are the special hearings held by various United States federal commissions such as the Interstate Commerce Commission (ICC), the Civil Aeronautics Board (CAB), the Department of Transportation (DOT), and various boards. We will discuss these in detail, but at this point we note only that such federal commissions do make up a part of the federal system of hearings and decisions.

There are other special federal courts as well, which deal with particular aspects of federal regulation and are often ways of appealing decisions awarded in the state courts systems.[5]

Federal Courts determine the intent of Congress in certain disputes. An example of this might be in interpreting the Act to Regulate Commerce. In the same way, state courts interpret laws formulated by state legislatures.

The Motor Vehicle Carrier Act of 1935 specifically denies Interstate Commerce Commission (ICC) control over in-state (intrastate) motor carriers operating legally under a state regulatory agency. Regulation at the state level is less pervasive in air commerce than in motor codes. (See the chapter on State Aviation Commissions and Laws.)

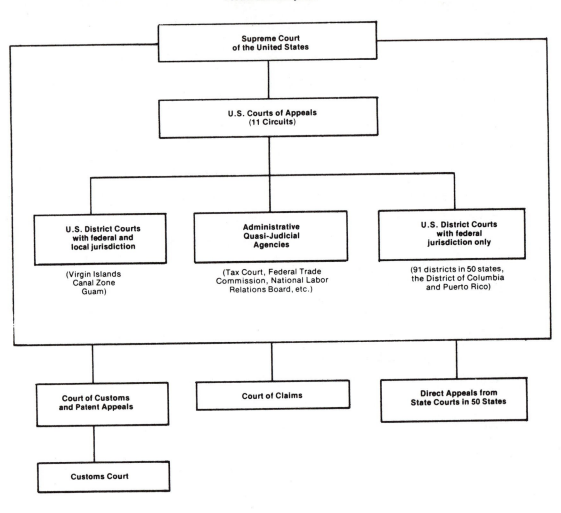

The Congressional Role

The Congress of the United States sets broad policies and delegates regulatory interstate commerce powers to commissions and boards. Congress controls these boards via its power to deny or appropriate funds.

In the U.S. House of Representatives and in the U.S. Senate legislation and action is studied via committees. For example, the Interstate Commerce and Foreign Commerce committees. These deny or recommend legislation to Congress. Proposals for new laws are heard, evidence sifted, opinions voiced, and compromises worked out.

The Executive Role

The President of the United States has great powers. The chief executive has the overall power to recommend legislation to Congress and to administer the laws of the Congress. Certain veto powers are his.

He, or she, appoints members of commissions, although there is a limit as to how many members of a single party may be seated on any one board. Likewise, no one President may appoint to a commission a majority of the members.

The President may order investigations and studies. Recent studies have been made at Presidential request in the fields or air and surface safety, urban transportation, and in other areas.

The national budget is drawn up by the President and its recommended appropriations are presented to Congress. All commissions are in this federal budget, of course, and must submit requests annually to the Bureau of the Budget.

In our discussion of international relations we will see further powers of the presidency in the President's power to negotiate by means of Executive Agreements with other heads of state.[6]

NOTES

[1] See Rene Wormser, *The Story of the Law* (New York: Simon & Schuster, 1962) 394-95, for the origin of U.S. state law policy.

[2] Wormser, 370.

[3] Rene David and John E. C. Brierley, *Major Legal Systems in the World Today*, 2d ed. (New York: The Macmillan Publishing Co., Inc., 1978), pp. 328-33.

[4] David and Brierley, pp. 393-94.

[5] Stuart M. Speiser and Charles F. Krause, *Aviation Tort Law*, I (San Francisco: Bancroft-Whitney Co., 1978), pg. 49-57. Also Vol. 2, pp. 435-37.

[6] Gerhard von Glahn, *Law Among Nation's*, 3d ed., (New York: Macmillan Publishing Co., Inc., 1976), pp. 422-24.

CHAPTER 5

U.S. Law: General, Torts, Contracts

The following definitions and discussions are intended to offer a general introduction to commonly used terms and concepts found in U.S. law. Some of the subjects mentioned here will be repeated in later chapters as applied to particular situations and conditions. It is, of course, important to consult an attorney for detailed information in actual cases.

Law in the United States is based on the Constitution, as discussed above. This document grants each citizen the right to live peaceably and unharmed, to enjoy a home, to own property and benefit from its use, to conduct businesses and many other rights. Citizens in turn are to respect the rights of others.

If existing laws fail, due to changing circumstances, to protect the rights of citizens, federal and state legislatures may revise or repeal laws or enact new legislation.

In effect, the law is a set of rules, regulations, and court decisions designed to settle disputes. If the parties involved cannot reach agreement, they may take the dispute to the courts for a decision.

"Case law," refers to that law which evolves from court decisions made prior to the case in question. These prior decisions, or "precedents," are cited by attorneys in the courts to support the arguments of plaintiffs and defendants.

A "plaintiff," is the party bringing action (suit) against another party.

The "defendant," is the party being sued who must defend himself against the charge.

The term "party," is used rather than list all the possible combinations of persons or organizations that might be involved in cases.

"Civil law," is that which determines and defines the rights of the individual in protecting his property or person.

"Criminal law," is written to protect the community against the harmful and criminal acts of individuals. It also protects the accused person by granting a fair and prompt trial.

A crime is an offense against the state and/or the people of the state. The public prosecutor brings suit against persons indicted (accused of) crimes in order to punish them and to deter crime.

A felony is a crime punishable by death (capital punishment) or with a state prison sentence. These are very serious crimes. (Example: assault with a deadly weapon.)

A misdeameanor is a crime but not a felony, a less serious crime in nature. (Example: simple assault, no weapon.)

An offense is not considered a crime but is punishable. Offenses are usually violations of local laws or rules of conduct or/and behavior. (Example: disorderly conduct.)

"Common law," is based on precedent, previous court decisions.

"Statutory law," is based on the acts of federal and state legislatures.

A "remedy," refers to some compensation or action taken to remedy the wrong done to a plaintiff, e.g., money paid, "damages".

Courts of equity deal with recompense involving more than money — an injunction, for example, to restrain some action, or to require the performance of some duty.

To make business transactions less complicated, most states have adopted the *Uniform Commercial Code.* This is a set of regulations relating to business transactions to offer uniform business law. Federal legislation, too, attempts to bring uniformity to business law with various acts, e.g., the *Federal Consumer Protection Act*, known as the "Truth in Lending Act."

Jurisdiction

Jurisdiction is the power, authority, capacity, or right to act. The term is a most comprehensive one and covers every sort of judicial action. It indicates the authority of a court to hear and decide cases. It may refer to a kind of case, and/or to geographical limits within which a court is empowered to act.

Jurisdiction is also used to indicate a nation's power to govern in certain geographical areas or situations. The term does not denote ownership.

The states of the United States have jurisdiction over non-federal matters within their borders.

Finally, the term indicates the power to govern persons being or residing in a particular state, nation, or place.

Venue

In practice the term "venue" means the place or county in which an injury is declared to have been done, or a fact declared to have happened. It also means the county or geographical division in which an action (a suit, a court action) is brought for trial. Venue does not refer to jurisdiction at all.

Attorneys often have a choice of venue in aviation cases. They may choose to sue a company in the state in which its headquarters are located, particularly if that state has high, or no, limits to liability. The attorney may choose the place in which the accident occurred, the state from which the flight departed or planned to land. To get the most favorable venue for his client's case, an attorney must check the laws of the available states in order to bring suit in the state offering his client the best chance for recovery of damages.

Liability

The term "liability" is a broad legal one which includes all manner of responsibilities, obligations, debts, and assumptions of risks by a person or an organization. To be liable is to be obligated or bound by law, answerable, chargeable; compellable to make restitution.

Limited liability is that which is legally limited in some manner. Owners of stock in a corporation, for example, are liable only up to the total amount of their investment. Other property they may own or money they may have cannot be reached by suits brought against the corporation.

Strict liability is "liability without fault." The case is one in which neither care nor negligence, good nor bad faith, knowledge nor ignorance, will save the defendant.

Negligence

Negligence is the omission to do something which a reasonable person, guided by ordinary considerations, would do. It also implies actions which would not be taken by a reasonable and prudent person.

Degrees of care to avoid being negligent vary with the situation. These degrees of care are known as: great care and caution, ordinary care, and slight care. These are discussed in detail later in this text.

One is not negligent unless one fails to use reasonable care, under existing circumstances, to avoid probable danger or injury. The term is synonymous with "careless."

Historically, the basis for liability in tort (see below) is that of negligence. One is negligent if one's actions resulted in damage or injury due to lack of care.

Res Ipsa Loquitur

Since aircraft accidents may completely destroy evidence as to the cause of the crash and all aboard may be killed, the doctrine of *res ipsa loquitor* is used as a reasonable inference which a jury may consider combined with other information which tends to show a lack of care. Under this principle, negligence is inferred when the injury is one which would not occur normally had reasonable care been used by those in control of the instrumentality causing the injury.

In cases where all physical evidence is destroyed the burden of proof of negligence (and the plaintiff must prove negligence) is very difficult to prove. Yet, if the thing causing the accident was under the exclusive control of the defendant and if the accident was one which would not occur as a rule when normal care is exercised, then the doctrine of *res ipsa loquitor* may be invoked.

The term *res ipsa loquitor* is defined as proving a fact "simply by being there." The theory being that, when the doctrine is applicable, the accident could not have happened without negligence in the ordinary experience of mankind.[1] For the doctrine to apply, it must be shown that the defendant was in control of the aircraft at the time of the accident.

If a variety of causes other than negligence may have brought about the accident, then the doctrine does not apply. It cannot be invoked, also, when the plaintiff is guilty of contributory negligence nor if the accident is due to an act of God, was an unavoidable accident, an inevitable accident, or caused by normally unforseen events.[2]

There are many exceptions and circumstances which will cause *res ipsa loquitur* not to apply to a particular case.[3]

Historically the doctrine has been used in those cases involving injuries to a passenger aboard a common carrier. A common carrier is a company which offers transport to the public for hire. The reason this doctrine is used is that the carrier virtually insures the safe carriage of the passengers aboard its aircraft. Also, the passengers are under almost the complete control of the carrier as to their well being and safety.[4]

Should the carrier be able to show no lack of care and no negligence, then the plaintiff normally cannot invoke the doctrine to advantage.

Bailment

In general, bailment is the delivery of goods or personal property to another for care or for some special object. The *bailor* is the person handing over the property; the *bailee* is the party receiving it. An example might be, the handing over of an aircraft for maintenance. The owner or leasor of the plane is the bailor; the operator of the maintenance shop is the bailee.

A detailed discussion of bailment may be found in discussion of aircraft ownership in this text.

Libel

A libel can be, in tort law, an accusation in writing or print against the character of a person which affects his reputation, diminishes his respectability, and which discredits him. Disparagement of goods is a form of libel. In general, libel in this sense means a false accusation which dishonors a person or product.

A libel can also be a legal term. In admiralty law it means to proceed against — to file a suit — to bring action — to "file a libel". It also may mean the process of seizing property under the admiralty process. This is the case in cases involving claims for payment of debts in maritime law.

Salvage

Since aircraft often operate over water, the laws of marine salvage sometimes apply.

Remember, the United States has an approach to territorial waters that differs from that of many European states. Navigable waters are those, under U.S. law, which are adjacent to the coastal areas of the nation, and those navigable waters connecting with the oceans. Navigable waters which are entirely inside a state are regarded as being under the jurisdiction of that state. These waterways are not considered U.S. territorial waters under federal jurisdiction, nor under the Death on the High Seas Act, nor other maritime legislation of a federal nature.

To illustrate the difference in these navigable waters definitions, consider these examples. Should an aircraft crash into waters under the jurisdiction of a state, then state law will apply and suit must usually be brought under state laws. Should the crash occur in navigable waters of the Mississippi River, however, suit can be brought in the appropriate federal court because the accident site was located in territorial waters.

In maritime law, salvage is the compensation due persons by whose assistance a ship or its cargo has been saved, in whole or in part, recovered from loss, saved from impending danger, or saved when derelict or abandoned.

In Anglo-American law (apart from maritime law) there is no duty to aid a person when he or his property is in peril. Such aid is purely voluntary. There is no legal right to a reward if a life is saved or property is preserved.

At sea, the legal obligation is specific. There *is* a duty to give aid and assistance and a right to a generous reward when property is saved. Those persons saving lives only are entitled to a part of the salvage payments should the property involved (ship or cargo) also be saved.

All those marine principles apply to aviation.

Freedom of Information

Under the Freedom of Information Act of 1966, which was strengthened in 1974, one is entitled to information from government files. To request this information, write to the appropriate federal agency, giving enough information so that the material in question may be located with reasonable ease. Send the statement that this is a "Freedom of Information Act Request. Do not delay."

Requests must be answered within ten working days, upon receipt by the proper office.

Torts

In general, tort law is that which is designed to compensate a plaintiff for the failure of a party to carry out a duty owed the plaintiff. To recover damages, a plaintiff must show a breach of duty and that injury or damage has resulted.

A "tort" is a civil wrong, an act, or a failure in one's duty toward another, causing property damage or loss, or injury to an individual. It may also be a breach of the peace, a crime, hence a cause for prosecution under criminal law. A tort may be cause for action in a court of law under either or both legal codes, civil and/or criminal law. The wrongdoer is termed the "tort feasor."

Civil law is divided into "equity" and "law." Wrongs resulting in damage or injury (torts) which can be corrected (remedied or relieved) by money payment (damages paid) come under the "law" portion of civil law. If money alone cannot remedy the wrong, then, in a more formal action, the courts may require action on the part of the person being sued (the defendant) to give relief to the person bringing suit (the plaintiff). For example, if a person wishes a certain aircraft only, the seller who refused to honor an original deal, may be compelled to go ahead and deliver the plane as promised.

Contract law is usually separate from tort law because court action may be brought for breach of the terms of a contract. Additional tort action is possible only if personal injury or property damage resulted and came from participation in the contract. Negligence must be proven to recover damages.

To review: "tort" is defined as coming from the Latin term, "to twist," "to wrest aside." It is a private or civil wrong or injury, independent of contract. It is a violation of a duty imposed by general law upon all persons in their relations to each other.

The three elements essential to every tort action are: the existence of a legal duty, the breach of that duty, and damage as proximate result.

When aviation was young, there was a tendency to apply absolute liability to what was then regarded, and indeed often was, an unusual and extra-hazardous activity. Later, tort law moderated toward aviation cases, as flying became safe and widely accepted.

Today, aviation has come to be ruled by the usual laws of negligence accorded other modes of transportation. There is an exception, however, in that aircraft product liability is still strict and absolute.

Contracts

Contract law is complex and is affected by the state laws in which contracts are made. The following is a general discussion only. No portion of this book is intended to replace the services of an attorney.

Contracts to be enforceable must be clear to all parties concerned and entered into without fraudulent intent. Contracts won by means of unwarranted pressures or threats are also unenforceable. The terms of the contract, then, should be clearly stated. All parties to the contract should examine all conditions of the contract before signing or otherwise assenting to the terms.

Contracts may be written, verbal, or implied. Written contracts are "express" contracts and are in force according to the terms when signed by all parties.

Verbal contracts are those not written but understood by all parties with verbal terms offered and accepted.

Contracts imply action and payment for action, or the transfer of some property for payment or other benefit. Placing a plane in the hands of airport maintenance personnel implies an order for work and an agreement to pay for the services requested. Offering to buy a plane implies willingness to accept the aircraft as described and to pay for it in a way agreed upon with the seller of the aircraft.

Since human memory is not infallible, it is good business practice to have a work order written out for maintenance and repair work and to have a sales contract for the purchase of a plane. In aviation, however, much business is, in practice, done with simple verbal agreements.

A contract has three essential parts: a subject, an agreement, and consideration. The *subject* is the object or goal of the contract. This must be a lawful one, since contracts to commit offenses or crimes are not enforceable. Also, whimsical and frivolous contracts are not enforceable. The *agreement* is based on the idea that a property or service is being offered on terms agreeable to another party. *Consideration* is, of course, the agreed upon compensation to be paid. This does not have to be money but must be to the benefit of the offering party. Again, contracts to perform unlawful ends are not enforceable.

The parties involved in an enforceable contract must be of age and mentally competent. Convicted felons cannot give assent that will be supported by the courts. One enters into agreement with felons with this risk in mind. Corporations are regarded by the law as persons and can enter into contracts.

Contracts begin with an offer communicated to a party. There must be a clear and explicit understanding of the offer on both sides. An offer with a serious intent and made in good faith is a binding one.

Recent court decisions have found an otherwise legal contract not binding because, viewed in the context of their commercial setting, the terms were so exploitive that they were an abuse of the bargaining process. (Example: District of Columbia, *Williams vs Walker-Thomas Furniture Company*.)

Implied contracts are those in which services or goods are offered by a business and accepted by a customer. It is implied that the goods are of reasonable quality as advertised and that great care will be exercised in performing services.

Insurance

Insurance is a contract entered into by the insurer and the insured. These contracts, commonly called policies, must contain the elements necessary for a valid contract. (See the contracts section of this chapter.) A policy usually provides, upon payment of a premium (a fee), that the insurer will reimburse the insured for any loss incurred by that person *from certain stated causes*. These causes are also known as "risks".

In insurance, as in other transactions, we get only what we pay for. Each additional coverage has an additional premium to take care of the greater risk that the insurance company is to bear.

To be insured a policy must have a subject — for example, the life of a stated person, a building, or an aircraft. The risk against which the property or life is insured must be specified in the policy. The amount for which the insuror agrees to cover losses must be given. The time period covered must also be plainly set forth in the policy.

One must have the right to insure. That is, if one has no financial interest in an aircraft, a hangar, or other property, one cannot recover money for damage or loss of the thing insured. An owner, or a partner (part owner), accurately described in the policy is insurable. A person who has property left in his possession for storage or repair (a bailee) has an insurable interest because should a loss occur he may be held responsible.

In life insurance if the insured takes out the insurance that person can make anyone he likes the beneficiary. The beneficiary may even be a complete stranger. Should a person take out insurance on the life of another person, a question arises. The beneficiary in this case must have an insurable interest in the life of the insured at the time the policy is issued.

Primarily, the items that affect enforceability of an insurance policy are concealment of relevant facts and failure to disclose facts that might cause an insuror to refuse insurance. Concealment, with fraudulent intent proved by the insurance company, voids the policy.

Policies may carry "waivers," which give up the right to reimbursement by the insurance company to the insured under certain circumstances. Suppose a plane was insured with a waiver that covered the aircraft except when carrying explosive materials or devices. Loss of the aircraft and cargo due to an accident while carrying a cargo of explosives would not be covered.

Insurance companies doing business through the mails consummate a contract according to the laws of the home state of the company. It is a valid contract. To sue the company, however, the insured will have to sue in the federal court or in the company's home state.

Any person legally capable of making a contract may enter into a contract of insurance.

A corporation may insure the life of key personnel and be the beneficiary since the corporation has an insurable interest in those persons. A partner may insure a partner for the same reason.

Buyers of aircraft, airports, buildings, or other property are strangers to the insurance company. A new owner is not automatically covered by existing insurance but must take out a policy himself on the property.

Insurance agents are authorized to represent a company and are, therefore, persons considered in the employ of the insurance company. The company is responsible for the actions and contracts made by its agents. Commitments made by the agents of the company bind that firm and are enforceable against it.

Insurance adjustors are not authorized to bind the company but may negotiate a settlement of a claim for the company. They are special agents hired by the insurance company to investigate and report losses under policies. If an adjustment is reached, they report it to the company and upon approval by that company it is binding.

Insurance brokers are not agents of the company but are independent businessmen who solicit insurance from their clients and then place it with a company they choose. Brokers are legally considered the agents of the insured. The broker owes his client a reasonable skill, judgment and care in obtaining a contract for insurance with a solvent company authorized to do business in the state. Brokers are licensed by the state governments.

A binder is a note or memorandum issued by an insurance company prior to the delivery of the formal policy to the insured. It is as binding on the company as a policy.

Losses caused by the insured for the purpose of being paid for that loss by the insurance company are, of course, illegal and not covered by the insurance company. An example might be the burning of a building or aircraft to obtain the amount for which the property was insured.

Reinsurance. Reinsurance is a term used to describe an insurance company's action to share the risks, in certain cases or under certain conditions, with another company.

There are two kinds of reinsurance: treaty and facultative. Treaty reinsurance is automatic reinsurance. This obligates one or both of the parties involved in a reinsurance contract to share the risk. The obligation is assumed via formal contract or treaty with specific terms stated in the document. Facultative is the older method of reinsurance and is handled on a case-by-case basis. The original company (the reinsured) gets in touch with the reinsurance company (the reinsurer) and offers that company full information about the proposed reinsurance. The two firms come to terms and a facultative transaction is made.

Photocraft courtesy Beech Aircraft Corporation.

The 1979 Beechcraft Duke B60.

NOTES

[1] Stuart M. Spicer and Charles F. Krause, *Aviation Tort Law*, 3 vols. (San Francisco: Bancroft-Whitney Co., 1978), 414-17, 601-3.

[2] *Johnson v. Western Air Express Corp.*, 45 Cal. App. 2d 614, 114 P. 2d 688 (1941).

[3] *Stoll v. Curtiss Flying Service, Inc.*, 236 App. Div. 664, 257 N.Y.S. 1010.

[4] Fred Biehler, *Aviation Maintenance Law*, (Basin, Wyo.: Aviation Maintenance Foundation, 1975), pp. 110-11. *Marvin Gerard v. American Airlines, Inc.*, U.S. Court of Appeals, 2d Nov. 27, 1959. 272 F. 2d 35 (CA-2) 1959; 6 Avi 17, 743.

PART III

AVIATION AND FEDERAL REGULATION

The McDonnell Douglas DC-9 Super 80.

CHAPTER 6

U.S. AIR LAW: ITS DEVELOPMENT VIA FEDERAL LEGISLATION

In the United States in 1916 the U.S. Post Office Department emerged as the patron saint of aeronautics. Several early flights had been made with mail aboard by this time, but were regarded more or less as stunts. These early mail flights were made in the United States as early as 1911 and 1912. The inability to fly cross-country at night and in poor weather limited the use of aircraft in mail carriage, to say nothing of the still uncertain reliability of aircraft engines and airframes. Still, the idea of air mail persisted.

Congress in 1916 authorized the launching of a regular airmail service by the Post Office Department with a small sum taken from its appropriation for steamboat or other powerboat service. The aircraft being regarded, apparently, as the "other powerboat service." Airmail service was planned, but the Post Office upon inviting bids for airmail carriage found no responsible takers.

At length Congress appropriated money for an experimental airmail route and on 15 May 1918 service began. Initially, army planes and pilots flew the routes. The Post Office ended its first year of airmail operation "in the black," with a profit of over $20,000.[1] The United States was the first nation to enjoy daily airmail service flown to a preset schedule. Before the end of 1918, the Post Office began operation of the airmail routes with its own planes and pilots.

Through the years 1918-21, air mail routes extended. On 22 February 1921 a day and night transcontinental airmail flight was made. Airmail continued to be flown for a time during the daylight hours only with the mail placed aboard railroads for night transport. Regular twenty-four-hour, day-night schedules began on 1 July 1924, when the Chicago-Cheyenne segment of the transcontinental airway was equipped with light beacons. Airmail was here.

In those early years, the Post Office Department built lighted airways. Not until 1927 were the construction and care of airways and early radio communication facilities turned over to the Department of Commerce. The demonstrated needs of the U.S. Airmail Service initiated the development of more reliable aircraft, radio aids, lighted airports and airways, plus better airport terminal facilities.

By the fall of 1927, the government completely stepped out of the actual flying of the mail in favor of contracting out this task. It had successfully shown the practicability of an airmail service. Thus, private interests were now willing to risk their capital, as they had not been in 1916. Newly organized airlines began to take over the Post Office routes. This new and stable source of income for the early airlines helped to establish U.S. commercial air transport.

As to legislation, Congress passed the Kelly Act, the *Airmail Act of 1925.* The first amendment of the act changed the process by which airlines were paid for carrying the mail. It no longer required the Post Office to pay airlines by the piece of mail, but rather by the pound of mail. In 1928 the second amendment passed, which reduced the price of an airmail stamp with a consequent public increase in airmail use. The Post Office airmail department was no longer legally forced to operate at a profit under the provisions of this second amendment; hence, the airlines could actually be subsidized. Mail reimbursement helped the airlines pay for better planes and more pilots. Airmail carriage was an important part of the early development of the U.S. airlines.

Air Commerce Act of 1926

It was soon apparent, however, that the few, new airlines which were carrying the mail needed still more and improved airways and radio aids. To foster the development of U.S. air commerce, the *Air Commerce Act of 1926* was passed. The first regulatory agency established by the Secretary of Commerce under the authority vested in him by this act was the Aeronautics Branch. (In 1934 the branch was reorganized and renamed the Bureau of Air Commerce.)

The Aeronautics Branch was the first U.S. air regulatory agency. It was set up to write regulations and enforce them in the interest of safety. The Bureau of Air Commerce was the predecessor of the Civil Aeronautics Administration and today's Federal Aviation Administration. For the first time, pilots and planes had to be licensed and registered.

From this beginning, although airline ownership and operation were left in the private sector, the government demonstrated a definite policy of encouragement and assistance to civil aviation, assuring the United States its place as a world leader in civil aviation.

President Herbert Hoover appointed Walter Folger Brown Postmaster General who took office in March 1929. Brown believed the airline industry needed unification in order to grow and to afford the expensive new equipment this growth would entail. He perceived an industry with scores of struggling companies cutting costs and possibly flying unsafe airplanes with poorly trained pilots in order to survive. The Postmaster General initiated the Airmail Act of 1930 which gave him the powers he wanted to develop a vigorous air passenger service. He believed that this could not be done until the fragmented route structure existing at that time was changed. Out of fifty-three established airline routes, forty-three were less than five hundred miles in length; eight ran over distances between five hundred and one thousand miles. Brown envisioned a few major east-west and north-south continental routes with secondary adjuncts. To fly these routes, he wanted to see big, financially stable airlines created through mergers and judicious dispensations of airmail contracts. At this time airlines lacked sufficient incentive to carry out such mergers and route extensions and to build a business based on passenger fares. Under the terms of the *Air Mail Act of 1925*, it was far more lucrative to carry mail than passengers. In fact, with the aircraft of the day, passengers were a losing proposition. Brown secured the needed incentive via the *Air Mail Act of 1930* which changed the formula for mail pay and actually rewarded carriers that carried passengers.[2]

Under the leadership of Postmaster General Brown, a second phase of airline development occurred. He urged the formation of three large transcontinental air carrier companies. With the great power over the air carrier industry given him by the *Air Mail Act of 1930*, the Postmaster General could carry out his plan. Brown had sought even greater power by asking for the right to contract for the carriage of airmail without asking for competitive bids, but Congress refused to grant this power. Still, under the 1930 statute, Brown could extend the life of existing contracts by converting them into route certificates; he could grant route extensions; or he could resort to competitive bidding. He could not grant a contract for a new route or to a carrier that did not possess a mail contract without competitive bidding. As a matter of fact, both the central and southern transcontinental routes where put up for bids (though Brown arranged it so that the lines he wanted to win the contracts did, indeed, win).

The Post Office offered routes that companies had to merge to qualify for in terms of equipment and personnel. In the new method of purchasing airmail carriage, the Post Office Department now paid for units of space and no longer paid for airmail by the pound. In response to this, airlines began to ask manufacturers to build planes with more cubic footage available. These were to be a new generation of aircraft, true multi-engine, passenger air transports.

The 1930 act also encouraged the aviation industry to solve the problems involved in flying in bad weather and during the hours of darkness. Radio navigational aids and aircraft "blind-flying" instruments were improved.

Brown's solution to the immediate problems of developing a strong airline industry was to have far reaching effects. What actually occurred was a regulation of competition among airlines and the forced consolidation of air carrier companies. His four years as Postmaster General gave the U.S. the airlines that were to fly almost free of competition for the next forty-five years! His policy was later to be carried on by the Civil Aeronautics Board, as we shall see in a later chapter.

Suddenly, with the newly elected President Franklin D. Roosevelt (FDR) in power, Postmaster General Brown was removed from office. He was accused of favoritism in contract awards. Charges flew, and in 1934 as a result of the so-called "Black Committee" investigation, all domestic airmail contracts were abruptly cancelled.

The Army Air Corps was ordered to begin flying the mail. From February to March 1934 the Army Air Corps pilots valiantly attempted to carry out this mission. After a number of crashes, many of them fatal, and four million dollars expended — all made much of by the press and FDR's detractors — President Roosevelt ordered the army airmail service flying stopped. The cost per pound of airmail carried, in addition to the tragic loss of lives, totaled four times the commercial cost. Politicians blamed various persons, but at the same time the former air carrier contractors were given their routes back for a temporary term of three months.

The Post Office advertised for bids on new contracts on 30 March, the day the Army suffered its last mail fatality. The first mail pouches under the new contracts were put on commercial carriers on 14 May, though the Army continued to fly some routes through 1 June.

Historian Dr. Nick A. Komons notes that the army near the end of the army airmail flying had gotten over its early inexperience and actually did a very good job of flying the mail between 19 March and 1 June. Moreover, he states, the twelve fatalities suffered by the Army Air Corps during that fifteen-week period was nothing unusual. Short periods with high fatality rates were not uncommon at that time. For example, the previous year during a ten-week period between 19 March and 1 June 1933, the Air Corps suffered sixteen fatalities, yet no one in the press or the Congress took notice.[3]

To make civilian airmail carriage by contractors a permanent arrangement, Congress wrote new legislation.

Airmail Act of 1934 (Black-McKeller Act)

The Airmail Act of 1934 was passed in an attempt to remedy the problems that had emerged during Brown's administration of the Post Office. It proved to be a stopgap measure creating as many problems as it solved. Control of the air carrier industry was placed jointly in the hands of the Post Office Department, the Interstate Commerce Commission, and the Department of Commerce. The role assigned the Department of Commerce was that of maintaining aviation safety and building and operating the airways.

The 1934 legislation did not actually open up free competition for mail routes. In practice it locked in all the routes awarded during the May 1934 bidding. The factor that introduced competition into the picture was actually something unforeseen in 1934: the appearance of the Douglas DC-3, the first air transport aircraft that could carry passengers only, without mail aboard, and still make a profit. This meant that anyone with sufficient financial resources could enter the business and compete against the airmail carriers for passengers. This was a frightening prospect for the mail contractors, who had bid low for mail contracts in 1934 and were becoming increasingly dependent on passenger-carrying for revenue.

The air carrier industry was still very new, still underfinanced, and faced with great operating expenses. From 1934 to 1941 the airlines struggled to stay in business.

During this time the case of former Postmaster General Brown was resolved. The historical consensus of opinion appears to show that Brown acted contrary to law in fostering the growth of a few big U.S. trunk carriers. He was sincere in his perception that this was best for the growth of U.S. air commerce and was never shown to have accepted compensation for his favoritism.

A number of airlines — Northwest, Western Air Express, TWA, American, and United Air Lines — filed suits in the U.S. Court of Claims asking for payment of withheld mail fees accrued prior to 19 February 1934 (the contract cancellation date), the return of performance bonds, and damages. In 1936 Northwest, American, Western Air, and TWA proposed to dismiss their suits with prejudice if the government would return their bonds and back pay. The government agreed to this solution. United Air Lines decided to press its suit to its conclusion. The Court of Claims found in favor of the government and awarded United only withheld pay earned during January and February 1934. In handing down its decision, the court said that United had entered into agreements and combinations for the purpose of preventing competitive bidding for airmail contracts and thereby excluding from the industry persons who desired to enter or continue in the industry.[4] The matter of the airlines and the former Postmaster General was thus resolved.

A provision of the 1934 act that affected the airline industry was the one requiring that no manufacturer also be a common carrier bidding on airmail routes. At this time airlines and aircraft and engine manufacturers were for the most part under holding company control.[5] The holding companies divested themselves of their airline interests. While the airlines did lose an important source of financial support, the divestiture was not all bad. Airlines could now shop around for their equipment, which they were not always free to do before, being constrained to buy equipment from their manufacturing affiliates.[6] The manufacturing companies emerging at this time were to become major U.S. aircraft manufacturing firms.

Progress was made. By the end of 1936 passenger revenue finally exceeded revenue realized from mail contracts. Airlines saw future prosperity linked to the market for passenger carriage and worked to build public confidence in air travel.[7]

In the public interest Congress decided that there was a need for the regulation of the aviation industry similar to that imposed on interstate surface transportation.

Civil Aeronautics Act of 1938 (McCarran-Lea Act)

The McCarran-Lea Act redesigned the government regulation of aeronautics. A single (but tripartite) agency, the Civil Aeronautics Authority (CAA) was set up to oversee U.S. aviation activities. This agency was composed of: a five-man board that wrote both safety and economic regulations; an Administrator responsible for fostering air commerce, controlling air traffic, and establishing airways; and an Air Safety Board that determined the probable cause of air accidents.

Under the 1938 act and its amendment, air carriers providing adequate service in the May to August 1938 time period were to be given Certificates of Convenience and Necessity. This "grandfather clause" found sixteen air carriers meeting the qualification. Most of these still lead the air carrier industry due to powerful growth and through various mergers.

Under powers granted by the Reorganization Act of 1939 President Roosevelt by executive order created the Civil Aeronautics Board (CAB) which assumed the powers of the five-man board (writing safety and economic regulations) and those of the Air Safety Board (deciding probable cause of aviation accidents). The Air Safety Board was abolished at this time. The CAB was a quasi-legislative, quasi-judicial, independent agency which reported to Congress. The president also created the Civil Aeronautics Administration (CAA) which assumed the powers formerly with the Administrator. The CAA was placed under the executive control of the Secretary of Commerce.

Federal Airport Act of 1946

In 1946 the federal government began to contribute funds to build or improve airports. Private industry could not be expected to provide airports any more than it could be expected to finance a federal highway system. Congress saw a need for a complete and effective system of airports. Air commerce was becoming increasingly important to the economy of the United States. The federal assistance was rendered under the Federal Airport Act of 1946. In 1953 this airport act was extended to provide funds for building or improving terminal building facilities. These legislative actions shifted a great deal of the cost of airport construction and maintenance from local governments to federal authorities. The Federal Airport Act was extended by Congress to run to 1970. It was then allowed to lapse with the establishment of a new airport program under the Airport and Airway Development Act of 1970.

Federal Aviation Act of 1958

Preceding the passage of the Federal Aviation Act of 1958 there had been a period of vehement protests by the (then) Civil Aeronautics Administration air traffic controllers over dangers they believed inherent in poorly equipped and undermanned Air Traffic Control (ATC) centers. Further, there was an urgent need to modernize not only the ATC equipment but control procedures. Aircraft speeds were now too high to allow pilots to rely as much as they formerly had on sighting aircraft on closing headings.

The advent of the jet transport plane created an even greater need for action. In 1956 the Boeing 707 jet prototype was unveiled. Time was running out. Only heroic dedication and effort enabled CAA's air traffic controllers to make the nation's overcrowded terminal area flyable. The big new jets also were soon to magnify such problems as undersized runways and crowded terminal buildings.

"Harnessing the technology to modernize the aging airways was difficult enough, but it was infinitely easier than resolving questions of policy."[8] Differences on operation philosophy found military and civilian interests both powerful and CAA barely able to make its presence felt in governmental councils among the diverse boards and committees taking part in air navigational decisions. There was a decided lack of central authority on questions regarding allocation of airspace and the nature of the new airway system. To resolve these diverse views, the White House in 1955 asked William B. Harding, a prominent broker experienced in aviation matters, to conduct a review of aviation policy. Harding found the airports, airways, and air traffic control systems lagging behind aeronautical developments and recommended a long-range study to develop a fresh approach to the problem. This study was begun 10 February 1956 by a board headed by Edward P. Curtis, appointed by President Dwight D. Eisenhower.

Harding had warned that airways and ATC facilities were so outmoded that midair collision risks had reached "critical proportions." His words proved prophetic when on 30 June 1956 two airliners collided over Grand Canyon killed 128 people. The crash hit federal policymakers and Congress with great impact. The accident pointed up the recommendations of the Curtis Board which were submitted to President Eisenhower in May 1957.[9] Congress, further pressed by three major midair collisions in the winter and spring of 1958 acted quickly. On 13 August 1958, a year after having created the Airways Modernization Board, it passed the Federal Aviation Act. President Eisenhower, in signing the measure, freed civil aviation policy from the problems inherent in divided responsibility and authority.[10]

Specifically, the Federal Aviation Act of 1958 responded to the needs for better aeronautical facilities and regulation by:

1. Abolishing the CAA and giving its responsibilities to a new and independent agency, the Federal Aviation Agency (FAA). (The CAA had been under the jurisdiction of the Department of Commerce.) The FAA answered to the President and to Congress.

2. Increasing the FAA's authority in the area of air safety. Budgets could now be written by FAA and submitted to Congress. Public demands for air safety made members of Congress amenable to FAA budget proposals and FAA now could make plans that stretched into the future in an orderly way.

3. Transferring to the FAA from the Civil Aeronautics Board the writing of safety regulations and standards. The FAA continued

the work of its predecessor agency the CAA of enforcing and administering these safety regulations.

4. Authorizing FAA-written aviation legislation.

5. Giving the FAA the power to revoke or suspend airmen certificates, another area of responsibility formerly held by the CAB.

6. Abolishing the Airways Modernization Board and giving its responsibilities to FAA. The FAA gained, too, a more clearly demarked power to allocate navigable airspace to both civilian and military users. [11]

Finally, the act gave the FAA responsibility for coordinating and carrying out necessary developmental and research programs concerned with air safety. This research today is not entirely an FAA function, however, for the National Aeronautics and Space Administration (NASA) also carries on certain air safety research in the fields of aircraft design.

The Civil Aeronautics Board retained economic control of U.S. air carriers in a practically unaltered way. The CAB also retained the task of investigating and declaring the probable cause of aviation accidents.

National Aeronautics and Space Act of 1958

The National Aeronautics and Space Act of 1958 is, "an act to provide for research into problems of flight within and outside the earth's atmosphere, and for other purposes." [12]

This act places a civilian agency in charge of United States aeronautical and space research and experimentation. A prime consideration is stated as the peaceful uses of air and space, yet the demands of national security are recognized. The Department of Defense directs the development of weapons and systems necessary for the defense of the United States.

Of interest to those in aviation is the stated goal of improvements to be made in "the usefulness performance, speed, safety, and efficiency of aeronautical and space vehicles." We are inclined to see NASA only as a space administration, yet NASA has taken over the research programs of the National Advisory Committee for Aeronautics which deal with improving aircraft design and safety. Further, ecological impacts, development of ground propulsion devices, and development of solar power devices are all specifically stated as goals of the act in a forward-looking, energy-conscious way.

Aircraft, under the Act, may be developed, constructed, tested and operated for research purposes. As we shall see in the chapter on supersonic flight, the government makes important contributions to aircraft design.

The act set up the National Aeronautics and Space Administration (NASA). This congressional and executive action was prompted by the successful launching of Russia's "Sputnik," the world's first artificial satellite. (Wernher von Braun, space scientist, stated in an interview that the United States had the capacity to place a satellite in orbit nearly a year before Sputnik was launched but inter-service rivalry prohibited the launch.) [13]

According to the act if invention is a part of a government employee's duty, or is the result of duty as a contractor's employee, then the invention shall be the exclusive property of the United States. The NASA Administrator can apply for a patent for the United States or can waive that right. [14]

Also as given in the NASA act: "Defense of Certain Malpractice and Negligence Suits: Sec. 207. (a) The remedy against the United States provided for by sections 1346 (b) and 2672 of title 28, U.S. Code, for damages for personal injury, including death, caused by the negligent or wrongful act or omission of any physician . . . (or other medical personnel) of the Administration (NASA) . . . while acting within the scope of his . . . employment . . . shall hereafter be exclusive of any other civil action or proceeding . . . of such suits against the government are to be defended by the Office of the Attorney General of the United States. If the case was instituted in a state court it is to be removed to a district court of the United States. Under some conditions, however, the case may be remanded to the State court. Generally, this occurs when no remedy is available under title 28 of the U.S. Code," [15] the legislation which allows the government to be sued under certain circumstances.

If assigned to a foreign country, health care and medical research people may be held harmless or liability insurance may be provided by NASA.

In 1977, the National Aeronautics and Space Act was amended 3 February

1978 to distinguish federal grant and cooperative agreement relationships from federal procurement relationships. [16]

Each executive agency is to use a written procurement contract between the federal government and a state (for example, Wyoming) or local government, or other recipient.

This amendment also established a bureau to be known as the National Air and Space Museum under the Smithsonian Institution.

Jurisdiction of United States District Courts

Under the National Aeronautics and Space Act as amended, the United States District Courts shall have original jurisdiction, concurrent with the Court of Claims, of civil actions or claims against the United States, not exceeding $10,000, founded on the Constitution, an Act of Congress, executive department regulation or any express or implied contract with the United States.

Subject to the provisions of Chapter 171 of the U.S. Code, District Courts have exclusive jurisdiction of civil actions on claims against the United States for money damages, injury, loss of property, or personal injury or death caused by the negligent or wrongful act or omission of employee of the United States government. This applies under circumstances where the United States, if a private person, would be liable to the claimant in accordance with the law of the place where the act or omission occured.

Pension suits and suits involving the Internal Revenue Service, however, do not come under the jurisdiction of United States District Courts.

The United States District Court has the power to remand cases to appropriate administrative or executive body. [17]

The relationship of NASA with FAA is given, too, in Title 49 of the U.S. Code 1349. The FAA coordinates airport improvement and construction. Further, new NASA or military missile launch sites, airports, and alterations to runway layouts must be described to the FAA Administrator well in advance of the NASA or military acquisition or construction.

Should the FAA, Department of Defense, and NASA be unable to agree on such matters, the problem is to be appealed to the President for final determination. [18]

President Lyndon B. Johnson asked that a twelfth Cabinet department be created to centralize transportation agencies. At that time, as the President noted, transportation revenue accounted for one-fifth the Gross National Product in dollar value. He predicted that transportation in the United States would double in the following twenty years.

The FAA was to lose its independent status and be placed under the new Department of Transportation (DOT). No radical change due to this reorganization was planned in the work carried out by FAA. The FAA Administrator testified that commercial aviation would not be harmed.

There were objections to the establishment of the new department, but these were overruled by Congress. The Department of Transportation Act of 1966 was passed and a $6.5 billion budget was appropriated to fund it.[19]

The new Department of Transportation was directed to lead and coordinate government transportation programs, develop U.S. transportation systems, and encourage cooperation within the transportation industry. The DOT was ordered to conduct research programs to advance safety in transport. Policies and needed legislation are to be recommended by DOT to the President and Congress.

A Secretary of Transportation is appointed by the President with the advice and consent of the Senate. The Secretary is to use the facilities of the DOT to help provide United States citizens with reasonably priced and efficient transportation. In the reorganization, agencies concerned with highway, rail, air, urban mass transit, and waterway transportation were placed under the DOT.

Aviation safety regulation, accident investigation, and the determination of the probable cause of aviation accidents were placed by the act under the administrative control of the Department of Transportation. The FAA carries out the aviation safety regulation function with the FAA Administrator being responsible for air safety.[20] A National Transportation Safety Board (NTSB) was set up to investigate aviation accidents and determine their probable cause. The NTSB also investigates and assesses other transporation accidents. The decisions of the Safety Board are final. To appeal, a plaintiff must take the case directly to the courts. The Safety Board was actually an independent

The control tower and terminal building at Dulles International Airport in Virginia.

Photograph courtesy FAA.

board lodged in the Department of Transportation for "housekeeping purposes," with the Secretary of Transportation exercising no control over it.

The Secretary of Transportation has an overall charge to maintain transportation safety, including air safety which is handled by the FAA. The act encourages the FAA to reform regulations to reduce paperwork and to encourage competition in the aviation industry. Energy conservation was made an FAA policy item as well as improved airport planning responsibilities. With air transport growing and changing at such an amazing rate, FAA's projection and research departments are hard at work keeping up with aeronautical technological advances.

Airport and Airway Development Act of 1970

To expand and improve the U.S. system of airports, Congress passed the Airport and Airway Development Act.[21] This 1970 legislation was designed to meet new demands for public air transportation needs, civil defense requirements, and postal air transport challenges.

Under the Planning Grant Program (PGP), as a first step to expand and improve airports, master plans were developed with funds largely provided by the federal government.

A controversial portion of the act is the requirement for airport operating certificates for those airports served by air carriers. According to critics of this part of the act, this gives the federal government considerable control over airports. To be awarded these Airport Operating Certificates, airports must meet minimum FAA safety standards listed in Federal Aviation Regulations, Part 139.

The Airport Development Aid Program (ADAP) is FAA's administrative plan for carrying out the programs of the 1970 act.

Airport and Airway Revenue Act of 1970

New and increased taxes were imposed on the users of the airport and airway system by Title II of the Airport and Airway Revenue Act of 1970, which amends the original act of 1950. Taxes are imposed on air freight waybills, non-commercial aviation fuel sales, most domestic airline tickets, and most international airline tickets originating in the United States; and a basic annual registration tax of twenty-five dollars is imposed on all U.S. aircraft. There are added charges for aircraft weighing over twenty-five hundred pounds, which includes most multi-engine aircraft and all transport aircraft.

The purpose of the taxes imposed on aircraft, fuel, and tickets was to impose more taxation on the users of the airways and airports than on the non-flying public. Since non-flying citizens benefit from a sound U.S. air transportation system, they do bear some of the tax burdens imposed by the need for air facilities used by military and commercial aircraft.

Noise Control Act of 1972

Congress moved to set federal noise emission standards by means of the Noise Control Act of 1972, to abate harmful and distressing noise. Aircraft are specifically singled out for attention.

The Administrator of the Environmental Protection Agency is assigned the duty of coordinating federal programs in research and taking appropriate actions for noise control. The primary responsibility for the control of noise still remains, however, with state and local governments. Federal action is aimed at obtaining national unity in treating major noise sources in commerce.

Airport construction has been affected with more attention being paid to runway orientation to avoid flight over congested areas and to allow air traffic patterns to be located over open country or open water when possible. Studies are made to assure that these measures are effective.

Noise abatement procedures have been added to the aircraft commander's responsibilities. The pilot must reduce power settings, plan angles of climb, and plan turns away from congested areas to reduce noise levels. At the same time the pilot must fly the plane in a manner which will not endanger passengers or freight with such reductions in power and flight paths.

Manufacturers have noise emission standards to meet in the early 1980s. New plane design now stresses quieter operation. Sonic boom is, of course, an obvious target for federal noise abatement programs. Noise problems were a major factor in aborting the U.S. development of a supersonic transport and drastically limits the use of foreign SST aircraft.[22]

68

Transportation Safety Act of 1974

The National Transportation Safety Board (NTSB) was taken out of the Department of Transportation and made an independent agency by the Transportation Safety Act of 1974.[23]

National Climate Program Act of 1978

The goal of the National Climate Program Act of 1978 is, "An act to establish a comprehensive and coordinated national climate policy and program and for other purposes."[24] Congress was prompted to act upon finding that the U.S. lacked a program to assess weather information, to make studies of climate, and to evaluate actions taken to affect climate. The act is designed to remedy this inasmuch as "weather and climate changes affect food production, energy use, land use, water resources and other factors vital to national security and human welfare."[25]

Under the Secretary of Commerce, a National Climate Program is established to gather, study, and disseminate climate research data. Aviation is involved with this program in several ways:

1. Ozone layer penetration by high-altitude aircraft may affect the earth's climate.

2. The "seeding" of hurricanes and other large storm systems may change the path of the storm or its intensity.

3. Local flying services "seed" clouds to attempt to increase rainfall over the land owned by their customers. Other farmers take legal action to prevent this "cloud rustling." Farmers have on occasion taken direct action to the extent that FAA has had to issue advisory notes to pilots to maintain a safe altitude over certain areas involved in these disputes.[26]

NOTES

[1] Robert M. Kane and Allen D. Vose, *Air Transportation* (Dubuque, Iowa: Kendall/Hunt Publishing Co., 1977), sec. 4, p. 5.

[2] Information from comments to author by FAA Agency Historian Dr. Nick A. Komons, June 1979.

[3] *Ibid.*

[4] *Ibid.*

[5] *Ibid.*

[6] *Ibid.*

[7] Martin T. Farris and Paul T. McElhiney, *Modern Transportation* (Boston: Houghton Mifflin Co., 1973), p. 116; Ted G. Misehhimer, *Aeroscience* (Los Angeles: Aero Products Research, Inc., 1976), pp. 688-89.

[8] Gianni Sellers, *FAA World,* vol. 8, no. 8, August 1978, pp. 4-5.

[9] Sellers, p. 5; Federal Aviation Act of 1958, Public Law 85-726, S. 3880, 85th Cong., signed by President Eisenhower 23 August 1958.

[10] Sellers, p. 5.

[11] *Ibid.*

[12] *National Aeronautics and Space Act of 1958, as Amended and Related Legislation,* committee print of the Committee on Commerce, Science, and Transportation, 95th Cong., 2d sess., published December 1978, p. 1.

[13] H.B. Walters, *Wernher von Braun* (New York: MacMillan Company, 1964), pp. 136-44; R. Cargill Hall, "Early U.S. Satellite Proposals," *The History of Rocket Technology,* Eugene M. Emme, ed. (Detroit: Wayne State University Press, 1964), pp. 67-93; and Wernher von Braun, "The Redstone, Jupiter, and Juno," op. cit., pp. 107-21.

[14] Sec. 207, 1346 (b) and 2672 of Title 28, U.S. Code.

[15] *Ibid.*

[16] Public Law 95-224, Sec. 4, 3 February, 1978.

[17] Authority to release funds for the settlement of claims and judgments is given under Title 31, U.S. Code 724a.

[18] Public Law 85-726, Title III, 23 August 1958, 72 Stat. 750.

[19] Public Law 89-670, 89th Cong., 15 October 1966.

[20] Department of Transportation Act of 1966, Sec. 6(c) (1).

[21] Public Law 91-258, amended in 1971 by Public Law 92-174, and in 1976 by Public Law 94-353.

[22] See chapter on supersonic aircraft development.

[23] See the chapter on the Safety Board (NTSB) for a full discussion of its objectives.

[24] Public Law 95-367, 17 September 1978.

[25] *Ibid.*

[26] See the chapter on agricultural flying and weather modification.

One of FAA's Air Route Traffic Control Centers.

CHAPTER 7

THE FEDERAL AVIATION ADMINISTRATION

Throughout its history the Federal Aviation Administration (FAA) and its predecessor agencies has served the airman well. In the field are thousands of men and women who have earned enormous respect — FAA's controllers, inspectors, and safety agents. The basic philosophy behind the establishment of the various federal aviation agencies was, and is, to promote and encourage the development of aviation and aviation safety. In the case of the FAA therefore, we find federal employees and pilots and aircraft owners working toward the same end, air safety and a thriving air commerce.

Oddly enough, factions within the aerospace industry itself tend to affect fairness. There is considerable alarm when federal regulations appear to threaten one sector or another of the aviation industry. Assignment of finite landing slots, use of altitudes and airspace near cities, airborne equipment requirements, all are high stakes in the "flying game."

Segments of the aviation industry fear that the top levels of FAA may favor one or the other segment, as general aviation interests and the airlines vie for airspace, and argue over regulations requiring certain airborne equipment in order to use large terminal areas. Involved in this fight are powerful interests and political considerations with billions of dollars at stake. The FAA has the thankless task of making decisions which will be fair to all airspace users and yet maintain air safety.

The removal of the probable cause of accident determination from FAA's jurisdiction over most of its history, has taken one complex and involved matter out of its hands. Huge sums and extensive legal suits are involved, with the play of power and politics, all making these determinations a most difficult work.

The separation of FAA and its predecessor agencies from involvement in making awards of air carrier routes, and in setting freight rates and passenger fares, allowed the agency freedom from other controversial factors and left it free to build a respected image as a service agency. Even its regulatory and enforcement actions have earned a reputation for fairness and forbearance. In 1979 this benign attitude began to change as the FAA administrator's policy shifted to favor stiffer prosecution of violations of the Federal Air Regulations (FARs).

General aviation interests currently fear that airline influence will cause regulations to be written which will require so much electronic equipment that light aircraft will become prohibitively expensive to buy and operate. Shall only the airlines and corporate jets fly, they ask? In fact, the requirements for costly encoding altimeters required to use certain large airports, and for transponders at many other large airports, has had the effect of legislating most small planes out of these terminal points.

There is a case for such legislative "fencing-out" of small planes from large, busy airports. Still, as the Aircraft Owners and Pilots Association (AOPA) spokesmen point out, the FAA is reserving more and more controlled airspace and requiring more and more sophisticated equipment.[1] Where can the aircraft owner of modest means fly? Also there is the problem of fewer general aviation airports being available to the public each year.[2]

The FAA faces many decisions in coping with the ever-changing technology of aeronautics and electronics. To date, it can look back over its fifty-three-year history with great pride. A huge federal agency, with an over-three-billion-dollar annual budget, it preserves a service image.

Part of the FAA's success lies in its mode of changing the Federal Air Regulations. Notices of proposed changes are widely disseminated and ample opportunity to comment is afforded. Pilots and aircraft owners are fairly vociferous regarding changes if these are perceived as unsafe, unnecessary, or unfair. The AOPA and other associations watch over airmen rights. Airline organizations and manufacturers associations with headquarters in Washington, D.C., likewise "watchdog" those interests.

In the 1920s the federal government was not involved in helping to build airports, light airways, or develop radio navigational aids. It soon became apparent that the struggling air carriers, manufacturers, and general aviation companies could not, nor should they, afford airport construction and navigational aid development on the scale required. Since highways are built with public funds it seemed logical that airways and terminal points should be likewise assisted.

In 1926 the federal government planned to assist aviation by means of the Aeronautics Branch. The branch was to write air regulations, license pilots, register aircraft, and investigate accidents. The lion's share of its budget went into airway development and navigational aids. The branch also built intermediate landing fields for emergency landings. Airport development, however, was prohibited by a provision in the Air Commerce Act.

As mentioned earlier, carriage of air mail proved to be the foundation of U.S. air commerce. Beginning in 1918, the Post Office Department set up airmail routes on the East coast. By 1924, by using lighted airways (beacons) trans-continental airmail service was available.

The Bureau of Air Commerce and the Civil Aeronautics Administration

In July 1934, the Aeronautics Branch of the Department of Commerce became the Bureau of Air Commerce. It was essentially the branch under a new name. The bureau was abolished in 1938, and its responsibilities were taken over by the new Civil Aeronautics Authority, an independent agency which took on a great deal more responsibility than had been carried by the bureau. In 1940, when the authority was broken up into two organizations, the Civil Aeronautics Board and the Civil Aeronautics Administration, the Civil Aeronautics Administration was placed under the jurisdiction of the Secretary of Commerce.

The Federal Aviation Agency

The Federal Aviation Act of 1958 abolished the Civil Aeronautics Administration (CAA) and gave its responsibilities to the newly created Federal Aviation Agency (FAA). The FAA also took over the responsibilities of the Airways Modernization Board, which was abolished at this time, plus the safety rule-making functions of the Civil Aeronautics Board.

The 1958 act grew from an obvious need to expand and improve air navigational aids, air traffic control, and airports.

As is only logical, both military and civil aircraft share a common system of navigational aids and air traffic control. Additional radio frequencies and equipment are available to military and commercial aircraft to supplement the common system, still both share airspace and basic navigational aids.

It has been said that the Federal Aviation Act of 1958 was generated by a crash. It is true that the needs of aviation were brought to national notice by several accidents, including mid-air collisions in 1957 and 1958.

The Federal Aviation Administration

The Federal Aviation Agency assumed its present name, the Federal Aviation Administration (FAA) in April 1967. The FAA lost its status as an independent agency at that time and was placed under the jurisdiction of the newly-created Department of Transportation.[3]

Accident Investigation

With this change in name and status, FAA's role in accident investigation and the assignment of the probable cause of accidents changed. To review, from 1926–1938 accident investigation was the responsibility of the Aeronautics Branch and the Bureau of Air Commerce in the Department of Commerce. In 1938, an Air Safety Board under the Civil Aeronautics Authority was set up to aid in accident prevention and to investigate aircraft accidents. The Civil Aeronautics Board (CAB) took over the duties of the Air Safety Board in 1940. Accident investigation and the determination of the probable cause remained with the CAB until 1967. The Federal Aviation Act of 1958 did not change CAB's accident investigative role. With the establishment of the Department of Transportation in 1966 by the Department of Transportation Act of 1966, accident investigation became the duty of a new National Transportation Safety Board (NTSB) in 1967, in the Department of Transportation.

All through the years the FAA and its predecessor agencies have played an important part in accident investigation. Upon request, FAA assists other government agencies with aviation accident investigations. The FAA checks all accidents to see if the FARs have been violated.

The National Transportation Safety Board

The NTSB has delegated investigation of light aircraft accidents (those aircraft weighing less than 12,500 lbs.) to FAA. The NTSB investigates accidents to aircraft weighing over 12,500 pounds and all air carrier accidents. The NTSB reports, after investigation and hearings, on the probable cause of all aviation accidents.

NTSB reports cannot be used or admitted as evidence in litigation involving aircraft accidents.

There are rules providing the FAA and the NTSB with assistance and information from other departments when both military and civil aircraft are involved in an accident. The military may reserve information only if such information's release would affect national defense. When only military aircraft are involved in an accident, two factors enter the picture: were FARs violated and will air safety be improved by release of appropriate information by the military?

NTSB can instigate special three-member boards of inquiry if the public safety is in question. It is no accident that we have the safest air carrier record in the world and that thousands of general aviation flights are made safely each day.

FAA Today

As the following review of the work being done by FAA today reveals, the FAA reaches everywhere that American airmen and planes fly. It touches every airman, mechanic, controller, airport and aircraft!

The National Tort Claims Act permits suits against the government of the United States, if damage or harm results from the actions of the government or its employees engaged in the performance of their duty. Hence, it is possible to sue the government. Aircraft controllers, for example, are liable to suit as a federal employee, and the FAA must defend such suits. This is not to say that the employee is personally liable, though this is not entirely ruled out; still it would be the FAA and the DOT that would be liable were a controller sued for his on-duty actions, or if one of FAA's many inspectors were found negligent.

The primary missions of the FAA, as set forth in the various Acts of Congress noted above, are to:

Regulate air commerce

Promote, encourage and develop civil air commerce and aviation

Promote air safety

Help meet national defense needs

Regulate the use of airspace for civil and military users

Install and operate air navigational facilities

Research and develop navigational facilities

Develop and operate a common system of air traffic control and a navigational system for civil and military use.

Further, the FAA exchanges information with the Secretary of Transportation, the National Aeronautics and Space Agency and the Secretary of Defense. Liaison between these three huge federal agencies develops plans to be followed in the event of war. Problems of air space use can also be solved by inter-agency meetings.

Some of the many actions taken during a real defense emergency are: grounding of civil aircraft temporarily, the take over of air carriers' aircraft earmarked for government emergency use, and the shutdown of civil radio broadcasting stations.

Still another service provided by the FAA is the supervision of the publication of aeronautical charts, instructional materials, and reports. An interesting series of FAA publications is the Advisory Circulars (ACs) which offer detailed instructions for a great number of aviation-oriented actions — how to mark obstructions, how to best remove snow from runways, etc.

The FAA provides air traffic control facilities and the personnel required to operate them for the protection and regulation of air traffic. Most control towers, for example, are manned by FAA controllers. These men and women do not necessarily have to be pilots. Control tower personnel can be non-FAA, and, of course, the various military branches use their own controllers.

Controllers can be sued as agents of their employers. Further, controllers do not necessarily have the last word in certain situations. Should a pilot see that complying with a controller's direction will result in an unsafe condition, the pilot can legally refuse or ask for a revision. In the interests of speed and efficiency, however, there is general compliance with air traffic controllers' directions. Arguments "on the air" over minor factors would not be wise, and would cause delays.

The FAA administrator may waive rules as he will. Such waivers cover one-time ferry permits, air show permits, aerial application, sign towing, and other operations.

To develop a national system of airports, the administrator oversees all airport planning and supervises the orderly development of navigable air space.

Aircraft design and modification are checked by the FAA. Aircraft equipment, too, is carefully monitored. Obtaining a manufacturing license is a slow and costly process. Further, approval of engines, parts and equipment is not an easy process. This slows adaption of new devices and technology at times, yet is, overall, a safe and careful process.

The FAA gives all written tests to pilots, engineers, mechanics, and other licensed persons involved in aviation. The FAA personnel (inspectors) give many flight tests, but FAA also delegates to non-FAA examiners, the bulk of private pilot flight tests.

The FAA administrator, presiding over this complex and extensive agency with its approximately 60,000 employees, reports to the Secretary of Transportation. All FAA activities and investigations are written into the Secretary's annual report to Congress.

The FAA administrator decides FAA's goals and priorities and plans ahead for the coming years. This necessitates sophisticated projections of aeronautical activities and needs. Acting on the most complete information available, the administrator submits needed legislation and submits the budget required to carry out the work of the FAA in the coming year. The FAA budget is part of the DOT budget and is first reviewed by the Office of the Secretary before going to the Office of Management and Budget.

The Deputy Administrator

The deputy administrator of FAA is responsible for the direction and execution of FAA operations. The deputy administrator coordinates technical staff offices and services, and coordinates regional operations and the activities of the Bureau of National Capitol Airports. (FAA operates both Washington National Airport and Dulles International Airport.)

The deputy can serve as acting administrator of FAA if necessary. The precise duties of this office vary from administrator to administrator. The deputy administrator's job is what an incumbent administrator says it is; it can be nothing, or it can encompass very substantial responsibilities. In general, the administrator functions as "Mr. Outside," determining broad policy matters

U.S. Department of Transportation
Federal Aviation Administration

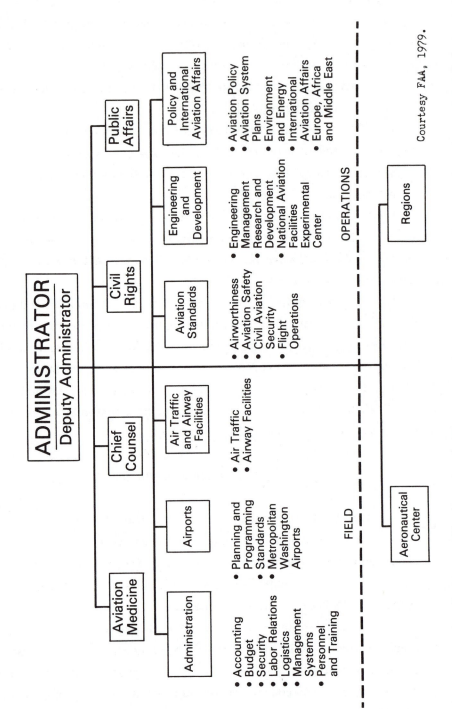

ADMINISTRATOR
Deputy Administrator

Aviation Medicine

Airports
- Planning and Programming
- Standards
- Metropolitan Washington Airports

Chief Counsel

Air Traffic and Airway Facilities
- Air Traffic
- Airway Facilities

Administration
- Accounting
- Budget
- Security
- Labor Relations
- Logistics
- Management Systems
- Personnel and Training

Civil Rights

Aviation Standards
- Airworthiness
- Aviation Safety
- Civil Aviation Security
- Flight Operations

Engineering and Development
- Engineering Management
- Research and Development
- National Aviation Facilities Experimental Center

Public Affairs

Policy and International Aviation Affairs
- Aviation Policy
- Aviation System Plans
- Environment and Energy
- International Aviation Affairs
- Europe, Africa and Middle East

FIELD

OPERATIONS

Aeronautical Center

Regions

Courtesy FAA, 1979.

and maintaining the agency's relationships with the Secretary of Transportation, the Congress, the aviation community, and the public at large. The deputy administrator as "Mr. Inside," involves himself with the agency's day-to-day internal affairs.

FAA Organization[4]

The four offices reporting directly to the administrator are:

Aviation Medicine — aviation standards, certification and programs

Chief Counsel — legal counsel and advice

Civil Rights — civil rights and equal opportunity matters

Public Affairs — public information, employee information, news media liaison

The six associate administrators who report to the administrator are:

Administration — administrative management support

Airports — administration of airport grant programs and certifications of airports and operation of two civil airports

Air Traffic and Airway Facilities — installation, maintenance and operations

Aviation Standards — safety of flight and certification of airmen, aircraft, air carriers, etc.

Engineering and Development — systems engineering, research and development and test programs

Policy and International Aviation Affairs — policy and planning and International activities

The FAA regions provide:

Agency operation in the field — this includes air traffic operational services, flight standards inspection, certification and surveillance, facilities and facilities and equipment maintenance and installation, airport development and airport development and certification, airman medical certification, civil aviation security services.

The Mike Monroney Aeronautical Center: Oklahoma City, Oklahoma, carries on:

Aircraft maintenance and modification

Airmen certification and aircraft registration

Central material inventory and distribution system

Technical training programs

NOTES

[1] *AOPA Newsletter*, May 1979.

[2] See the chapter on airports for discussion of this factor.

[3] *Department of Transportation Act of 1966.*

[4] Interview with Dr. Nick A. Komons, FAA Agency Historian, June 1979.

CHAPTER 8

THE CIVIL AERONAUTICS BOARD

Economic regulation of domestic transportation by the federal government began about a century ago with legislation concerning railroads. By 1910 federal regulation spread to communications and by 1916 to ocean shipping. In the 1930s, with the U.S. economy at a standstill due to the depression, more federal controls were placed on American business with the addition of regulations concerning interstate motor transport and airlines.

For years it seemed that nothing could stop the implacable spread of federal regulation into every corner of our business and personal lives. That is why the story of the deregulation of the U.S. air carrier industry is such an encouraging and significant one. It promises to be what CAB Board Chairman Marvin Cohen calls, "the cutting edge of what could be a historic movement."[1]

U.S. Regulatory Commissions

U.S. regulatory commissions set up regulations and exercise economic controls.

The courts actually carry out enforcement actions not coming under a commission's enforcement sanctions of license and certificate revocation. The commissions and the courts act in a partnership relation.

Courts can review a commission's decisions if Constitutional issues are in question. The provisions of the 5th and 14th Amendments to the Constitution of the United States say that a person cannot be deprived of property without due process of law.

On the other hand, Article I, Section 8 (3) of the Constitution gives Congress the power to "regulate commerce among the several states." Power not included in this and other statements in the Constitution revert to (belong to) the states. For example, interstate commerce is regulated via the Interstate Commerce Commission (ICC), the CAB, and other commissions, while intrastate commerce is regulated by state commissions.

Overall, federal regulatory agencies are designed to help develop service, promote safety, offer service to all, refrain from discriminatory practices, and to offer reasonable rates to all.

CAB — Early Developmental Factors

The Air Commerce Act of 1926 imposed no economic regulation on aeronautics, stressing only safety regulation.[2] Any person who complied with these safety rules could operate an airline. In actual practice, however, the Post Office Department's contracts largely controlled airline competition.

Under the Airmail Act of 1925, the "Kelly Act," sponsored by Rep. Clyde Kelly of Pennsylvania, private contractors could bid for airmail contracts. The provisions of the Airmail Act of 1930, the "McNary-Watres Act" gave the newly-appointed Postmaster General Walter Brown methods of controlling air carrier development to a great extent.

The Postmaster General saw airline companies struggling to survive often without adequate capitalization which had the effect of slowing the introduction of expensive, larger aircraft. Only with modern, passenger-carrying aircraft could the national air carrier system develop in Brown's view. Hence, with mail contract awards, a few strong lines survived and many smaller companies failed. The matter was not as simplistic as this, of course, but in general this was the situation.

By 1938 the airlines, airmail contractors, now offered regularly scheduled passenger and airmail service over set routes. Some air freight was carried. Another segment of the aviation industry was the manufacturers and suppliers. Still another portion of the national aviation business was made up of flying schools, airport operators, aerial applicators, and itinerant air show operations. Charter flights were offered by flying schools and airport operators.

Economic Regulation Begins

With the passage of the Civil Aeronautics Act of 1938, the 1926 act and the airmail acts were largely replaced. The Civil Aeronautics Act of 1938 brought air carriers under federal economic control with regulation of the sort usually placed on public utility companies.

Air mail contracts were almost all eliminated, and instead air carriers were awarded certificates of public convenience and necessity, authorizing transportation of mail, persons and property, once a public need was demonstrated via public hearings. In effect, very nearly dictatorial powers were exercised by the CAB under the provisions of the act. The act gave subsidy in the form of mail payment, controlled domestic rates, and controlled mergers and other relationships between airlines.

"Grandfather provisions" enabled the then-existing airlines to automatically gain certificates, an enormous advantage over airlines seeking entry into the field. A further advantage granted operating carriers was the exemption allowed by CAB under the 1938 act relieving these carriers from some of the economic regulations. Also, certified carriers were granted exemptions to conduct special activities such as one-time charters, temporary service.

Local fixed-base operators were exempted from most air carrier requirements and subsidy. Air taxi services were allowed under an exemption to provide service to certain points.

Supplemental air carriers developed following World War II under a blanket exemption originally meant for fixed-base operators, providing air taxi type transport of passengers and freight. In this way, hampered as they were from gaining certification by CAB requirements, hearings, paperwork, and decisions, the new airlines grew and hoped to gain entry into the U.S. air carrier business.

So important did these large supplementals grow that the CAB designed regulations specifically for their operation. Just at the time that the CAB planned to grant the supplemental airlines certification, powerful opposition developed and adverse court decisions threatened the survival of supplemental air carriage. In 1962 the Congress granted the supplementals (by now far too large to ignore) certificates by amending the Civil Aeronautics Act of 1938. Their certificates, however, were limited to charter flights to supplement the larger regular route carriers (the trunk airlines).

The CAB, constrained by legislation which its members perceived as a mandate to protect existing air carriers from competition, stood firmly across the door offering entry to new certification of air carriers. One might object to this statement by pointing to the cargo carriers, to Trans Caribbean, Wright Airlines (serving Cleveland and Detroit), and Air New England as examples of new entries allowed to enter the air carrier industry. These, however, seldom directly threatened the large trunk carriers. For nearly forty years in a truly awe-inspiring demonstration of monolithic bureaucratic obstructionism the CAB carried out its perceived role effectively indeed.

Provisions of the Civil Aeronautics Act of 1938

Originally the 1938 Civil Aeronautics Act was administered by three groups. There was a five-member Civil Aeronautics Authority to regulate and enforce regulation; three-member Air Safety Board which investigated aviation accidents, reported on their probable cause and made accident prevention recommendations. Finally, there was an Administrator of Civil Aeronautics whose duty was to assist the Civil Aeronautics Authority to develop landing areas, civil airways, and air navigational facilities.

Reorganization Plans — 1940

By 1940 under reorganization plans the Air Safety Board was abolished. The five-member Civil Aeronautics Authority absorbed the work of the now defunct Air Safety Board. The Civil Aeronautics Authority was renamed and became the Civil Aeronautics Board with the status of an independent regulatory agency.

The Administrator of Aeronautics by 1940 headed an organization known as the Civil Aeronautics Administration (CAA), and this, in the reorganization, was placed under the Department of Commerce.

An Independent CAB

Under the Civil Aeronautics Act of 1938 and the 1940 reorganizations, the duties of the CAB were now:

(a) The economic regulation of United States air carriers both nationally and internationally. This included the power to offer or withdraw airline operating authority. Further, the CAB was to fix rates in many areas, to control mergers, to rule on whether routes might be abandoned and to require service as deemed necessary.

(b) In cooperation with the Department of State, to decide on reciprocal air agreements. Also, CAB controlled the entry of foreign air carriers into the United States.

(c) To set safety standards for commercial civil aviation, including air carriers. This involved suspension of safety certificates by the CAB if deemed necessary.

(d) The investigation of aircraft accidents and the determination of probable cause of the accidents.

The Federal Aviation Act of 1958

The Federal Aviation Act of 1958 made virtually no changes in the economic regulation of air carriers by CAB. Also, the board kept its aircraft accident investigative role. The duty of safety regulation passed to the new Federal Aviation Agency (formerly CAA). The FAA was now an independent agency and set regulations and standards for U.S. aviation. The CAB remained an interested party to safety regulations. The FAA could now recommend revocation of safety certificates, as could CAB.

Generally, with the above exceptions, the CAB's powers were unchanged. Indeed, a clearer authority was given to CAB to decide matters of air space usage, allocations of navigable air space between civil and military users.

Transportation Act of 1966

With the establishment of the Department of Transportation (DOT), on 1 April 1967, a reshuffling of agencies took place. The CAB remained an independent agency but lost its accident investigation and related functions. These went to the new DOT and were placed under the responsibilities of the National Transportation Safety Board (NTSB). The NTSB investigates with the aid of federal and state authorities not only aircraft accidents but rail and motor carrier accidents as well. The NTSB determines and publishes the probable cause of the accidents.[3] Many of the investigations and findings of the NTSB are not in themselves admissable as evidence in litigation.

The CAB was governed not only by the Federal Aviation Act of 1958 but by other legislation such as the Transportation Act of 1966 discussed above.

The Civil Aeronautics Board is made up of five members serving six-year terms. The terms expire on a staggered schedule to allow continuity. Board members are appointed by the President with the advice and consent of the Senate. Only three of the board members may be of the same political party. Each year the President designates one member of the board as chairman, and another as vice-chairman. Three members present constitute a quorum at meetings. Board decisions are reviewable in the Courts of Appeals. Decisions on foreign air carrier permits and matters involving international routes are submitted to the President for his approval. Presidential decisions are not appealable.

CAB Organization

The Managing Director: is responsible for devising, installing and otherwise implementing operating procedures for the administration and enforcement of the statutes and regulations under which the board operates; develops and, under a broad delegation of authority from the chairman, executes the administrative policies of the board and consults with and advises the board members with respect to carrier-judicial policies, decisions, orders, rules and practices as they may affect, or be affected by, operational or administrative policies.

The Comptroller: serves as the top level executive assistant to the Managing Director in the development and execution of financial, budget, information management, data processing and general management policies and programs.

The Secretary: holds and distributes CAB documents, reviews documents, and processes formal CAB actions.

CAB established an Office of Economic Analysis (OEA) in August 1977 to help the Board define and achieve its work. The OEA through studies of interrelated factors is to determine some of CAB's future actions with regard to rates charged by the airlines and services needed. Both airfreight shippers and air travellers are expected to benefit from these analyses.

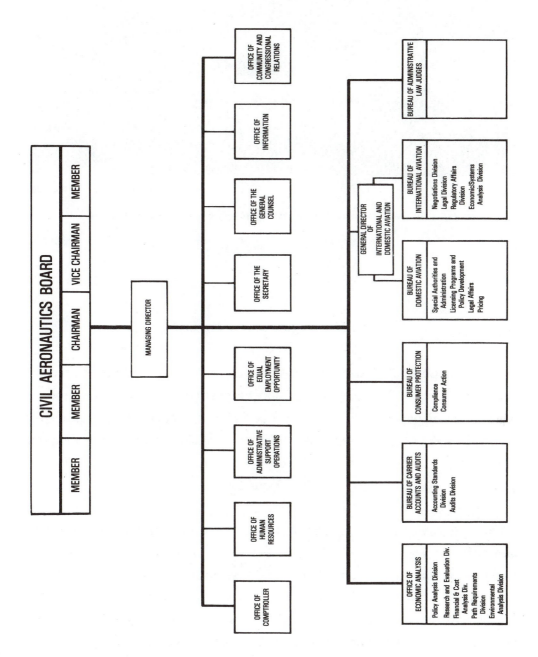

CIVIL AERONAUTICS BOARD

| MEMBER | MEMBER | CHAIRMAN | VICE CHAIRMAN | MEMBER |

MANAGING DIRECTOR

OFFICE OF COMPTROLLER

OFFICE OF HUMAN RESOURCES

OFFICE OF ADMINISTRATIVE SUPPORT OPERATIONS

OFFICE OF EQUAL EMPLOYMENT OPPORTUNITY

OFFICE OF THE SECRETARY

OFFICE OF THE GENERAL COUNSEL

OFFICE OF INFORMATION

OFFICE OF COMMUNITY AND CONGRESSIONAL RELATIONS

OFFICE OF ECONOMIC ANALYSIS
Policy Analysis Division
Research and Evaluation Div.
Financial & Cost Analysis Div.
Path Requirements Division
Environmental Analysis Division

BUREAU OF CARRIER ACCOUNTS AND AUDITS
Accounting Standards Division
Audits Division

BUREAU OF CONSUMER PROTECTION
Compliance
Consumer Action

GENERAL DIRECTOR OF INTERNATIONAL AND DOMESTIC AVIATION

BUREAU OF DOMESTIC AVIATION
Special Authorities and Administration
Licensing Programs and Policy Development
Legal Affairs
Pricing

BUREAU OF INTERNATIONAL AVIATION
Negotiations Division
Legal Division
Regulatory Affairs Division
Economic/Systems Analysis Division

BUREAU OF ADMINISTRATIVE LAW JUDGES

The wide body Rockwell Commander 700, a new business transport.

Who May Appear Before the CAB?

The U.S. Code of Federal Regulations, Section 30211 (a) states that any party to a proceeding may appear and be heard in person or by attorney. No register of persons who may practice before the board (Civil Aeronautic Board) is maintained and no application for admission to practice is required.

In 1974 in the Senate

In California and Texas competing, unregulated intrastate airlines prospered and offered good service at reasonable prices for over twenty years. This experience prompted action at a national level in the 1974-76 period. Senator Edward M. Kennedy held hearings on "Oversight of the C.A.B. Practices and Procedures." Upon examining CAB past and present goals and actions, both CAB and the Gerald Ford administration advocated a relaxation of the maze of regulations which bound U.S. air carriers.

Senator Howard Cannon, Chairman of the Commerce Committee, and Senator Edward Kennedy in 1974, proposed a regulatory reform bill, and the CAB greatly loosened its restrictions on charter flights.

In response to charter liberalization, American airlines introduced its "Super Saver" transcontinental fares. Others followed suit. The energetic English businessman Freddie Laker with his "Skytrain" to Europe soon placed more pressure on all airlines to reduce fares.

How is this possible? How can one airline offer transportation over the same route at 50 percent or more off the standard fare? The answer is that there are fixed costs to making the flight at all. The airplane must be purchased or leased, the fuel and supplies must be used, and the ground hangar, maintenance and terminal facilities must be paid for. The crew and ground personnel must be present.

If the airline can fly with only 50 percent of the seats filled, the other 50 percent of the plane is wasted. The airline can fill these seats, asking any fare, and be ahead. A filled aircraft can operate at a lower cost per passenger.

Other situations which offer lower fares are flights which must be made in any case by the airline: (a) to return planes and reposition them, (b) to reposition aircraft at unpopular middle-of-the-night times, (c) to keep schedules in off season or mid-week times. Also, "no-shows" of passengers with reserved seats, can be filled by "stand-by" passengers who will pay lower fares but at least will pay the airline something for the seat.

In effect, much airline capacity was being wasted. Once allowed to offer seats at reduced prices, in return for the passenger flying when seats were available and for prepayment of fares, the airlines made more money.

Further, once lower fares were made available, the response of the public proved to be overwhelming. A huge hitherto unexploited market was revealed.

STATEMENT OF SENATOR EDWARD M. KENNEDY DURING SENATE CONSIDERATION OF S. 2493 (April 19, 1978) [4]

Only slightly more than four years ago the Subcommittee on Administrative Practice and Procedure looked at the performance of the Civil Aeronautics Board and discovered that the Board's procedures were unfair to some industry groups, inadequate to protect the interests of the traveling public, inefficient, and biased in favor of existing major carriers. Underlying our report on the CAB, issued in 1975, was the firm conviction of the Subcommittee members that the existing Federal Aviation Act needed substantial overhaul if both the industry and the public were to be best served.

It is now clear beyond doubt that the aviation regulatory scheme devised in the depression to protect an infant industry has resulted in higher fares, less service — especially to smaller communities, fewer competitive alternatives and generally less competition than the public deserves, and has a right to expect, from a mature industry.

Our studies have shown, for example, that in those intra-state markets where airlines are free to enter and compete on their merits, prices are lower and service better than the prices and service offered by regulated inter-state carriers over comparable routes.

Over the past several months we have seen additional proof of the popularity, and profitability, of competition. Under the leadership of President Carter and Chairman Kahn[5] of the CAB carriers have been freed to increase their competitiveness both here in the United States and abroad.

The result has been the lowest air fares in history — and higher profits than the industry has enjoyed in more than a decade.

S. 2493 reforms the present law in four fundamental ways.

First, the bill substitutes carrier rate flexibility for government control of rates. Predatory pricing below cost is forbidden. But so long as a carrier's rates are profitable, it has the right to engage in the same competitive bidding for the public's patronage that we depend on in other industries to provide consumers with better products and lower prices. The lower fares that such competition brings about are highly popular with consumers — we would expect this as a matter of common sense; this has now been proven by the experience of intrastate carriers and by the recent interstate experience as well. The experience also shows that such competition can be highly profitable for the carriers as well.

Second, the bill reduces the presently overly restrictive limitations on entry. Since 1938 not one new trunk carrier has been certified by the CAB in the face of 80 applications for such certificates since 1950. The CAB under this bill will, of course, continue to regulate entry. But now it will be possible for a limited number of competitors to enter selected markets. Such new entry will provide new competitive alternatives for consumers and new competitive opportunities for carriers. The threat of such entry will also act as a spur to improved service and lowered prices by existing carriers.

Third, the bill is fashioned to provide improved service to small communities. This feature of the legislation is the result in large part of the work of Senator Pearson. Studies have shown that service to smaller communities was seriously deteriorating. S. 2493 contains provisions which will halt that trend and encourage better, more flexible service to small communities. The easing of entry restrictions will also benefit smaller communites seeking new or improved service.

Fourth, this bill refines the standards for the granting of antitrust exemptions to airline carriers. It provides that the CAB can tailor the antitrust exemption granted to fit the air transportation needs of a particular case, instead of committing itself to a blanket exemption every time an agreement is approved. This provision, like the bill as a whole reduces unnecessary restriction on com-

92

petition while preserving the CAB's authority to regulate where necessary to promote legitimate air transportation objectives.

By October of 1978, traffic on certificated carriers ran 20 percent above the record levels of 1977, with well over 40 percent of the travellers flying at discounts. CAB Chairman Alfred E. Kahn stated that these gains in traffic and revenue represented the benefits of competition.

Winds of Change

The appointment on 10 June 1977 of a new CAB chairman, Alfred E. Kahn, proved to be a momentous one for the air transportation industry. It is interesting to see how Kahn's direct actions brought about the deregulation first proposed by Senators Kennedy and Cannon.

The CAB's 1977 *Report to Congress* noted many winds of change sweeping the CAB. Working under the same legislation as previous Civil Aeronautics Boards, the 1977 CAB members instituted what Chairman Kahn called "innovative legal practices." Objections poured in from airlines, the exception being United Air Lines, largest carrier in the world. It was now unclear as to whether the air transportation industry feared being eaten alive by National or scared to death by the vigorous removal of their former protections by Chairman Kahn and the CAB.

Historically, since the time of Postmaster General Walter Brown in the 1930s, the philosophy of federal air carrier regulation had been to make certain that the U.S. had the benefit of a few strong, well-financed, air carriers.

In the 1920s and 1930s, lacking funds, fledgling airlines failed to buy new aircraft and were unable to equip and staff them well or maintain the aircraft they had or required. These were several reasons to build a few, strong airlines via protective legislation which awarded routes, paid subsidies for mail carriage, and allow major airlines immunity from U.S. antitrust laws.

In the 1970s the federal authorities realized that safety regulations now in effect would protect the public. As to financial stability, there are now enormous sums available to properly capitalize airlines. This is true today because markets await development. Air travel has become necessary and well accepted. Further, just over the horizon is a shift from surface carriers to air freight of giant proportions. In a word, the air transport industry has grown up.

93

What were the objections to continuing to regulate the air lines? Here, according to the statements of Chairman Alfred E. Kahn, are some of the outmoded practices of federal air carrier control:

> CAB doesn't have the ability to say what markets are, what routes should be flown, and what aircraft should be used. A competitive market, allowing businessmen to invest freely, will regulate air commerce better than CAB or any federal agency can. This points to a future with revenues up, prices down, and more services available.[6]

Antitrust immunity may no longer be as justified. For forty years the air carriers had virtual antitrust immunity in order that strong financial backing could be attracted to a new industry. Today's mature aviation industry stands in less need of this immunity and, indeed, growth of air commerce may well be hampered by the cartelization of the U.S. air carrier industry. Further, CAB now sees complete control over all airline mergers and proprietorship as constrictive and unfair to both American business and to the public interest.

Legislation affecting CAB activities in revision of antitrust immunity practices is the Hart-Scott-Rodino Antitrust Improvements Act of 1976 (Public Law 94-435) approved 30 September 1976. This measure affects certain areas of antitrust law, civil procedures regarding antitrust complaints, pre-merger notification requirements, and *parens patrie* actions (guardianship of persons or organizations needing it by a government, "parental" agent) by state attorneys general.[7]

Outmoded Practices: Routes

For CAB to continue to award routes as before makes no sense Dr. Kahn stated. Airlines must serve routes they hold or give them up, also certificated carriers may wish to suspend a route and service will be provided by a commuter air carrier.

There are over three hundred U.S. commuter air carriers conducting scheduled service. The development of planes with speed, range and short-haul efficiency has made commuter service safe and comfortable at a lower cost

94

than that provided by large airlines which operate transports often more suited to transoceanic or transcontinental use.

Nearly three thousand air taxi and commuter operators filed reports with CAB in 1977.

The CAB in 1977 began to approve certification of more air carriers, approved more routes, and approved multiple service on many routes.

Air Cargo

Air cargo was virtually deregulated in November 1977 by Public Law 95-163. No more huge stacks of papers had to be submitted for route permissions. If a company was stable, and able, then the route was awarded.

In the first six months of 1978 air freight ton miles went up 14 percent over 1977 levels. Seventy-five new all-cargo carriers were certified. Free to set prices generally where they would, these freighters found that customers would pay steep prices for special handling projects. On the other end of the price scale, freight air carriers could offer big discounts for off-peak-hours transportation.

When the public discovers how much weight and cubic footage aircraft can handle and how fast it can be moved, air freight will grow. Further advantages are (a) less damage generally to freight and (b) competitive rates obtainable by contracting for off-peak, over forty-eight-hour delivery, and space available options.

Containerization is growing in favor with airlines and customers. Handling costs are lessened and damage claims reduced.

Animals in air transit are protected by both CAB and U.S. Department of Agriculture regulations. Airlines may reject certain hostile creatures but must exercise general care and humane treatment of live stock accepted for transport.

Air Freight Forwarders

Oddly, some companies in the business of providing customers with air freight service are not actually "in the business," since these companies may not be operators of airlines or aircraft at all. The freight forwarder contracts with a customer to take freight from one location to another. The forwarder accomplishes this by arranging loading, carriage, transfer from one mode of carriage to another (from truck to aircraft, for example), paperwork and payments to the carriers, off loading and delivery. The forwarder pays for all of this and is in turn reimbursed by his customers. Forwarders can relieve their clients of much paperwork, including customs forms.

Freight forwarding is an important and growing business. In 1977 over 33 percent of all U.S. interstate air freight and about 12 percent of international air freight received by U.S. airlines was air freight forwarder traffic.

Need for Legislation

CAB member Elizabeth E. Bailey in February 1978, joined Chairman Kahn as she urged Congress to pass explicit and permanent legislation deregulating the air carrier industry.[8] The work toward this end done by the CAB in 1977 might well be reversed by the courts and by later boards she stated. Further, an examination of the CAB in recent years shows "cumbersome and lengthy procedures." She cited applications for fare reductions which were refused a hearing for five years and others requesting permission to provide needed services going unheard. Applications to offer services and new routes were not being heard in 1977, in spite of CAB's efforts to do so, due to cumbersome procedures imposed by 1958 legislation. Chairman Kahn and other members of the board appeared before Congressional committees urging strong and explicit legislation to open up entry, reduce regulations, and afford more flexible pricing of air transportation.

Chairman Kahn noted that during 1976-1978 and, in spite of changing membership, the five CAB members have unanimously urged the House and Senate to pass reform legislation swiftly. Kahn mentioned that since November 1974, eight sets of hearings were held by five separate Congressional committees — a total of more than sixty days of testimony. The CAB during this time made several presentations and testified frequently. Dozens of reports and studies were submitted by the CAB, DOT, General Accounting Office and several Congressional committees. Nearly twenty thousand pages of evidence in all. Kahn urged that reform not be "talked to death" but acted on and swiftly.

He praised the House of Representatives Bill 11145 under consideration and urged its passage. He feared that even though the present CAB was allowing competition and streamlining procedures, future boards might not. Further, court decisions could reverse even the work done so far unless Congress acted to give CAB firm legal mandates to continue its pro-competitive, anti-regulatory efforts.

In the early 1960s there were few new air carriers admitted, certified by CAB. In mid and late 1960s changes began.

The character of local service carriers changed and CAB granted a significant competitive authority. Then suddenly, starting in 1969 and continuing through 1974 a route moratorium prevailed! There were virtually *no competitive route awards for five years!* Just as suddenly as it began, in 1975 the route moratorium ended.[9]

In February 1978 Dr. Elizabeth E. Bailey, CAB member, urged a Congressional Forum on Regulatory Reform to give CAB ". . . a statute with provisions for procedural expedition including the ability to create classes of applications subject only to the most minimal procedures. You (the Congress) can give us (the CAB) as much automatic authority as possible and expand our policy options well beyond an occasional multiple award, and/or grant of permissive or back-up authority."[10]

Seven major reasons for urging new CAB legislation, all requiring legislation to be possible, were given by CAB Chairman Alfred E. Kahn:[11]

1. Complete overhaul of small community air transportation program long needed.

2. Fundamental changes are needed in *removing regulation from air transport industry.* Competition is superior to regulation in serving the public interest. It holds prices in check, stimulates cost, price and service innovations.

    Let airline management, not government make decisions as to *where to fly* and *what to change.* CAB is not as capable as management.

    (In March, Dr. Kahn still advocated gradual change in the deregulation

97

process, due to industry need to adjust from its long history of government protection.)

Automatic entry is needed to pass decision-making over to business.

3. We must get out of our *procedural* morass. (Mentions one case which has lasted eleven years!) Routine work needs legislation to speed it up.

4. "Glowing reports of the Board's recent successes are . . . both premature and exaggerated. We have taken bold initiatives on a number of fronts." The courts and present legislation make these *subject to reversal* unless Congress comes through with legislation to make these changes permanent.

   As it is, "our flexibility is grossly restricted by the present law and by its interpretation over the last forty years."

   A revision of charter rules in process at CAB "will give *supplemental carriers* for the first time genuine opportunities to compete. But every such step poses serious legal problems. . . . Those who oppose many of the changes we are making have forty years of CAB precedent to back them up."

   Kahn noted that the present CAB was reinterpreting a forty-year-old statute but the courts might not agree. Airlines, too, oppose changes and are good at litigation! A whelter of indecision will result as the CAB wins some concessions, loses others.

5. Kahn noted that under present legislation CAB is doing what no democratic government should do: May a business sell and a buyer accept? How many seats may an air taxi aircraft be allowed? May a certificated carrier pick up stranded charter passengers and fill seats otherwise empty? These and scores or other ridiculous (for a government) decisions are posed to CAB daily the chairman stated.

6. The forty-year-old statute no longer applies and CAB needs new

orders. In 1938 flying was a risky financial venture with only a few small airlines in existence. Today the industry is huge and can expand more if allowed to do so. Congress is urged to remove prescriptions and proscriptions.

7. Only Congress can prevent the reversal of the present CAB's work in making important and needed changes.

On 16 May 1978 Dr. Kahn spoke before the International Aviation Club, Washington, D.C., mentioning the drastic shift in federal regulatory policies at CAB. He then tackled several issues.

First, in international negotiations Kahn advocated bilateral agreement and frank economic and air service pressures to gain competitive opportunities for U.S. airlines operating abroad. He advocated access by airlines to compete in services, routes offered, and prices charged. Only regulation to prevent predatory practices should be required. Recent agreements with government of the Netherlands and Belgium were cited as good ones.

Kahn urged that artifical and discriminatory barriers be removed by bargaining. Incentives that may be held out to foreign governments included access to American markets and reciprocal concessions, with no concessions on part of the U.S. alone. Work must go forward to prevent cartelization under Bermuda-type agreements. Bilateral horse trading is required, Kahn noted.

Doomsayers to free competition can now look about and see results of less government intervention, more competition: "traffic surging, tourism burgeoning, employment growing, and aircraft orders recovering."

A second issue is the determination of the proper role of charters and scheduled service. No one can know, but free competition can soon answer the question. There seems to be a market for both scheduled and charter service. Perhaps the outcome will be tied to costs, somewhat — very high fares for scheduled transport and low fares for charters (with high load factors, hence lower per passenger costs). Kahn suggested that the CAB get out of the way and let business decide what kind of service is to be offered. He would certify supplemental carriers for scheduled service and allow scheduled carriers freer access to charter mode.

Finally, Kahn asked what should be the future role of International Air Transport Association (IATA)? Basically, IATA violates price-fixing and antitrust laws by setting rates with the agreement of member airlines. On the other hand, IATA serves the public interest by standardizing airline forms, interline billing, providing for interline baggage checking, assigning of flight numbers, and many more valuable interairline liaison work.

The CAB approved the initial IATA agreement in 1946. CAB had no power over fares and rates charged by the world's airlines and even directly, over its own international air carriers. The IATA gave CAB an opportunity to participate indirectly in influencing international price setting. The only alternative to setting prices in traffic conferences seemed unilateral control by other governments of rates charged by U.S. carriers.

In 1972 CAB was given the power to cancel, investigate, and suspend international tariffs considered unlawful by the board.

Do foreign governments then give up ultimate sovereign authority over rates their airlines charge and authority to regulate the rates of airlines operating into their countries? Some have to a limited extent. For example, Israel, Thailand, Korea, Singapore, Belgium, and Jamaica have agreed to a "double disapproval" of fares plan. This means that both the U.S. and the foreign state must disapprove a fare before it can be suspended.

Several governments of foreign countries have seen benefits in allowing freer international price competition. The U.S. has signed treaties with the Netherlands and the Federal Republic of Germany. Some relaxation of regulation is seen, too, in bilateral treaties signed between the U.S. and the Netherlands, Great Britain, and Belgium. Temporary agreements have been signed with Australia, Papua-New Guinea, Peru, and Fiji. In these last-mentioned agreements the governments concerned allow airlines to set their own rates for flights originating in the foreign country. Consultations may be called at any time and the bilateral agreement may even be cancelled.

CAB chairman Kahn in May 1978 expressed a tendency to pull out of the IATA conference in favor of such bilateral agreements. The chairman denied that such agreements were designed to "divide and conquer" foreign groups of nation; yet, of course, this is what insues in practice. It also puts economic pressures on neighboring nations, when one country signs such bilateral agreements. The government of the United States does have considerable leverage in the IATA through U.S. power to approve or disapprove IATA agreements.

Kahn noted in May 1978 that tidy solutions tend toward cartelization of the air carrier industry. He suggested that pragmatic and innovative action dictated by real conditions might be the best policy.

In a talk given before the American Bar Association in August 1978, Kahn denied that the CAB was in effect carrying out regulatory reform without legislation or due process of law. He preferred to call the board's recent actions creative reinterpretation of CAB's original mandate in the light of a now mature industry.

Dr. Kahn described the basic unfairness of a CAB which denied entry to willing an able companies. The injustice of hearings and applications denied and the cumbersome procedures of the CAB in the past were not consistent with American freedoms, Dr. Kahn stated, and cited historic decisions of CAB. The opening up of the air carrier industry to new companies and the deregulation proposed by CAB would lower costs, offer lower prices for carriage and increase airline revenue.

"The CAB," Dr. Kahn said, "had come full circle from lusty youth to ineffective senility and no longer fitted the needs of today's air industry. It hasn't the ability to regulate them." Dr. Kahn challenged the attorneys before him to seek less protection of established interests and open up their minds to new and exciting ideas.

The Economics of Deregulation

"Simply getting out of the way," CAB Chairman Alfred Kahn admitted to the American Economic Association (AEA) members in August 1978, was almost impossible with CAB's outmoded role buttressed by forty years of precedent and cases. He described the way in which he had, in the prior fifteen months, tried to cope with a transition in the air transportation industry from cartelization to free competition.

At first he had favored gradual deregulation but later saw that it would offer unfair opportunities to some segments of the industry. He told AEA members it seemed that deregulation should proceed rapidly, that the doors to the

101

industry should be thrown open, and that the market place should dictate routes served and prices charged. The CAB's future role, Kahn stated, should be to watch for violations of antitrust legislation, assist in consumer protection, aid the development of air services to small communities, and watch the airlines for evidences of predatory trade practices.

Dr. Kahn told AEA members that the statement that CAB has since 1938 permitted no entry into the airline business, or at least into the part served by the "trunk carriers," is wrong in detail yet true in describing CAB's spirit. Revenue passenger miles (RPM) had increased three hundred times in the period between 1938 and 1977, but the grandfather carriers continued to fly over ninety percent of the RPM in the continental United States.

The remaining ten percent of RPM flown by local and regional certificated carriers often serve markets never operated by the trunk airlines, or routes abandoned by them. With very few exceptions virtually no firms directly competed in the forty-eight states with the trunk airlines. Thus, the CAB policies in 1977 represent a radical break with tradition, Kahn said.

Slots

Smaller carriers applying to serve a congested airport may have to accept a less desirable "time slot" because (a) the big certificated carriers have the most desirable (landing time) slots reserved and (b) taking a large plane out of a slot in order to let a smaller plane use it means fewer people moved. Chairman Kahn suggested a uniform policy at airports across the nation that would charge more for the best time slots, rewarding carriers willing to take other than peak traffic hours slots. Likewise, a reduction in fees at less used airports and increase of fees at high-traffic-density airports would tend to spread the traffic around.

The CAB in 1977 also began to rethink the route antitrust exemption given large carriers which permitted them to get together and allocate slots.

The Laker Decision

In September of 1977 the CAB attempted to place some limits on how much transatlantic fares could be cut by certificated carriers who wanted to do so to compete with charter flights and in particular with Laker Airway's "Sky-train." The board felt that had it not been for Laker and the charters, the trunk airlines would have continued to deprive consumers of discount trans-atlantic fares. The board also recommended a lower limit to fare reductions by the trunks in order to continue to give the charter carriers a chance to compete with the trunks.

President Carter vetoed this lower limitation, however, and fares dropped, though often with certain restrictions imposed. Allowing trunk carriers to drop fares made it urgent that the CAB certify more supplemental carriers so that they could get into the marketplace and share in markets now opening up with these fare reductions.

Statement of Senator Edward M. Kennedy On the Occasion of the Presidential Signing of the Airline Deregulation Bill (S.2493) October 24, 1978

> Less than four years ago, when I began hearings on airline regulatory reform virtually no one predicted that any meaningful reduction of government regu-lation would be politically possible. Even two years ago, airline regulatory reform was a controversial and highly contested issue. Today, the clear need to reduce airline regulation is accepted not only by many of the original skeptics but even by many of those who initially argued that reducing regulation would result in airline bankruptcies and a destruction of our air travel system . . .
>
> Industries reluctant to leave the regulatory incubator or seeking governmental pricing protections should also heed the airline example. In an age of spiralling inflation, the airline industry has returned record profits by cutting prices.[12]

"All of us have a big stake in seeing that this country gets its act together on international aviation" wrote former CAB Chairman John E. Robson, in an article in *The Washington Post,* on 15 October 1977. (During his chairmanship Robson supported deregulation yet ran the CAB as constrained by the 1935 legislation.)

Robson noted that the International Air Transport Association aviation price-setting cartel was accepted as necessary and had worked smoothly. He warned that foreign governments had to be won over individually to allow American carriers to land and to obtain efficient service. Further, each country naturally wants to favor its own carriers. In the face of *de facto* deregulation, Robson cautioned, foreign governments might roll up the red carpet and penalize U.S. airlines.

President Carter and Congress, Robson continued, have a good opportunity to give international aviation a close scrutiny and evolve a coherent international aviation policy.

The Airline Deregulation Act of 1978

The Airline Deregulation Act of 1978 amends section 102 of the Federal Aviation Act of 1958 in important ways.[13]   The new "Declaration of Policy" removes CAB's old protectionist policy and has now made competition an end in itself. Safety is still stressed as the foremost concern of the government via standards to be imposed by the Federal Aviation Administration. The CAB is directed to encourage entry by new and existing carriers into new markets. An explicit goal in the 1978 legislation is to make CAB decisions prompt. Applicants for new certification and/or new routes long complained of CAB's cumbersome and time-consuming application machinery.

Another goal of the 1978 legislation is air service at major urban areas to be provided by more secondary and/or satellite airports. Continued and continuous air service to small communities and isolated areas is provided for by means of direct subsidies in the act.

Small carriers are to be strengthened and opportunities are to be made available to them. More than one or two carriers may serve the same route under the CAB's multiple permissive authority program.

These and other goals were set by the Airline Deregulation Act. A discussion in more detail follows.

Small Communities Air Service Program

It is not profitable for an airline to stop at small cities to pick up or discharge only a few passengers, yet these communities need air transport. The federal government plans to step into the picture with subsidized flights. In previous years the CAB pressed airlines to maintain quite a number of unremunerative routes. Today, under the provisions of the Airline Deregulation Act of 1978, airlines may abandon routes that are not profitable simply by notifying the board on sixty or ninety-day notice. If the abandonment of service by that airline adversely affects the essential level of service to a community, the board may block the action until a suitable replacement carrier is found.

During the early part of 1979 CAB representatives met with local authorities and interested parties in a series of nine regional meetings to determine the best methods of meeting community needs at a reasonable cost to the government. Small, isolated, and medium-sized communities may now be served by air carriers paid by the federal government.

Cities eligible under the small-communities program are promised a formal decision by the end of October 1979 of what their guaranteed essential level of service is for ten years. A list of points served and currently certificated as of Junary 1979 (555 points) are automatically eligible. An additional 129 points may qualify. [14]

Dormant Routes

Airlines in the past have obtained routes which were not profitable simply to keep a competitor from getting it, to monopolize an area, on the chance that the route might later develop. Just enough service was provided to retain the route. To stop this practice, as we have seen, CAB adopted a policy of multiple permissive entry (permission to enter markets freely if qualified). The CAB also has adopted the policy of almost always freely allowing airlines to leave routes found uneconomic to serve.

Shortly after the signing of the deregulation legislation in October 1978, CAB in a major action awarded 248 dormant (unused, unserved at a level acceptable to CAB) routes to twenty-two airlines. Six of these airlines were certificated for the first time.

Under the new 1978 law, airlines may file applications for routes on which other airlines are certificated but not serving at a minimum level acceptable to the CAB. Airlines may file notice to resume service on those routes and will have only thirty days to resume service. An airline with new authority to fly a route has forty-five days to begin service.

Industry-wide regulation of travel agents began in the late 1930s as the Air Traffic Conference, a subdivision of the Air Transport Association of America (ATA), began its work. The ATA is a trade association of certificated airlines. The Air Traffic Conference became responsible for all agreements on traffic (number of customers planned for), sales, and advertising. The CAB had no objection to the way Air Traffic Conference operated and exempted it from antitrust regulation which forbids price fixing and business cartels.

Federal legislation policies in 1979 are aimed at attempting to lessen government regulation yet retain laws to achieve health, safety, and consumer protection goals. In the transition period travel agents were at first annoyed when airlines proved hard to reach due to busy telephones. But gradually agents realized new markets were opening up and that their revenues could rise. Further, old restrictions imposed by CAB and the Air Traffic Conference on where travel agents might locate offices may soon be eased.

CAB Chairman Marvin Cohen, in a November 1978 speech before an organization of travel agents, mentioned that the CAB plans to scrutinize industry agreements for possible antitrust violations. The CAB is lifting much of the immunity to antitrust laws so long given to air carriers and to travel agents.

Is it, for example, a restriction of free trade for the Air Traffic Conference to prevent travel agents from locating offices at airports and hotels? Can the Air Traffic Conference set advertising policies for agents?

Some new requirements may be written to safeguard the members of the public who pay in advance for tours and flights, such as requiring escrow accounts for refunds for services not provided. In recent years groups of passengers have been stranded abroad, or have lost money paid to a travel agency, when the agency collapsed for one reason or another.

Business is increasing, Chairman Cohen stated in November 1978, with air carrier profits up one-half billion dollars. Chairman Cohen viewed travel agents as very much needed and, if efficient and innovative, he is confident they will prosper.

CAB's Consumer Protection Offices

The CAB advocates a policy of offering the consumer full information regarding air carrier services, fares, and restrictions, allowing him or her to choose from the various options offered.

To help customers avoid misunderstandings and to hear complaints, CAB opened consumer oriented field offices early in 1979 in six large U.S. cities. The offices, in addition to other duties, offer consumers information on discount air fares, new air routes, overtaxed airport facilities, and crowded jet liners.

Aggrieved customers should act promptly to obtain redress. To be sure, travellers can avoid some problems if they refuse to deal with obviously unscrupulous agents. The CAB and the American Society of Travel Agents work together to obtain sound business practices in the field and to handle complaints.

The Sunset Clause

There is a "sunset clause" written into the Airline Deregulation Act of 1978 which requires that the CAB relinquish all authority over domestic routes by 31 December 1981. The board will continue to assess carrier fitness. On 1 January 1983 the Board's authority over domestic fares expires. Also on that date, its authority over domestic mergers and interlocking agreements is transferred to the Department of Justice.

On 1 January 1985 the CAB will cease to exist unless Congress takes action to the contrary. Its subsidy authority will be transferred to the Department of Transportation (DOT). Authority over foreign air transportation will also go to DOT, which must exercise this authority in consultation with the State Department. Authority over agreements, foreign mergers and foreign interlocking agreements will go to the Department of Justice. Determination of domestic mail rates will be made by the Postal Service.

By 1 January 1984 CAB is to report on the overall implementation and the effects of the Deregulation Act. At that time the board is to recommend whether it should continue to exist past the sunset date of 1 January 1985.

Various safeguards are written into the Airline Deregulation Act to ease the transition period. Yet this is a most daring piece of legislation. It may be the forerunner of deregulation movements in other industries also to let free competition operate, restricted only by antitrust and antipredator legislation.

Benefits followed the lifting of tight airline regulation. Ticket prices went down, new services were offered, more passengers were attracted to air travel, there were more jobs in airline work, and airlines began making more money. This effectively quieted those who opposed such deregulation, yet concern continues in the airline industry. Is the yield on investment adequate? Time will tell.

The new act:

1. requires expedited CAB procedures

2. promotes free entry of airlines into markets and into certificated status

3. grants airlines flexibility in pricing fares

4. places onus on opponents, not applicants, for new routes and entry

5. promotes a CAB policy of faith in competitive market forces and on actual and potential competition.

The CAB now has a sound legal basis for what it had begun doing in 1977 and 1978. The act endorses the idea of allowing multiple, permissive route awards. (This allows airlines to decide if a market justifies starting service on routes.)

The Airline Deregulation Act has three route award provisions:

1. Airlines may pick up almost immediately the authority to fly another airline's routes which are going unserved. This right to serve a dormant

108

route is available on a first-come, first-served basis.

2. Each airline may select one new route each year for the next three years without CAB proceedings. Each airline may also protect one of its dormant routes a year from this "automatic entry."

3. The Act holds the CAB to a one-year timetable on applications for domestic route authority unless the CAB finds that the award would not be consistent with the public interest.

The burden of proof will be on the opponent to the route award. World Airways' eleven-year wait for permission to apply for half-price scheduled transcontinental air service has ended. Such long waits are no longer permitted under the 1978 act.[15]

The act also removes the "closed door" stops formerly used to protect carriers from competing with one another. For example: United on the route from Baltimore to Kansas City to Denver was previously allowed to take passengers to Kansas City and Denver but could not pick up passengers at Kansas City. Now it can.

Fares can be reduced under the act up to 50 percent without CAB approval and raised 5 percent on competitive routes (those on which the carrier does not hold 70 percent of the passenger traffic). The CAB has the option of increasing the downward zone limit. Board intervention and control over fares ends at the end of 1982.

Mergers may now come under antitrust scrutiny as the CAB contemplates removing the traditional immunity enjoyed by the airlines to antitrust laws. If a merger is not anticompetitive, it will not be opposed by CAB.

The President of the United States has the authority under the 1978 Act to reverse the CAB and award routes only on grounds of national defense or in the interests of improving foreign relations.

Marvin Cohen, New CAB Chairman

Almost immediately following the signing of airline deregulation legislation, Dr. Alfred E. Kahn resigned after an eventful sixteen months as chairman of the Civil Aeronautics Board. At a press conference held 27 October 1978, Dr. Kahn turned the leadership of the board over to Marvin Cohen, an Arizona attorney. Chairman Cohen plans to continue Dr. Kahn's programs, to continue to ease entry restrictions, and generally to reduce federal intervention in industry affairs as required by the Airline Deregulation Act of 1978, signed by President Carter earlier that same week.

Fares Float

Before the end of October 1978, the CAB gave permission to float domestic air fares (that is, to raise and lower rates within certain broad limits on routes inside the forty-eight contiguous states). The air carrier industry reacted with fare shifts up and down.

The CAB hopes that new cost-related fares will become the rule.

Airlines still must file all such tariff changes with the CAB, sixty days in advance of an increase, thirty days before a decrease. In some cases rates applied for never materialize and are abandoned if competing airlines' fares make such changes unattractive to the consumer.

When an airline can book a flight ahead of time and ask advance payment for the ticket, then it has revenue and traffic that it can rely on. Filled planes mean that the per-passenger costs to the airline go down. If airlines can pre-book flights to a high percentage of capacity with paid fares, then the airline can pass a portion of this reduction in its costs along to the passengers. Peak-hour arrivals and departures require the maximum amount of aircraft and personnel. If passengers are willing to fly at other times of the day or night, then the airline, repositioning planes for the next peak-hour traffic demand, can take them aboard at little additional cost. These passengers can again benefit from the airline's lower costs which can be reflected in their lower ticket prices. Mid-week travel offers fare bargains for the same reason — planes must be repositioned and must continue schedules so the aircraft may as well fly passengers as they go.

International Response to U.S. Deregulation

"The world is not the United States" remarked members of international conferences as they watched in 1977, 1978, and 1979, what they termed the U.S. "deregulation experiment." Still be early 1979 directors of foreign air carriers had to admit that the increased traffic due to "deregulation" across the North Atlantic did give them food for thought. Spurred by increased competition, fares were lower in 1979 with more flights offered. Both revenues and traffic rose. Since airlines throughout the world are in business to make money and to provide service, this increase in business was not lost on foreign air carrier managers.

Still, it was difficult for airline executives around the world to abandon a system that was well organized and had worked well. This established system offered an airline network which could send cargo or passengers around the globe using uniform ticketing, baggage handling, and waybilling procedures. Further, standards of planes and crews were established to provide a high degree of international airline safety. Would open competition threaten this system?

In the U.S., while foreign observers speculated, CAB Chairman Kahn in September 1977 appointed a young but experienced attorney, Donald A. Farmer, Jr., to head the Bureau of International Aviation (formerly known as the Bureau of International Affairs). Significantly, Farmer's experience included federal prosecution of antitrust cases involving the transportation industry.

The CAB plans expanded programs to evaluate existing international aviation systems and to forecast changes that may develop under "alternative" (deregulated) price and service assumptions. Routes, rates, charters, and capacity are being studied as parts of an international aviation system. Further, the Bureau will develop "negotiating strategies" for international aviation agreements designed to benefit the traveling and shipping public.[16]

International Routes Awarded

Early in December 1978 nonstop service to Germany was granted by the CAB to three U.S. airlines, and to another airline was authorized to fly from Los Angeles to Amsterdam. Due to the Deregulation Act of 1978, several routes formerly assigned to Pan American Airways were suspended. A new United States-Germany bilateral agreement was signed 1 November 1978.

Three more carriers were awarded nonstop authority to Germany 17 January 1979.

Also in December 1978 the CAB tentatively instituted Chicago-Texas-Southeast U.S. to Western Mexico route proceedings.

By 14 December 1978, U.S. and Australian negotiators reached agreement to allow new low scheduled airline fares between the two countries. The agreement with Australia established a "country-of-origin" system under which each country accepts new prices for traffic originating in the territory of the other on both one way and round trip tickets. Both Australia and United States governments announced their intention to allow low fares.

International Objections Voiced

Even with several important agreements signed, there remained in early 1979 areas of misunderstanding and anxiety in the world aviation community. These were voiced at a February 1979 meeting in Jamaica of fifty airlines and negotiators from more than two dozen nations.

The increased competition offered by deregulated U.S. airlines worried many governments. Dependence on U.S. airlines by less developed nations was one major concern. Others feared that the "experimental" U.S. policy could dismantle a smoothly working, well understood, international air transportation network.

Foreign aviation interests voiced fears regarding what seemed to be the U.S. intent to force U.S. policy on all nations. To counter this anxiety, CAB representatives said that only willing partners were sought in attempting to open up routes and allow flexible fare setting by airlines. When one country rejects U.S. carriers, however, in favor of its own airline, it may well risk tourists and dollars pouring into a nearby country that has a more liberal aviation policy.

The Director General of the Air Transport Association cautioned that the world is one in which the principles of national sovereignty rule. Participants from around the world at the Jamaica meeting seemed generally unconvinced of the benefits of the new freedoms offered air carriers by deregulation. Still, air carriers around the world are watching the U.S. experience to determine whether lower fares will in the long run result in higher profits or whether the old, controlled fares system is better.

U.S. representatives noted that both old and new modes are still available in international aviation. The U.S. will not force new policies on nations preferring more conservative air transport agreements, CAB representatives stated.[17]

Support came from several countries which had signed bilateral agreements with the U.S. allowing considerable competition. Also, Air India voiced approval of the new competitive policies for international air carrier operation proposed by the U.S.

The Jamaica meeting was valuable in that it offered national representatives an opportunity to talk together, voice fears, and receive explanations and reassurances.

The service experience of the years 1979 through 1983 will prove or disprove the U.S. contention that competition and profits go together.[18]

Photograph courtesy Boeing Company.

Modernized interior of the Boeing Advanced 727 aircraft.

NOTES

[1] Remarks by Marvin S. Cohen, Chairman CAB at 2d Annual American Tourism Awards Dinner, New York, 27 November 1978. Courtest CAB Office of Information.

[2] 44 Stat. 568.

[3] See chapter on NTSB for more information. The Safety Board is now an independent agency.

[4] Press release, office of Senator Edward M. Kennedy, 19 April 1978.

[5] Dr. Alfred E. Kahn, then Chairman of the CAB.

[6] CAB press release, 4 October 1978.

[7] The 1977 CAB Report to Congress.

[8] Dr. Elizabeth E. Bailey, Member CAB to Congressional Forum on Regulatory Reform, Rayburn House Office, Building, 7 February 1978.

[9] *Ibid.*

[10] *Ibid.*

[11] Statement of Dr. Alfred E. Kahn, Chairman CAB before the Aviation Subcommittee of the House Public Works and Transportation Committee, on H.R. 11145, 6 March 1978.

[12] Press release, office of Senator Edward M. Kennedy, 24 October 1978.

[13] Airline Deregulation Act of 1978, Public Law 95-504, 24 October 1978.

[14] Statement by CAB Chairman Marvin S. Cohen, CAB press release, 5 January 1979.

[15] The eleven-year wait experienced by World Airways is an extreme example of CAB delay, even before deregulation; yet airline applicants often did wait years for applications to be heard and/or decided upon.

[16] CAB press release, 29 October 1977.

[17] CAB press release, February 1979.

[18] The author is indebted to the Civil Aeronautics Board, Office of Information for press releases, copies of speeches, CAB Reports to Congress, and other material.

CHAPTER 9

THE NATIONAL TRANSPORTATION SAFETY BOARD

The National Transportation Safety Board (NTSB) was created by the Transportation Act of 1966. It began operations in April 1967 and functioned as an autonomous agency under the Department of Transportation. Later, in 1974, Congress enacted the Independent Safety Board Act, which was signed by the President in January 1975. This established the safety board as a totally independent agency of the federal government and gave it additional investigative duties to investigate surface modes of transportation. Under this new act, the board began operations on 1 April 1975.

The board has responsibility for investigating and determining the probable cause of:

All U.S. civil aircraft accidents

Railroad accidents involving a passenger train, loss of life, or substantial property damage

Pipeline accidents involving loss of life or substantial damage

Major marine casualties

Highway accidents involving five or more fatalities

The board issues safety recommendations and requires corrective actions to reduce transportation hazards. To enhance transportation safety, the board also conducts special studies and investigations, assesses techniques and methods of accident investigation, and evaluates transportation safety effectiveness of other government agencies. The board evaluates the safeguards and procedures involved in the transportation of hazardous materials.

The safety board has authority to review on appeal, orders of the Administrator of the Federal Aviation Administration (FAA) and the Commandant of the U.S. Coast Guard suspending, modifying, amending, or revoking operating certificates or licenses issued by these agencies.

Each year the safety board formally reports its activities and recommendations to Congress. Needed administrative and legislative action is suggested.

The act requires that all safety board accident reports, special studies, safety recommendations, and replies thereto shall be made available to the public. Notices of the issue and availability of such reports are published weekly in the *Federal Register*. Details on publications are available by writing to the Publications Section, National Transportation Safety Board, Washington, D.C. 20594.

The safety board is made up of five members. These are appointed by the President and confirmed by the Senate for five-year terms. The board is one of the smallest agencies of the federal government. Most of its authorized positions are filled by specialists in various categories of transportation technology. To date about 388 positions are authorized. The board headquarters are located in Washington, D.C. There are twelve field offices.

The mission of the safety board is to improve transportation safety. This is primarily done by determining the probable cause of accidents through direct investigations and public hearings, and through staff review and analysis of accident data, plus the activities listed in the above discussion.[1]

In Air Transportation

In air transportation the Safety Board determines the cause of all civil aircraft accidents that occur in the United States. This function cannot be delegated to any other agency or department. The board has, however, temporarily authorized the Federal Aviation Administration to investigate most non-fatal light plane accidents and helicopter accidents, but keeps the statutory duty to determine probable cause in each case. The board investigates all air carrier accidents, most fatal light plane accidents, and other selected accidents.

When a civil aircraft of U.S. registry or U.S. manufacture is involved in an accident in a foreign country, the NTSB may send an accredited representative to participate in the investigation, in accordance with the standards and recommended practices of the International Civil Aviation Organization (ICAO).

Teams of investigators proficient in the various specialized segments of aeronautical technology are maintained in Washington, ready to move immediately to the scene of any major air disaster in the United States. The investigators, usually accompanied by a board member, work to gather factual evidence at the scene of the accident. This is presented at subsequent public hearings and used by the board for evaluation as to the cause of the accident.

General aviation fatal accidents of the non-air carrier category are usually handled by the NTSB field office nearest the site. The board decides the probable cause of these based on an analysis of the investigator-in-charge's findings. No public hearings are held as a rule.

Other NTSB Transportation Safety Work

In a like manner to the one described above, board experts are available to investigate railway and pipeline accidents. The board is required to determine the cause of all major marine accidents and investigate those major accidents in which U.S. Coast Guard operations are so involved that independent investigations are needed.

Hearings and Records Availability

All safety board hearings are public. Parties are invited to testify at these in order that all facts and circumstances may be gathered. In its Washington, D.C. headquarters, the Safety Board maintains records of all accident investigations, safety recommendations, and safety enforcement proceedings. These records are available to the public. Copies of reports and safety research publications are also available to the public.

Organization

The NTSB is headed, as noted above, by its five-member board, one of whom is the chairman, and another, vice chairman.

The Office of the Managing Director assists the chairman of the Safety Board in his executive and administrative duties. This office is responsible for planning, day-to-day operation of the board, general management, legislative affairs, executive secretariat activities, and program analysis.

The NTSB Office of General Counsel provides legal advise and assistance to the board. This office also prepares opinions for board approval on matters of appeal from Board Administrative Law Judges and the Coast Guard. It represents the board in the U.S. courts on appeals taken from board opinions, and in both the U.S. District Courts and State Courts in connection with the enforcement of board orders, collection of civil penalties, and in opposing requests that board employees be required to testify at civil trial proceedings arising out of transportation accidents.

This last may seem a contradiction of the NTSB role, yet were all requests for employee presence at various trials assented to, there would be little time for the employees to carry out their prime role of accident investigation and safety research. The reports of the NTSB are not admissible in civil litigation as evidence. NTSB employees can give factual statements but cannot serve as expert witnesses.

The Office of General Counsel prepares board comments on proposed legislation requested by Congressional committees, by the Office of Management and Budget, and by NTSB members. The office also prepares drafts of legislative proposals, rules and amendments to existing rules. Legal assistance is rendered to the NTSB's Bureau of Accident Investigation during investigations, preparation of reports, public hearings, and processing of requests for taking depositions (statements) in private litigation arising out of accidents.

The Office of General Counsel, then, is a key office in the NTSB.

The Public Affairs office is the official spokesman for the board on public announcements and explanations of board decisions and actions. Public affairs programs of the NTSB, too, are prepared by this office. This office maintains the important line of communications between the agency and all news media and in such matters advises the chairman and the board members. Press releases, initial releases of accident reports, statistical reviews, technical studies, appeal decisions, and safety recommendations are announced and distributed by the Office of Public Affairs.

The Office of Administrative Law Judges conducts formal proceedings involving petitions for review from applicants who are denied airman and medical certificates by the FAA. The office also hears appeals from FAA orders suspending or revoking certificates issued to pilots, navigators, mechanics, dispatchers, air traffic controllers, air carriers, and air agencies authorized by the FAA to perform aircraft maintenance and to certify aircraft as airworthy.

Administrative law judges serve as trial judges, issuing supoenas, administering oaths, holding prehearing conferences, ruling on procedural requests and motions, receiving relevant evidence, and performing other duties.

A law judge will prepare and issue an initial decision analyzing the evidence and deciding the merits of the issues raised during a hearing. These become final and the decision of the board, in the event no appeal is filed. If an appeal is taken, then the full board will issue an opinion or order affirming, reversing, or modifying the judge's initial decision. Further, the certificate holder may also appeal a final order of the board to the appropriate U.S. Court of Appeals.

Nearly all hearings on petitions for review and certain other appeals are held outside the Washington, D.C. area, in the states and Puerto Rico, since the place of the hearing must be convenient to all parties.

The NTSB Bureau of Accident Investigation is, as the name states, the section that carries out accident investigations conducted by the Safety Board in rail, pipeline, highway, marine, and civil aviation transportation. It may also participate in the investigation of civil aviation accidents involving U.S. registered, or U.S. manufacturered aircraft occurring in foreign countries, pursuant to Annex 13 of the Chicago Convention, multinational treaty.

The Bureau of Technology is a NTSB reservoir of technical expertise in a wide range of disciplines. This bureau provides support for both the investigative and accident prevention activities of the board. Specialists are available from human, vehicle, and operational areas of expertise, as well as from the Hazardous Materials Division. These experts participate in public hearings as members of the technical panel. They examine vehicle parts, aircraft flight data and voice recorders, and maintain an automated accident data system which is used by both the United States and other countries in their efforts to assess reasons for accidents and the way to prevent future occurrences.

The Bureau of Plans and Programs coordinates and manages accident prevention and safety promotion programs. It conducts an intricate series of special studies and evaluations. The bureau trains employees in accident investigation and in NTSB methods. It conducts liaison with other government agencies, private agencies and industry, and foreign government agencies in matters pertaining to both the board's safety products and oversight responsibilities.

The Bureau of Administration executes all administrative support programs for the board. The Safety Board Publications Section makes documents published by the board available to the public.

Since the NTSB is such a small agency with limited numbers of employees, FAA is often asked to assist it in the investigation of accidents involving aircraft. Other agencies, too, may be called upon to assist the NTSB in its work. For example, certain accidents may require assistance from the Federal Bureau of Investigation, from the Treasury's experts, or from Coast Guard men equipped

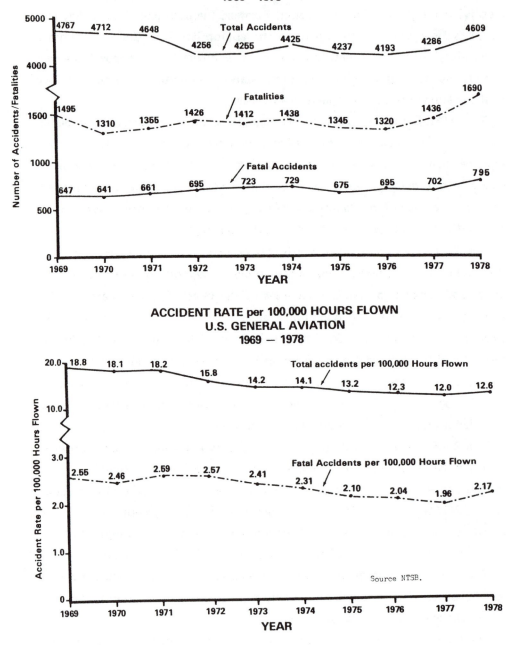

ACCIDENTS, FATALITIES
U. S. GENERAL AVIATION
1969 - 1978

Number of Accidents/Fatalities

Total Accidents

4767 4712 4648 4256 4255 4425 4237 4193 4286 4609

Fatalities

1495 1310 1355 1426 1412 1438 1345 1320 1436 1690

Fatal Accidents

647 641 661 695 723 729 675 695 702 795

YEAR
1969 1970 1971 1972 1973 1974 1975 1976 1977 1978

ACCIDENT RATE per 100,000 HOURS FLOWN
U.S. GENERAL AVIATION
1969 — 1978

Accident Rate per 100,000 Hours Flown

Total accidents per 100,000 Hours Flown

18.8 18.1 18.2 15.8 14.2 14.1 13.2 12.3 12.0 12.6

Fatal Accidents per 100,000 Hours Flown

2.55 2.46 2.69 2.57 2.41 2.31 2.10 2.04 1.96 2.17

Source NTSB.

YEAR
1969 1970 1971 1972 1973 1974 1975 1976 1977 1978

120

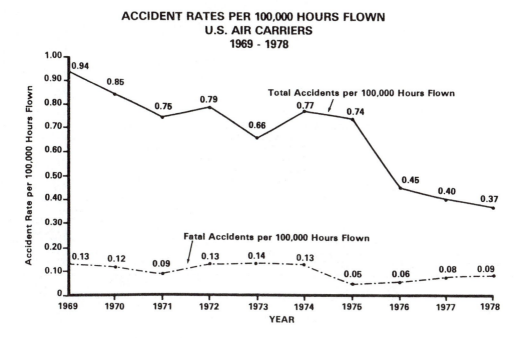

ACCIDENT RATES PER 100,000 HOURS FLOWN
U.S. AIR CARRIERS
1969 - 1978

ACCIDENTS, FATALITIES, RATES
U. S. GENERAL AVIATION

1969 - 1978

Year	Accidents Total	Fatal	Fatalities	Aircraft-Hours Flown (000) c/	Aircraft-Miles Flown (000) c/	Accident Rates Per 100,000 Aircraft-Hours Flown Total	Fatal	Per Million Aircraft-Miles Flown Total	Fatal
1969	4,767	647	1,495 b/	25,351	3,926,461	18.8	2.55	1.21	0.164
1970	4,712 a/	641 a/	1,310	26,030	3,207,127 d/	18.1	2.46	1.47	0.200
1971	4,648	661	1,355	25,512	3,143,181	18.2	2.59	1.48	0.211
1972	4,256 a/	695 a/	1,426 b/	26,974	3,317,100	15.8	2.57	1.28	0.209
1973	4,255 a/	723 a/	1,412	29,974 r/	3,728,500	14.2 r/	2.41 r/	1.14	0.193
1974	4,425 a/	729 a/	1,438	31,413 r/	4,042,700	14.1 r/	2.31 r/	1.04	0.180
1975	4,237 a/	675 a/	1,345	32,024 r/	4,238,400	13.2 r/	2.10 r	1.00	0.159
1976	4,193 a/	695 a/	1,320	33,922 r/	4,476,014	12.3 r/	2.04 r/	0.94	0.155
1977	4,286 a/	702 a/	1,436	35,792 r/	4,786,400	12.0 r/	1.96 r/	0.90	0.147
1978 P	4,609	795	1,690 b/	36,600	4,519,900	12.6	2.17	1.02	0.176

a/ Suicide/sabotage accidents included in all computations except rates (1970-1, 1972-3, 1973-2, 1974-2, 1975-2, 1976-4, 1977-1).
b/ Includes air carrier fatalities (1969-82, 1972-5, 1978-142) when in collision with general aviation aircraft.
c/ Source: FAA
d/ Beginning in 1970, the decrease in aircraft-miles flown is the result of a change in the FAA standard for estimating miles flown.
r/ Revised

NATIONAL TRANSPORTATION SAFETY BOARD
Washington, D.C. 20594
January 3, 1979

ACCIDENTS, ACCIDENT RATES, AND FATALITIES
U. S. AIR CARRIERS
(CERTIFICATED ROUTE, SUPPLEMENTAL, AND
COMMERCIAL OPERATORS OF LARGE AIRCRAFT)
ALL OPERATIONS
1968 - 1978

YEAR	ACCIDENTS		FATALITIES				HOURS FLOWN	MILES FLOWN (000)**	ACCIDENT RATES PER 100,000 AIRCRAFT-HOURS FLOWN		PER MILLION AIRCRAFT-MILES FLOWN	
	TOTAL	FATAL	PSG	CRW	OTH	TOT			TOTAL	FATAL	TOTAL	FATAL
1968	71	15*	306	37	6	349	6,404,260	2,498,848	1.109	0.203	0.028	0.005
1969	63	10*	132	22	4	158	6,740,199	2,736,596	0.935	0.134	0.023	0.003
1970	55	8	118	24	4	146	6,470,351	2,684,552	0.850	0.124	0.020	0.003
1971	48	8*	174	23	6	203	6,386,662	2,660,731	0.752	0.094	0.018	0.002
1972	50	8	160	17	13	190	6,302,160	2,619,043	0.793	0.127	0.019	0.003
1973	43	9	200	26	1	227	6,504,819	2,646,669	0.661	0.138	0.016	0.003
1974	47	9	421	46	0	467	5,978,480	2,464,295	0.769	0.134	0.019	0.003
1975#	45	3	113	11	0	124	6,040,841	2,477,764	0.745	0.050	0.018	0.001
1976	28	4	39	6	0	45	6,228,487	2,568,113	0.450	0.064	0.011	0.002
1977	26	5	381	17	257	655	6,541,168	2,684,072	0.397	0.076	0.010	0.002
1978PREL	25	6	141	12	10	163	6,783,000	2,797,000	0.369	0.088	0.009	0.002

* INCLUDES MIDAIR COLLISION ACCIDENTS NONFATAL TO AIR CARRIER OCCUPANTS—— NUMBER ACCIDENTS EXCLUDED FROM FATAL ACCIDENT RATES (1968-2,1969-1,1971-2).

** NONREVENUE MILES OF THE SUPPLEMENTAL AIR CARRIERS ARE NOT REPORTED.

BEGINNING 1975,INCLUDES ACCIDENTS OF COMMERCIAL OPERATORS LARGE AIRCRAFT.

NOTES—SABOTAGE ACCIDENT(9/8/74)IS INCLUDED IN ALL COMPUTATIONS,EXCEPT RATES.

IN 1977,FATALITIES(OTHER)INCLUDES 248 ON AIRCRAFT OF FOREIGN REGISTRY.

NATIONAL TRANSPORTATION SAFETY BOARD
WASHINGTON, D. C. 20594
JANUARY 3, 1979

ACCIDENTS, ACCIDENT RATES
CERTIFICATED ROUTE AIR CARRIERS
ALL SCHEDULED SERVICE
1968 - 1978

ACCIDENT RATES

YEAR	ACCIDENTS		AIRCRAFT- MILES FLOWN (000)	AIRCRAFT- HOURS FLOWN	DEPARTURES	PER MILLION AIRCRAFT-MILES		PER 100,000 AIRCRAFT-HOURS		PER 100,000 DEPARTURES	
	TOTAL	FATAL				TOTAL ACCIDENTS	FATAL ACCIDENTS	TOTAL ACCIDENTS	FATAL ACCIDENTS	TOTAL ACCIDENTS	FATAL ACCIDENTS
1968	56	13*	2,146,038	5,521,931	5,299,987	0.026	0.005	1.014	0.199	1.057	0.208
1969	51	8	2,385,082	5,892,254	5,377,302	0.021	0.003	0.866	0.136	0.948	0.149
1970	43	4	2,417,550	5,780,503	5,100,201	0.018	0.002	0.744	0.069	0.843	0.078
1971	43	7*	2,380,664	5,706,270	4,999,093	0.018	0.002	0.754	0.088	0.860	0.100
1972	46	7	2,347,864	5,659,485	4,966,256	0.020	0.003	0.813	0.124	0.926	0.141
1973	36	8	2,448,114	5,898,575	5,133,816	0.015	0.003	0.610	0.136	0.701	0.156
1974	43	7	2,258,136	5,474,495	4,725,783	0.019	0.003	0.767	0.110	0.889	0.127
1975	30	2	2,240,505	5,422,665	4,704,052	0.013	0.001	0.553	0.037	0.638	0.043
1976	22	2	2,319,967	5,587,601	4,835,138	0.009	0.001	0.394	0.036	0.455	0.041
1977	20	3	2,418,652	5,800,843	4,934,094	0.008	0.001	0.345	0.052	0.405	0.061
1978PREL	20	4	2,490,000	5,985,000	4,995,000	0.008	0.002	0.334	0.067	0.400	0.080

* INCLUDES 2 MIDAIR COLLISIONS NONFATAL TO AIR CARRIER
OCCUPANTS, EXCLUDED IN FATAL ACCIDENT RATES.

NOTE--SABOTAGE ACCIDENT OCCURRING 9/8/74 IS
INCLUDED IN ALL COMPUTATIONS EXCEPT RATES.

NATIONAL TRANSPORTATION SAFETY BOARD
WASHINGTON, D. C.   20594
JANUARY 3, 1979

to analyze data or provide certain specialized information.

Why is the NTSB a separate agency? If one thinks a moment, the reason is clear. Decisions in major air, ground, and sea disasters involve great sums of money, important legal considerations, and politically sensitive issues. In the NTSB all such accident investigations are coordinated and centralized to make the process of determining probable cause of the accidents and to plan for better rules to enhance transportation safety more effective, fair, and less sensitive to local pressures.

Courtesy of the Boeing Company.

The cockpit of the Boeing 737.

NOTES

[1] Interview with NTSB public relations director, Edward Slattery, July 1979.

PART IV

STATE REGULATION

Photograph courtesy Piper Aircraft Corporation.

The 1979 Piper Super Cub.

126

CHAPTER 10

STATE AVIATION COMMISSIONS

The Constitution of the United States specifically declares that all rights not held by the federal government shall revert to the states. States' rights are jealously guarded by the states on the premise that a local government is closer to the people governed and more in touch with their needs. Also, each state in the union has its particular history, ethnic composition, and set of state laws.

Federal law takes precedence over state law in some cases, as discussed in this text in the chapters on air carriers, aircraft ownership, and supersonic flight. For example, the Civil Aeronautics Board asserted 28 December 1978 that with the passage of the Airline Deregulation Act (Public Law 95-504) a state may no longer exercise authority over air carrier fares.

In the past some states required intrastate air carriers to hold fare levels down, which had the effect of discouraging out of state entrants into the area market. Once this state regulation was removed large intrastate carriers which had achieved a monopoly over state routes jumped fares by as much as 40 percent.

The CAB favors reliance on the marketplace to set fares, but has a duty to prevent the transition from state utility regulation to federal jurisdiction from leaving the public vulnerable to monopoly power. When price increases occur in an area in which an air carrier has a monopoly over services offered, the CAB will call attention to such unfair practices and as a next step consider direct action.[1]

There is a clause in the Constitution of the United States that requires all states to give full faith and credit to all of the public acts, records, judicial proceedings and determinations of sister states. Sales in one state, for example, are valid in another state with proper documentation as proof of lawful sale.

Damages in the event of death in an aircraft accident vary widely from state to state. In some states damages amounting to millions of dollars can be collected while in other states a human life is legally worth only a few thousand dollars. One of the primary problems in the lawsuits resulting from a crash of a public air carrier is this diversity of state law. Federal multi-district litigation is a system by which a federal court tries more than one case at a time to prevent re-trying what is essentially one case many times. For example, should an air carrier accident result in 275 fatalities, the multi-district litigation consolidates the lawsuits before one court. This court will have the power to decide who is liable for the accident. The court also has the power to decide what damages may be awarded each plaintiff in the case. Compensation will vary widely as various state liability limits and other state laws are taken into account. Attorneys, however, may advise their clients to try the case singly and choose the applicable forum in the jurisdiction which will provide for the plaintiff the most sympathetic atmosphere.[2]

The "supremacy clause" in the Constitution of the United States states that the "Constitution and the laws of the United States . . . shall be the supreme law of the land." Aviation is so much under federal regulation that we tend to see federal law as always supreme, thereby preemptive over state law. Yet a great body of criminal law has been developed primarily in state laws.

Criminal actions by pilots such as the operation of an aircraft under the influence of alcohol or certain other drugs violates not only the Federal Aviation Regulations but state laws as well. The state may impose fines and prison sentences upon such persons even though the FAA also has taken action[3] It is important for aircraft owners, operators, and pilots to contact their state aviation department to ascertain the regulations extant in that particular state.[4]

State Aviation Regulation

About three-fifths (33) of the states rely wholly upon the Federal Aviation Regulations. Seventeen states reported in a 1979 poll that they have separate state aviation regulations.

Alaska reported an aviation code on hand but noted that in general the state relied upon the FARs and the discretion of the Alaskan pilots. Certain survival and emergency gear is required in Alaska which is required by law and common sense. Alaska aviation officials revealed a great respect for the pilots flying in that state. Further, Alaska has an extensive assortment of airport and seaplane facilities. Aviation is a most essential portion of the transportation system in Alaska.

States having separate aviation regulation used in conjunction with the FARs are: Alaska, Connecticut, Delaware, Illinois, Maine (new regulations, 1978),

Maryland, Massachusetts, Michigan, Minnesota, New York, North Dakota, Ohio, Pennsylvania, Rhode Island, Utah, Vermont, and Virginia. All of these codes seem to be fairly flexible and are imposed more in the interests of promoting aviation and air safety than as burdensome rules for pilots.[5] Enforcement varies from state to state. So far as the survey revealed, strict enforcement does not seem to be the rule in any state. The FAA is relied upon extensively. Only the most flagrant violations of responsibility seem to arouse state officials to prosecute operators and pilots.

Master Airport Plans

Over forty-three states reported having master plans for the development of aviation and airports in the state. Pennsylvania reports having a state-wide airport plan in effect. Indiana went under the airport planning grant in February 1979. West Virginia is working toward a master plan by 1980. State airport planning is of course, greatly assisted by the FAA's federal airport planning grants, and airport improvement funding. Autonomy is at the state level, however, for it is there that the applications and planning begins.

Pilot Registration

In the fifty states, thirty-four state governments do not require that pilots apply for state pilot certificates. The federal (FAA) pilot certificates are accepted as proof of qualification and a certain competency. In thirteen states pilot certificates are required with varying degrees of enforcement of this requirement exercised. Alaska, Kentucky, and Minnesota have legislation empowering the state transportation and aeronautics departments to require pilot registration but choose not to exercise this option at the present time.[6] In Puerto Rico all aviation activities are ruled by the FAA. Pilot registration in Puerto Rico, other than normal FAA certification, is not required.

Pilots living or working in the following states do not need state pilot registration or certificates: Alabama, Arkansas, Arizona, California (in-lieu license law), Colorado, Florida, Georgia, Hawaii, Indiana, Iowa, Kansas, Maine, Maryland, Massachusetts, Michigan, Mississippi, Missouri, Nebraska, Nevada, New Jersey, New Mexico, New York, North Carolina, Ohio, Oklahoma, Pennsylvania,

Rhode Island, South Carolina, Tennessee, Texas, Utah, West Virginia, Wisconsin and Wyoming. Two states do not have aviation departments.

Pilots in the following states are required to have state registration certificates and pay the fees indicated: Connecticut, Delaware ($1 annually, but not enforced); Idaho ($2 annually); Illinois ($5 annually); Louisiana (registration not enforced); Montana ($1 annually); New Hampshire ($6 annually); North Dakota ($3 for private, commercial, and mechanics certificates; $1.50 for student pilots; all fees on biennial basis); Oregon ($2 annually); South Dakota ($1 annually); Vermont ($10 biennially); Virginia ($2 annually); and Washington ($3 annually).

State Aircraft Registration

The registration for purposes of showing the ownership of an aircraft is a function of the state government in which the aircraft operator resides, does business, or chooses to base the aircraft. The FAA registers aircraft ownership in Oklahoma City, Oklahoma, but should contrary title, ownership, or lien information be registered at the state level, the state information prevails. There is presently the possibility of creating a supreme federal title registration to facilitate checking titles of aircraft but at this writing this is not the case.[7]

Having said this, we now note that registration for the purposes of ownership will not be the subject of the following discussion of aircraft registration in the various states. Rather, state registration now to be surveyed, is the required listing of all aircraft owned or based in a state. Often this is a requirement for the purpose of collecting taxes on the aircraft or levying property taxes upon the aircraft owner at the state level.

In the 1979 M. H. Press survey of state aviation authorities, twenty-one states reported no need for the state registration of aircraft; two states, Alaska and Kentucky noted that no registration is required at present but that the aeronautics commissions are empowered by state legislation to do so; twenty-seven states reported that aircraft state registration is required.[8]

The states which have no requirement for registration are: Alabama, Arkansas, California, Colorado, Connecticut, Florida (registration discontinued 1 July 1978), Georgia, Hawaii, Kansas, Mississippi, Missouri, Nebraska, Nevada,

New York, North Carolina, Pennsylvania, Tennessee, Texas, Utah, West Virginia, and Wyoming.

Aircraft should be registered at the state level, and fees paid, as shown in the following listing: Arizona; Delaware ($1, registration not enforced); Idaho; Illinois ($10 annually); Indiana; Iowa; Louisiana (registration not enforced); Maine ($10 annually); Maryland; Massachusetts (annual fee charged based on weight of the aircraft, amounting to $32 to $100 biennially); Michigan; Minnesota; Montana ($4 annually. Montana law requires that aircraft owners register their aircraft with the aeronautics division; however, registration cannot be accepted without proof of payment of personal property taxes. The aeronautics division does not receive any of the tax money collected but serves, in effect, as the enforcement arm for the counties in which the aircraft are based).

Registration is required in New Hampshire; New Jersey (fees charged vary with aircraft); New Mexico (fees are based on aircraft weight and model year. New Mexico charges a registration fee of the owner or lessee of the aircraft in the possession of the aircraft prior to 1 March of each year. Fines are levied on owners failing to register aircraft within fifteen days of bringing an aircraft into the state for more than a brief stay. The registration fee is based on the maximum gross weight of the aircraft. There is a flat fee of $10 for balloons. Registration fees in New Mexico are in lieu of all other state and local property taxes assessed on the aircraft).

Registration at the state level is required in North Dakota; Ohio (fees are based on the number of seats in the aircraft and range from $6 to $15 and up. Glider fees are $3. Transfer of ownership fees are $1. There is no Ohio license tax on hot air balloons). Oklahoma requires aircraft registration annually by weight and by model year. The fee is also affected by the aircraft classification, such as turbo-prop, turbine, multi-engine, single-engine. (The Oklahoma fee is in effect primarily for tax purposes).

Oregon law requires the registration of aircraft. Fees are based on the aircraft classification and the model year of the aircraft. Lighter-than-air aircraft are required to register and pay an annual fee of $20. Rhode Island requires aircraft registration and payments of annual fees ranging from $30 to $250. The fees are based on the gross weight of the aircraft. Dealers' aircraft are taxed at $50 each, annually. South Carolina requires registration and bases the fees charged on the aircraft weight and model year. Vermont requires biennial registration and payment of a fee of $60. Virginia has an extensive set of aircraft regulations ($5 annually). Washington requires that aircraft be registered ($20 per single engine aircraft and $30 per multi-engine aircraft, annually). Finally, Wisconsin also requires aircraft registration with an annual fee based on the aircraft model year and its gross weight.[9]

State Taxes: Privately Owned Aircraft

A survey of the states reveals that thirty-three states report taxes imposed upon privately-owned aircraft. These taxes are imposed for the most part as annual private-property taxes and generally are based upon the value and age of the aircraft. Five states reported that their annual registration fee was charged in lieu of an annual property tax on aircraft. South Dakota imposes only a one-time registration fee on aircraft bought or brought into the state.

Fourteen states reported no taxes imposed on privately-owned aircraft. These are, as of June 1979: Alaska, Delaware, Florida, Georgia, Hawaii, Illinois, Massachusetts, Nebraska, New York, Pennsylvania, Tennessee, Texas, Vermont, and Washington. No information was received to this question from Colorado, Nevada, or North Carolina.

We can see that a privately-owned aircraft is a prime target for state taxation. The states need the income to provide the services that the public demands — improved airports, better terminals, access roadways, and other expensive items.

If an individual buys a plane out of state this may not exempt that person from state taxation. A requirement to register the aircraft or to pay a use tax may impose a tax upon the plane owner or user. If one can show that a sales tax has been paid, however, it is often possible to get credit for this amount.

Some states exempt agricultural aircraft from taxation, aircraft used by a dealer for sale or demonstration, and aircraft used for training purposes. State law varies so greatly that every owner should contact the state aviation authorities to learn the exact regulations governing aviation in that state. We are endeavoring here to show trends in state regulation and taxation.[10]

Casual and occasional sales of aircraft are often exempt from state taxation. A check of the aviation authority will reveal whether or not this is true in your state. Definitions of what comprises a casual sale vary from state to state. There is an exemption, too, in many states for the sale of a low-priced aircraft. Again, check the regulations of the state involved.[11]

State Taxation: Air Carriers

In a 1979 survey nineteen states reported various taxes imposed upon air carriers. Virtually all states impose normal real estate and real property taxes on airlines which own facilities in the state. These are usually levied at the county level.

According to the replies to the survey received from the states the following taxes are charged air carriers each year:

Arkansas	3 percent aviation fund tax
Arizona	taxed by Department of Revenue
California	taxes air carriers
Georgia	3 percent state sales tax
Hawaii	4 percent state sales tax
Iowa	has a sales tax and taxes airline aircraft
Kentucky	taxes airlines on an allocated unit value
Maine	taxes all aircraft based in the state
Minnesota	taxes airline aircraft
New Hampshire	charges an annual fee ($30)
New Jersey	5 percent sales tax
New Mexico	imposes a gross receipts tax
Ohio	taxes air carrier aircraft
Oklahoma	imposes a 2 percent sales tax
Oregon	taxes aircraft and other air carrier facilities via a formula, county assessment
Pennsylvania	sales and use taxes
South Carolina	aircraft taxed
South Dakota	airlines taxed
Wyoming	airlines taxed by the county in which they base facilities or aircraft

Again, the data presented here is representative only and for exact information the state aviation authorities in each state must be consulted. From this listing we can see that few states impose taxes on airline aircraft or on aviation activities other than the usual business taxes and sales taxes.[12]

State Taxes: Aviation Fuels

A 1979 survey has shown that forty states charge taxes on each gallon of aviation fuel. Three states refund taxes charged. They are Louisiana, Oklahoma, and Wisconsin. The refunds are made since the taxes usually are imposed for state highway funds.

From the results of this poll it is evident that most states impose taxation via fuel sales as a means of obtaining revenue. A few of the states pay the taxes charged into an aviation fund for use in improving facilities and promoting aviation safety in the state.

State Taxation: Aviation Businesses

Thirty-six states reported some form of taxation imposed upon aviation businesses such as charter services, flight schools, repair stations, and aircraft sales. Flight schools were most often exempted from taxation. The most frequent target for taxation proved to be aircraft sales and aircraft use taxation.

In general aviation businesses were not subject to special taxation but required to pay the same taxes as any other such enterprise operating within the state.

State Financial Responsibility Laws

All states, the District of Columbia, and Puerto Rico have laws that require financial responsibility of automobile owners and operators. Aviation law is following this pattern. At present, the 1979 survey reveals only ten states with specific aviation laws on financial responsibility. These states are: Alaska (with a requirement that air carriers carry insurance or give assurance of financial responsibility); California; Illinois (which has a financial responsibility statue); Indiana; Maryland; Michigan (a financial responsibility law); Minnesota; Montana; Virginia; and Wyoming (for air taxi operators specifically).[13]

Should FAA impose what the state considers insufficient penalities upon violators of FARs or state laws, the state's attorney may file suit as well. Further, a plaintiff in a state may sue for recompense for injury or damage caused by aircraft under laws extant in all states.

Strict liability is now being applied to fixed-base operators renting aircraft. This trend makes it essential that the managers of such businesses acquire a knowledge of state law and insure themselves responsibly.[14]

States with liability insurance or financial responsibility laws sometimes require proof of this prior to allowing aircraft to be registered in the state.[15]

Photograph courtesy Cessna Aircraft Company.

1979 Cessna Skylane.

135

NOTES

[1]CAB press release, 28 December 1978 (CAB 78-261).

[2]F. Lee Bailey, *Cleared for the Approach* (New York: The New American Library, 1978), pp. 150-52.

[3]Alfred L. Wolf, "Does Federal Law Preempt State Prosecuting a Pilot for a Crime?" *AOPA Pilot*, November 1977, p. 18.

[4]For a listing of state aviation commissions consult AOPA's *Handbook for Pilots* published annually and available from AOPA, 5100 Wisconsin Ave., Washington, D.C. 20016.

[5]For a discussion of the state regulation of weather modification and aerial application see the chapter on the flyer and the farmer.

[6]The information given in this chapter, referred to as a 1979 survey or poll, is obtained from an M. H. Press, Lanham, Maryland, survey made in the spring and summer of 1979. State aviation authorities were asked to answer questions relating to state regulation, taxation, and airport planning. For specific information check your state aviation laws by contacting the appropriate state aviation authority.

[7]Interview with member of FAA Office of the General Counsel, 30 July 1979.

[8]See note 6.

[9]M. H. Press survey.

[10]*Ibid.*

[11]John S. Yodice, "Aircraft Sales and Use Taxes," *AOPA Pilot*, September 1977, p. 17.

[12]M. H. Press Survey.

[13]*Ibid.*

[14]John S. Yodice, "Strict Liability in Aircraft Rental," *AOPA Pilot*, May 1979, p. 131.

[15]*Ibid.*

PART V

U.S. LAW AS APPLIED TO THE COMPONENTS OF AVIATION

The 1978 Cessna Citation I.

CHAPTER 11

AIRCRAFT OWNERSHIP

Buying a plane is very much like buying an automobile. You may purchase the aircraft for cash or via a conditional sale contract. Banks now offer loans for the purpose of purchasing aircraft.

Buying or selling a plane is made simpler by the standardization of the forms and documents required by the Federal Aviation Administration (FAA). Also, titles and liens are registered centrally in FAA's Aircraft Registry in Oklahoma City Oklahoma.[1] This does not mean that the title is clear, however, for titles of aircraft are recorded at the local level, so a further check is indicated.

When you buy, of course, you must check that you have a clear title. Citizens may go the FAA and their county files themselves or may hire authorized title companies to check the ownership of the aircraft in question. The Aircraft Owners and Pilots Association (AOPA) has such a title search service and offers title insurance as well. The FAA will provide a list of qualified title companies upon request. These companies will check FAA and local government registries.

A bill of sale should be obtained. Use an FAA or other form for this to expedite re-registration of the aircraft. Payment should be arranged with clear understanding between both parties to the terms of the sale contract. (See Chapter 5 for a discussion of contract law.)

A conditional sale contract implies that the sale will be made upon completion of certain conditions by the buyer. The title generally remains with the sellor until payment is completed. A conditional sale contract should be filed in appropriate county, town, or city offices, as well as with the FAA in Oklahoma City.[2]

Liens

A lien can be in effect without actual possession of the aircraft. A lien is different from credit extended to an owner, and this point should be made clear by those placing a lien on property.

Recording a sale or lien with FAA gives one first priority from the date of recording in showing an interest in an aircraft. Suppose a mechanic's lien is

UNITED STATES OF AMERICA — FEDERAL AVIATION AGENCY

STANDARD AIRWORTHINESS CERTIFICATE

1. NATIONALITY AND REGISTRATION MARKS	2. MANUFACTURER AND MODEL	3. AIRCRAFT SERIAL NUMBER	4. CATEGORY

5. AUTHORITY AND BASIS FOR ISSUANCE
This airworthiness certificate is issued pursuant to the Federal Aviation Act of 1958 and certifies that, as of the date of issuance, the aircraft to which issued has been inspected and found to conform to the type certificate therefor, to be in condition for safe operation, and has been shown to meet the requirements of the applicable comprehensive and detailed airworthiness code as provided by Annex 8 to the Convention on International Civil Aviation, except as noted herein.
Exceptions:

6. TERMS AND CONDITIONS
Unless sooner surrendered, suspended, revoked, or a termination date is otherwise established by the Administrator, this airworthiness certificate is effective as long as the maintenance, preventative maintenance, and alterations are performed in accordance with Parts 21, 43, and 91 of the Federal Aviation Regulations, as appropriate, and the aircraft is registered in the United States.

DATE OF ISSUANCE	FAA REPRESENTATIVE	DESIGNATION NUMBER

Any alteration, reproduction, or misuse of this certificate may be punishable by a fine not exceeding $1,000, or imprisonment not exceeding 3 years, or both. THIS CERTIFICATE MUST BE DISPLAYED IN THE AIRCRAFT IN ACCORDANCE WITH APPLICABLE FEDERAL AVIATION REGULATIONS.

FAA Form 1362 (7-65)   0052-040-8000   (8100)

FORM APPROVED:
OMB NO. 04-R0076

UNITED STATES OF AMERICA
DEPARTMENT OF TRANSPORTATION -FEDERAL AVIATION ADMINISTRATION

AIRCRAFT BILL OF SALE

FOR AND IN CONSIDERATION OF $ THE UNDERSIGNED OWNER(S) OF THE FULL LEGAL AND BENEFICIAL TITLE OF THE AIRCRAFT DESCRIBED AS FOLLOWS:

UNITED STATES
REGISTRATION NUMBER **N**

AIRCRAFT MANUFACTURER & MODEL

AIRCRAFT SERIAL No.

DOES THIS   DAY OF   19
HEREBY SELL, GRANT, TRANSFER AND
DELIVER ALL RIGHTS, TITLE, AND INTERESTS
IN AND TO SUCH AIRCRAFT UNTO:

Do Not Write In This Block
FOR FAA USE ONLY

NAME AND ADDRESS
(IF INDIVIDUAL(S), GIVE LAST NAME, FIRST NAME, AND MIDDLE INITIAL.)

PURCHASER

140

recorded with FAA on 10 March 1980 and the plane had been sold 1 March 1980, and the bill of sale signed as of March 1. When the new owner registers his ownership with FAA, the mechanic's lien is effective. Recording with FAA gives one priority, not the date on a bill of sale.

The matter is not made less complex by the fact that some local jurisdictions also record such liens and these can also cloud a title. Yet, in any state according to common law a lien yields to the federal requirement, which is registration of aircraft titles and liens with the FAA. Aircraft liens can, then, be locally recorded, or recorded with FAA in Oklahoma City, Oklahoma, or both.

A mechanic's lien, an airport lien, for storage or tie-down, or a bank lien can constitute a cloud on the title of an aircraft. Remember, recorded liens can be in effect without possession of the aircraft.[4]

If a lien holder is not paid as agreed upon and reasonable efforts have not resulted in payment, the holder of the lien can locate the aircraft and begin suit by "filing a libel." This advises "all interested persons" to show up on a certain date to show why the aircraft should not be condemned and sold to satisfy the lienholder (the libelant).

A marshal of the court attaches and holds the plane, keeping it in a safe and secure manner. Expenses involved will be paid out of the forced sale. If the owner comes forward the sale can be prevented by the owner's payment of the lien and costs.

A lien can grow "stale"! If the aircraft has changed hands, the purchaser in good faith is liable for liens presented only up to a certain time. After this period, the lien has grown "stale" and is less apt to be enforceable. If the owner who incurred the lien retains the aircraft, then this time limit is less applicable.

You may check with local government record offices and with the FAA Aircraft Records Division in Oklahoma City, Oklahoma, to determine whether liens are recorded against a particular aircraft.

Warranties

New aircraft carry the manufacturer's warranties. These are usually of about six months duration. Buyers should check to see if the warranty period begins

141

with the delivery of the aircraft to the customer, or with delivery to the dealer.

An express warranty is a promise made by the seller that the aircraft is in a described condition at the time of the sale.

An implied warranty is one in which the law requires of every seller. Among the things that a sale implies is that the seller has the authority to sell the aircraft and possesses a good title to it. A sale implies that the purchaser will find the aircraft fit for the uses for which it was purchased. Also it is implied that the aircraft is in reasonably good condition unless a note is included in the sale contract that the aircraft is being sold "as is," or "with all faults."[5]

Kinds of Ownership

An individual may own an aircraft alone, a type of ownership termed a "sole proprietorship."

Partnerships are common forms of plane ownership in which two or more persons share a plane for social and economic reasons. Unless such a partnership is incorporated, all of the partners are exposed to liability claims on their entire net worth. When forming flying clubs this same liability risk should be considered.

Incorporating makes the share holders in the corporation liable only up to the amount they have invested in the corporation. Corporations may be non-profit or profit-making. They are formed in the state in which the flying club, or other entity, is based.

Incorporation, then, limits one's liability. Even so, it is the responsible course for the corporation to carry reasonable amounts of liability insurance. Corporations must be operated in an overt (open, honest) manner to conform to the stated purposes of incorporation. They should be properly and legally set up according to appropriate state laws.

Any proven intent to defraud or deceive is reason for the courts to pierce the "corporate veil" and reach to the assets of members of a corporation.

Civil Air Patrol (CAP) ownership of aircraft is formed under a somewhat similar mode. The Civil Air Patrol is a volunteer organization, an auxiliary of the U.S. Air Force. The CAP members are insured with policies that carry a $500 deductible clause. They have strict operating regulations and a system of pilot checks to maintain safety and to carry out the CAP missions. The

142

CAP members often carry additional personal liability insurance.

Assistance for Buyers

Any FAA general aviation safety office may assist an individual in locating and completing the necessary forms involved in purchasing or selling an aircraft. The FAA publishes regulations and advisory letters to guide buyers and sellers.

Among several excellent books which offer information on aircraft ownership are: AOPA's *Handbook for Pilots* (published annually); Fred A. Biehler's, *Aviation Maintenance Law.* 1975; and Timothy R. V. Foster's *The Aircraft Owner's Handbook, 1978.*

Financing and Funding

Aircraft can now be financed much as automobiles are financed, through your local bank. Legal considerations are much the same. The holder of the conditional sale contract, or other such lien, can hold the title until repaid in full. This does not relieve the purchaser of ownership nor the liabilities associated with ownership.

The Federal Aviation Regulations (FARS) Part 47 outline the procedures involved in the registration of all U.S. aircraft. The party registering the aircraft must be a citizen of the U.S., or a corporation organized and doing business under U.S. laws with aircraft based and primarily being used in the U.S., or a person who is a citizen of a foreign country but lawfully admitted for permanent residence in the U.S.

Since aircraft registration is a federal affair, the forms are available everywhere in the United States at FAA offices (FAA Forms 8050-1). This form with a fee ($5.00 at this writing) and proof of ownership is sent to FAA Aircraft Registry:

> DOT
> FAA Aeronautical Center
> Aircraft Registration Branch
> Oklahoma City, Oklahoma 73125

Proof of ownership is usually a bill of sale from the manufacturer or a previous owner.

As you can see by consulting the chapter on state aviation authorities, some states require that all aircraft based inside state boundaries be registered.

State taxes are imposed on aircraft in several states. Your aircraft may be listed and taxed in your state as personal property.[6]

Liabilities

Aircraft owners must be prepared to act with due care, be financially responsible or carry reasonable liability insurance, and lend the use of their plane only cautiously. Further, owners should be aware that attorneys, seeking recompense for their clients may seek to "deepen the pocket," in aircraft cases. This means that, should an owner not have the financial resources to satisfy a suit, an astute attorney may well look about for other parties to sue.

Did the mishap which caused the suit occur as you flew on a business trip for your firm? Then your employer may be found partly liable and with greater financial means. Are you a government employee, carrying out some part of your work, via the use of your aircraft? Then the government might be reached via the Torts Claims Act.

In this same manner, partners, estates, manufacturers, airports, maintenance and overhaul facilities are scanned by the trained aviation attorney in an attempt to find parties wholly or partially liable for the accident who may bear a portion of the damages if found negligent.

If the title holder is operating, or in actual possession of the aircraft, that person is liable. Simply owning a plane, however, does not automatically involve that owner in all liability associated with the use of the aircraft.[7]

The person operating the aircraft under a properly drawn lease of thirty days or more, is responsible for its safe operation and liable for injury or damage which may involve the aircraft.

This assumes that the plane was provided the lessee in a reasonable and airworthy condition. Another important consideration is that the firm or person to which the aircraft has been leased could reasonably be expected to be a responsible and able operator of the equipment leased.

Financial Responsibility Laws

The general rule is that in absence of a statute imposing liability the owner of a motor vehicle (or aircraft) is not liable to strangers for injuries occurring from the negligent use of the auto by one to whom it has been loaned or hired.[8] Most states where liability laws exist provide that owner and lessee are jointly liable.

Florida holds owners liable via the use of an old-fashioned rule, that the person whom the owner allows to use the vehicle is his agent. The majority of the states reject this, yet it is a factor to be carefully considered before leasing or lending an aircraft.

Some states have rules of liability insurance to cover possible negligent use by renter before the registration of a vehicle; some only if an accident occurs. Nearly every state and D.C. have some such financial responsibility law. Most define "owner" to include "lessor". A lessor often risks the grounding of a whole fleet if he fails to comply with state insurance laws.

Several states have aircraft financial responsibility acts patterned after the Uniform Aircraft Financial Responsibility Act which by requiring responsibility would, in effect, cause most owners and lessors to carry liability insurance; only Indiana exempts passengers from this coverage. Virginia and Maryland both have acts differing from the uniform one by requiring financial responsibility liability insurance. (These uniform acts are not federal acts but rather are suggested statutes which are written by a body of jurists and attorneys. These uniform codes are recommended as uniform state codes.)

"Vicarious liability," thus, is now a fact of life.

Aircraft Insurance

Aviation insurance firms are, of course, most knowledgeable about aircraft insurance. You may deal with either an agent or a broker. (See Chapter 5 for a general discussion of insurance considerations.) The term "underwriter," means the firm actually carrying the insurance and the one paying claims.

Liability insurance may be required by your state laws. It is required by common sense, in any case. Liability insurance covers persons outside the aircraft and/or persons carried by the aircraft.

An aircraft owner may decide to carry the full risk of damage to the aircraft himself. This is an owner's legal right. Various coverages are available for the owner to choose from should he or she decide to purchase insurance.

An owner may elect to carry "hull" or "full crash" coverage. This covers the aircraft itself. Some owners may choose the less expensive type of policy that insures only against certain items — ground damage only, in-flight damage only, for example. There are "named risks," policies and there are "all risks," policies with exclusions.[9] The amounts the owner must first pay himself of the damage costs, or "deductibles," vary. If the owner agrees to a high deductible amount, then his insurance will cost less.

The owner must observe the uses that he has stated on his policy or the insurance company can refuse to honor the policy. Private use, business use, and aircraft used for hire, all these carry different insurance premiums and must be used as described in the policy to be covered by the policy.

The type of flying and the pilot's experience affect the cost of insurance coverage. Naturally, the value of the aircraft also affects the cost of insurance.[10]

An owner should check his policy carefully: is the policy invalid with an inadvertent violation of the Federal Aviation Regulations? Negligent operation can invalidate all or a part of the policy. Acts of God may well not be insured by the policy. Should an owner lease a plane, a check of the lessor's insurance coverage is in order. An owner may wish to retain certain insurance coverage for his own benefit.

An owner who willfully damages or destroys an aircraft to collect insurance may be prosecuted under state laws, or, it the incident occurs in a federal or maritime jurisdiction, under federal statutes. Unlawful use of an aircraft voids the insurance coverage.

The aircraft insurance policy is void with a transfer of ownership. Persons buying aircraft must make new arrangements to insure the aircraft.

Finally, insurance policies are contracts and contain coverages, exclusions and terms. (See Chapter 5 for a discussion of contract considerations.)

The owner-operator is primarily responsible for keeping an aircraft in an airworthy condition.[11] This person must also see that all inspections are complied with and that work to satisfy any outstanding Airworthiness Directives (ADs) is done.

All U.S. aircraft must pass an inspection each twelve calendar months to retain their airworthiness certificate. If the plane is used for hire or used by student pilots, 100-hour inspections are also required.

Aircraft engines are extremely reliable due to careful manufacturing techniques and to FAA's inspection requirements. There are measurements called "tolerances," for parts of the aircraft engine. When an engine can no longer meet these tolerance checks it must be overhauled. [12]

Is an aircraft owner responsible to successor owners for failing to maintain the aircraft in accordance with the Federal Aviation Regulations? The Georgia Court of Appeals has ruled that the owner is not responsible to later owners.[13]

The registered owner of an aircraft is responsible for maintaining the aircraft in an airworthy condition.[14] The owner must have maintenance properly recorded. Should an aircraft be discarded, "junked," for any reason, the FAA Aircraft Registry, Oklahoma City, Oklahoma, must be notified immediately. The Registry also must be notified immediately if the aircraft is sold, or if there is a change in the permanent mailing address of the owner.

Most aircraft manufacturers publish maintenance manuals.

Each twelve calendar months, the aircraft must undergo an "annual inspection." A certificated air frame and power plant (A&P) mechanic must do this, but parts of the inspection may be done by an assistant (who can be the owner) under the A&P's supervision. The A&P mechanic must write up the appropriate engine and aircraft logbooks and complete any forms associated with certain equipment changes. [15]

In general, any work done on an aircraft which can alter its airworthiness or flight characteristics (for example, resetting control cable tension) must be performed by, or under the supervision of, an A&P mechanic.

Owners can, exercising due care, do routine minor maintenance: oil changes, brake fluid addition, clean or replace spark plugs, replace battery, and replace fairing fasteners. Under the supervision of an A&P mechanic much more maintenance may be done by an owner. Since the A&P mechanic is responsible for the work, however, he may elect to delegate tasks with care and may choose to do many himself.

There are separate log books for airframe and engines, since engines can be removed, sold, rebuilt, and installed in another aircraft. The log travels with the engine.

To avoid repetition at this point, it is suggested that legal factors relating to maintenance and shop control of aircraft will be found in the chapter on airports. Also, aircraft owners may be interested in the chapters describing state court systems which will give them information on jurisdiction in certain cases. The chapter on state aviation laws will give owners data about taxes, required liability insurance, and registration of aircraft required by their state.

Emergency Locator Transmitter

Emergency locator transmitters (ELTs) are required in U.S. aircraft. Crop dusters, flight testing aircraft, single-seaters, jets and airliners are excepted, as are planes flown within a 50-mile radius of their base.[16]

Taxation

Exempt from the annual federal use tax are: aircraft without engines, aircraft owned by tax-exempt organizations, military aircraft, and aircraft being delivered, demonstrated or in process of import/export.

States often impose sales taxes on aircraft. These laws vary widely.

The tax benefits from leaseback arrangements are considerable. If you lease 100 percent of the aircraft's use to a flight school or charter company, you may deduct all expenses relating to owning the aircraft.

Should you reserve a portion of the use of the aircraft for personal use, then all expenses are not deductible. If the aircraft use is for business purposes, however, this use is deductible.

Some lease agreements retain the investment tax credit ot the lessor, others pass it on to the lessee. [17]

Notice to Aircraft Owners

You may be required to file a Federal Use Tax Return on Civil Aircraft, Form 4638, if an engine-powered aircraft is registered, or required to be registered, in your name and is used in U. S. navigable airspace.

Tax Rates

The Federal use tax on civil aircraft includes an annual $25 tax on the use of any taxable aircraft during the reporting period. There is also a "poundage" tax of either 2 cents or 3½ cents a pound, depending on the type of aircraft, based upon the maximum certificated take-off weight.

A piston-powered aircraft with maximum certificated take-off weight over 2,500 pounds is taxed annually at 2 cents for each pound over 2,500 pounds. The 2,500 pound exclusion does not apply to turbine-powered aircraft. They are taxed annually at 3½ cents for each pound of maximum certificated take-off weight.

When to File

For newly acquired aircraft, the return is due on or before the last day of the month following the month in which the first taxable use of the aircraft occurs. For other aircraft, returns are due on July 31 of the taxable period which begins July 1 and ends June 30 the following year.

More Information

You can get more information about the filing requirements from any Internal Revenue Service office. Ask them for Publication 582, Federal Use Tax on Civil Aircraft.

Department of the Treasury
Internal Revenue Service   Notice 465 (1-78)

GPO 926-143

Chartered Aircraft

A charter is a contract. There are two types. One type turns over the control and operation of the aircraft to a person or organization. In this type, the care, operation and crewing of the aircraft is assumed by the charterer, who also assumes great and owner-like liability. The owner is constrained only to charter to parties who seem reasonably able to carry out such aircraft operation. If, however, an owner leases a plane with knowledge that illegal or willful misconduct is probably, the owner remains liable to a degree.[18]

A second type of charter is one in which control over the plane, its staffing and navigation are not surrendered, but only the use of the plane for a stated time. The owner selects a crew and pays all operating expenses. Liability in this case remains with the owner.

The owner should write into any charter a contract provision against charterers incurring liens.

Reporting Accidents

Minor mishaps need not be reported by owners, or operators, to the National Transportation Safety Board (NTSB). "Accidents" are incidents involving serious personal injury or death and/or "substantial damage" to an aircraft. This includes any damage affecting the structural stength and operation of the aircraft.[19]

Immediate notification of accidents, by the owner or operator, must be given the nearest NTSB field office. Also, the Board is to be notified of overdue aircraft which it is believed may be involved in an accident.

Wreckage protection rules provide for recordation and leaving wreckage alone until surrendered to the custody of NTSB investigators. It is permissable, of course, to remove survivors or to protect the public safety. [20]

General Aviation Safety

Over ninety percent of all aviation accidents are classified as "pilot error." Few accidents are due to the failure of the aircraft or its engine. The following figures, then, reflect the lack of training or judgement of pilots and not the unairworthiness of aircraft.

U.S. civil aviation safety records released by the National Transportation Safety Board revealed that the calendar year 1978 produced a decline in general aviation safety.

In U.S. general aviation, including air taxi and commuter operations, there were 4,609 total accidents. Of these 795 were fatal accidents with 1,690 persons killed. This compares with 4,286 total accidents, 702 fatal accidents, and 1,436 fatalities in 1977.

We can see that the 1978 figures comprise an 8 percent increase in total accidents with a 13 percent increase in fatal accidents, and an 18 percent increase in fatalities. [21]

For the past twenty years general aviation has grown enormously, yet each year the number of accidents remains between four and five thousand with fatalities of about 1,000 persons. Each year the number of flights and people carried increases. There seems to be, oddly enough, a "normal" number of aircraft accidents and a "normal" number of automobile accidents. (Automobile accidents account for about 50,000 deaths a year, 150,000 permanent disabilities, and a total of nearly two million injuries a year according to recent figures collected by the Department of Health, Education and Welfare.)

Stolen Aircraft

An owner immediately upon discovering that an aircraft has been stolen, or parts from it taken, should notify the police. Next, he should report the theft to the insurance company, which will set to work to find the plane, or, failing that, render payment to the owner. The insurance company or the owner must notify the FAA as soon as possible.

Aircraft theft is a federal offense. If it is proved that the theft related to the import of narcotic drugs (including marijuana), a pilot's certificate will be suspended for a year plus other penalties. [22]

Salvage Laws

Salvage law is as old as the sailing of merchant vessels, dating back to Rhodian and Roman times. Salvors of derelict, sunken, or wrecked vessels or cargo were permitted an award. There were also laws penalizing those looting disabled or wrecked vessels. Modern maritime law encourages salvage awards, since it can turn an entire loss to a partial one.

Salvage is defined as a service voluntarily performed by those with no legal obligation to do so, to save property from approaching marine peril on the seas or other navigable waters. [23]

U.S. law extends navigable waters (navigable in law) to include navigable inland waters as well as the seas. These waters are public ones serving interstate or international commerce, such as the Mississippi River, Columbia River, and Hudson River. If a river does not flow into the sea or into a navigable body of water, and is all within one state — it does not come under admiralty law and courts.

State courts cannot grant salvage awards. So aid lent voluntarily in vessels and cargo in intrastate waters is a purely altruistic action. Legally, such assistance is not entitled to a salvage award.

If vessel is not occupied by captain or crew, a salvor needs no permission to save it, take it to safety, and claim salvage. Retrieving a stranded vessel, saving a vessel from fire, or raising a sunken vessel is salvage. Saving a life, *if* associated with saving a vessel, entitles one to award. Other types of salvage are: advice, standing by, lending aid, lending personnel, and recapture from pirate (hijacker).

If working for the rescued vessel's owners or a professionally contracted salvage vessel, only salary or a fee is paid and the salvor is entitled to no other award.

Passengers have the duty to assist crew members if they are needed but need not stand by to the last. If a passenger exerts special skill, effort, and/or risk to help save a ship he is entitled to an award.

Public officers such as Coast Guard personnel, pilots (in the maritime sense of the work), and ship's agents, if serving beyond the call of duty, can also be rewarded. In general, officers and crew members are not given recompense for their efforts to save their own vessel since this is their paid duty in any case. There are certain exceptions to this rule.

For anyone to earn an award, however, success is necessary. Contributing to this success is rewardable. If a vessel is a total loss, or if salvors in conditions not beyond their control abandon efforts to save it, then no award is made. Further, acts of misconduct on the part of salvors are legal offenses.

The salvor gains a lien on the vessel but not title to it. He takes the vessel to safety and asks the owner for a salvage award. If the owner cannot reach agreement with the salvor, the salvor then takes the matter up with the admiralty court. Should the owner fail to appear in court to claim his property or to arrange to award the salvor, the property can be sold by a marshal under a court order. Sale proceeds are given to the salvor for his award and the remainder is paid to the owner. The salvor may buy the vessel at the public sale as can any other qualified person. It is the salvor's right, under maritime law, to retain possession of the vessel.

Non-contracted-for salvage is called "pure salvage," with no prior arrangements having been made for the reimbursement of the salvor. In such cases the Federal District Courts set salvage reimbursement fees.

Contract salvage, on the other hand, involves an oral or written agreement as to payment for services prior to the salvage operation. Payment can be made contingent on success if this is so written into the agreement. Contracts made under duress are not enforceable.

The maritime laws of salvage apply to aircraft in maritime jurisdictions.

Homebuilt and Experimental Aircraft

An aircraft owner can legally fly his, or her, home-built aircraft or experimental plane and can install and fly experimental equipment. This cannot be done without FAA advice and applicable FAA waivers to certification rules of aircraft manufacture. Generally, passengers cannot be carried. These planes cannot be manufactured and offered for public sale until certification as an approved type is awarded.

The FAA upon request will send an expert airframe and powerplant inspector to the place at which a person is building the aircraft. The inspector can warn the builder of hazards in welding, forming, and assembly. Stage by stage the FAA inspector will aid the builder with advice. The FAA is interested in new designs and also in having aircraft meet reasonable safety standards before flying over the general public.

Some certificated aircraft have type approval and may be built "at home," with FAA checks at certain stages. [24]

Restored aircraft are more and more popular. Glistening Stearman trainers and World War II fighters are flown to "Antique Aircraft" shows. Again, FAA will come by shops on request to help owners with advice and registration of these older aircraft.

Border Crossings and Export

Owners, or persons in control of an aircraft (lessee or borrower), may cross national boundaries freely by adhering to the Federal Aviation Regulations (FARs) governing such flights. [25] Personnel documents, a passport and several aircraft documents are required. The FARs state these requirements clearly. Further assistance may be obtained from appropriate FAA field offices.

The first landing in another country must be at an entry (port of entry) airport. Flight plans are required. The Aircraft Owners and Pilots Association has a valuable advisory service for members flying personal aircraft to other countries.

The export of U.S. aircraft for sale involves additional export documents obtainable from the FAA and from the State Department.

Pilots should notify U.S. Customs Service of their wish to leave the U.S. to obtain outward bound clearance. If freight or passengers are carried for hire, this is a mandatory requirement; otherwise it is not. To ease reentry into the U.S., it is a good idea to have expensive equipment such as a survey instrument or cameras listed by customs on the outbound flight. Aircraft owners should check their policies to be certain that their insurance coverage is valid for foreign flights.

All aircraft inbound into the U.S. must clear customs and must enter at either an international airport or one to which customs officials will come by prearrangement (a landing-rights airport). In either case, advance notice to customs is required.

Pilots should check the FARs for special regulations which pertain to flights over the northern and southern U.S. borders and for transoceanic flights.

No penetration of the Defense Visual Flight Rules zones is permitted without filing a flight plan.

NOTES

[1] Rowland W. Fixel, *The Law of Aviation*, 4th ed., (Charlottesville, Virginia: The Michie Company, 1967), pp. 406-15. Also FAR Part 49.

[2] Timothy R. V. Foster, *Aircraft Owner's Handbook*, (New York: Van Nostrand Reinhold Co., 1978), pp. 92-98.

[3] Gerard Pucci, *Aviation Law*, 3d ed., (Dubuque, Iowa: Kendall/Hunt Publishing Co., 1974), Chapter 14, p. 4.

[4] Fred A. Biehler, *Aviation Maintenance Law*, (Basin, Wyo.: Aviation Maintenance Foundation, Inc., 1975), p. 13.

[5] Stuart M. Speiser and Charles F. Krause, *Aviation Tort Law*, Vol. 2, (San Francisco: Bancroft-Whitney Co., 1979), pp. 473-77.

[6] See the chapter on state legislation of aviation.

[7] Biehler, pp. 123-24.

[8] Pucci, Chapter 14, p. 5.

[9] Biehler, p. 24.

[10] Foster, pp. 14, 16, 110.

[11] See FAR Part 91.163.

[12] See FAR Parts 91.175; 91.165; and 41.13(a).

[13] Tanner v. Revel Aviation, Inc., (Ga. Ct. App. 1978) 15 CCH Avi. 17, 158.

[14] See FAR Part 91.165.

[15] See FAR Part 43.

[16] See FAR Part 91.52.

[17] Foster, pp. 33, 35.

[18] See FAP Part 91.54, "Truth in Leasing."

[19] See FAR Part 830.

[20] *Ibid*. See also National Transportation Safety Board regulation Part 830.2.

[21] NTSB press release, March 1979.

[22]Biehler, p. 64; Foster, pp. 126-27.

[23]Fixel, pp. 73-74.

[24]Biehler, pp. 28-29.

[25]For example, if planning a flight to Mexico or Canada, pilots should consult FAR Part 91.84.

Photograph courtesy Piper Aircraft Corporation.

1979 Piper Chieftan.

CHAPTER 12

AIRPORTS AND AIRPORT BUSINESSES

First of all we must differentiate between airport ownership, airport management, and the businesses conducted at airports. True, at a small airport the ownership, management and businesses operated may all be a one-person proposition. On the other hand, the owner of an airport, be it an individual or corporation, may choose to delegate operation of the airport to one company, and maintenance facilities and the sale of various goods and services to several other companies. We shall, therefore, consider each phase of the airport and its various businesses separately in the following discussion.

Kinds of Airports

Airports in the United States range from short turf strips to huge facilities laid out over square miles of land.

The least federal regulation is exerted over the party owning a plane and also the land on which it is based. An example of this, the farmer who uses a stretch of private pasture or roadway for his take offs and landing. This owner may build a hangar for his plane or simply tie it down.

This "airport" may not appear on charts at all. If the owner has set aside a definite landing space, the "airport" may appear on charts marked as a plain circle with the letter R inside. Pilots now know that a landing area is there but restricted to a private owner's use. The "airport" is legally available only to the owner, and his guests, and to pilots in trouble due to some mechanical malfunction or unexpected navigational or weather problems. These may claim sanctuary and be given assistance as reasonably determined by the owner of the landing area.

By not inviting the public, nor offering any facilities or services to the public, the owner of a private landing area is liable for only a moderate and reasonable care of planes and pilots choosing to trespass onto his property. They do so at their own risk.

An airport open to the public is so designated on aviation charts and listed in various FAA publications. For information regarding construction, altera-

157

tion, or closing an airport FAR Part 157 should be consulted.[1] The FAA must be advised of all changes in status whether or not of a temporary nature.

Once an airport is open to the public an entirely new set of legal responsibilities are undertaken. In general, reasonable care over all those eventualities that a normally prudent individual might foresee is required. Owners and/or operators of businesses on the airport should be prepared to carry insurance coverage or to bear liability risks themselves.

When planning a new airport, whether public or private, the FAA will give advice and helpful publications.

The "international airport" is also known as an "airport of entry" or "port of entry." Here, at any time of the day or night, customs services are available to aircraft entering the United States. Before entry the pilot should advise the airport authorities of his estimated time of arrival (ETA). This automatically grants permission to land in most cases. Fourteen states and the District of Columbia have U.S. international airports.

An airport located near a U.S. customs office may make a practice of granting landing rights to pilots entering the United States. These are known as "landing rights airports." To use these, pilots must transmit both a proposed ETA and a request for landing permission.

Other information is needed, of course, by pilots planning flights into and out of the United States. The FARs should be consulted. The FAA offices will assist pilots with needed forms and information.

Airports are now being termed: "air carrier," "commuter service," "general aviation," and "reliever," airports.

As the titles indicate, airports range in size from unpaved, unlighted grass strips to the unbelievably complex metropolitan airport. At the small airport, days may pass without an aircraft approaching to land. At major airports, the activity resembles a busy city, awake 24 hours a day. Here air carriers come in from the ends of the earth to disgorge thousands of souls. Other thousands of people are there to meet the arrivals and thousands more are there to wave off thousands of departing passengers.

Major airports have an airport control center apart from the air traffic control. Here, around the clock, airport security is supervised, parking and automobile traffic monitored, runway condition reports received, and all problems anticipated and coped with. Is aviation fuel arriving on schedule? Are there any plumbing, cooling, heating problems? The answers are formulated in the airport control room.

Airspace Approval

To open an airport you require a "permit" from FAA, and "air space approval." This is needed to insure that airport traffic patterns do not overlap, or that there is no conflict with air traffic control systems such as the approaches to established airports, or high density air traffic areas. Once an airport owner has this approval, the airport can begin operation.

Certificated Airports

Use by air carriers, however, does require an airport certificate from FAA. If the airport is to be served by CAB–certificated air carriers, then FAA standards must be met.

FAR Part 139.1–139.27 gives requirements to meet FAA standards as an airport certificated for use by CAB-certificated air carriers.

Photograph courtesy the Boeing Company.

The Boeing 737.

Limited Certificates

If an airport wishes to serve non-scheduled air carriers only, FAA may issue a "limited certificate." This certificate has fewer and less costly requirements than the certificate awarded airports serving CAB-certificated scheduled air carriers.

A resort area, for example, may have seasonal air transportation needs. Once the FAA is satisfied that the airport can be used with reasonable safety, for such non-scheduled flights, a limited certificate is issued for the operation of aircraft of over 12,500 pounds.[2]

The airport can then offer public non-scheduled transport services without the major investments which would be required for regular use by CAB-certificated scheduled air carriers.

Non-certificated Airports

Airport locations, conditions, and needs, vary widely in the United States. Rather than try to write standards and regulation to fit all U.S. airports, the FAA does not certificate, regulate, or close down airports used for other than air carrier flying.

Private airports opened only for personal use need not allow landings by the flying public save in emergency situations. The owner may, however, choose to allow landings. The pilots using the private strip are "guests" and accept the same risks as does the owner.

Some private airports have serious approach obstacles, or short, rough surfaces and other hazards. If open to public use the owner must advise FAA of these possible dangers so that FAA publications may carry the warnings.

Privately-owned airports open for business purposes face more exposure to liability because the public is invited to the premises. Even so, the FAA has no set requirement for runway length, approach angles, or other items.

Factors which cause airport owners to seek and take FAA advice on runway siting, surfacing, drainage, approaches and other factors are (a) benefits of a safe operation (b) more cooperation from local authorities with a safe and thriving business, (c) improved financing options, and (d) use by scheduled and/or non-scheduled carriers.

160

Federal Financial Assistance

Many airports, usually publicly owned, may qualify for federal funds to improve their landing and terminal area facilities. In these cases, compliance with antidiscriminatory and pro-competitive standards are required. Businesses must be allowed to open at the airport in fair competition. Persons seeking to use the airport facilities must not be denied such use on an unjustly discriminatory basis.

General

The FAA checks virtually every public use airport in the United States to see if appropriate information has been published and to see if the information is correct. Such information includes runway lengths, landing area lighting available, and approach obstructions.

Education and persuasion rather than rigid regulation keynote FAA's approach to airport owners and operators.

FAR Part 135 Operation

FAR Part 135 applies to those parties wishing to offer air taxi and commercial operator services.

Operations specifically excluded from FAR 135 and which may be carried on without a Part 135 certificate are:

Ferrying aircraft

Training flying

Student instruction

Crop dusting, seeding, weeding, spraying

Commercial bird chasing

Banner towing

Local sightseeing flying

Aerial photography

Reserve operations

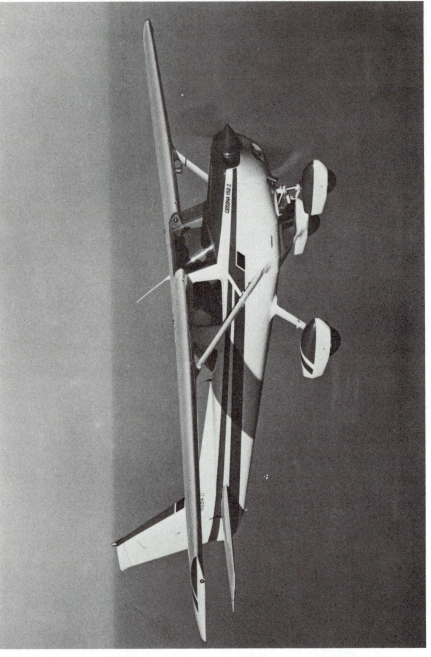

1979 Cessna 152 II.

Fire fighting

Survey flying

Pipeline or powerline patrol

Certain construction work done by helicopters.

In the interests of safety, not to mention sanity, student pilots may not land or take off from many of the larger air carrier airports such as Washington National, O'Hare, and others.

Aircraft flying into the busiest United States airports, air carrier airports, must be flown by a rated pilot and have transponders, encoding altimeters, and two-way radio communications equipment.[3]

Large airports with less total air carrier roles may be used by rated pilots flying aircraft equipped with two-way radio and transponders.

Airport Traffic Patterns

A system of approaching and leaving an airport has been devised which is known as "standard traffic pattern." Aircraft approach the field by entering the downwind leg of this pattern, parallel to the runway in use. Visual symbols and wind indicators tell pilots which runway to use. All turns are made to the left. These are also known as "left-handed patterns." Standard entry and departure procedures are taught to all pilots. No radio contact is needed at "uncontrolled airports," that is, airports without manned control towers. Pilots simply give way to aircraft according to a set right-of-way system. Avoidance is by visual reference only.

A uniform communications system (UNICOM) is used at most small airports on a voluntary basis. Pilots may ask for advisory comments on the runway in use and other information such as wind strength and direction.

Standard patterns are used unless there is a reason for a non-standard one. The FAA works with airports and local authorities to set patterns that will enhance safety, reduce noise, and offer pilots reasonable approach and departure paths. If a non-standard pattern is used, again ground markers indicate this

163

and the FAA notes the fact in its airport directories and pilots' information publications.

Airports with control towers use published patterns, but can direct pilots by radio to deviate from these as necessary for improving the flow of traffic.

Small airports generally require no radio equipment for operation at the landing facility; larger airports require two-way radio; and still larger airports require transponder (radar response radio) equipment and encoding altimeter equipment (altimeters which report to airport traffic controllers the height of the aircraft). Requirements are published by the FAA in its publications and charts.

Noise Abatement Factors

In recent years noise abatement regulation has affected large airports. Pilots are required to adhere to certain flight patterns, turn away from populated areas, and reduce power on takeoffs as soon as possible. Small airports, as well, have pattern restrictions. Curfews also are used in noise abatement programs.

"Taking." The constitution of the United States guarantees to U.S. citizens the right to own property, to use and enjoy their property, to own and benefit from their businessess. Any disruption, therefore, of one's enjoyment and use of a home or business is illegal. Aircraft noise and low flight can constitute a "taking." That is, an action that in effect takes away or limits the full use of one's property. This taking is considered an unlawful act.

When the noise and/or vibration caused by aircraft deprive a land owner of one or more useful functions of his property, the owner may sue for compensation for the easement (the right to cross his land, a right of way). If damages or injury can be proved, the aircraft or airport operator may have to pay for such injuries or damages.

Noise has been ruled by the courts in some instances a "tort," a failure of the airport or the aircraft operator's duty toward a fellow citizen, an injury.

Not all noise, vibration, lights at night, or other annoyance from low-flying aircraft can be considered a taking. The needs of the public and the requirements of normal air commerce must be considered. The navigable airspace, as described by the Federal Air Regulations, is open to common use, to public transit. Proven damage or injury can generally be considered a taking as can proven loss of money or property.

State laws vary regarding what may legally be considered a taking. The wording of state constitutions varies. Also, case law varies from state to state.

Defendants

The owner of an airport may be sued for impairment of a business, property loss or damage, and personal injury due to low flying aircraft.

When the aircraft or airport operator is a private individual or partnership the plaintiff has no trouble in filing suit. If the airport operator is a corporation, the corporation is sued as though it were a person.

When the airport operator (or operator of a particular aircraft) is a city, county, or state — and many are — these may be reached through the courts. State laws prevail in these situations. A state can be sued only by its own consent. This consent is found in the state constitution or in acts of the state legislature. Since state constitutions and laws vary so widely, persons doing business in a state should engage legal assistance and should familiarize themselves with state laws.

When the aircraft or airport involved is military, the federal government is the defendant. When any federal employee in the course of his duties is involved, again the federal government is the defendant. Should the federal government be the operator of aircraft or airports, again the federal government is open to suit.

Since a sovereign state, such as the U.S. government, can only be sued with its consent, how are such suits possible? The U.S. permits suits against itself under the authority of the Federal Tort Claims Act. This act permits a citizen to sue the federal government for torts committed by a federal employee in the course of his duties.[4]

There are five additional situations in which the U.S. will agree to be sued: (1) claims arising from contracts with the government; or (2) based on an act of Congress; (3) or the regulation of the Executive; or (4) claims referred to it by either house of Congress; or (5) claims for exoneration by a disbursing officer.

When offering special events and airshows open to the public, the airport operator is required to obtain a waiver from FAA to allow low and acrobatic flying and to give notice that on a particular day the airport will temporarily be closed. This must be done well ahead of the time of the event in order to allow proper notification to airmen.

Liability risks are increased during airshows. Special insurance plus considerable thought and care will help reduce possible claims.

Attractive Nuisance — Reasonable Care

An "attractive niusance" is an object(s) or activity one maintains on his premises which is dangerous to young children and may be expected to attract them to the premises.

An operator of certain businesses may reasonably expect that children may be brought onto business premises. Reasonable care involves fencing and warning signs to prevent children from wandering onto ramps and taxiways.

When airshows or other demonstrations are in progress, reasonable provision must be made for crowd and traffic control. Extra personnel and clearly marked areas for expected audiences must take into consideration the fact that children may be present. Signs and personnel should be provided to adequately warn parents of possible hazards.

Airport Lighting

The FAA has recommendations not only for runway, threshold, and taxiway lighting of airports at night but also standards for lighting obstructions near airports. Any towers or other structures extending into the navigable airspace must be marked and/or lighted according to FAA standards.

Many small airports do not have lighting for night operation. Others have quite limited lighting.

Large airports have extensive night illumination plus high-intensity lighting for the runways and approaches. This assists pilots making landings during the hours of darkness and during periods of poor visibility.

A fixed base operator (FBO) may operate an entire small airport and manage all the services offered there or be one of several businessmen located on an airport.

The FBOs rent, lease, sell, and repair aircraft, and offer instruction to pilots. In about half of the states, the FBOs have a "vicarious liability" and may be held responsible for the negligence of pilots flying for them. The owner/leasor of the aircraft is seen as operating the aircraft, hence is held responsible. There may well be no state limitation on damages collectible. State laws vary. Approximately twenty-five states have some form of vicarious liability statutes.

Persons leasing aircraft to the FBO are also subject to vicarious liability. Operators and owners should therefore either insure against liability or be prepared to bear the costs that may arise.

"Negligent entrustment" is a liability run by a FBO who has reason to believe that a pilot is not capable or qualified to fly an aircraft, but allows the pilot to rent the aircraft. To recover damages one filing suit must prove the negligence of such a pilot and also prove that the FBO should have foreseen the possibility of the accident.

Today's courts expect an operator to check a pilot's license, medical certificate, ratings, and his plans for use of the aircraft. Further, in most cases a check ride is indicated. The operator is expected to give weather information and local hazards information.

"Negligent instruction" is a possible cause for court action brought by passengers against an operator for damages because the pilot had been trained by the FBO but had not received adequate instruction.[5]

Flights in rented aircraft impose responsibilities on the FBO to ascertain the qualifications of the pilot, assure airworthiness of the plane, and to furnish careful briefing prior to flights.

Do flying schools customarily assume responsibility for damage occurring as the result of carelessness by one of the school's student pilots? It seems that flight schools generally are lenient with students; yet, unless an understanding has been reached, a contractual agreement as to the responsibility of the school, legally the student may face suit for damages.

The school is responsible, of course, for providing good training, careful preflight briefing and sound aircraft. On the other hand, once a student acts in a careless, reckless negligent manner, the responsibility shifts to the student.

Over the years, the FBOs face more and more possible liability risks and should be alert to these exposures.[6]

Guest Statutes and Business Invitees

A person who enters airport property seeking services offered there has the right to a higher degree of care than a guest, and a lesser degree of care than a bailee.[7] (A guest takes the same risks as the operator of the business, or vehicle involved. A guest does not pay for services.)

An invitee may be a person contemplating buying an aircraft, taking a sight-seeing ride, or contracting for flight or ground instruction. Such an individual may expect some form of protection from known hazards on the airport such as warning signs and fences. A considerable degree of care is given business invitees.

Another invitee might be a person landing an aircraft to buy fuel. The airport fuel service operator owes this business invitee ordinary care and warnings of any known hazards. Beyond this the customer assumes responsibility for safe operation.

Types of Ownership

A sole proprietorship is a business owned by one person. In the event of a claim for damages, based on negligence, the sole proprietor is required to pay to the full extent of his resources. Few persons choose to expose their entire net worth to this risk.

Likewise, two or more persons, who own a business as a partnership, also are responsible to the full extent of their resources for possible claims. The acts of one partner do not involve just that partner, but all partners. Again, few persons wish to expose themselves to such unlimited liability risks.

Corporations (incorporated businesses) are responsible for liabilities only up to the amount of worth existing in the corporation. Each shareholder can lose only the amount he has invested. Claimants generally cannot reach back to shareholders' personal net worth.

Hence, incorporation under the laws of the state in which the company headquarters are located helps many businesses to limit liabilities. Another method of reducing liability risks is to insure against possible claims.

Overall, companies should exercise due care and close supervision of employees and agents to reduce opportunities for claims against the firm.

Truth in Leasing

Truth in leasing clause requirements in leases and conditional sales contracts are included in FAR Part 91.54 as reproduced below:

91.54   TRUTH IN LEASING CLAUSE REQUIREMENT IN LEASES AND CONDITIONAL SALES CONTRACTS.

(a)   Except as provided in paragraph (b) of this section, the parties to a lease or contract of conditional sale involving a United States registered large civil aircraft and entered into after January 2, 1973, shall execute a written lease or contract and include therein a written truth in leasing clause as a concluding paragraph in large print, immediately preceding the space for the signature of the parties, which contains the following with respect to each such aircraft:

(1)   Identification of the Federal Aviation Regulations under which the aircraft has been maintained and inspected during the 12 months preceding the execution of the lease or contract of conditional sale; and certification by the parties thereto regarding the aircraft's status of compliance with applicable maintenance and inspection requirements in this Part for the operation to be conducted under the lease or contract of conditional sale.

(2)   Identification of the person the parties consider responsible for operational control of the aircraft under the lease or contract of conditional sale and certification by that person that he understands his responsibilities for compliance with applicable Federal Aviation Regulations.

(3)   A statement that an explanation of factors bearing on operational control and pertinent Federal Aviation Regulations can be obtained from the nearest FAA Flight Standards District Office, General Aviation District Office, or Air Carrier District Office.

(b)   The requirements of paragraph (a) of this section do not apply—

(1)   To a lease or contract of conditional sale when:

(i)   The party to whom the aircraft is furnished is a foreign air carrier or certificate holder under Part 121, 123, 127, 135, or 141 of this chapter; or

(ii)   The party furnishing the aircraft is a foreign air carrier, certificate holder under under Part 121, 123, 127, or 141 of this chapter, or a certificate holder under Part 135 of this chapter having appropriate authority to engage in air taxi operations with large aircraft.

169

(2) To a contract of conditional sale, when the aircraft involved has not been registered anywhere prior to the execution of the contract, except as a new aircraft under a dealer's aircraft registration certificate issued in accordance with 47.61 of this chapter.

(c) No person may operate a large civil aircraft of U.S. registry that is subject to a lease or contract of conditional sale to which paragraph (a) of this section applies, unless—

(1) The lessee or conditional buyer, or the registered owner if the lessee is not a citizen of the United States, has mailed a copy of the lease or contract that complies with the requirements of paragraph (a) of this section, within 24 hours of its execution, to the Flight Standards Technical Division, Post Office Box 25724, Oklahoma City, OK 73125; and

(2) A copy of the lease or contract that complies with the requirements of paragraph (a) of this section is carried in the aircraft. The copy of the lease or contract shall be made available for review upon request by the Administrator.

(d) The copy of the lease or contract furnished to the FAA under paragraph (c) of this section is commercial or financial information obtained from a person. It is, therefore, privileged and confidential, and will not be made available by the FAA for public inspection or copying under 5 U.S.C. 552(b)(4), unless recorded with the FAA under Part 49 of this chapter.

(e) For the purpose of this section, a lease means any agreement by a person to furnish an aircraft to another person for compensation or hire, whether with or without flight crewmembers, other than an agreement for the sale of an aircraft and a contract of conditional sale under Section 101 of the Federal Aviation Act of 1958. The person furnishing the aircraft is referred to as the lessor and the person to whom it is furnished the lessee.

Legal Relationships With Employees

The negligence of an employee binds the employer if injury or loss results from the negligence of an employee performing the work which he is paid to perform. This is known as "respondeat superior." It is the same theory as in the law which makes a principal responsible for the promises and acts of agents. For example, a corporation acts through its agents.

Independent Contractors

When an employee is hired on a temporary basis, the employee may elect to work as an "independent contractor." That is, the employee assumes all responsibilities for payment of taxes, health care, retirement, Social Security matters and receives no holiday pay.

Time periods vary according to state laws, but in general, once an employee works more than 50 percent of a normal work week (a forty-hour week), for more than three years, the employer must make provision for retirement and other benefits.

Employee Benefits

Full time, permanent employees are entitled to several benefits.

Social Security payments are contributed by the employee and these funds are matched by the employer.

Unemployment Insurance is paid, via wage withholding arrangements, by the employee. A firm or person employing four or more workers is required to pay a tax for the calendar year of the employee's employment.

Workmen's Compensation provisions vary from state to state. In each state, however, employers in certain occupations and industries must assure reimbursement of the employee for medical care made necessary by a job-related injury or disease. This provision may be provided by company insurance or other means.

Retirement funds set up by employers must comply with the Retirement Security Act. An employee with three years employment must be covered. Employees who start work within five years of the normal retirement age are excluded.

The contributions of employees to a retirement fund are nonforfeitable. That is, retirement must be paid, at retirement or all funds credited to an employee must be refunded if the employee ceases to work for a firm and requests reimbursement, prior to retirement.

An employer cannot forbid picketing and unionizing by employees if these activities conform to state law. Breach of the peace or danger to the public safety, of course, is illegal.

Discrimination

Discrimination is illegal under federal codes. No state law may support discrimination. Any facility open to the public, whether privately or publicly owned, may not discriminate due to race or religion against persons seeking use of the facilities offered.

Discrimination due to sex is largely now repealed but still a lingering practice. In some states a married woman must have the signature of her husband upon the sale of her property due to his interest in her property under state community property law. Otherwise, a married woman has the right to acquire, own, possess, control, convey, lease, use, or mortgage property. She can make contracts and pledge her separate property without the signature of her husband. She may be sued and may sue, and is liable for her torts.

Unmarried women have no legal restrictions imposed by state laws or federal laws.

There remain some gallant statutes in some states. For example, the Constitution of the State of Maryland makes a man liable for the debts of his wife, yet she is not liable for his debts! A knowledge of the law in the state of operation is necessary for operators of businesses since they do vary so widely.

Security

Even small airports are not immune to hijackers. It is impracticable to screen all persons entering and leaving such airports. Yet, operators should be aware that a hijacker may well be a solitary male who will attempt to charter an aircraft, and who has a history of mental illness or a criminal record. All pilots should consult the *Airman's Information Manual* for a code number which, set into a transponder, will alert FAA air traffic control centers to the pilot's predicament.

The FAA has full primary authority over aircraft hijacked in flight, that is, from doors shut to doors opened.[8]

Tie Down Care

If a plane is handed over to an airport employee for fueling, taxiing and tie down, the owner of the business furnishing this service is responsible for damage that may occur through the negligence of the line crew, that is, the "agents" of the business.

172

When an aircraft blows away from its tie down space with resultant damage, the operator who leased the space may or may not be liable. Affecting liability are the following factors:

(a) What basic understanding exists between tie down leasor and aircraft owner (lessee). Is it clearly understood which is responsible for securing the plane? If it is the owner's responsibility, then the leasor need exert only slight care.

(b) What control over the plane is given the airport operator (leasor)? If the plane has been moved for any purpose by the airport operator then it becomes his responsibility to exercise care in moving and re-securing the aircraft.

(c) Was an Act of God involved? That is, were there factors which a reasonably prudent person could not reasonably have foreseen? (For example, tornado, unusually violent winds.) Acts of God relieve the operator of liability.

Overall, then, the legal condition existing may be one of simply a contract for the leasing of space. If a degree of control is exercised by an airport operator, then a contract of bailment exists.

Bailment

Bailment for hire is a contract in which the bailor agrees to pay for the safe-keeping of the thing trusted to the custody of the bailee. The bailee agrees to keep it and return it, on the request of the bailor, in much the same condition as it was received. The bailee is not responsible for normal wear, or for injury or loss from causes for which he was not negligent or responsible.

An example is that a bailor, the owner of a Cessna 172, entrusts her plane to the bailee, an FBO offering hangar space for rent. Another example might be a plane left for repair at a maintenance facility. Once the company accepts the aircraft, it must be cared for in a reasonable and prudent manner. If the person accepting custody is acting for his employer, both the employee and employer are responsible.[9]

Should a hangar burn with planes entrusted to the bailee inside, if no negligence of the bailee was involved, then the bailee is not liable. Further, such losses of aircraft do not relieve insurance companies of payment to the owner of the plane.

Who has custody over an aircraft? We can answer this with the the following examples:

1. An owner who ties down her or his aircraft must accept liability for the security of the aircraft tethering. (Further, many airports have a clear understanding that ropes or chains required for securing aircraft, are the responsibility of the tiedown space user.)

2. If a pilot or mechanic moves a plane for an owner, to fuel or repair it, then the pilot or mechanic and their employer are responsible for the safety of the plane and re-securing it at a tiedown or hangar space.

3. If a plane is left at a gasoline pump for fueling and tiedown, the FBO accepting it from the owner or user is responsible.

4. Unforeseeable and unusual events that occur do not imply negligence. Persons are responsible only for due care and normal prudence. "Acts of God" come under this theory of relief from liability exposure.

If a plane is in such condition that reasonably careful handling results in damage, the bailee is not liable. (Example: fabric so rotted that hands go through it.)

Persons accepting a plane in order to perform free maintenance or services are under less constraint and legally can exercise slight care, liable only for gross negligence, willful damage, fraud, or bad faith.

Should you lend your aircraft to a friend and accept no pay for its use, the borrower is legally responsible for exercising extraordinary care in safeguarding your property. He must return the aircraft in the same condition as when it was borrowed. The borrower is not responsible of course, for normal and reasonable wear and tear, nor if the aircraft is lost due to no fault of the borrower.

If you return to the maintenance shop for your aircraft and the shop owner cannot return it to you through no negligence on his part, then you, the owner of the aircraft, must accept the loss.[10]

Any condition in which the mechanic or shop exercised reasonable care but still damage or loss occurred does not justify suit. The owner of the aircraft has the burden of proving negligence.

If while acting as bailee, a plane is damaged or stolen, prompt notice of the event must be given the owner of the aircraft. Further, if the plane is stolen or vandalized, law enforcement agencies must be promptly notified by the bailee.[11]

Mechanics' Responsibilities

A mechanic is responsible for his work and records, notwithstanding pressures or instructions given him by his employer.

Should a mechanic note a defect in an aircraft or a potentially dangerous condition, that mechanic has a duty to warn the user or owner. Should a plane be considered unsafe to fly by the mechanic, he should leave a notice in the cockpit in the event the condition is something a pilot might miss while making a normal and reasonable preflight inspection.[12]

The rule of what a reasonable man might be expected to do is in effect here. Should a mechanic be asked to make a minor repair he cannot reasonably be held accountable for some defect not associated with the initial repair.

Repair Stations

The repair station has the primary responsibility for its selection and direction of its employees.

When a shop agrees to repair or alter an aircraft there is a legal principle that this implies a warranty. It implies that the person accepting the job can perform the work in a competent manner to reasonably satisfy a customer. If the repairs or alterations are not performed in a reasonably competent way, then the aircraft owner has recourse to the shop or mechanic.

Airworthiness Directives (ADs) are published by the FAA to correct some defect or potential part failure in aircraft based on service experience and accident investigation. Unless pertinent ADs listed for an aircraft are complied with, the aircraft is technically unairworthy.

Mechanics may, as a practical matter, assume that AD's recorded in a log book as having been done were in fact done. The FAA holds, however, that the last mechanic is legally responsible for checking that previous ADs were done.

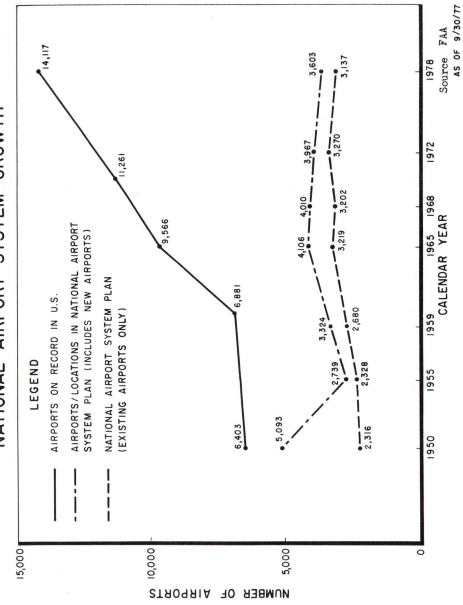

NATIONAL AIRPORT SYSTEM GROWTH

LEGEND

AIRPORTS ON RECORD IN U.S.

AIRPORTS/LOCATIONS IN NATIONAL AIRPORT
SYSTEM PLAN (INCLUDES NEW AIRPORTS)

NATIONAL AIRPORT SYSTEM PLAN
(EXISTING AIRPORTS ONLY)

NUMBER OF AIRPORTS

CALENDAR YEAR

Source FAA
AS OF 9/30/77

176

"Let the buyer beware" as a business concept is waning in the light of new federal, state, and local consumer protection legislation. The Federal Consumer Product Safety Act is designed to protect consumers from unreasonable risks or injury from the normal use of products.

Conditional sales are those, for example, of an airplane to a person on the condition that payment will be made in some agreed upon manner. Title to the aircraft may remain with the seller until payment is completed. The plane serves as collateral on the loan of funds needed to buy the plane.

Retention of title does not imply ownership per se, since control and use of the aircraft goes to the purchaser of the aircraft. The buyer bears the liability risks involved in operating the plane which he has purchased via a conditional sales contract.

Aircraft leasing control and liability likewise go to the operator, the lessee.

False advertising, of course, opens a firm to the possibility of legal action or other community sanctions.

U.S. Airports

The surging growth of air travel, the increase in mail carried by air, and air freight carriage is astonishing. Most major airports are expanding terminal facilities, lengthening runways, adding ramps and taxiways.

By the end of 1978 the number of landing facilities in the United States and its possessions totaled 14,574. Included in this total were 12,007 airports, 1,987 heliports, 536 seaplane bases, and 46 short takeoff and landing (STOL) facilities.

Of the total number of landing facilities, 4,751 are publically owned. Privately owned landing facilities numbered 9,823 but only 2,573 of these were open to the public. All in all, about 7,000 airports were open to the public. The total number of landing facilities includes those military fields which are open to civil aviation operations (joint use).

Of the total number of airports, 4,567 locations have lighting facilities and 5,484 have paved runways. Thus, roughly two thirds of all airports are not paved and/or do not offer lighting for night operation. Only 69 U.S. airports have runways over 10,000 feet in length.

Out of the total of 14,574 airports, 730 are served by CAB-certificated air carriers.

General Aviation

All flying which is not military or air carrier is termed "general aviation." A general aviation aircraft may be a $40 million corporate jet or a $4 thousand two-place aircraft.

Well over a quarter of a million persons in the United States work in general aviation. The following industry figures are conservative. There are:

50,000 employees of manufacturers

70,000 persons who work fo the approximately 5,000 fixed base operators (FBOs)

50,000 employees of firms making subcomponents

10,000 self-employed mechanics and flight instructors

25,000 people in agricultural flying

35,000 employees involved in corporate flying

General aviation contributes over four billion dollars a year to the nation's economy. The industry also generates the world's largest pool of trained aviation personnel of many types — pilots, mechanics, and skilled workers.

General aviation airports constantly generate interest in aviation. Here young people can find out about flying careers and begin their training. They may enter the scores of careers in general aviation, or follow a military aviation career, or work for the airlines.

Free Passage Right

The public right of freedom of transit in navigable airspace is affirmed by the Federal Aviation Act of 1958.[13] Any United States citizen may use the navigable air space in the United States. This means that a property owner does not "own" all air above his land and that the United States government has supremacy over his rights to the navigable airspace above his property.

The term "navigable airspace" is defined as airspace above minimum flight levels set by U.S. Federal Aviation Regulations (FARs). This air space includes that needed for safe approaches to land and air space required for safe take off paths.

These rules of the right of free passage were set by the Civil Aeronautics Board before 1958. The Board ruled that freedom of peachful transit allowed aircraft to overfly property below without being considered a trespasser. Even so, should this passage interfere with a landholder's enjoyment and use of his property, the landowner has certain rights against what becomes in those instances a "taking" of his airspace and use of the land below it. State laws might then be invoked against the person unlawfully "taking" the property.[14]

The Impact of Deregulation on Airports

Airlines are now free to serve fewer airports.[15] Air carriers will naturally find large air terminal points the best markets for their services. Air lines will concentrate on services between major hub airports. With planes feeding passengers and freight from small communities into these hub airports to connect with the large carriers, traffic congestion seems probable.

More general aviation runways are needed at major airports so that the main runways can be used only for transport aircraft. Smaller, slower planes can then be safely landed on their own runway. At the Baltimore-Washington International Airport, a taxi-way has been converted into a general aviation runway. Light planes use this very adequate strip and then taxi to the nearby general aviation ramp and hangar area. The long runways are less congested and airline ramp areas free of general aviation traffic.

New reliever airports and upgraded facilities at smaller airports are badly needed. Under-used military fields could be converted to civilian use or used by both military and commercial aircraft.

The owner of a personal plane is finding it difficult to find a small airport today. If he bases his plane at a large airport, he may encounter delays in taxiing and takeoffs. The owner may have to pay high fees for hangar space and for fuel. Further, he often will find himself impeding transport traffic.

U.S. LANDING FACILITIES

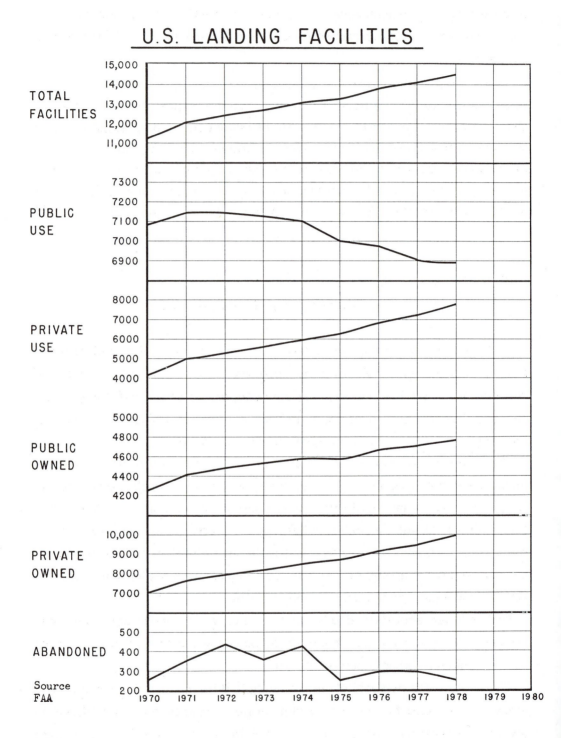

TOTAL
FACILITIES

PUBLIC
USE

PRIVATE
USE

PUBLIC
OWNED

PRIVATE
OWNED

ABANDONED

Source
FAA

Unless well equipped with radio, transponder, and other devices, the small plane can slow traffic. It would be much more convenient for the small plane owner, in many cases, to have an adequately equipped small airport to use.

Airport capacity in the U.S. must be increased, for safety and for the fair and orderly growth of air commerce.

Need for Small Airports

In the 1970s a trend developed in which fewer airports were open to the public each year, particularly small privately-owned airports. During this same time period, more planes each year were sold, air travel for business and pleasure was up, and more persons used aircraft for more commercial purposes than ever before.

With fewer small airports available, the general aviation and air carrier aircraft are pressed into the remaining larger airports. What is meant in this discussion by a "small" airport is a general aviation field, located on as little as forty acres of land, serving aircraft of less than 12,500 pounds weight. "Larger" airports are those serving planes of 12,500 pounds weight and up with some air carrier service available and having, of course, paved runways, lighting, control towers, and paved taxiways and ramp areas.

Land near the small airport is often improperly zoned thus encouraging real estate development near the airport. This may even extend to the erection of high rise structures on runway approaches or the erection of powerlines near the airport. Land values tend to rise.

Owners of privately-owned airports must pay taxes on their land. As the value of the land rises, taxes rise. Quite a bit of land is needed to build an airport and the value of a large parcel is naturally higher. Eventually the owner finds the parcel too valuable to retain. The money represented in the land is not bringing in revenue as it would if invested in bonds, for example. Further, the land owner finds an ever-increasing tax burden with the only escape the sale of the property.

The airport service may be considerable to a community while the revenue to the owner may well be low. Since land values are rising, owners often hesitate to make long-term investments in runways and buildings.[16]

These privately owned airports do not qualify for federal assistance under present legislation. As a consequence, there is a decrease in the number of landing areas for general aviation aircraft just as their numbers are increasing.

Lawrence, in his study, learned that interest in aviation has drawn many of the individual owners into airport operation. Adequate planning, development and profit-making business practices are often missing.[17] Cost accounting and economic planning, too, were lacking in approximately 75 percent of the airports studied. Both airport design considerations and management skills were largely lacking.

In Maryland, realizing the dilemma faced by owners of public use airports in financing improvements and repairs, the Maryland General Assembly, guided by the State Aviation Administration, passed legislation in 1979. The bill (Senate Bill No. 885) became law on July 1, 1979, and enables the owner of a public use airport in Maryland to take advantage of low interest money available through the Maryland Industrial Development Financing Authority Act. This money may be used for the acquisition, refinancing, rehabilitation or improvement of a public use airport or public use airport facility. It is this type of innovative and responsible aviation legislation that is needed at both the state and federal level.

Airport Planning

The complexities involved in planning a major airport are stunning. Even smaller airports have scores of items to consider. Planning improperly carried out may offer cause for a suit against the airport operator.

Some considerations in the provence of airport planning are:

Financing for land, buildings, paving, mobile equipment, aircraft.

Land acquisition.

Zoning.

Plans for runway, taxiway, and ramp area construction.

Plans for adequate drainage of all airport areas.

Plan for proper approach and departure areas.

Tie-down area provision.

Plans for fuel supply and storage. Fueling vehicles.

182

Plans for adequate power supply and emergency generators.

Plans for hangars, shops, terminal facilities, office space.

Location of radio navigational and communications equipment needed.

Selection of such equipment.

Parking areas for airport vehicles, employees, emergency vehicles, arriving and departing customers, customers requiring long-term parking.

Control tower design.

Roadways on the airport.

Access roadways allowing arrival and departure from the airport.

Security provisions: communications, personnel, equipment, fencing.

Food service provision.

Maintenance shops.

Flight school provision.

Provision for aircraft sales offices and hangar areas.

Runway, taxiway and ramp lighting.

Control room to supervise airport and offer emergency coordination.

Fire equipment selection; fire station placement.

Plans for snow removal equipment.

Selection of support vehicles such as forklifts, baggage trucks, and other service vehicles.

Mowing equipment.

Provisions for sanding runways to offer traction during periods of ice or snow. Mobile broom vehicles to remove the sand when the hazards of ice are past.

Bird suppression program.

Provision of all airport vehicles with radio equipment and special lights.

The items listed above are only a few of the things that have to be considered in airport planning. Ecological impact studies must be made for proposed construction of large airports. Surveys must be taken to assess the impact of noise on surrounding businesses and residences.

The airport operator must decide whether or not to "groove" his runways. Factors to be considered are: a significant number of accidents occurred due to hydroplaning; the frequency of rainfall and its intensity; the slope or grade of the runways, depressions, abnormalities affecting water runoff; surface texture quality as to slipperiness under dry or wet conditions; terrain limits such as a dropoff at the end of a runway; adequacy of the runways as to length for current and projected aircraft use; cross wind effects; and the present strength and condition of existing runway pavements. By cutting small grooves in the runway surface, water runs off more rapidly thereby enhancing aircraft braking and crosswind control on the ground. There are other advantages to grooving and suggestions regarding its applicability obtainable from local FAA offices.

Airport planning can be as simple as mowing a grass strip on one's farm and tying an aircraft down in a fence corner. The larger the airport, however, the larger the number of items to be considered to provide services and to protect the public from harm.

Original Goals, ADAP

The original goals and authorization of the 1970 Airport Development Aid Program (ADAP) were:[18]

AIRPORT DEVELOPMENT AID PROGRAM

Section 14 of the Airport and Airway Development Act of 1970 (P.L. 91-258), as amended in 1971 by P.L. 92-174, and in 1976, authorizes the Secretary of the Department of Transportation to make airport development grants in order to bring about, in conformity with the National Airport System Plan (NASP), the establishment of a nationwide system of public airports adequate to meet the present and future needs of civil aeronautics. The Airport and Airway Development Act Amendments of 1976 (P.L. 94-353), enacted on July 12, will have a considerable impact on the Airport Development Aid Program (ADAP). This Act, the third amendment to the Airport and Airway Development Act of 1970, contains additional funding and adds several new eligible items of development.

The 1976 amendment raised the annual program level from $310 million, established in 1973, to a range of $500 million to $610 million over the 5-year period through Fiscal Year (FY) 1980. This provides $435 to $525 million annually for airports serving all segments of aviation including a category of air carrier airports identified as commuter. It further provides $65 million to $85 million annually for general aviation airports including airports that relieve congestion at high density locations. It also revised the percentage of Federal participation in eligible airport development upward from previous levels of 50 and 75 percent. ADAP participation at all except the busiest airports is 90 percent until September 30, 1978, and then drops to 80 percent for FY 1979 and 1980. Air carrier airports other than commuter airports whose total annual passenger enplanements are one-quarter of one percent or more of the total annual passenger enplanements of all such airports receive Federal participation at 75 percent. There are slight upward adjustments in a few states containing a high percentage of public land that results in Federal participation up to 93.75 percent of project costs.

In the case of airport development projects involving safety and/or security equipment, the 1976 amendment provided for the same rate of Federal participation as for other items of development. This revises a 1973 amendment that allowed 82 percent funding for these purposes.

The following items were made eligible under the 1976 amendment: (1) snow removal equipment; (2) noise suppressing equipment; (3) physical barriers and landscaping to diminish the effect of aircraft noise; and, (4) terminal, development (including multi-modal terminal development) limited to nonrevenue producing public use areas directly related to passenger movement at airports serving air carriers certificated by the CAB. (A maximum of 50 percent Federal share is allowed for terminal development with no more than 60 percent of a sponsor's enplanement funds for any fiscal year to be obligated for this purpose.)

The latest amendment also allows a maximum of four states to administer the general aviation airport development portion of ADAP within their states. This State Demonstration Program will be evaluated and findings are to be reported to Congress by March 31, 1978.

Four special studies are authorized by the amendment. They are related to (1) airport land banking; (2) establishment of major new U.S. airports; (3) sound-proofing public buildings near airports; and, (4) airports threatened with closure. The results of the first three studies must be reported to Congress by July 12, 1977, and results of the airport closure study must be reported to Congress by January 1, 1978.

The amendments permit certifications to be accepted from sponsors indicating that they will comply with all program statutory and administrative requirements. Other significant ADAP provisions of the amendment are: allowance for multi-year grants for projects extending over several years; and funding for grants to states to assist them to develop their own general aviation airport development standards, other than standards for safety of approaches. A maximum of $25,000 may be granted to a single state for development of standards.

PRIMARY GOALS

The primary goals of the ADAP are to:

Encourage the development and implementation of airport development programs consistent with national transportation goals and with goals determined locally through areawide planning programs.

185

DISTRIBUTION OF CONTRACT AUTHORITY FOR
AIR CARRIER / COMMUTER FUNDS (ADAP)
(SECTION 15(a)(3))

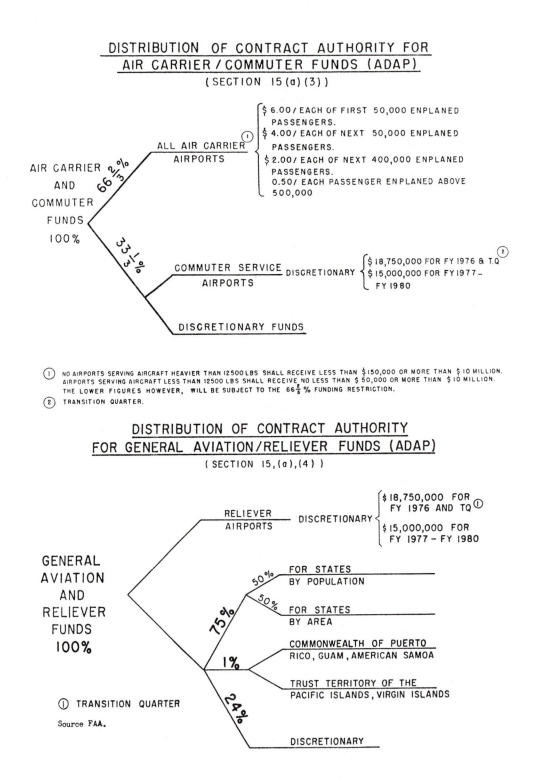

AIR CARRIER AND COMMUTER FUNDS 100%

66 2/3%

ALL AIR CARRIER AIRPORTS ①

$ 6.00/ EACH OF FIRST 50,000 ENPLANED PASSENGERS.
$ 4.00/ EACH OF NEXT 50,000 ENPLANED PASSENGERS.
$ 2.00/ EACH OF NEXT 400,000 ENPLANED PASSENGERS.
0.50/ EACH PASSENGER ENPLANED ABOVE 500,000

33 1/3%

COMMUTER SERVICE AIRPORTS — DISCRETIONARY ②

$ 18,750,000 FOR FY 1976 & T.Q
$ 15,000,000 FOR FY 1977 – FY 1980

DISCRETIONARY FUNDS

① NO AIRPORTS SERVING AIRCRAFT HEAVIER THAN 12500 LBS SHALL RECEIVE LESS THAN $ 150,000 OR MORE THAN $ 10 MILLION.
AIRPORTS SERVING AIRCRAFT LESS THAN 12500 LBS SHALL RECEIVE NO LESS THAN $ 50,000 OR MORE THAN $ 10 MILLION.
THE LOWER FIGURES HOWEVER, WILL BE SUBJECT TO THE 66 $\frac{1}{3}$ % FUNDING RESTRICTION.
② TRANSITION QUARTER.

DISTRIBUTION OF CONTRACT AUTHORITY
FOR GENERAL AVIATION/RELIEVER FUNDS (ADAP)
(SECTION 15,(a),(4))

GENERAL AVIATION AND RELIEVER FUNDS 100%

RELIEVER AIRPORTS — DISCRETIONARY

$ 18,750,000 FOR FY 1976 AND TQ ①
$ 15,000,000 FOR FY 1977 – FY 1980

75%

50% FOR STATES BY POPULATION

50% FOR STATES BY AREA

1%

COMMONWEALTH OF PUERTO RICO, GUAM, AMERICAN SAMOA

TRUST TERRITORY OF THE PACIFIC ISLANDS, VIRGIN ISLANDS

24%

DISCRETIONARY

① TRANSITION QUARTER

Source FAA.

186

Assist investments of airport sponsors in airport facilities.

Improve the safety and economic efficiency of the system by encouraging uniformity in development within appropriate safety and design standards.

Promote the timely development of airport facilities needed to minimize delays due to congestion in the system.

Assure consistency of airport development with other aviation facility installations programmed under the Facilities and Equipment Program for the Federal Aviation Administration (FAA).

Assure permanency of the national airport system by financially assisting in the acquisition of nonpublic-owned airports needed for the system.

Mitigate, to the extent practical, adverse environmental effect of aircraft operations.

Airports Programs

The following discussion was taken from a 1977 FAA publication, The *Eighth Annual Report of Operations Under the Airport and Airway Development Act of 1970 as Amended by the Airport and Airway Development Act Amendments of 1976*. In this report to the Congress the FAA states its present official position with regard to the various airport development programs and legislation.

EIGHTH ANNUAL REPORT OF OPERATIONS UNDER THE AIRPORT AND AIRWAY DEVELOPMENT ACT OF 1970 AS AMENDED BY THE AIRPORT AND AIRWAY DEVELOPMENT ACT AMENDMENTS OF 1976

Section 24 of the Airport and Airway Development Act of 1970 (Public Law 91-258) requires that the Secretary, Department of Transportation, submit an annual report to Congress of operations under Part II of the Act for the preceding fiscal year. This report covers operations for the fiscal year ending September 30, 1977.

INTRODUCTION

With the enactment of the Airport and Airway Development Act of 1970 (P.L. 91-258) the Nation moved toward improving the efficiency and safety of the airport and airways system. Reflecting the role of aviation in the economy and the benefits derived from safe and efficient operation, that statute (1) found the airport and airway system inadequate to meet the requirements of the then current and projected growth in aviation, (2) declared substantial expansion and improvement was required to meet the demands of interstate commerce, the postal service, and national defense, and (3) established an expanded program of federal matching grants to sponsors of airports serving commercial and general aviation. Moreover, the Act established a system of user taxes paid into a trust fund to provide an assured, long-term source of funding.

The Act has now been amended three times.

The Act was amended in 1971 (P.L. 92-174) to incorporate provisions involving the use, preservation, and priority for expenditure of funds from the trust funds. The Airport Development Acceleration Act of 1973 (P.L. 93-44) made further amendments to the 1970 Act, increasing annual authorizations for fiscal years 1974 and 1975 and increasing the Federal contribution for grants at most airports. Most recently the Airport and Airway Development Act Amendments of 1976 (P.L. 94-353 approved July 12, 1976) made several major changes to the Act, affecting among other things project eligibility, increased overall funding levels, distribution of funds, the project approval process, the percentage of the Federal contribution for most projects, extension of the planning grant program and the revisions to the National Airport System Plan.

THE AIRPORTS PROGRAM

The Airports Program covers the identification, planning, and development of the Nation's system of public airports to serve the needs of civil aviation in the fifty states, Guam, Puerto Rico, American Samoa, the Trust Territory of the Pacific Islands, and the Virgin Islands.

It is based primarily on provisions of the Airport and Airway Development Act of 1970 (Public Law 91-258), and the Airport and Airway Development Act Amendments of 1976 (P.L. 94-353) which amended P.L. 91-258. These laws provide legislative recognition of an important national need for improvement in the national airport and airway system. Airport system improvements aimed at increased system capacity and the accommodation of higher performance aircraft has been the goal of the Airports Program. Federal involvement is designed to assist municipalities and other public agencies that own and operate the civil airports of this country in funding airport planning and development that will (1) help assure environmental acceptability and (2) provide for increased safety in airport operations.

Principal activities in this program include: preparation of a National Airport System Plan and other airports planning activities; administering a program of grants–in–aid for airport planning and airport development engineering and safety standards; airport certification and inspection for safety of operations; participation in transfers of Federal land and property for civil airport use; field collection of data for the airport data program; assuring that public agencies receiving Federal assistance continue to operate their airports for the benefit of the public in accordance with their agreements and a general aviation grant state demonstration program.

-AIRPORTS PROGRAMS-
HISTORY OF PROGRAM FUNCTIONS
FISCAL YEARS 1947 THROUGH 1980

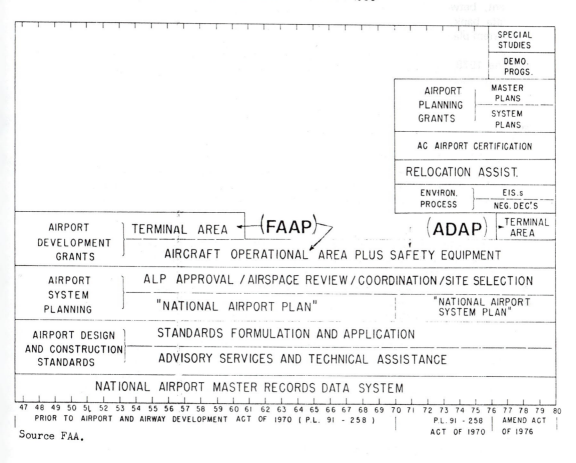

Source FAA.

National Airport System Plan (NASP). The Airport and Airway Development Act of 1970, as amended, requires the Secretary of Transportation to prepare a ten-year National Airport System Plan for the development of public airports in the U.S. adequate for the needs of civil aeronautics, the requirements of national defense, and the special needs of the Postal Service. In developing the plan, the Secretary is directed to give due consideration to the relationship of each airport to local transportation systems, forecast technological developments in aeronautics, other modes of intercity transportation, and factors affecting the quality of the national environment. Prepared by FAA, the first edition of the NASP covering the years 1972 through 1982 was submitted to Congress in June 1973 and released to the public in September 1973. A revised NASP, 1978-1987, was delivered to Congress in January 1978. The NASP is kept current, between major editions, by continuing revisions to a computer-stored data bank. Many of the revisions include the findings of airport master and system plans funded under the Planning Grant Program (PGP).

The 1978-1987 NASP includes about 3,600 locations. The NASP recommends more than $10.6 billion in eligible development for the ten-year period.[19]

PLANNING GRANT PROGRAM (PGP)

The Airport and Airway Development Act of 1970, as amended (Section 13), authorities the FAA (through delegation from the Secretary of Transportation) to make grants to public and planning agencies for preparation of airport system and master plans. The program is designed to promote the effective location and development of publicly owned airports and to develop a national airport system plan.

System plans are developed by a state or areawide planning agency to formulate air transportation policy, determine airport facility requirements needed to meet forecast demands, and to establish the framework for detailed airport master planning. Airport master plans, which are developed by the airport owner, focus on the nature and extent of development required to meet the future aeronautical demand at a particular facility over a 20-year period.

Since the inception of this program in Fiscal Year 1971, 1,387 planning grants have been issued totaling $57.8 million. Of these, 1,250 were for master plans ($42.1 million) and the remaining 137 were for system planning projects ($15.7 million). Included in the latter were the initiation of state system plans for 43 states, the Commonwealth of Puerto Rico, and the Trust Territory of the Pacific Islands.

When the program first began, the Federal Government provided up to two-thirds of the cost of planning grant projects. However, the enactment of the Airport and Airway Development Act Amendments of 1976 increased the Federal share of planning projects. The Federal Government now provides 75 percent of the cost of airport system plans. The Federal participation rate in the cost of airport master plans is 90 percent for general aviation airports and varies from 75 to 90 percent for air carrier airports depending upon the number of passengers enplaned. The participation rate in master plans may be higher in public land states.

AIRPORTS PROGRAMS

HISTORY OF AUTHORIZED GRANT-IN-AID PROGRAMS
FISCAL YEARS 1947 THROUGH 1980

FAAP-FEDERAL-AID AIRPORT PROGRAM
ADAP-AIRPORT DEVELOPMENT AID PROGRAM
PGP-AIRPORT PLANNING GRANT PROGRAM

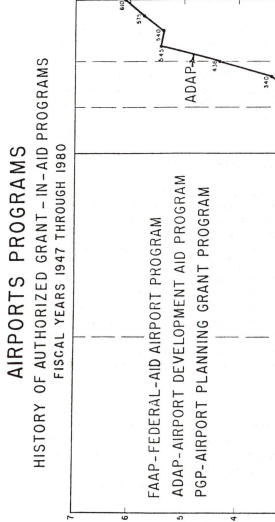

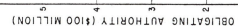

During Fiscal Year 1977, $12,193,597 was obligated through the PGP for 205 projects. Recoveries from closeout of prior-year grants resulted in net obligations for Fiscal Year 1977 totaling $11,767,673. This amount virtually exhausted all available program funds and significantly exceeded the previous obligational record of $9.7 million in Fiscal Year 1975. Fourteen of the 205 projects ($953,237 in PGP funds) were for airport system planning. The remaining 191 projects ($11,240,360 in PGP funds) were for airport master plans at 70 air carrier and 121 general aviation locations. A breakdown by location of the grants is shown in Appendices A and B.

Emphasis in airport planning and development will be placed upon maintaining the viability of our existing airports to accommodate the projected increase in aviation demand. A critical issue affecting the viability of the existing system is the annoyance caused by noise from aircraft taking off and landing at these facilities. The airport owner is primarily responsible for the effect of aircraft noise on the community and developing action plans to reduce the impact of the noise. To assist airport owners in carrying.

ENVIRONMENTAL CONSIDERATIONS

All Federal airport development actions are subject to environmental consideration as required by the Airport and Airway Development Act of 1970, as amended, the National Environmental Policy Act of 1969 (NEPA), and numerous other laws and regulations. Section 16(c) (4) of the Airport and Airway Development Act and Reorganization Plan No. 3 (1970) require consultation with the Environmental Protection Agency and the Department of the Interior with regard to the effect that a project involving the location of an airport, location of a runway, or a major runway extension may have on natural resources. Section 102(2) (C) of NEPA requires an environmental impact statement and a more comprehensive Federal review when an action would produce a significant impact on the environment. Other laws have specific requirements relative to specialized concerns such as air quality, water quality, public recreational lands, coastal zones, and endangered and threatened species of plants and animals.

Initial review of airport development actions identifies the extent of environmental assessment and coordination required. This results in the preparation by the Federal Aviation Administration of a detailed environmental impact statement or a negative declaration. A negative declaration includes a finding that the proposed action does not significantly affect the quality of the human environment or otherwise require full coordination and review pursuant to Section 102(2) (C) of NEPA.

In Fiscal Year 1977, approximately 374 environmental actions were processed as negative declarations. Another 39 airport actions were environmentally approved through full coordination procedures required by Section 102(2) (C) of NEPA.

Our commitment to dealing with environmental issues has resulted in utilizing experience gained since the 1970 NEPA legislation to improve the environmental process, to assure more thorough analysis and evaluation of significant impacts, to identify projects with negative or minimal impact early in the process, and overall to speed the process for many Federal actions. Nevertheless, some actions are so complex or controversial that the resolution of the issues involved has been and continues to be a major time-consuming factor in reaching Federal decisions on proposed airport development.

On occasion sensitive environmental issues exist which must be resolved before a final decision can be made on an airport project. For example, the issue of possible jeopardy to the continued existence of an endangered species, the Florida Everglade Kite, is currently being addressed in connection with completion of the final environmental impact statement for a replacement airport for the Everglades Jetport in Southeast Florida. Controversy over hydraulic fill of a wetlands area for a runway extension had to be settled on the North Bend, Oregon, airport, requiring a year of research and negotiations to resolve the State's requirements for a permit.

POLICIES AND PROCEDURES
LAND ACQUISITION UNDER THE AIRPORT DEVELOPMENT
AID PROGRAM

All matters pertaining to land acquisition and relocation of persons will be accomplished in accordance with the Uniform Relocation Assistance and Real Property Acquisition Policies Act of 1970, PL 91-646, Part 25 of Regulations of Secretary of Transportation, Advisory Circular 150/5100-11, and all applicable state and local laws and ordinances (*Maryland*-Article 1-A, Sections 4-401, 5-501, 7-703f, 14c, 15f, Maryland Annotated Code; *Virginia*-Chapter 6, Title 25, Code of Virginia). Each property to be taken in fee or easement shall be appraised, except that for uncomplicated takings which do not involve relocation of persons and which have a value of less than $1,000 a nominal value finding may be made in lieu of an appraisal. *The appraisal must be performed prior to going under Grant and be submitted to the FAA District Office for approval.*

There will be a separate file established for each property taken. All matters pertaining to a parcel will be documented and recorded in the parcel file, including records of each contact with the owner and/or tenant of that parcel.

All land acquisition will be accomplished by negotiation, if possible. Condemnation will be used only when all reasonable means of negotiation have been exhausted, or in the case of defects in title which require condemnation action to clear.

PRELIMINARY ACTIONS

As soon as a decision to acquire land interests is made the Sponsor will determine whether such acquisition will result in the dislocation of any person, business or farm operation. If persons are to be relocated, the Sponsor will determine that adequate decent, safe, and sanitary housing, at least comparable to that being taken, is available and on the market.

Should there not be adequate replacement housing, the sponsor will decide whether it is in their best interests to construct and make available such housing or to abandon the proposed acquisition.

193

When any decision to proceed with acquisition involving relocation is made, a relocation plan will be prepared. The relocation plan will be submitted to FAA for review and concurrence and must follow the requirements set forth in Advisory Circular 150/5100-11.

APPRAISALS

With regard to the number of appraisals to be obtained, this is covered by the Advisory Circular No. 150/5100-11. The airport sponsor will obtain at least one appraisal for each parcel to be acquired. Where property acquisition will be of a complex or unusual nature or whenever the appraised value is expected to exceed $50,000 at least two appraisals should be obtained.

. . .

Recent Trends

Airport Development Aid Program allocations for the first quarter of Fiscal 1979 included work on 172 projects in 44 states and in U.S. territories. Of these, 68 general aviation projects received $17.3 million.

A higher priority for reliever airports is being urged by Rep. Glenn Anderson (D. Calif.), Chairman of the House Aviation Subcommittee. This would make sure that general aviation has airport facilities available at major cities which would reduce general aviation activity at the large hub airports.

In the new ADAP proposal (1979) FAA showed a new willingness to allow privately owned, public use airports to receive federal funding. Funds for development with suitable controls would be available, under the proposed legislation, for privately owned reliever airports in states that administer their own ADAP programs. The states would receive funds and enter into direct contractual relationships with the airports. With more ADAP funds available under the new proposals, however, FAA believes that acquisition of privately owned airports by local governments will be more likely than the granting of funds to privately-owned airports. This indicates that the smaller airports in private hands, still face the problem of rising taxes, increasing pressure to sell out and close down these small but very useful landing facilities.

U.S. Civil and Joint-Use Airports, Heliports, and Seaplane Bases on Record by Type of Ownership and Landing Facilities, by FAA Region and State, December 31, 1977

FAA Region and State	Total facilities[1]	By ownership		Paved airports		Unpaved airports	
		Public	Private	Lighted	Not Lighted	Lighted	Not Lighted
Total	14,117	4,708	9,409	3,564	1,749	919	7,885
United States—total[2]	14,069	4,678	9,391	3,547	1,734	918	7,870
NEW ENGLAND—total	542	139	403	128	104	9	301
Connecticut	103	14	89	27	29	9	47
Maine	162	49	113	26	16	—	116
Massachusetts	139	31	108	41	35	4	62
New Hampshire	54	16	38	15	13	1	23
Rhode Island	24	8	16	8	5	3	10
Vermont	60	21	39	11	6	1	43
EASTERN—total	1,906	298	1,608	387	259	115	1,145
Delaware	32	3	29	6	4	10	12
District of Columbia	17	8	9	5	7	—	5
Maryland	142	24	118	34	27	8	73
New Jersey	254	34	220	45	45	12	152
New York	490	70	420	93	72	38	287
Pennsylvania	651	76	575	108	65	38	440
Virginia	249	56	193	68	24	8	149
West Virginia	71	27	44	28	15	1	27
GREAT LAKES—total	2,832	668	2,164	612	170	253	1,797
Illinois	876	96	780	103	62	59	652
Indiana	306	67	239	84	20	32	170
Michigan	413	133	280	113	19	43	238
Minnesota	336	143	193	83	6	40	207
Ohio	569	125	444	134	49	52	334
Wisconsin	332	104	228	95	14	27	196
CENTRAL—total	1,274	447	827	364	64	141	705
Iowa	253	115	138	92	6	49	106
Kansas	351	123	228	92	15	44	200
Missouri	365	116	249	115	28	25	197
Nebraska	305	93	212	65	15	23	202
SOUTHERN—total	1,666	699	967	628	213	98	727
Alabama	142	93	49	85	21	3	33
Florida	438	126	312	114	63	28	233
Georgia	275	121	154	106	34	9	126
Kentucky	97	54	43	42	21	6	28
Mississippi	154	77	77	64	19	6	62
North Carolina	258	72	186	76	17	25	140
Puerto Rico	27	12	15	10	12	—	5
South Carolina	126	63	63	52	8	15	51
Tennessee	144	77	67	77	18	3	46
Virgin Islands	5	4	1	2	—	—	3

(Continued on next page)

195

U.S. Civil and Joint-Use Airports, Heliports, and Seaplane Bases on Record by Type of Ownership and Landing Facilities, by FAA Region and State, December 31, 1977

FAA Region and State	Total facilities[1]	By ownership		Paved airports		Unpaved airports	
		Public	Private	Lighted	Not Lighted	Lighted	Not Lighted
SOUTHWEST—total	2,123	627	1,496	616	319	63	1,125
Arkansas	167	76	91	65	15	7	80
Louisiana	282	72	210	68	46	10	158
New Mexico	139	62	77	42	22	2	73
Oklahoma	285	127	158	114	26	10	135
Texas	1,250	290	960	327	210	34	679
ROCKY MOUNTAIN—total	961	466	495	272	93	77	519
Colorado	261	82	179	61	45	11	144
Montana	169	115	54	60	9	12	88
North Dakota	211	95	116	49	7	22	133
South Dakota	134	74	60	37	6	30	61
Utah	93	58	35	38	17	—	38
Wyoming	93	42	51	27	9	2	55
WESTERN—total	1,140	450	690	321	330	29	460
Arizona	209	96	113	57	34	10	108
California	813	296	517	242	275	16	280
Nevada	118	58	60	22	21	3	72
NORTHWEST—total	841	339	502	176	148	58	459
Idaho	190	130	60	32	23	5	130
Oregon	301	93	208	61	52	19	169
Washington	350	116	234	83	73	34	160
ALASKAN—total	763	543	220	45	16	74	628
PACIFIC—total	69	32	37	15	33	2	19
Hawaii	53	18	35	10	30	1	12
South Pacific[3]	16	14	2	5	3	1	7

Source: FAA

[1]Includes U.S. Civil and joint use airports, heliports, seaports, and seaplane bases.
[2]Excludes Puerto Rico, Virgin Islands, and South Pacific.
[3]American Samoa, Guam, and Trust Territory.

NOTES

[1]FAR Part 157, "Notice of Construction, Alteration, Activation, and Deactivation of Airports."

[2]After World War II when schores of "gypsy" non-scheduled carriers began operation, FAA (then CAA) decided to place planes over 12,500 pounds in a transport category in order to improve safety procedures for non-scheduled transport. The engineering and mechanic's regulation also benefitted from this demarcation line, relieving light aircraft from certain procedures and standards which were demanded of the transport aircraft. At that time no planes usable in the transport mode were manufactured under 12,500. (This has recently changed.)

[3]The transponder is a device which causes a radar image on the Air Traffic Control (ATC) radar screens and may also signal for identification and be interrogated by ATC. The transponder can be set to indicate to ATC an emergency situation without pilot voice communication. The encoding altimeter likewise transmits ATC information. It sends the aircraft altitude to the ATC computer upon interrogation of the transponder by ATC's ground radar. Altitude encoders are required for IFR and VFR flight within controlled airspace above 12,500 feet (except when that airspace lies at and below 2500 feet above the surface as in mountainous regions) and in certain terminal control areas. See also, Timothy R. V. Foster, *The Aircraft Owner's Handbook*, (New York: Van Nostrand Reinhold Company, 1978), pp. 189-90.

[4]Federal Tort Claims Act as amended in 1966 by Public Law 89-506, 80 Stat. 306.

[5]Paul Engstrom, "Liability of the Fixed Base Operator — Legal Impact," *The L. E. News*, Vol. 22, No. 2 (October 1978), p. 13.

[6]*Ibid.*

[7]Bailment is discussed later in this chapter.

[8]See the chapter on hijacking for more information.

[9]Fred A. Biehler, *Aviation Maintenance Law* (Basin, Wyo.: Aviation Maintenance Foundation, Inc., 1975), pp. 63-64.

[10]Biehler, p. 84.

[11]Biehler, p. 80; Foster, pp. 127-28.

[12]*Lock v. Packard Flying Service, Inc.* 193 NW 2d 516 (Neb Sup; 1970; 11 Avi. 17, 402.

[13]Federal Aviation Act of 1958, 85th Cong., Public Law 85-726, S. 3880, passed 23 August 1958.

[14]For a discussion of "taking" see the chapter on U.S. law.

[15]Airline Deregulation Act of 1978. The act relieves certificated air carriers from serving non-profitable points and contains provision for air services to small or isolated communities via subsidized, non-certificated operators.

[16]John R. Lawrence, "The Financial Future of Privately-Owned Utility Airports," unpublished paper, 1978, Wilmington College, Business Aviation Management program, New Castle, Delaware, pp. 33-34.

[17]Lawrence, p. 17.

[18]Source: FAA Office of Airports, Federal Aviation Administration, Washington, D.C., June 1979.

[19]*Ibid.*

Photograph courtesy Cessna Aircraft Company.

1979 Cessna 310.

CHAPTER 13

AIRMEN: RIGHTS, RESPONSIBILITIES, ORGANIZATIONS

FARs: The Airman's "Bible"

To the U.S. pilot, the Federal Aviation Regulations (FARs) constitute the airman's "Bible." The only difference being, some assert, that the FARs are longer! Fortunately, the FARs are also well indexed and compartmentalized. A pilot need not know all the FARs. Those pertaining, for example, to aircraft manufacture or maintenance need not be mastered in detail by pilots.[1]

The airman can select, too, the type of flying planned and the particular parts of FAR that apply. "Part 91 pilots," for example, operate aircraft sans passengers or property carried for hire. An entirely different set of FARs pertains to "for hire" carriage with stricter limits and more care required of airlines, air taxis and airfreight.

It is possible, then, for pilots to learn well the FARs under which they plan to operate. Every pilot has a basic set of rules pertaining to Visual Flight Rules (VFR) and Instrument Flight Rules (IFR) weather conditions; regarding medical standards; general safety rules and air traffic regulations.[2]

The FARs have been written by the Civil Aeronautics Board (CAB) and the (now) Federal Aviation Administration (FAA), with industry contributions, in a forty-year time span. The FAA Administrator has the responsibility of enforcing these regulations.

The Responsibility of the Pilot

The responsibilities of a pilot, whatever his rating or area of flight, are staggering. To a degree you may liken the pilot to the driver of a motor vehicle, but over the years, the direct responsibility of the pilot has far exceeded this comparison.[3]

The reason for this heavy and specific responsibility is that the pilot is on the spot. He is the only person facing a particular problem, and often the only person in the aircraft equipped with expertise. Further, one person in command offers less confusion and delay in decision making and action.

A pilot has the duty of planning his flight, of preflight examination of the aircraft and making a determination as to its airworthiness; the safe fueling and loading of the aircraft; the operation of the plane with proper navigational and weather data on hand to fly the plane and its contents safely to its destination. He is, literally, the captain of his ship.[4]

A pilot flying an aircraft, alone or carrying passengers, accepts these and other responsibilities. A flight instructor takes on complete responsibiiity for the training of the student, the safety of the aircraft, plus the performance of the student while flying solo training exercises. Obviously, other commercial pilots, too, have additional, serious responsibilities; for example, the airline captain, the crop duster, and the cargo aircraft captain.

Pilot Exposure to Liability

You have an exposure for pilot service liability if you fly in the performance of the following functions:

(a) test flying a plane you do not own.

(b) for the business or pleasure of an owner, flying that airplane (not yours).

(c) demonstrating a plane for an owner.

(d) selling a plane for someone.

(e) aircraft ferrying (not in your aircraft).

(f) giving flight instruction in a plane you do not own.

All pilots are, as noted, responsible for the safe operation of the aircraft. Ignorance of the law whether local, state, federal or FAA regulations, is no defence.[5]

Only by careful study of FARs and adherence to these regulations can pilots avoid possible suits. By avoiding "willful negligence," and/or "malicious intent," or "careless and reckless operation," the pilot is fairly safe from legal consequence of his actions.[6]

Pilot Negligence

A violation of the FARs is generally viewed as evidence of negligence. A pilot's duty is to fly safely, avoid endangering other aircraft, endangering persons and property on the ground, and safeguarding, too, his passengers and cargo.

If flying for hire the pilot must exercise even a greater degree of care.[7]

In many jurisdictions the theory of *contributory negligence* prevails, in others it is termed *comparative negligence*. Both show that in an accident, one party may carry more of the blame and be therefore more culpable (responsible) to make restitution.

This can be a pilot, an air traffic controller, a manufacturer, a maintenance facility, or other party.

The "last clear chance" theory is somewhat of an exception to the doctrine of contributory negligence. If the defendent was aware of danger but did not act to avoid the accident, then the contributory negligence of the plaintiff will not defeat his recovery of damages.[8]

FAA Enforcement

The FAA is an administrative agency and thus holds hearings which are quasi judicial in nature; all the standards of procedure required by the courts are not adhered to. Agency personnel serve as judges, prosecutors, and agency rules are being applied. This is quite different from a judicial system, an impartial tribunal.

"Due process of law" is a feature both the courts and the administrative hearing, however, must adhere to. Due process means that there is a system of hearings before condemning.

Since situations can vary so widely in aviation no set of regulations can cover all of them. Further, safety demands that rules be violated, on occasion. The standard that decides the pilot's liability is — has the pilot acted in a reasonable and prudent manner? If so, he is less apt to be held liable.[9]

The following description of airmen's rights and FAA enforcement procedures is quoted from an article written by Jonathan Howe, Regional Counsel, Northwest Region, FAA, and distributed by FAA in August 1977.[10]

AIRMAN'S RIGHTS — FAA ENFORCEMENT PROCEDURE

I. INTRODUCTION

Enforcement of FAA's regulations is a statutory responsibility of the Administrator under the Federal Aviation Act of 1958, as amended (ACT), (49 U.S.C. 1301 *et seq.*). In a policy statement issued in January 1973 (FAA Order 1000.9B (1-26-73), the Administrator stated that the purpose of the enforcement program is to "bring about compliance with the regulations and the Federal Aviation Act so as to promote aviation safety and protect the public interest." The Administrator strongly emphasized the enforcement program be carried out in an equitable but firm manner.

The statutes and regulations provide several enforcement alternatives. Section 609 of the Act (49 U.S.C. § 1429) authorizes issuance of orders amending, modifying, suspending, or revoking certificates where aviation safety and the public interest require. Section 901 of the Act (49 U.S.C. § 1471) provides for imposition of civil penalties of up to $1000 for each violation. In addition, the Administrator is authorized to issue cease and desist orders, and orders for seizure of aircraft, where specific circumstances warrant such actions. (49 U.S.C. § 1471(b), 1473(b), and 1485(a); 14 C.F.R. §13.17 and 13.20).

The provisions cited above also authorize the Administrator, in emergency situations, to take summary action; and in these cases appeal by the party affected will not usually stay the enforcement action (*See, e.g.,* 49 U.S.C. §1429).

In non-emergency cases, airmen have several alternative informal methods, discussed *infra*, to seek relief from the Administrator's enforcement processes. If these informal avenues fail to satisfy the parties, more formal proceedings take place in United States District Court or before the National Transportation Safety Board (NTSB). Appeals from either the NTSB or District Court are to the United States Court of Appeals (49 U.S.C. § 1486; 28 U.S.C. § 1291). In emergency cases, the informal processes are bypassed, and expedited review by NTSB and the federal court system is available.

The procedures for implementation of the FAA Enforcement Program are outlined below.

II. TYPES OF ENFORCEMENT ACTION

The FAA enforcement program consists of "administrative" and "legal" enforcement actions. These terms have meanings different from those which an attorney reading them for the first time might expect. The "administrative" actions (provided for in 14 C.F.R. 13.11) are, in effect, warning notices analogous to the warning ticket a driver might receive from a traffic policeman for a minor driving infraction. No substantive rights privileges, or property, are denied the party against whom an "administrative" action is taken; accordingly, as with the warning ticket, there is no right of appeal provided from an FAA administrative action.

The nature of the violation and its impact on aviation safety will determine the type of enforcement action which will be undertaken. The FAA is not limited to any single action. In the interest of safety, any or all of the enforcement actions discussed *infra* may be initiated.

Also covered in this section are FAA actions to deny applications for licenses and certificates. These really are not "enforcement" actions in the same sense as the legal actions, in that they constitute a discretionary decision not to grant a privilege, rather than an action to remove or revoke a license or certificate in being. In legal actions, the FAA has the burden of proof, as distinguished from the discretionary denial cases in which the applicant has the burden of proof.

A. *"Administrative" Action*

This action may only be used where no significant unsafe condition or lack of competency exists. The violation must have been inadvertent, and the violator must have a good attitude. Successful corrective action by the violator will avoid any further enforcement action. However, failure of the violator to correct the problem may result in the initiation of legal enforcement proceedings. Administrative actions may take the form of a warning notice or letter of reprimand where the violation is a single occurrence, or correction has already been successfully completed. (See 14 CFR § 13.11(a)); or may consist of a letter of correction where the violation is continuing and correction has not yet been successfully completed. (See 14 CFR § 13.11 (a)). [Authority: 49 U.S.C § § 1354, 1421; 14 CFR § 13.11; *Enforcement Policy*, FAA Order 1000.9B; *Enforcement Handbook*, FAA Order 2150.2A.]

B. *"Legal" Actions*

When administrative actions prove to be ineffective or the severity of the violation demands more stringent enforcement, the Federal Aviation Act authorizes certain legal actions which may be instituted by the FAA. Selection of an appropriate action is the mutual responsibility of the investigatory officials and legal staff of FAA, and to ensure equal and fair treatment must be based on existing case or policy precedent.

1. *Certificate Actions*

Section 609 of the Act (49 U.S.C. § 1429) authorizes the amendment, modification, suspension, or revocation of any certificate or authorization issued by FAA. Prior to such action, the FAA must give notice and hearing to the alleged violator unless an emergency demands immediate action.

a. *Suspension*

This action is generally used for operational violations, or where an operator's practices have shown a lack of qualification which can be corrected by remedial action. Suspensions may be disciplinary, as well as remedial in nature.

b. *Revocation*

Revocation of a certificate will not be sought unless there is a deficiency in qualification which is incapable of near-term correction; an unwillingness to comply with air safety regulation demonstrated by repeated offenses; or, in other cases, where public policy demands. (See *Enforcement Handbook, supra*). *Specht v. CAB*, 254 F.2d 905 (8th Cir., 1958) states that the FAA has the authority to revoke even where the violator possesses the technical operating skills required, but shows a lack of good judgment.
[Authority: Sec. 609 of the Federal Aviation Act of 1958, as amended, (49 U.S.C. § 1429), 14 CFR § 13.19, *Enforcement Handbook, supra*.]

2. *Civil Actions*

In circumstances where certificate action could result in undue hardship because of economic dependency on continued operation, or where a certificate action is insufficient to assure compliance with the regulatory standards, civil actions may be implemented.

a. *Civil Penalties*

Section 901 of the Act (49 U.S.C. § 1471) states that any person who violates the Federal Aviation safety regulations shall be subject to a civil penalty. In most cases the maximum penalty is $1000 for each violation, but in cases involving shipment of hazardous materials, a $10,000 maximum is provided. Where a violation is continuous, each day of the violation shall constitute a separate violation. The determination of the actual amount of the penalty will take into account the nature, circumstances, extent and gravity of the violation. As a matter of FAA policy, a civil penalty action usually will not be instituted where there has been certificate action or criminal punishment for the same offense, to avoid the appearance of "double jeopardy." Further, the Administrator has the power to compromise the penalty. (See, 49 U.S.C § 1471; 14 C.F.R. 13.15; *Enforcement Handbook, supra).*

  b. *Seizure*

         Section 903 of the Act authorizes seizure by FAA of an aircraft subject to a lien for a civil penalty instituted under Section 901 of the Act. (See, 49 U.S.C. § § 1471, 1473; C.F.R. 13.17.) The constitutionality of FAA's seizure of an aircraft prior to filing of civil penalty action has been upheld where the violation presented an "unusual situation" justifying postponing of notice and hearing. (*Aircrane, Inc. v. Butterfield*, 369 F. Supp. 598 (D.C. Pa. 1974) (3 Judge court).) However, in *U.S. v. Vertol H21C*, 545 F. 2d 648 (9th Cir. 1976), the Court found that the Government had not demonstrated a "special need" for prompt action in collecting a civil penalty and that the seizure prior to notice and hearing was violation of due process. *Vertol* did not overrule *Aircrane v. Butterfield, supra*, and did not find statute and regulations allowing seizure unconstitutional.

         The various U.S. Supreme Court cases dealing with preseizure notice and hearing requirements do not provide a precise guideline upon which FAA's statute and regulations can be confidently predicted to be either valid or void. (See, *e.g., Mathews V. Eldridge*, 424 U.S. 319 (1976); *North Georgia Finishing, Inc. v. Di-Chem, Inc.*, 419 U.S. 601 (1975); *Calero-Toledo v. Pearson Yacht Leasing Co.*, 416 U.S. 663 (1974); *Mitchell v. W. T. Grant Co.*, 416 U.S. 600 (1974); *Fuentes v. Shevin*, 407 U.S. 67 (1972); *Sniacach v. Family Finance Corp.*, 395 U.S. 337 (1969); *Cafeteria and Restaurant Workers Union, Local 473 v. McElroy*, 367 U.S. 886 (1961); *Ewing v. Mytinger and Casselberry*, 339 U.S. 594 (1950); *Fahey v. Mallonee,* 332 U.S. 245 (1947).

         A new aircraft seizure case now before the Ninth Circuit may eventually provide a definitive answer. *U.S. v. Lockheed L-188 Aircraft*, C.A. No. 77-1131 (9th Cir.), filed September 9, 1976, is presently docketed for hearing in the Ninth Circuit. The district court upheld the constitutionality of a seizure without prior notice or hearing. (See *U.S. v. Lockheed L-188 Aircraft*, D.C. No. CV 74-123 (D.C. Ore., July 12, 1976).)

  c. *Cease and Desist*

         Section 1005(a) of the Act (49 U.S.C. § 1485(a)) gives the FAA broad emergency powers to deal with hazards to air safety. These powers may be used to issue cease and desist orders under appropriate circumstances. (14 CFR § 13.12). The statute requires an "emergency requiring immediate action . . . in respect to safety in air commerce;" and proceedings pursuant to a cease and desist order are given preference over all others. *Id.*

  d. *Injunction*

         Section 1007 of the Act (49 U.S.C. § 1487) grants jurisdiction to the District Courts of the United States to enforce compliance with the statutory provisions of the Act and regulations promulgated thereunder by issuance of injunctions restraining violators from further violations.

C. *Denials of Applications*

  1. *FAA Authority to Issue Certificates*

         The statutory enforcement actions enumerated above are remedial or disciplinary in nature and as such place the burden of proof on the FAA to show a violation has occurred which warrants that enforcement action be taken. However, prior to issuance of a certificate or authorization, the FAA can exercise preventive discretion which is reviewed by a different standard. Section 602 of the Act empowers FAA to issue airman certificates. (49 U.S.C. § 1422). Section 602(b) states that the Administrator shall issue a certificate to such applicants as have the proper qualifications and are physically capable of performing duties pertaining to the certificate sought. Parts 61, 63, 65 and 67 of the Federal Aviation Regulations set forth the standards necessary for certification of an airman. (See 14 CFR Parts 61, 63, 65 and 67.) *Specht v. CAB*, 354 F.2d 905 (8th Cir. 1958), states that the Administrator may require "good judgment" as an element of qualification for certification. The power to issue certificates is a discretionary one and as such shifts the burden of proof to the applicant to show qualification. *Doe v. Dept. of Transportation*, 412 F.2d 674 (C.A. Mo., 1969).

2. *Denial of Certificate and Appeal*

Section 602 of the Act (49 U.S.C. 1422) provides for an appeal to the National Transportation Safety Board (hereinafter referred to as NTSB) by an airman upon denial of an application for a certificate. The NTSB is not bound by the FAA's factual determination and its decision is binding on the FAA. If the NTSB affirms the Administrator's denial of the applicant's certificate, thereby exhausting the administrative appeal, the Administrative Procedure Act of 1947, as amended, provides for judicial review in the United States Courts of Appeal, 5 U.S.C. § 704. It should be noted that there is no statutory administrative appeal provisions for denial of non-airman certificates (49 U.S.C. § § 1423, 1424, 1426, 1427), and as such, the Administrative Procedure Act defines the denial as a final action which is subject to direct appeal to the U.S. Court of Appeals without a formal Administrative hearing (See 5 U.S.C. § 704, 49 U.S.C. § 1486, *Club International v. CAB*, CA. No. 75-1033 (9th Cir., 1975)).

D. *Sanction for Operation Without a Certificate*

Section 610 of the Act (49 U.S.C. § 1430) states that it shall be unlawful to operate an aircraft or serve as an airman without an appropriate certificate. With the obvious exception of certificate action, the legal sanctions enumerated above, including civil penalties, cease and desist orders, seizure, and injunctions, all apply to enforce the requirement of certification by FAA.

IV. *FAA PROCEDURES*

A. *Investigation*

The FAA has the power and duty to investigate reported violations of the Federal Aviation Act and Regulations, or Orders promulgated pursuant thereto. (See 49 U.S.C. § § 1354, 1482; 14 CFR § 13.1). Section 13.3 of the Federal Aviation Regulations (14 CFR § 13.3) states, "Under Part 313 of the Act (49 U.S.C. § 1354), the Administrator may conduct public hearings or investigations and take evidence and depositions, issue subpoenas, and compel testimony in a manner provided in Section 1004 of the Act (49 U.S.C. § 1484.)" Section 1002 of the Act (49 U.S.C. § 1482) provides for both formal and informal initiation of investigative proceedings.

1. *Formal Complaint*

Any person may file a complaint in writing with respect to a violation of the Act or Regulations and Orders pursuant thereto, and where there is reasonable ground the FAA shall investigate. (49 U.S.C. § 1482(a), 14 CFR 13.1(a).)

2. *Informal Initiation of Investigation*

The FAA is empowered at any time to institute an investigation on its own initiative as to any matter within its jurisdiction, concerning which complaint is authorized to be made.

B. *Procedure in Non-Emergency Situations*

1. *Notice of Proposed Action*

Following investigation indicating that violations have occurred, the FAA investigators are responsible for submitting a complete report to FAA Counsel (in Washington, D.C. Headquarters or various Regions around the country), which includes a recommendation for the action required in the public interest. Upon agreement with the investigators regarding the merits of the case and the sanction to be applied, the FAA Counsel issues a letter notifying the alleged violator of the proposed action. This letter must include detailed factual allegations and a recitation of the specific violations alleged to have occurred. In the instance of a civil penalty action, the letter is in the form of an offer of compromise, which specifies the amount the FAA will accept in full settlement of the alleged violation. A Notice of Proposed Certificate Action is issued in a similar way, but identifies whether revocation or susupension, is proposed, and, in the case of suspension, the specific duration.

Included in the letter of proposed action is a list of alternative responses available to the alleged violator. The respondent may:

a. Transmit the amount suggested in the offer of compromise, or surrender the certificate for suspension or revocation.

b. Submit an answer to the letter of proposed action and request that such answer and any information attached thereto be considered in connection with the allegations set forth in FAA's letter, and final disposition of the case.

c. Request an opportunity to discuss the matter informally with the FAA Counsel (Informal Conference).

d. Request formal disposition of the case through NTSB or District Court Proceedings.
[Authority: 49 U.S.C.§§1429, 1471; 14 CFR §§13.15, 13.19.]

2. *Informal Conference with FAA Counsel*

These conferences provide an opportunity to arrive at what a-mounts to a consent agreement through a quasi-plea-bargaining process. The respondent may be accompanied by counsel or any other person. The FAA may modify, amend or dismiss its proposed action as a result of the informal conference. Circumstances surrounding the alleged violation and potential ramifications of the proposed sanction may persuade FAA Counsel to mitigate the action ultimately taken. The resulting agreement may, where circumstances warrant, revise a certificate action to a civil penalty action, and conversely, where agreement is not reached between the respondent and the FAA Counsel, formal proceedings will commence (See 49 U.S.C. § § 1429, 1471; 14 CFR §§13.15(b), 13.19(c)).

3. *Formal Action*

In the event of a certificate action, following the completion of alternative informal procedures outlined above, the FAA then issues a formal Order of Certificate Action, which includes the Administrator's findings of fact, specification of regulations violated, and sanction imposed. (See 49 U.S.C.

§1485). This order is an administrative determination, rather than an adjudication of the airman's rights. Its finality is entirely at the option of the respondent. Section 609 of the Act (49 U.S.C. § 1429) gives the respondent the right to appeal the administrative determination to the National Transportation Safety Board (NTSB) for an adjudication on the merits (See 14 CFR § 13.19).

  In a Civil Penalty action, failure to reach a compromise will result in initiation by FAA of proceedings in a U.S. District Court under Part 903 of the Act (49 U.S.C. § 1473; See also 14 CFR § 13.15(2)). In such actions, FAA routinely pays for the maximum statutory penalty

C. *Procedure in Emergency Situations*

  Section 1005 of the Act (49 U.S.C. § 1485) provides that where an emergency requires immediate action in respect of safety in air commerce, the FAA is authorized to issue such orders as are necessary without prior notice or opportunity to be heard by those who are adversely affected by the Order (See also Sections 302, 313 and 601 of the Act for general regulatory authority (49 U.S.C. 1303, 1345, 1421). The following actions have been employed in emergency situations:

1. *Emergency Certificate Action*

  Section 609 of the Act (49 U.S.C. § 1429) specifically provides for immediately effective certificate action where an emergency warrants. It further provides, in protection of the respondent's due process rights, for an accelerated appeal procedure to the NTSB. NTSB must finally dispose of the appeal within sixty (60) days from the date the NTSB is notified of the emergency nature of an order. *Air East, Inc. v. NTSB*, 512 F.2d 1227 (3d Cir. 1975), *cert. denied*, 423 U.S. 863 (1975), upheld the constitutionality of the statute, permitting the FAA to dispense with a prior hearing in an emergency demanding immediate revocation of a certificate.

2. *Emergency Cease and Desist Orders*
[See above "Revocation"]

3. *Emergency Seizure Orders*
[See above "Legal" Actions]

4. *Airworthiness Directives*

  Section 601(a) of the Act (49 U.S.C. § 1421) generally authorizes the Administrator to prescribe such reasonable minimum standards as are necessary to provide adequately for national security and safety in air commerce. Section 603 of the Act (49 U.S.C. § 1423) provides for airworthiness certification by FAA for aircraft. Federal Aviation Regulations, Part 39 (14 CFR §39), promulgated under the authority of the above two statutes, provides for Airworthiness Directives (AD's) when an unsafe condition exists and that condition is likely to exist or develop in other products of the same type design. (Only applies to aircraft, aircraft engines, propellers, or appliances.) No person may operate a product to which an AD applies, except in accordance with its requirements. AD's are normally issued where a mechanical or design defect has been discovered as a result of a malfunction, and can be corrected. Serious consideration is given to the economic impacts on the aviation community, in balance with the safety considerations.

5. *Injunctive Relief*

  The United States District Court has jurisdiction under 49 U.S.C. §1487 to enforce obedience to any provision of the Act and Orders issued thereunder. In an emergency situation, a temporary restraining order may be issued by the court subsequent to a filing of a complaint by FAA, until such time as there can be a formal hearing.

V. *NATIONAL SAFETY TRANSPORTATION SAFETY BOARD (NTSB) PROCEDURES*

A. *Right of Appeal to the NTSB*

Section 303 of the Independent Safety Board Act of 1974 (49 U.S.C. 1902) establishes the National Transportation Safety Board (NTSB) as an independent agency to serve, among other duties, as a review board for the actions of the Federal agencies within the Department of Transportation. Sections 602 and 609 of the Federal Aviation Act (49 U.S.C.§§1422, 1429) provide specifically for review by NTSB of the FAA's actions with regard to certificates. Where the Administrator has denied the issuance or renewal of an airman's certificate (49 U.S.C.§§1422), the applicant may petition for review of such action by NTSB. The petition must be filed within sixty (60) days. The burden of proof is on the applicant to show he/she meets the standards for certification. (49 CFR §§ 821.24 and 821.25). Where a certificate has been suspended or revoked by the FAA, the certificate holder may appeal such action (49 U.S.C. §1429). The appeal must be filed within twenty (20) days from the time of service of the Order suspending or revoking the certificate. The Administrator shall have the burden of proof in these proceedings to show the certificate was justifiably suspended or revoked.

B. *NTSB Proceedings*

Upon petition or appeal, the NTSB assigns an Administrative Law Judge, who conducts a formal proceeding under 49 C.F.R. Part 821 and makes initial findings of fact and conclusions of law. The law judge is not bound by any finding of fact made by the Administrator, and has the power and duty to ascertain the facts. (49 CFR § 821.35.) All parties have the opportunity to present evidence and argument in support of their case. A formal record is made of the proceedings. (49 CFR §§ 821.37 to 821.40.) The initial decision of the Administrative Law Judge will become final where an appeal to the full NTSB is not timely filed by either party; or the NTSB on its own initiative does not decide within twenty (20) days of the decision to review it. (49 CFR §821.43.)

Either party may appeal the initial decision of the law judge to the full NTSB by filing and serving notice of appeal upon the other parties within ten (10) days after the rendering of the initial decision. (49 CFR § 821.47.) The NTSB is limited in its consideration to the following issues on appeal (49 CF℞ 821.49):

1. Are the findings of fact each supported by a preponderance of reliable probative and substantial evidence?

2. Are the conclusions made in accordance with precedent and policy?

3. Are the questions on appeal substantial?

4. Have any prejudicial errors occurred?

The findings of the full Board are final and, as such, exhaust the appellant's administrative remedies.

VI. *JUDICIAL REVIEW*

Ultimately, all enforcement actions by the FAA are reviewable by the courts of appeals of the United States or the United States Courts of Appeals for the District of Columbia. The Administrative Procedure Act (5 U.S.C. §704) and the Federal Aviation Act (in 49 U.S.C. § 1486) both provide that all final administrative actions are reviewable by the courts. Where the Federal Aviation Act provides for review by the NTSB, judicial review will not be available until the NTSB has issued a final decision, thereby exhausting administrative remedies. As noted above, Sections 602 and 609 of the Federal Aviation Act provide for review of certificate denial, amendment, suspension or revocation by the NTSB. (49 U.S.C. §§ 1422, 1429). Cease and Desist Orders are final and, as such, are directly appealable to the courts of appeals of the United States. (14 CFR § 13.20). Civil penalty actions and seizure orders are enforced by initiation of proceedings in an appropriate District Court for the United States by the District Attorney, upon notification by the FAA (14 CFR §§ 13.15, 13.17). These Federal District Court actions proceed as do other federal court actions, and final judgments are appealable under 28 U.S.C. § 1291.

ENFORCEMENT PROCEDURE FOR VIOLATIONS BY MILITARY PERSONNEL

Sections 609 and 901 of the Act (49 U.S.C. 1422 and 1471), providing for certificate and civil penalty enforcement proceedings, expressly limit the FAA's jurisdiction to civil airmen acting in violation of the Federal Aviation Act or Regulations. However, Section 1002(a) of the Act (49 U.S.C. 1482) provides for referral to the Secretary of the military department concerned, of alleged violations of the Act or Regulations by members of the Armed Forces of the United States, acting in their official capacity. Any enforcement action taken against the military airman is at the discretion of the appropriate Secretary. Under 1002(a), the Military Secretary is required to inform the FAA of the disposition of the alleged violation within ninety (90) days of the referral.

ENFORCEMENT PROCEDURE FOR VIOLATIONS BY FOREIGN AIRMEN

The FAA has exclusive jurisdiction with respect to use of navigable airspace within the United States and the promulgation of safety regulations for the use thereof. Any alleged violation of the Federal Aviation Regulations by a foreign airman, which would normally result in a certificate action, is referred to the Secretary of State to direct to the appropriate foreign government for disposition. Where the enforcement action is a civil penalty, the FAA may initiate proceedings against the foreign airman, and the aircraft involved, if the circumstances warrant. The standard rules for obtaining jurisdiction against a foreign citizen apply. (28 U.S.C. 1330, et seq.; and the Federal Rules of Civil Procedure.)

A complaint against a foreign citizen will allege a violation of the Federal Aviation Regulations, but, where applicable, will incorporate by reference the correlative violation of the appropriate foreign law.

Immunity

The FAA has experimented with a program in which pilots and air traffic controllers may report near-misses, near-collisions, and be granted immunity from prosecution for breaking the air regulation forbidding flight closer than five hundred feet to another aircraft. This is called the Aviation Safety Reporting System (ASRD). FAA does not have access to NASA's ASRS data.

In 1979 FAA Administrator Langhorne M. Bond objected to granting blanket immunity to pilots reporting near-misses. Bond stated that pilots involved in such near-miss flying might file a report in order to escape FAA enforcement action for negligence. The Aircraft Owners and Pilots Association (AOPA) worked with the FAA to work out a way to save the reporting system. The AOPA noted that should pilots fear to report near-misses, areas of traffic congestion in which collisions might occur could not be located prior to a serious accident.[11]

In June 1979 the AOPA was able to report to its members that immunity would be granted to reporters of unsafe incidents except those involved in accidents or criminal offenses. Although a person reporting may have violated the FARs, there will be no civil penalty nor certificate suspension if the violation was not criminal, not deliberate, not because of lack of competence or qualifications, and if the person had not violated the FARs since June 1975, and finally, if he or she had filed a report of the current incident with ASRS within 10 days.

These modifications went into effect 1 July 1979, the date that the FAA had planned to revoke immunity. An Advisory Circular (AC 00-46B) has been sent to all airmen explaining the changes.[12]

Violations that come to the attention of the FAA from other sources will be followed up.

Pilots may claim immunity when obliged to break an air regulation in order to safely continue or complete the flight. If the FAA, upon the pilot reporting the violation and the circumstances, considers that the pilot used good judgement, immunity may be granted. Likewise, when conditions of flight are of such a nature that the pilot with no reasonable amount of foresight or planning, or competence, could have prevented the FAR violation, again immunity may be claimed.[13]

Degrees of Care

Guest Statute. Should an individual accept without paying, a sightseeing ride or transport in one's automobile or aircraft, that individual comes under the "guest statute." The operator is responsible for only so much due care as

210

he might reasonably exercise to protect his own well being. Shared expenses do not constitute "payments." Private pilots fly passengers on this basis, as guests.

Should an aircraft operator accept payment for his services as a pilot, then he is responsible for a much greater degree of care. Flying for hire is an implied contract for services performed with care.

Our discussion thus far gives the impression that flying as a nonpaying guest exempts the pilot and/or aircraft operator from liability except in the case of gross negligence. One might infer that guests in an aircraft are owed only the care due guests in an automobile, that slight degree of care which a reasonably prudent man would exercise. The law relating to aerial "guests," is not quite this simple.

Rather, we find that where no aviation guest statute exists, guests flown in aircraft can sue on the grounds that the pilot was exercising a degree of ordinary negligence (as opposed to gross negligence). The reason for this is that the aerial guest has not the opportunity to leave the aircraft that an automobile guest has to leave an automobile when alarmed or displeased at the operation of the vehicle. The aerial guest is more under the control of the pilot and at the mercy of the pilot's care and attention in planning and executing the flight.[14] The courts further hold that a pilot's slight negligence in piloting the plane might have more serious results than a similar slight negligence of the driver of an automobile.[15] The writer does not agree with the assessment of the court, yet the judgement is of interest in that it reveals the lingering tendency to see flying as more hazardous than driving.

Social versus business intent of the flight also affects whether or not the flight was instigated as a free and generous action of the host or did the host-operator of the aircraft expect a business benefit to result. A pilot carrying a prospective aircraft buyer aloft falls within the latter category. Less obviously, so does the pilot of a plane carrying a passenger to a business conference.[16]

Should a firm or individual, provide a pilot and plane for hire to transport passengers, that firm or individual warrants the safe transport of the passengers. Extreme care is then the responsibility of the aircraft operator. For all passenger-carrying flights it is legally necessary that airworthy aircraft and properly certificated pilots be provided.

Invitee. A person invited upon business premises for flying training, aircraft sales, is entitled to great care on the part of the operator of the business.[17]

Hijacked Pilots

"Pilots wishes are to be fully considered," the Antihijacking Act of 1974 notes, yet on occasion they are not. The pilot is responsible for the safety of his flight. Pilots, to assure the safety of themselves, passengers and aircraft, however, must decide *whether or not* to call in the FAA and the FBI. The pilot's decision is based on his judgement of how to safely end the flight.

The FAA is legally in control of the situation, once called upon, and coordinates the actions of assisting agencies such as the FBI and others.

Pilots should know hijacking radio and radar codes from the *Airman's Information Manual*.[18]

Waivers and Special Conditions

For many rules there are waivers. If this were not so, the air regulations could hamstring aviation business and development.

Until the new FAR Part 137 was written, for example, all agricultural pilots flew under waivers allowing them to fly close to crops and other property in the course of their work. Pilots may ferry planes which are not legally airworthy but found by FAA to be ferryable, to shops for maintenance and overhaul. Sign towing is carried on under a waiver.

The owners of experimental, homebuilt, and antique aircraft call upon FAA for various waivers in order to fly such aircraft.[19]

Public Right of Transit

The Federal Aviation Act of 1958, Section 104, contains a declaration of a public right of freedom of transit through the navigable airspace of the United States. "Navigable airspace" is defined by Section 101 (24) as "airspace above the minimum altitudes of flight prescribed by regulations issued under this act (by the Federal Aviation Administration), and shall include airspace needed to insure safety in take-off and landing of aircraft."

Such altitudes are prescribed by the FAA. The courts have supported this freedom of transit, relieving aircraft operators from technical claims of trespass but not denying a landowner's rights in the case of an actual "taking" of property caused by low-flying aircraft. Should low flights endanger persons below, harm them, prevent their use and enjoyment of their property — then the low flight may well be considered a "taking." The person harmed or whose property loses value therein may sue for damages and/or relief.[20]

The Causby Case

A landmark case was United States vs. Causby (1946). An army airport was built near Mr. Causby's chicken farm. Planes approaching to land, worried Causby and played havoc with his chickens. Causby sued for damages.

The case eventually went to the Supreme Court. The Court held that, indeed, the government had "taken" Mr. Causby's property by taking an easement over his land and without payment. The 5th Amendment of the Constitution grants a right — private property may not be taken for public use without just compensation.

Ancient land law held that a property owner owned the air above his land. Today the air above the minimum height approved for air navigation by the Administrator of FAA is considered in the public domain — open to public use.[21]

Even so, cases have followed the Causby case, and when an unlawful "taking" again was found, damages have been paid.

Military Airmen

The air traffic control and radio navigational aids systems in the United States serve both civil and military aircraft. The FAA plans, administers, mans, and coordinates the use of the nation's airways. Military pilots adhere to the FARs with the aid of special corridors, areas, and FAR exemptions that enable them to carry out their missions.

An individual who has served in one of the services as a rated military pilot in the preceding twelve months may apply for a private or commercial certificate, or an aircraft or instrument rating, according to FAR Part 61.73. After passing a written examination, the certificate and appropriate ratings are issued.

Military pilots who are not currently rated must pass both written and flight tests. Properly documented military flight training and experience is accepted by the FAA.[22]

The Civil Air Patrol

The Civil Air Patrol (CAP) pilots are usually civilians and are pilots certificated by the FAA. Pilots flying Civil Air Patrol aircraft obey all FARs plus a body of regulations written by the CAP. The CAP is a civil volunteer organization, an auxiliary of the U.S. Air Force.

The organization's mission is to search for downed aircraft, lost children and hikers. The CAP flies disaster relief on occasion and may be called on for a variety of search and mercy missions.

The CAP pilots are covered by the organization's insurance so long as they adhere to FARs and CAP regulations. Even so, the policy has a $500 deductible feature. The state CAP Wing Headquarters may assist the pilot with all or part of this deductible after a hearing.

Certificates, Ratings, Categories

Certificates. A pilot "certificate" certifies that a pilot has proven a certain level of competency and knowledge. There are several kinds of certificates: the private pilot certificate, the commercial pilot certificate, the Airline Transport Pilot certificate, and the flight instructor certificate.

Ratings. To pilot certificates, "ratings," may be added. There are airplane, rotorcraft, glider, airship, free balloon, and instrument ratings.

Categories. A rotorcraft category includes the gyroplane class rating or a helicopter class rating. The lighter-than-air category takes in free balloon ratings and airship ratings. The airplane category covers fixed-wing aircraft. Finally, there are certain aircraft which require special flight tests to achieve a type rating. These are large aircraft, transport aircraft, helicopters, turbojets, and other aircraft specified by the FAA Administrator as requiring special flight tests.[23]

Active and Forecast Pilots by Type of Certificate

As of January 1	Total	Students	Private	Commercial	Airline Transport	Helicopter	Glider	Instrument Rated[1]	Other
1973	750,869	181,477	323,383	196,228	37,714	7,987	4,080	187,909	1,970
1974	714,607	181,905	301,863	182,444	38,139	5,968	4,288	185,969	2,942
1975	730,541	180,795	305,848	192,425	41,002	5,647	4,824	199,323	3,187
1976	725,059	176,978	305,867	189,342	42,592	4,932	5,348	203,954	3,132
1977	741,272	188,801	309,005	187,801	45,072	4,804	5,789	211,364	2,974
1978	783,900	203,500	327,400	188,800	50,100	4,800	6,200	226,300	3,000
1979*	844,100	214,700	363,600	198,800	52,300	4,700	7,000	241,900	3,000
1980*	899,700	222,300	387,400	220,100	54,400	4,700	7,800	265,200	3,000
1981*	941,500	227,800	407,100	234,000	56,500	4,600	8,500	287,200	3,000
1982*	970,100	227,900	421,400	245,600	58,500	4,600	9,100	306,100	3,000
1983*	987,000	225,400	430,000	254,000	60,300	4,600	9,700	324,600	3,000
1984*	1,008,600	228,200	441,700	259,000	62,000	4,500	10,200	341,700	3,000
1985*	1,038,800	231,800	459,200	265,800	63,800	4,500	10,700	358,300	3,000
1986*	1,064,200	231,200	474,800	276,100	63,500	4,500	11,100	375,800	3,000
1987*	1,088,500	229,600	487,200	285,200	67,300	4,600	11,600	393,200	3,000
1988*	1,107,600	227,200	499,200	292,500	69,000	4,600	12,100	408,700	3,000
1989*	1,131,300	227,200	513,700	299,500	70,600	4,600	12,700	423,500	3,000
1990*	1,155,800	225,000	529,600	308,100	72,200	4,700	13,200	438,400	3,000

Source: FAA

*Forecast
[1]Not included in total.

Note—The total count includes all pilots with current medical certificates; it also includes pilots who no longer fly but desire to keep their active status by periodic medical examinations. At the close of 1973 the active pilot count totalled 714,607, compared with 750,869 at the end of 1972. The decrease in the number of airmen resulted from a purging of the Airmen Certificiation files. During the process approximately 26,000 duplicate or faulty records were eliminated. Helicopter pilots include pilots who hold only a helicopter certificate.

215

This pressurized Rockwell Commander Model 690B propjet visited 15 countries on a sales tour in 1979. The executive aircraft was completely decorated in a pinstriped motif to stress the efficiencies of propjet business flying.

Pilots — General. All pilots must pass at least a biennial flight review; must hold a current medical certificate appropriate to the flying being done; and have a Federal Communications Commission (FCC) radiotelephone permit to operate an airborne radio transmitter. All pilots are trained to fly cross country and most have night proficiency training. Not all pilots hold instrument ratings and many are not legally qualified to fly under instrument conditions.

The only pilots who are not certificated and are exempt from the above requirements are those flying man-propelled or foot-launched aircraft such as hang-gliders, super-light aircraft, and man-powered aircraft.

Student Pilots. No flying experience or ground instruction is needed to obtain a student pilot certificate. Before solo flight, however, at least a Class III medical certificate and the proper endorsements by a flight instructor are required. Flight instructor endorsements are required for student cross country and night flying. Student pilots may not carry passengers nor fly for hire.

Private Pilots. A private pilot may fly any aircraft for which he is rated, may fly anywhere he likes, and may carry passengers. He may earn an instrument rating and a flight instructor rating. Private pilots can add seaplane and multi-engine ratings to their certificates. At least a Class III medical certificate is required each twenty-four months.

Private pilots must pass FAA written examinations and a flight test given by an FAA-appointed examiner or an FAA inspector. There are definite proficiency and experience requirements given in FAR Parts 61.101 and 61.120.

Private pilots may share expenses but may not fly for hire.

Commercial Pilots. Commercial pilots must hold an instrument rating unless holding a commercial certificate obtained at a time before this became a requirement. Experience and proficiency requirements are high.

The commercial pilot must hold at least a Class II medical certificate. The regulations pertaining to commercial pilot certificates may be found in FAR Parts 61.121 and 61.139. Commercial pilots may fly for hire and may carry passengers for hire.

Civilian Flight Instructor (CFI). The civilian flight instructor certificate is awarded pilots meeting the requirements for a commercial pilot certificate with an instrument pilot rating. In addition, the flight instructor must pass comprehensive written, oral, and flight tests given by the FAA. A private pilot may hold a CFI rating, but most CFI's hold commercial pilot certificates.

The CFI is the key to the FAA's safety program. The instructor trains students and rated pilots in flying techniques. The CFIs automatically holds the privileges of a ground instructor and can, for example, write recommendations allowing student pilots to take the FAA written tests. Before a student may solo (fly alone), practice solo, fly at night, or go cross-country, the instructor must issue a written endorsement of the student's competency. Once the instructor is satisfied that the student pilot is ready for his private pilot flight test, the CFI writes a recommendation. The instructor may also recommend applicants for commercial and flight instructor ratings. If the CFI holds an instrument instructor's rating then he may recommend applicants for instrument ratings. These instrument instructor's are known as "double-I's" that is CFIs. Flight instructors may also give biennial flight reviews ("Biennials," are required of all pilots.)[24]

The legal responsibilities of a flight instructor are heavy. Instructors should keep records of persons trained and endorsements written. The instructor's liabilities are many, and it would seem only prudent to carry liability insurance. Most instructors, however, rely on the insurance they presume to be carried by their employers.

Flight instructors with commercial certificates may fly for hire. The FAR regulations pertaining to flight instructors are to be found in FAR Part 61.[25]

Airline Transport Pilots

The Airline Transport Pilot (ATP) must hold a valid Class I medical certificate.

To qualify for an ATP certificate a pilot must pass demanding written and flight tests. At least fifteen hundred hours of total flight experience, with extensive instrument and night flying skills, are required.

An ATP may fly transport type aircraft for hire.[26] The ATP is the "Ph.D of airmen."

Reporting of Accidents

An "accident" is defined as any occurence in which (a) death or serious

218

injury results or in which (b) there is substantial damage to the aircraft or other property, or (c) when an aircraft is overdue and believed involved in an accident.

The "operator" is the person causing or authorizing operation of the aircraft — the owner, lessee, or bailee.

The aircraft operator must immediately notify the National Transportation Safety Board in the event of aircraft accidents, certain incidents involving fire-in-flight, collision, certain mechanical and control failures, and serious crew disabilities. FAA, if notified, will assist the operator with reports.

The operator is responsible, too, for the preservation of aircraft wreckage, mail cargo and records. Aircraft wreckage may be moved, of course, when it interferes with the public safety.[27]

Pilot Insurance

Recently, pilots have become aware that airport, or company, insurance does not necessarily cover all situations. Whenever a pilot flies a borrowed, rented, or club-owned aircraft and has an accident, the possibility of liability arises.

Rather than risk personal bankruptcy pilots often buy liability insurance known as "non-owner" policies. This can cover personal injury, other property, and even damage to the aircraft being flown.

Pilots no longer have difficulty in buying personal life insurance, yet it is wise to be sure that your insurance policy does not carry an aviation exclusion clause.

A business firm is responsible for the actions of its agents, hence a charter company or a flight school may be held liable for the negligence of a pilot employed by the firm.[28]

Some states require pilots to register with a state aeronautics commission. (See the chapter on state aviation law.) Several states require liability insurance coverage.

Tax Deductible Flying?

Portions of money spent for flying may be tax deductible. (Consult your tax advisor for specific information.)

Civil Air Patrol pilots may deduct most fees associated with flying CAP corporate aircraft. They may deduct travel expenses to and from the airport, and to CAP meetings. Books, uniforms, supplies, and CAP dues are also deductible.

All pilots may deduct expenses for flights made for charitable use of the aircraft. Further, interest fees and taxes are in general deductible.[29]

If used for business, that percentage of use and portion of the operating costs of an aircraft, its depreciation, and an investment tax credit may be claimed. Auto mileage to and from the airport can be deducted. Should a plane be rented or leased for business, all leasing costs are tax deductible.

The investment tax credit is *not* just a deduction from taxable income but is a credit against tax payable. The rate of credit depends on the value of the aircraft you are depreciating and the time span allotted for depreciation. Check with your tax advisor for the best way to list this tax credit.[30]

Airman Organizations

Airmen are served by scores of organizations, some of which are listed below:

Academy of Model Aeronautics, 815 — 15th St., N.W. Washington, D.C. 20005.

Aerobatic Club of America, Box 401, Roanoke, Tex. 76262.

Aerospace Education Foundation, c/o H. Fisher, 628 Mountain Rd., Smoke Rise, Kinnelon, N.J. 07405.

Airborne Law Enforcement Association, Inc., 2639 Maplewood Dr., Columbus, Ohio 43229.

Aircraft Owners and Pilots Association (AOPA), Air Rights Bldg., 7315 Wisconsin Ave., Bethesda, Md. 20014.

Air Force Association, 1750 Pennsylvania Ave., N.W., Suite 400, Washington, D.C. 20006.

Air Line Pilots Association (ALPA), 1625 Massachusetts Ave., N.W., Washington, D.C. 20036.

Air Traffic Control Association, 525 School St., S.W., Suite 409, Washington, D.C. 20024.

Allied Pilots Association, 2621 Ave., "E" East, Suite 208, Arlington, Tex. 76011.

American Association of Airport Executives, 2029 K St., N.W., Washington, D.C. 20006.

American Aviation Historical Society, P.O. Box 99, Garden Grove, Calif. 92642.

American Bonanza Society, Chemung County Airport, Horseheads, N.Y. 14845.

American Helicopter Society, Inc., 1325 18th St., N.W., Suite 103, Washington, D.C. 20036.

American Navion Society, Box 1175, Municipal Airport, Banning, Calif. 92220.

Antique Airplane Association, P.O. Box H, Ottumwa, Iowa 52502.

Association of Aviation Psychologists, c/o R. Besco, 3982 San Bonito, Los Alamitos, Calif. 90720.

Balloon Federation of America, Suite 430, 821 — 15th St., N.W., Washington, D.C. 20005.

Canadian Owners & Pilots Association, Box 734, Station B, Ottawa, Ont. KIP 5S4, Canada.

Cessna 120/140 Association, Box 92, Richardson, Tex. 75080.

Cessna 190-195 Owners Association, c/o T. Pappas, P.O. Box 952, Sioux Falls, S. Dak. 57101.

Cessna Skyhawk Association, Box 779, Delray Beach, Fla. 33444.

China, Burma, India Hump Pilots Association, c/o H. Fisher, Director, 628 Mountain Road, Smoke Rise, Kinnelon, N.J. 07405.

Christian Pilots Association, Inc., Box 5157, Pasadena, Calif. 91107.

Civil Air Patrol, Hq., Maxwell AFB, Ala. 36112.

Confederate Air Force, Rebel Field, P.O. Box CAF, Harlingen, Tex. 78550.

Continental Luscombe Association, 5736 Esmar Rd., Ceres, Calif. 95307.

Early Birds of Aviation, Inc., c/o Paul Garber, President, 310 N. Jackson St., Arlington, Va. 22201.

Ercoupe Owners Club, 3557 Roxboro Rd., P.O. Box 15058, Durham, N.C. 27704.

Experimental Aircraft Association, P.O. Box 229, Hales Corners, Wis. 53130.

Flight Safety Foundation, Inc., 1800 N. Kent St., Arlington, Va. 22209.

Flying Architects Association, 203 St. Paul Federal Bldg., 8th & Cedar St., St. Paul, Minn. 55101.

Flying Chiropractors Association, 215 Belmont St., Johnstown, Pa. 15904.

Flying Dentists Association, 5410 Wilshire Blvd., Los Angeles, Calif. 90036.

Flying Engineers International, Box 387, Winnebago, Ill. 61088.

Flying Funeral Directors of America, 10980 Reading Rd., Sharonville, Ohio 45241.

Flying Optometrist Association of America, 311 N. Spruce, Searcy, Ark. 72143.

Flying Physicians Association, 801 Green Bay Road, Lake Bluff, Ill. 60044.

Flying Psychologists, c/o P.W. Clement, Exec. Sec., 190 N. Oakland Ave., Pasadena, Calif 91101.

Flying Veterinarians Association, 10519 Reading Road, Cincinnati, Ohio 45241.

Helicopter Association of America, 1156 — 15th St., N.W., Suite 610, Washington, D.C. 20005.

International Aerobatic Club, P.O. Box 229, Hales Corners, Wis. 53130.

International Cessna 170 Association, 29010 E. Highway 160, Durango, Colo. 81301.

International Comanche Society, Inc., M. E. Tipton, 600 E. 4th St., Bellwood, Pa. 16617.

International Flying Bankers Association, c/o J. E. Eubanks, Exec. Dir., P.O. Box 11187, Columbia, S.C. 29211.

International Flying Farmers Association, Mid Continent Airport, P.O. Box 9124, Wichita, Kans. 67277.

International Flying Nurses Association, Inc., c/o Ms. Gary Wheeler, 162 Woodbridge Apts., Greenville, S.C. 29607.

International Mooney Society, 2202 Oakhill, San Antonio, Tex. 78238.

International Swift Association, Box 644, Athens, Tenn. 37303.

James XD-5 Club, Box 151, Pasadena, Calif. 91104.

Lawyer-Pilots Bar Association, 2908 First National Bank Tower, 1300 S.W. Fifth Ave., Portland, Ore. 97201.

Lighter Than Air Society, c/o R. L. Wolcott, 1800 Triplett Blvd., Akron, Ohio 44306.

National Aeronautic Association (NAA), Suite 610, 806 — 15th St., N.W., Washington, D.C. 20005.

National Aerospace Education Association, P.O. Box 59, Middle Tenn. State University, Murfreesboro, Tenn. 37132.

National Association of Air Traffic Specialists, Wheaton Plaza North Bldg., Suite 415, Wheaton, Md. 20902.

National Association of Flight Instructors, Ohio State University Airport, Box 20204, Columbus, Ohio 43220.

National Association of Priest Pilots, 5157 S. Calif. Ave., Chicago, Ill. 60632.

National Association of State Aviation Officials (NASAO), 444 N. Capital St., N.W., Washington, D.C. 20001.

National Business Aircraft Association, One Farragut Sq. S., Washington, D.C. 20006.

National Intercollegiate Flying Association, Parks College, St. Louis University, Cahokia, Ill. 62206.

National Pilots Association, 805 — 15th St., N.W., Washington, D.C. 20005.

National Police Pilots Association, Box 45, Shenorock, N.Y. 10587.

National Real Estate Fliers Association, Box 6200 E., Norfolk, Va. 23502.

Ninety-Nines, Inc., Box 59965, Will Rogers World Airport, Oklahoma City, Okla. 73159.

Organized Flying Adjusters, Box 2501, Airport Station, Oakland, Calif. 94614.

Pilots International Association, Suite 500, 400 S. County Rd. 18, Minneapolis, Minn. 55426.

Professional Air Traffic Controllers Organization (PATCO), 444 N. Capitol St., Washington, D.C. 20001.

Silver Wings Fraternity, Russ Brinkley, Pres., Box 1228, Harrisburg, Pa. 17108.

Soaring Society of America, Inc., Box 66071, Los Angeles, Calif. 90066.

Society of Automotive Engineers, Inc., 400 Commonwealth Dr., Warrendale, Pa. 15096.

Society of Flight Test Engineers, Inc., P.O. Box 4047, Lancaster, Calif. 93534.

Society of World War I Aero Historians (Aerospace), 10443 S. Memphis Ave., Whittier, Calif. 90604.

Swift Association, Box 644, Athens, Tenn. 37303.

Taildragger Pilots Association, 3039 Kingsgate, Memphis, Tenn. 38118.

United States Air Racing Association (USARA), 16425 Hart St., Van Nuys, Calif. 91406.

United States Parachute Association, 806 15th St., N.W., Suite 444, Washington, D.C. 20005.

United States Seaplane Pilots Association, c/o D. Quam, Pres., Little Ferry Seaplane Base, P.O. Box 43, Little Ferry, N.J. 07643.

Wheelchair Pilots Association, c/o T. E. Lewandowski, Pres., 12623 111th Lane N., Largo, Fla. 33540.

Whirly-Girls, 1725 DeSales St., N.W., Suite 700, Washington, D.C. 20036.

NOTES

1. For the latest listing of the Federal Aviation Regulations, see the Department of Transportation, Federal Aviation Administration, Advisory Circular AC 00-44L, 2 April 1979.

2. Timothy R. V. Foster, *The Aircraft Owner's Handbook* (New York: Van Nostrand Reinhold Company, 1978), p. 129.

3. *Ibid;* Gerard Pucci, *Aviation Law* (Dubuque, Iowa: Kendall/Hunt Publishing Company, 1977), Ch. 14, pp. 5-6.

4. Pucci, p. 14-5.

5. FAR Part 91.3 explains these responsibilities in detail.

6. See the chapter on general law and contracts for further useful legal background. See also Stuart M. Speiser and Charles F. Krause, *Aviation Tort Law*, I, (San Francisco: Bancroft-Whitney Co., 1978), pp. 337-38.

7. Speiser and Krause, I, 350-51.

8. Fred Biehler, *Aviation Maintenance Law* (Basin, Wyo.: Aviation Maintenance Foundation, 1975) p. 88; Speiser and Krause, I, 338-39, 342-43.

9. Speiser and Krause, 364-65.

10. Jonathan Howe, "Airman's Rights — FAA Enforcement Procedures," FAA Regional Counsel, Northwest Region, FAA, Seattle, Washington, Ausust 1977, made available courtesy FAA, Washington, D.C.

11. AOPA *Newsletter*, June, 1979.

12. FAA press release June 1975; see also Advisory Circular AC 00-46B, July 1979.

13. *Ibid.*

14. Speiser and Krause, *Aviation Tort Law* (San Francisco: Bancroft-Whitney Co., 1979), II, pp. 12-21; Biehler, pp. 88-89.

15. Speiser and Krause, II, p. 14.

16. *Ibid;* also p. 19 and note 45.

17. Biehler, p. 83.

18. Michael J. Hart, *Outline of International Aviation Law*, (St. Louis: Parks College of St. Louis University, 1975), pp. 65-68; "Hijacking Convention," the Convention for the Suppression of Unlawful Seizure of Aircraft, was completed 14 September 1971 and entered into force on 14 October 1971; Robert M. Kane and Allan D. Vose, *Air*

Transportation (Dubuque, Iowa: Kendall/Hunt Publishing Company, 1975), chap. 12, p. 15.

[19]FAR Parts 23, 43, 137.

[20]Rowland W. Fixel, *The Law of Aviation* (Charlottesville, Va.: Michie Company, 1967), pp. 84-91; Pucci, chap. 2.

[21]*Ibid.*

[22]FAR Part 61.73; Speiser and Krause, II, pp. 1-5.

[23]FAR Part 61; Biehler, pp. 24-27.

[24]*Ibid.*

[25]FAR Part 61, Subpart G, 61.181 through 61.201.

[26]FAR Parts 61 and 135.

[27]FAR Part 830 deals with the reporting of accidents.

[28]Biehler, p. 24; Foster, pp. 99-104.

[29]See the aircraft ownership chapter for tax benefits associated with leaseback arrangements.

[30]Foster, pp. 30, 33-38.

Photograph courtesy Piper Aircraft Corporation.

The 1979 Piper Tomahawk.

CHAPTER 14

MANUFACTURERS OF AIRCRAFT AND COMPONENTS

General Aviation Aircraft

All flying, exepting military and airline flying, is known as "general aviation." There are around 200,000 aircraft in this fleet of U.S. aircraft in the general aviation sector. This represents 98.7 percent of all U.S. civil aircraft.

As 1978 ended, the general aviation industry marked up the seventh consecutive year of record aircraft billings. Sales worth $1.78 billion were made in 1978, an increase of nearly 20 percent over 1977.[1]

The 1978 sales figures according to General Aviation Manufacturers' Association (GAMA), included:

Single Engine: During 1978, our industry posted single engine factory net sales of $482 million, up 10.8% from 1977, on deliveries of 13,651 units. In 1979, we expect the single engine market to produce factory net billings of $532 million, up 10.4%. That would represent shipments of 14,000 single engine airplanes. New training aircraft will continue to be introduced, and recently introduced high-performance single-engine aircraft — offering such features as pressurization and all-weather equipment — have contributed to the growth of this market segment. We expect this trend to continue.

Multi-Engine Piston: In 1978, this market segment showed good gains over 1977. Shipments provided factory net billings of $492 million, up 26.5%, and we delivered 2,630 new multi-engine piston powered aircraft in 1978, 230 more than forecast. We see dollar billings for 1979 of $489 million in this category, with shipments at 2,500 new multi-engine aircraft. However, in view of the recent strong performance of multi-engine aircraft, and the introduction of new models, we believe our forecast could be conservative.

Agricultural Aircraft: In 1978 we ended the year below forecast with sales of $33 million and 748 units delivered, down from $37 million and 890 aircraft in 1977. For 1979, we are forecasting an increase in factory billings to $40 million and 800 units in the agricultural category. The market condition reflects the continued depressed state of agricultural economics. But we still firmly believe this is an excellent market in the long term, since the potential of the agricultural airplane in worldwide food production is virtually unlimited. Just last month, while leading a U.S. aviation trade delegation in Africa, I was made aware of the growing interest and tremendous potential by officials and private businessmen in several developing nations on that continent.

Turboprop: In 1978 turboprop aircraft accounted for $393 million, up 33.2%, in factory net billings, with deliveries of 548 units. Our turboprop forecast

Trade barriers erected by a number of countries continue to seriously hamper our export market. Brazil, Japan, Mexico, and the Philippines are the chief problems. If some of these barriers can be removed, through positive actions on the part of our own government, or through multi-lateral negotiations, it would have an extremely beneficial effect on U.S. general aviation exports. Also, it is difficult for us to understand why export licenses for our industry are delayed by the U.S. government — for human rights and other considerations — at a time when our nation faces record trade deficits. Such delays, imposed through the bureaucracy, threaten the growth of our industry abroad. But there is hope on the international scene. We see the possibility of multi-lateral negotiations resulting in the worldwide free trade of civil aircraft. This should mean zero tariff on aircraft and the discouragement of non-tariff barriers throughout the free world.

This year, 1979, will be the industry's first 2 billion dollar year. Only four years ago in 1975, we reach our first billion dollar year. Consequently, you' can see how far we have come in just four years.

Photograph courtesy Cessna Aircraft Company.

The 1979 Cessna Conquest.

TABLE 1

Estimated Active General Aviation Aircraft by Type of Aircraft

(In Thousands)

As of January 1	Total	Fixed Wing Piston Single-engine	Fixed Wing Piston Multi-engine	Turboprop	Turbojet	Rotorcraft	Balloons Dirigibles Gliders
1974	153.3	126.1	18.7	1.9	1.4	3.1	2.2
1975	161.0	131.5	19.7	2.1	1.6	3.6	2.5
1976	168.1	136.6	20.3	2.5	1.7	4.1	2.8
1977	178.0	144.8	21.3	2.5	1.9	4.4	3.2
1978	184.3	149.3	21.5	2.9	2.3	4.7	3.6
1979*	198.8	160.6	24.1	3.2	2.3	5.0	3.6
1980*	208.6	167.8	25.4	3.7	2.6	5.3	3.8
1981*	219.6	176.3	26.8	4.0	2.9	5.6	4.0
1982*	230.0	184.2	28.3	4.3	3.1	5.8	4.3
1983*	240.4	192.3	29.6	4.6	3.4	6.1	4.4
1984*	251.1	200.4	31.1	4.9	3.6	6.4	4.7
1985*	261.9	208.6	32.5	5.2	3.9	6.7	5.0
1986*	272.4	216.7	33.8	5.6	4.2	6.9	5.2
1987*	282.5	224.2	35.3	5.9	4.5	7.2	5.4
1988*	292.1	231.4	36.5	6.4	4.8	7.4	5.6
1989*	301.6	238.3	37.7	6.9	5.1	7.7	5.9
1990*	310.8	245.0	38.9	7.4	5.4	8.0	6.1

Source: FAA

* Forecast

Note—An active aircraft must have a current registration and have been flown during the previous calendar year. It should be noted that historical data are estimates. Detail may not add to total due to independent rounding.

229

During 1978 a number of major aerospace systems passed significant milestones. Omitting the portions of the report that deal with missiles, space vehicles and satellites, the "Aerospace Highlights of 1978," published by the Aerospace Industries Association (AIA) gives current aircraft projects status:

Defense

. . . .

- The Navy/McDonnell Douglas F-18A Hornet strike fighter flew for the first time on November 18. Northrop Corp. is principal subcontractor on the F-18 program.

- The McDonnell Douglas AV-8B Advanced Harrier, new version of the British-designed VTOL fighter for Navy and Marine Corps use, made its initial flight on November 9.

- In August, the first production model of the General Dynamics F-16 USAF/NATO fighter was delivered to the Air Force.

- A new and advanced version of the Lockheed U-2 reconnaissance plane, called the TR-1, went into development for the Air Force.

- The first production model of the Army/Sikorsky UH-60A Black Hawk helicopter, designed to airlift an infantry squad for tactical assaults and related combat missions, was delivered October 31.

- Development was essentially completed on the USAF/Boeing E-3A Sentry Airborne Warning and Control System (AWACS) and the first operational airplane was to go into continental air defense service on January 1, 1979.

Civil Aviation

- In July, Boeing Commercial Airplane Company launched development of its advanced technology widebody twinjet, the 767. In August, Lockheed Aircraft Corporation announced plans for an advanced technology, flexible-range version of its L-1011 TriStar called the Dash 400. Also in August, Boeing announced still another new development, the twinjet standard body 757, a companion to the 767 aimed at a different segment of the market. McDonnell Douglas Corporation continued development of its DC-9 Super 80, initiated in 1977. These airplanes are the advance members of a new generation of U.S. jetliners which will begin airline service in the early 1980s.

- On November 21, the Sikorsky S-76 12 passenger twin-turbine helicopter received its Federal Aviation Administration type certification. Initial

FULL HOUSE AT BOEING
Latest photograph of the final assembly area at Boeing Commercial Airplane Company's 707/727/737 production plant shows a full house. Increased production rate, reflecting rising orders from airlines, will hit 12 a month on the 727 trijet and seven a month for the 737 by the end of 1979. Eight 727s are visible in the foreground and five 737s in background. The 707 remains in production in a nearby building, at the rate of ½ airplane each month.

231

deliveries of the S-76 began in December. The introduction of the S-76 is particularly notable in that it represents the first time that a helicopter was developed from the beginning as a civil transport, rather than as a derivative of a military helicopter.

- Development flight testing continued on Bell Helicopter Textron's 6-10 passenger twin-turbine transport helicopter, the Bell 222. The company expected certification in 1979 and first deliveries in October 1979.

- Undergoing ground testing during the year were two types of engines in NASA's "clean and quiet" research program: the Quiet, Clean Shorthaul Experimental Engine, under development by General Electric Company., and the Quiet, Clean General Aviation Turbofan, two models of which were being developed for NASA by Avco Lycoming and The Garrett Corporation's AiResearch Manufacturing Company.

- Flight test activity continued on three rotorcraft research vehicles in programs co-sponsored by NASA and the military services. During the year, the Sikorsky S-72 Rotor Systems Research Aircraft (RSRA) successfully completed a series of flights in the compound helicopter configuration. Bell Helicopter Textron's XV-15 Tilt Rotor Research Aircraft completed wind tunnel and hover tests and late in the year was being readied for conversion tests, in which the plane's rotors tilt forward after vertical take-off to become propellers for forward flight. The Sikorsky SH-59A Advancing Blade Concept (ABC) vehicle began the high speed phase of its flight test program.

- In April, the American Microwave Landing System (MLS) was selected as the international standard by the World Wide All Weather Operations Panel of the International Civil Aviation Organization. The American MLS, which employs a Time Reference Scanning Beam (TRSB) technique, has been under development by the Federal Aviation Administration since 1971; the contractor team is headed by The Bendix Corporation and Texas Instruments.

AEROSPACE EMPLOYMENT AND PAYROLL
Calendar Years 1968-1979

Year	EMPLOYMENT AS OF DECEMBER (In Thousands)			ANNUAL PAYROLL (Millions of Dollars)		
	TOTAL	Production Workers	All Other	TOTAL	Production Workers	All Other
1968	1,403	738	665	$14,397	$ 6,582	$ 7,815
1969	1,295	658	637	14,649	6,401	8,248
1970	1,069	528	541	12,275	5,322	6,953
1971	924	448	476	10,480	4,409	6,071
1972	944	473	471	11,197	4,565	6,632
1973	962	474	478	12,257	5,114	7,143
1974	973	483	490	13,250	5,454	7,796
1975	925	444	481	14,561	5,822	8,739
1976	898	420	478	14,908	5,766	9,142
1977	894	410	484	15,948	6,173	9,775
1978(p)	999	467	532	19,230	7,527	11,703
1979(e)	1,024	480	544	20,844	8,157	12,687

Source: Employment: Aerospace Industriea Association.
        Payroll   : Bureau of Labor Statistics, estimates by AIA.
(e) Estimate
(p) Preliminary

CIVIL AIRCRAFT SHIPMENTS
Calendar Years 1968-1979

Year	NUMBER OF AIRCRAFT SHIPPED				VALUE (Millions of Dollars)			
	TOTAL	Commercial Transport Aircraft	Helicopters	General Aviation	TOTAL	Commercial Transport Aircraft	Helicopters	General Aviation
1968	14,922	702	522	13,698	$4,267	$3,789	$ 57	$ 421
1969	13,505	514	534	12,457	3,598	2,939	75	584
1970	8,076	311	482	7,283	3,546	3,158	49	339
1971	8,158	223	469	7,466	2,984	2,594	69	321
1972	10,576	227	575	9,774	3,308	2,660	90	558
1973	14,709	294	770	13,645	4,665	3,718	121	826
1974	15,325	332	828	14,165	5,090	3,993	189	908
1975	15,236	315	864	14,057	5,086	3,779	274	1,033
1976	16,460	238	775	15,447	4,726	3,192	305	1,229
1977	17,989	185	884	16,920	4,756	2,889	316	1,551
1978[p]	19,125	235	890	18,000	6,287	4,087	400	1,800
1979[c]	19,505	375	950	18,180	8,770	6,230	440	2,100

Source: Commercial Transport Aircraft and Helicopters: AIA Company Reports.

        General Aviation: AIA and GAMA.

p Preliminary

e Estimate   Source   Aerospace Industries Association.

233

The needs of the several parts of the U.S. aviation industry are real and must immediately and imaginatively be met. As the industry reports just quoted show, each year aircraft sales are increasing.

Americans by the millions are flocking aboard airliners. They have the right to expect safe airways and airports. The heavy, powerful, fast airliners are more or less monopolizing major airports to meet the demands of Americans for passenger, mail, and freight transport.

Yet, as we have just seen in our account of general aviation manufacturing statistics, soon two billion dollars a year will be spent on light and medium-weight aircraft. These are engaged in training, business, and agricultural flying and need airports not crowded with airliners. U.S. general aviation, too, has a right to safe airways and airports.

The problem has developed due to the fact that major airports are publically owned and thus qualified to receive federal, state, and local funds for airport and facility maintenance and improvement. Smaller airports, on the other hand, are generally privately owned. They receive virtually no subsidy and are taxed as real estate and as businesses. The owner must also bear many insurance burdens.

As towns grow, the airport real estate increases in value. Homeowners build near the airport and may complain about the noise and possible hazards associated with aircraft. Taxes on the airport land tend to rise.

Airport owners grow old and often can no longer afford to leave money invested in the land which the airport occupies. They need cash income for retirement. Owners grow weary of the responsibilities involved in the operation of the airport. Taxes, complaints, and insurance costs increase until the owner is forced to sell out.

Hence, the owner of the airport cashes in on his land and retires. Where do the planes and pilots go? A good question. Today small airports open to the public are decreasing in number.[2] It is a serious problem and one which must soon be faced.

The answer is subsidy and tax relief for private owners of airports, or more investment by municipal, county, and/or state governments in the smaller airports and in satellite airports.

There will be many business benefits from this kind of small airport encouragement. One large benefit, too, will be the increase in safety for both the airline and general aviation airborne public.

Type Certificate

To obtain a "type certificate" from the Federal Aviation Administration (FAA) for a newly designed aircraft, propeller, or engine, requires development of the entire design, building a prototype, and exhaustive tests. The FAA oversees the process from start to completion. After much testing, a type certificate is awarded. The new plane is inspected by the FAA and an airworthiness certificate issued.[3]

Changes in design, too, are subject to FAA approval. Type certificates can be sold by the holder. In its entirety a type certificate is in effect a form of design protection or patent.

Production Certificate

Once a type certificate is obtained, a firm wishing to manufacture the aircraft for sale must satisfy the FAA as to its capability and standards of workmanship before the manufacturer is awarded a production certificate. As manufactured items (engines, planes, or propellers) come off the production line, the manufacturer issues a statement of conformity which says that the type certificate has been adhered to. The FAA can then issue an airworthiness certificate without further inspection.

Inspections of such manufactured planes, production facilities, and manufacturing personnel may be made by the FAA and production certificates can be revoked or suspended by the FAA.[4]

Airworthiness Certificates

Standard airworthiness certificates remain in effect indefinitely while an aircraft is maintained according to FAR Parts 43 and 91.

If for some reason (lack of annual inspection, for example) the airworthiness certificate lapses, a mechanic may renew it by performing the inspection, certifying that all Airworthiness Directives (ADs) have been complied with, and signing off the aircraft as airworthy.[5]

Airworthiness Directives

Airworthiness Directives (ADs) notify the owner of record of any mechanical problem with the aircraft after it leaves the factory. This mode of requiring that a plane or engine be modified or specially inspected has kept flying safe from hundreds of possible problems in flight. Does a landing gear tend to crack after a time? Does a propellor blade fail after prolonged operation at a particular RPM? Then an AD is written and distributed. Before the planes involved can pass their next required inspection, the AD must be taken into consideration.[6]

The aircraft industry is stringently regulated. Production certificates can be revoked if FAA perceives unsafe production procedures.

All of a particular aircraft can be grounded by FAA if an accident reveals a potentially dangerous mechanical problem. Scores of planes then have to sit, awaiting FAA's release once the problem is solved.

Proximate Cause

"Proximate cause" is the predominent cause of injury or damage. This term is used when several parties are involved in a casual relation, that is, whose negligence set in motion a train of events leading up to the mishap. If a plane is sold by a manufacturer in a defective condition, the manufacturer is liable due to this theory of law.[7]

Duty to Warn

An aircraft manufacturer has the legal duty to warn users of known dangerous conditions in aircraft built by that manufacturer. Further, this duty continues long after manufacture and the initial sale. Service Bulletins and Service Letters are sent to appropriate owners of record by the manufacturer. If a manufacturer does not provide information on defects on the aircraft, the firm is faced with possible liability actions. Dealers and distributors of the planes automatically are sent service information.

Mechanics should locate this information on the makes of planes they regularly service.

At one time, several years back, it was not easy for independent or unfranchised mechanics to get service information from a manufacturer. Now, however, since adequate notice of product defects must be available to those persons likely to service the product, manufacturers have made this information more easily available.

Factory training for both mechanics and pilots is also more generally available now. This again, is a part of the manufacturers "duty to warn," in that training is a portion of the manufacturers adequate information responsibility.

Adequate manuals are another part of the manufacturer's "duty to warn." The manufacturer must provide adequate information on the product, aircraft, propellers, and engines.

The FAA, mechanics, and manufacturers work together to locate patterns of part failures. The National Transportation Safety Board, too, analyzes accidents so that mechanical defects may be discovered and future accidents prevented.[8]

An interested person may obtain a set of service bulletins and letters by writing to the manufacturer and giving the serial number and model of the aircraft. One may ask to be put on a mailing list to get past/and future advisory letters and bulletins. These will not necessarily be free publications.

Implied Warranties

Pilots, owners, passengers, and even third parties not associated with the operation of the aircraft can hold the manufacturer liable for a defective product which has caused property loss or injury. Also, lack of information provided by the manufacturer may also hold that manufacturer liable. The reason for this is that a manufacturer by offering a plane (or component) for sale to the public implies that the product will perform its intended function. The product, it is implied, is a reasonably safe one to use.

The defect to cause the manufacturer to be liable, however, *must* be the proximate cause of the property loss or injury and *one existing* at the time the product left the factory. If discovered later, then, it must be one about

237

which, after in-service defects appeared, the manufacturer gave no proper warning to users of the defect and steps needed to correct it.[9]

Sellers' Express Warranties

When a manufacturer sells an aircraft, he may have shown a demonstrator aircraft, may have described the aircraft, and may have promised the buyer certain things about the aircraft. All of these comprise an express warranty by the seller. The product must live up to warranties (guarantees, promises).

A manufacturer's warranty customarily includes phrases which promise a product free of defects in normal use, manufactured with reasonably good workmanship, and lists all equipment to be provided by the manufacturer. A time limit is usually contained in the warranty — usually six months or a year. During this time the manufacturer will replace defective parts without charge.[10]

Factory Documents

In addition to the usual documents such as airworthiness and registration certificates, the factory provides an aircraft log book, engine(s) log book(s), a weight-and-balance report, the airplane flight manual, a pilot's operating handbook, an equipment list, and applicable warranties.

Either in the manual, in the handbook, on placards, or by instrument markings, the normal operating limits of the aircraft and engine(s) are given. Warnings may be either placarded and/or listed. The information must be made available by the manufacturer.

Adequate records of planes manufactured are required for the manufacturer. A reasonable stock of parts must be kept for a reasonable length of time by the manufacturer. [11]

The Laws of Products Liability

A manufacturer can be held liable for:

(a) Negligence in fabrication and workmanship.

238

(b) Defects in quality control.

(c) Inadequate testing.

(d) Use of materials of inadequate quality.

(e) Not exercising reasonable care in the design of a product.

Strict Liability

The seller of a defective product is "strictly liable," in spite of disclaimers, for personal injury caused by the defect. By offering a product for sale, such as an aircraft, the manufacturer implies a warranty that the item will adequately perform the purpose it was designed to perform. The liability is not assumed by agreement or contract, but comes under the law of strict liability in tort. Over two-thirds of the states support this view. [12]

A person suing a manufacturer must prove that, while using the aircraft in the way it was supposed to be used, he (or she) was injured because of a defect in the product of which the user was not aware. A product must be safe for its intended use.

NOTES

[1]Statistics taken from General Aviation Manufacturers Association (GAMA), *General Aviation Statistical Data*, 1979 edition. GAMA represents 37 firms which manufacture over 90 percent of the aircraft, engines, supplies, and avionics in the United States.

[2]See the chapter on airports for statistics on the number of U.S. airports open to the public.

[3]FAR Part 21; Fred Biehler, *Aviation Maintenance Law* (Basin, Wyo.: Aviation Maintenance Foundation, Inc., 1975), pp. 27-28.

[4]Biehler, p. 28.

[5]FAR Part 21, H; FAR Part 21.187; FAR Part 43; FAR Part 91.27; and FAR Part 91.42. Also see Biehler, pp. 28-29.

239

[6]Biehler, pp. 40-42; Stuart M. Speiser and Charles F. Krause, *Aviation Tort Law*, II, (San Francisco: Bancroft-Whitney Co., 1979), pp. 477-83.

[7]Speiser and Krause, II, pp. 29-35; Gerard Pucci, *Aviation Law* (Dubuque, Iowa: Kendall/ Hunt Publishing Co., 1977), chap. 9, pp. 1-3.

[8]Biehler, pp. 34-35; 45, 96-97; Speiser and Krause, II, pp. 30-35.

[9]Continental Motors v. Antonio V. Joly and Darr Services, Inc. 483 P 2d 244 (1971); 11 Avi 18, 057.

[10]Timothy R. V. Foster, *The Aircraft Owner's Handbook* (New York: Van Nostrand Reinhold Co., 1978), pp. 78-79; Biehler, pp. 92, 97.

[11]Biehler, pp. 23-28; Foster, pp. 108-9.

[12]Biehler, pp. 88, 105; Pucci, chap. 9, pp. 1-3; Speiser and Krause, II, pp. 515-24. See also cases such as: *Greenman v. Yaba Power Products, Inc.* 59 Cal. 2d 57, 377 Pac. 2d 896, (1963); *Liberty Mutual Insurance Co. v. Williams Machine and Tool Co.*, 62 Tel. 2d 77; and *Buehler v. Whalen*, 10 Tel. 2 d. 51, (1977).

Photograph courtesy the Boeing Company.

CHAPTER 15

THE U.S. AIRLINES

Air carriage has developed in sometimes strange, yet upon examination quite logical ways. It is startling to find, for example, such a modern-day device as the airplane in undeveloped and primitive areas of the world. Yet these very places need a machine that requires no expensive roadway, no railbed, only a clearing in the trees or desert. The airplane has won acceptance in Alaska, in South America, in Africa, and Asia — wherever ground and water transport fails, the airplane fills a special need.

Obviously, too, the speed of air travel was its first and most powerful attraction. Early passengers braved frail, noisy, open aircraft to (literally) leap mountains, seas, and long miles of land.

Looking back over the short history of air travel and air cargo transport, one sees markets awaiting only the development of the technological capability — the planes, the instruments, the navigational aids and landing facilities — in order to expand.

As soon as planes could carry passengers — they did so. As soon as the Post Office Department in the 1920s and 1930s could send mail by air — it was done. In the 1930s with new planes developed by Douglas, Lockheed, Boeing, Stinson, Fairchild, Beech, and others, the airlines formed and became an important part of our national mail and passenger transportation system.[1]

World War II generated planes with ocean-spanning capabilities, new engines, new instruments, new navigational aids, plus a pool of trained airmen. The shift into the air since World War II has been an astonishing phenomenon. Railroads soon lost their long-distance passengers to the airlines. Transoceanic travellers turned to the air and left many ocean liners to be turned into cruise ships and tethered hotels. Only the private automobile transports more people interstate than do the airlines.

The advent of the passenger jet aircraft in the 1960s revolutionized airline travel. Air carrier companies risked huge amounts of capital to put large jet aircraft into service. Transport speeds doubled. Everything in the air carrier industry was affected. Airports built longer and stronger runways, and expanded terminals and parking areas. Access roadways were built. Hordes of passengers swarm in and out of airports today using this new generation of aircraft. Virtually every airport in the United States is building new facilities with more expansion and growth ahead. Finally, pilots, mechanics, and air traffic controllers had to be retrained to handle the new jets.

When the changeover was complete, in the 1970s, the airlines of the world were giving passengers travel speeds of over five-hundred mph. Only the problems of supersonic flight drew the line for airline speeds at around six-hundred mph.

The supersonic transport (SST) will create another air transportation revolution in the late 1980s and early 1990s. (For a discussion of the SST, see the chapter devoted to the development of supersonic flight.)

Today, however, it is important to note that all air carriage is not flown in jet equipment. Propeller-driven planes continue to fill a need. Passenger and air freight service is available using propeller-driven aircraft. As airlines replace this equipment, the older aircraft are purchased for use as charter transports, air freighters, executive transport, intra-company air freight — to offer just a few examples. Further, foreign governments often buy planes from the airlines for various civil and military uses.

The future will find the skies of the world flown by a variety of air carrier aircraft — the SSTs, jets, propeller-driven aircraft, rotorcraft, and the Short Take Off and Landing (STOL) aircraft. All designed to meet specific needs.

Airline History

The story of the airlines of the United States is an exciting one. Several excellent histories have been written on this subject. It is, however, beyond the scope of this volume to give the details of airline development here.

The legal complexities faced by airline companies naturally grew with the industry. In our discussion of international air law we note the ever-increasing liabilities shouldered by the air carriers. We also see how the decisions of the U.S. Post Office Department have affected initial airline development in the United States.

The Civil Aeronautics Board has played a major role since the 1940s in shaping the development of airline law. The CAB carried out a U.S. policy of fostering only a few strong, well-financed, and experienced major air carriers (trunk

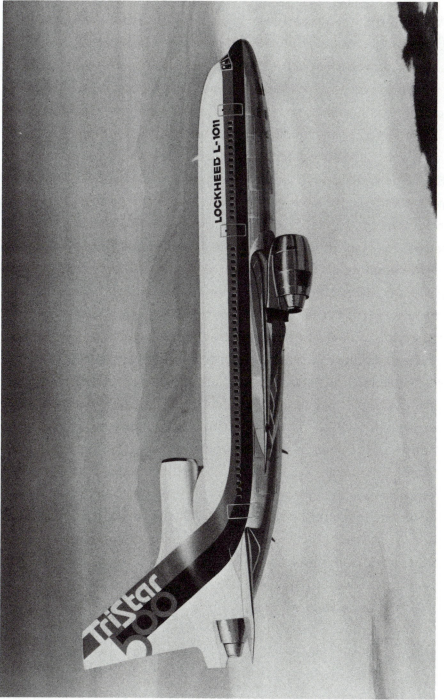

Artist's conception of the new Lockheed L-1011 TriStar, the "Dash 500."

243

carriers). By demanding enormous amounts of research and many reports, the CAB incidentally created an airline industry highly skilled in litigation and air law as well. Airline legal staffs also gained expertise as the years went by in contract and tort law litigation involved in the complex field of air transport.[2]

As noted in the discussion of CAB and air carrier deregulation, in the 1930s the CAB was given virtually dictatorial powers in assigning routes, determining rate structures, certificating companies and regulating those companies. The normal U.S. rules against monopolies, cartels, and price-fixing were suspended in the interests of building a safe and financially sound air carrier industry. The reasoning behind this U.S. policy was that, in the early days of airline development, competing companies were often poorly financed because too much competition cut profits and did not attract capital. To attract passengers, rates were cut. This lack of investors made it difficult for air carrier companies to replace old aircraft and to maintain their planes in safe operating condition. Then, too, it was most difficult for small airlines to initially finance the ever more costly new aircraft being designed. It seemed in the 1930s to the Post Office Department and later to the CAB, that to build a strong U.S. air transportation system, airlines must be sheltered from competition and guaranteed the security of holding lucrative routes. Further, rates were not allowed to react to the marketplace. Limits often involved the CAB's refusal to lower rates rather than refusal to raise rates. This was intended to prevent price wars and damage to the financial resources of the airlines. Likewise, the mergers and sales of airline companies were regulated and guided by the CAB to prevent undue financial damage to other airlines.

In the 1970s the monolithic nature of the U.S. air carriers, less than twenty in number, was challenged by scores of financially sound, able, companies requesting admission into the certificated air carrier industry. Suddenly the doors were thrown open to free competition by the Airline Deregulation Act of 1978. This was a staggering reversal of policy. How U.S. and world air transport will be affected is yet to be seen. Certainly new vigor and innovative services are being injected into the industry. Flying is now a safe, mature, and advanced mode of transportation and believed able to now withstand competition. Financial regulation has also matured to insure against unsound corporate structures. Governmental aviation regulation has matured and copes well with the safety needs of the air carrier industry.

The consumer now has a generous assortment of fares, schedules and services from which to choose. The marketplace will largely determine fares, services, and the eventual profits of the air carrier industry.

Consumer Protection

To deal with consumer inquiries and complaints in the welter of airline offers, charter flight and tour packages, travel agencies, auto rental and hotel offers involved in air travel today, the CAB has set up a Bureau of Consumer Protection. Field offices in major cities stand ready to assist the aggrieved traveler.

In general the travel industry, and in particular the airlines, have been responsive to the problems of the consumer. Complaints have, however, been numerous enough to attract the attention of prosecuting attorneys, better business offices, and municipal offices of consumer affairs.

Some complaints are, of course, unjustified. Many can be settled with a telephone call or letter. The CAB advises travelers to avoid obviously shoddy and unfair travel offers.

The American Society of Travel Agents has a set of procedures to follow up complaints made against any of its over 13,500 members.

In most states, the consumer can seek aid from the attorney general of that state. Few cases are prosecuted unless numerous complaints are filed. Adequate laws are lacking in many states.

Under CAB regulations, which became effective 3 September 1978, airlines must first solicit volunteers to give up their seats in an oversale situation before "bumping" anyone involuntarily. "Bumped" passengers are given monetary compensation.

"Forum — Shopping"

Attorneys representing parties bringing suit against a company or individual, seek the jurisdiction that may best compensate their clients. F. Lee Bailey, a well known attorney and pilot, notes in his book *Cleared For the Approach* that a knowledge of the various state limitations can greatly affect the amounts recoverable. Attorneys who deal with aviation cases should be familiar with the laws of the states involved.

Bailey recommends one set of laws for the entire country. This would eliminate the need for aviation attorneys to research the laws of several states involved. The lawyer-pilot also says that the "point of origin" rule should not govern the amount of damages which can be recovered for clients.[3]

A federal court sitting in one state can allow laws of other states to apply. For examples, the law, of the site of the accident, the laws of the point of departure and/or even laws of intermediate stopping points. Knowledge of the various state limitations then can greatly affect aviation litigation.

The citizenship of passengers involved in an air carrier incident is an added complication. If the accident occurred abroad, then the laws of the place of the accident, the country of origin and the national registry of the carrier enter into the matter of where the case may best be heard and what laws apply.[4]

Fixing Responsibility

In the course of litigation over an aircraft accident, the essential fact to be determined is — who is responsible for the accident? Was it the airline through its policies and procedures? Can the cause be placed on an agent of the airline, a pilot, a mechanic or a company meteorologist? If so, the airline is liable for the actions of its employees while they are engaged in carrying out their work.

Blame may be shifted back, however, to an equipment overhaul company which has worked on an engine, a radio, or other component for the airline. Attorneys may choose to reach back even further to the manufacturer for known design or in-service faults in the aircraft or its parts.

Under the Federal Tort Claims Act, the government of the United States waives its sovereign immunity to suit. If an employee of the federal government during the course of his duties, causes injury or loss through negligence, then the federal government may be sued for damages. In aviation this act has wide application. Was the government at fault in certificating an aircraft? Did a controller give the wrong clearance or fail to note planes on converging paths? Was federal navigational equipment faulty? Were military aircraft involved?

If the cause of an air carrier accident can be placed on a manufacturer, on a government employee, or even on a passenger's wrongful act or negligence, the airline is generally not liable.

246

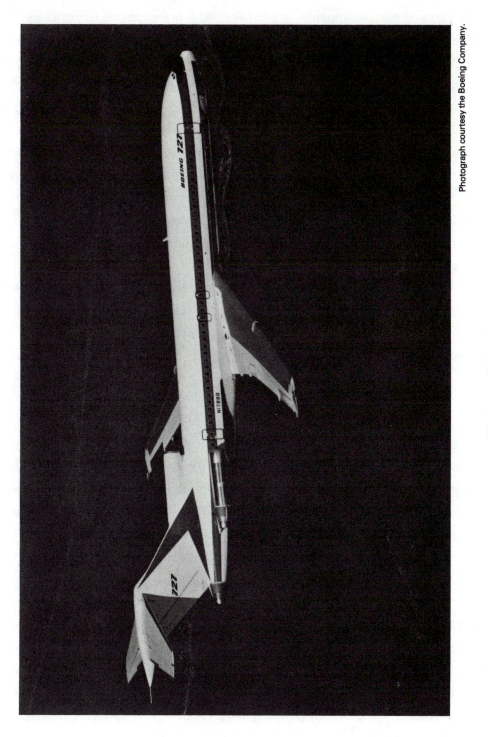

The Boeing 727 transport.

247

Airlines, being common carriers, that is, soliciting public business and offering air carriage for recompense, must exercise a great degree of care. Every foreseeable condition must be prepared for and the highest degree of care taken, to insure the safety of passengers, the general public, and property. Airlines, charter, and air taxi operators promise (warrant) safe travel. This places a great burden of liability upon air carriers. Insurance, attention to detail, and a capable legal staff help air carriers face these responsibilities.

At times, responsibility is shared. A manufacturer, for example, may accept a part of the blame for a loss, and the airline a portion. To be "joint tortfeasors," the parties must either act together in committing the wrong, or their acts, if independent of each other must unite in causing a single injury.

About the only accident cause that finds everyone non-negligent, and so not open to suit, is the so-called "Act of God." This term indicates a situation in which no reasonable human forethought could anticipate its occurrence. An example might be an abrupt or virtually "unforecastable" weather condition. Acts of God find those suffering injury or property loss "without remedy," with no party to sue for negligence, no party responsible for the losses.[5]

Multi-District Litigation

Large amounts of court time are involved in the hearing of cases involving small planes. These are heard singly in the appropriate court. Accidents involving large, air carrier aircraft involve much more complex litigation, with massive amounts of data submitted to the court. Depositions (statements, interviews taken under oath) from witnesses and experts with knowledge pertaining to the case are submitted by plaintiffs and defendants.

In air carrier accident litigation, to avoid trying the same case two-hundred to four-hundred times, a consolidation of suits is possible. This is a federal system known as "multi-district litigation." There is a federal courts provision, in which most of these aeronautical cases are tried, to place all of the pleas (plaintiff's requests for recompense) before one court. This court has the power to decide who is liable in the cases. Further, the court has the power to decide what damages each plaintiff may receive. This can vary widely as to individual plaintiffs.[6]

If a person should die in an air carrier accident, for example, his or her heirs may sue for recompense. If the deceased was the sole support of other family members, the amounts awarded are larger than if the deceased had no dependents.

Time Limitations

If a claim is not made promptly, generally speaking, the plaintiff has more difficulty in recovering damages. Further, there are statutory limitations in many state laws as to how much time is allowed before a claim is filed.[7]

Contributory Negligence

It seems strange that a passenger might contribute to his own injury, yet this has happened. This contributory negligence takes place when a passenger does not use reasonable care for his own safety and so is fully or partially responsible for his own injury. Some state laws do not allow such plaintiffs any recovery of damages.[8]

Employee's Rights Waiver

An airline employee riding on a pass may be required to give up the right to sue the airline in the event of injury.

Railway Labor Act

The Railway Labor Act (Public Law No. 257) was approved by Congress 20 May 1926 and was amended in 1936. The act applies to all air carriers carrying mail, engaging in interstate and foreign commerce, and their employees. The act was designed to avoid interruption of commerce, to allow employees freedom to join unions, and to assist in the prompt and orderly settlement of labor disputes.

Both employers and unions have the duty to engage in collective bargaining over the wages, hours, and working conditions involved in labor disputes. Once the National Mediation Board (NMB) has made a determination, there is no provision for judicial review. (The NMB is a board set up by the Railway Labor Act.)

The act deprives the states of some of their regulatory powers in labor disputes involving interstate transportation. So, an airline employee cannot seek to recover his position, if discharged under union agreements, under common law action. When necessary, the National Mediation Board may order the carriers and unions to set up a four-member "National Air Transport Adjustment Board."

The Railway Labor Act gives rules for hearing employee grievances, collective bargaining, picketing, and other factors involved in labor disputes and affecting U.S. national and international air transportation.[9]

Limits of Liability: Baggage

Tariffs filed by air carriers with the Civil Aeronautics Board constitute the contract of carriage between passengers and airlines.[10] A common limit set on the actual loss of a piece of luggage in the U.S. is $500.

The Warsaw Convention sets liability limits for baggage claims for international travel at about $9.07 per pound for checked baggage and $400 per passenger for unchecked luggage.

To date, passengers have found it difficult to obtain further payment than that given above for lost or damaged baggage. The airlines generally refuse to carry more dollar responsibility and ask passengers to keep their valuables (jewels, currency) in the personal possession of the passenger.

Limits of Liability: Passengers

In case of death or injury, in the United States, to be awarded compensation a plaintiff must prove the negligence of the airline. The amount of such compensation varies due to several factors. One limiting factor is the law of the state in which the accident occurred, or from which the flight originated. The status of the passenger involved affects the amount of damage recoverable. If the passenger is highly paid, then the loss to the heirs is greater. If the passenger was the sole support of his or her family, this too, is taken into account. A great number of such claims against airlines are settled out of court.

Passengers lost on international flights face no such ambiguity over the value of a human life. Under the terms of the Warsaw Convention a present-day valuation is set at about ten thousand dollars as of September 1973. In cases in which the place of departure, a destination, or a planned stop is in the United States, the Montreal Agreement of 1966 applies. This supersedes the liability limit set by the Warsaw Convention.

It is in the interest of the airlines of the world to limit liabilities for property loss and death. A set limit allows the airline to better insure its risks and to avoid ruinous claims. On the other hand, plaintiffs and their attorneys are seeking higher compensation for losses — often by most ingenious legal strategies.

The delivery of a ticket creates a legal contract between the air carrier and the passenger. It is important for plaintiffs suing airlines to be certain that the passenger involved was properly ticketed, otherwise the airline can be said not to be a party to the contract.

An airline is *not* an insurer of passengers. Once great care has been exercised, the airline's responsibility ceases.

Airlines have the duty to make their terminal area, boarding and deplaning, waiting areas, and access corridors as safe as they can using a considerable degree of care. Air carriers are not responsible for items which fall in the area of responsibility of the terminal operator and airport management. Also, the passengers and others at airline areas must exercise due care for their own safety.[11]

Air Carrier Liability Limits: Air Cargo

Common law regarding carriers is ancient and strict. It requires a carrier of goods to be an insurer of property entrusted to the carrier for transport. The exceptions are few — Acts of God, or an act or omission of the shipper and other factors beyond the control of the carrier. The burden of proof of non-liability rests with the carrier.

This common law is so strict because the carrier is peculiarly in a position to know how to safely deliver goods entrusted to him and to exercise control over the goods.

The provisions of the Federal Aviation Act completely govern contracts for other than intrastate carriage. The act preempts state laws. Common law does not apply to airlines filing tariffs in compliance with the act. The Civil Aeronautics Board has jurisdiction over U.S. domestic and foreign carriage of passengers and cargo by air.[12]

There is an important legal difference with regard to intrastate cargo or passenger operation. If air carriage is completely inside the boundaries of one state (intrastate), then the laws of the state govern. The regulations of the state aviation administration or other department of transportation will determine how tariffs are to be filed and the limits of liability to be assumed by the carrier.

Tariffs filed by air carriers with CAB for interstate and/or foreign air freight or cargo operation, and approved by CAB, generally have the effect of limiting the liability of the carrier for loss or damage to goods.

The filed tariff is in effect a contract of carriage between shippers and carriers. No variation in tariffs is possible without the risk of making the contract invalid. A declaration of value by the shipper will assist his being compensated should the shipment be lost or damaged. Shippers can insure for a higher than usual value if they wish. Shippers' instructions must be adequate and clearly marked. The liability of the carrier eneds when the freight is delivered to the consignee.

There are time limitations on shippers' placing claims for damages to goods. The shipper must report the loss or damage within approximately fifteen days and legal action to recover damages must be filed within a year of the carrier (or forwarder) disallowance of the shipper's claim.

Waybills (airbill, bills of lading) are lists of items being shipped and contain instructions to the carrier. It serves as the shipper's receipt, as a contract of carriage, and written evidence of title. The waybill automatically insures the shipper's goods according to the terms it contains.[13]

Common Carriers

Common carriers are those who undertake to carry persons or goods for hire or reward and are available to the general public. These firms are legally bound to offer transportation services to all "indifferently," that is, without discrimination.

It is easy to see that a trucking company or an airline can be a common carrier. It is at first less apparent that a freight forwarder might also be considered a common carrier. Yet, the forwarder, too, offers transportation services to the public for hire.

Freight forwarding is a thriving, growing industry. The forwarder may offer such services as picking up freight from a customer, carrying it to the airline freight terminal, then at another point, taking the consignment by other means to its ultimate destination, or, freight forwarders may offer service only from one of their terminals to another. Generally several modes of transport are involved. The freight forwarder attends to all needed customs work and paper work associated with getting the consignment from consignor to consignee. Are travel agents also common carriers? They are not unless they are also charter tour operators who file programs with the CAB regarding financial and safety considerations. These tour operators must be bonded and show contracts they are to use with air carriers. With CAB approval of these and other data, a tour operator is then termed an "indirect air carrier." No certificate is awarded.

CAB regulations, Part 212, apply to charter trips by foreign air carriers. Changes which went into effect 24 January 1979 liberalized CAB regulations for indirect cargo carriers. [14]

Foreign air carrier permits authorizing charter transportation only are covered by CAB regulation, Part 214. Part 378 applies to Inclusive Tour Charters. An inclusive tour means a roundtrip tour combining air transportation of at least seven days duration with hotel accommodation and land transport.

These CAB regulations and others are designed to help provide safe, financially sound, and economical transportation for U.S. and foreign travellers.

Air Travel Plans

A plan to investigate an inter-carrier credit program for the purchase of airline tickets was announced by the CAB in December 1978.

The Universal Air Travel Plan (UATP) has over 160 members including both domestic and international airlines. Under the plan, Air Travel Cards may be issued by members of UATP to customers paying an interest-bearing deposit of $425 to join the program. The cards may be used on any UATP-member airline to buy tickets. An additional "Silver Card" is proposed by UATP to

253

allow customers to charge hotel and motel reservations and to rent cars as well as to buy airline tickets.

In 1978, as it had done in 1975, the CAB disclaimed jurisdiction over items other than air transport.

To answer the UATP proposal, the board had checked (a) whether UATP is an illegal joint venture under the antitrust laws; (b) will any of UATP's practices restrain trade; (c) are there anticompetitive aspects to UATP; and (d) if UATP is approved should the board grant antitrust immunity?

Private Air Carriers

Not all air carriers are available to the general public for transportation for pay. Some air carriers carry people and goods for only one company, or person, or organization. These are termed private air carriers.

Generally, the duty of a private air carrier is to exercise ordinary care under the conditions existing at the time of the flight. If an accident occurs caused by the negligence of the pilot or aircraft operator, the private carrier is liable for injury, death of those carried, and property losses in the air or on the ground.

Death on the High Seas Act

In the days of sail, embarking upon the high seas was thought to be so hazardous that all persons choosing to travel the high seas waived all rights to sue the carrier. In traditional maritime law there was no action possible for wrongful death (death caused by some negligence on the part of the carrier or other parties).

In 1920, with only deaths at sea in mind, a U.S. statute was written. The Congressional act was titled Death on the High Seas Act (DHSA) (46 U.S.C., section 761).

The act enables the family of a person killed "beyond one marine league from the shore of any state, or the District of Columbia, or the territories or dependencies of the United States," to file a suit for damages in the district courts of the United States. The act makes the "vessel, person, or corporation," liable for wrongful deaths at sea.

Today, this DHSA, once used only for ships, now deals for the most part with aeronautical cases. An aircraft need not be operating in interstate or foreign commerce to come under DHSA and admiralty law.

There are no dollar limits set on the amounts that may be recovered by a plaintiff. Further, contributory negligence (negligent acts of the person injured) do not prevent suit for recompense for injury or death. The law of the place involved controls the case in question, admiralty law holds.

The DHSA states that suit must be brought within two years unless the defendant is not available. Recovery is apportioned out among those plaintiffs named in proportion to the loss they have suffered.

Since the Constitution of the United States places maritime matters under the control of the federal government, U.S. federal courts hear cases brought under the DHSA. Indeed, most maritime matters come under admiralty law and are heard in U.S. district courts. State courts, most agree, do not have jurisdiction of wrongful death actions based on the act.

The place of departure and intended destination play an important part in determining whether DHSA applies, even if an aircraft crashes into navigable waters. Further, whether or not the aircraft was engaged in traditional maritime activity (such as transoceanic transportation) is a consideration in determining whether the act applies to a case.[15]

Some Major Airlines

The following list of some of the major American airline companies reveals the impact of the policies of the U.S. Post Office, and later the Civil Aeronautics Board. Until the late 1970s most large, certificated air carriers in the United States had their origin in the 1930s.[16]

Air California	Founded in 1966 as an intrastate airline.
American Airlines	Founded in 1934 to succeed American Airways and earlier firms from 1926. In 1971 American Airlines and Trans Caribbean Airways merged.
Braniff Airways	Began service in 1930; formed from 1928 companies.

The McDonnell Douglas DC-10 air transport.

Continental Airlines	Began as Varney in 1934, renamed Continental in 1937.
Delta Airlines	Founded 1925 as agricultural application company. Passenger service began in 1929. Delta is now one of the largest U.S. airlines.
Eastern Air Lines	Began in 1926 as Pitcairn Aviation; taken over by North American Aviation 1929; reorganized as EAL in 1938.
Flying Tiger Line	Founded in 1945 as National Skyway Freight Corp. and was the first U.S. all-cargo airline; named FTL in 1946. One of the largest U.S. airlines.
Hughes Airwest	Founded 1968 as Air West; took present name in 1971.
National Airlines	Founded in 1934. One of the world's largest airlines.
Northwest Airlines	Began service in 1926 as Northwest Airway, Inc.; present name in 1934; also known as Northwest Orient Airlines.
Overseas National Airways	Founded in 1950 as worldwide charter operator.
Pacific Southwest Airlines	Founded in 1945 as intrastate airline in California.
Pan American Airways	Began service in 1927 and is one of the world's leading airlines. Pan Am has led the way in international passenger carriage.
Trans World Airlines	Through mergers, founded in the 1920s; in 1930 was Transcontinental and Western Airlines; present name, 1950. An important U.S. air carrier.
United Airlines	Founded in 1930 with merger of four earlier airlines. Merged in 1960 with

	Capital. One of the world's largest air carriers.
Western Airlines (WAL)	Began service in 1925 as Western Air Express; named WAL in 1941. Serves U.S. and foreign routes.
World Airways	In 1948, founded as a non-scheduled air service. World-wide charter airline for both cargo and passengers.

Today, according to a list published by CAB in September 1978, there are thirty-eight U.S. certificated air carriers. There are ten supplemental air carriers listed and over four hundred air freight forwarders at this writing.

There is within this huge air transport system a civil air reserve capability which may, under present law, be immediately drafted for use as military air transport if needed. Certain aircraft are so designed as to be quickly converted to military troop carriers and cargo carriers. The plan is known as the Civil Reserve Air Fleet (CRAF) and is subject to call to duty on 24-hour notice. It is based on an Executive Order signed by President John F. Kennedy in 1963.[16]

The Airplanes

Today's workhorses are the Boeing 747 and 727, the Lockheed 1011, and the McDonnell-Douglas DC-10.

Boeing Company, late in 1978 announced plans for jets with an investment of over $2.5 billion. These will be the Boeing 767, a medium-range, wide-body jet which will be able to carry two hundred passengers; the Boeing 757, a narrow-body airplane; and the Boeing 777. All are designed to fly quieter, and with more fuel efficiency than previous designs.

How much do popular Boeings in service now cost? Prices vary a great deal, of course, according to the use (passenger, or cargo, or both). A general dollar value, however, is around $15 million for the Boeing 727 and $50 million for the 747.

McDonnell Douglas Corporation presently markets the DC-9 and the DC-10 priced at around $15 million and $37 million respectively. Again these are very general figures. McDonnell Douglas plans a DC-9 Super 80 jet, to sell for

U.S. AIR CARRIER FREIGHT REVENUES,
INTERNATIONAL & TERRITORIAL OPERATIONS

By Type of Services

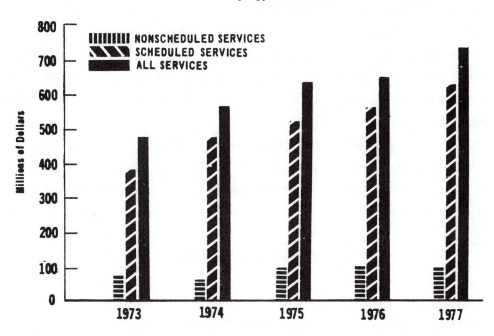

By Carrier Group, All Services

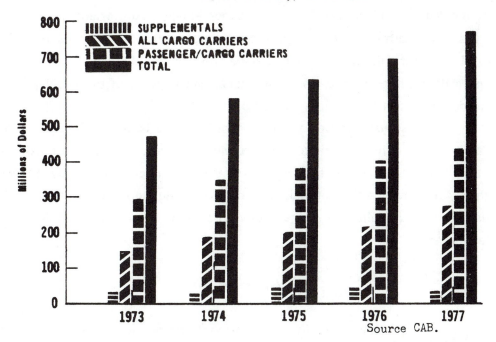

Source CAB.

259

around $17 million, which will meet all the government noise level standards of the 1980s.

Lockheed Aircraft Corporation today sells C-130 cargo planes to civilian air carriers, the Lockheed L-100 and L-1011 jets for civil passenger use. A general price for the L-1011 is about $35 million. The Lockheed L-1011 Dash 500 model, a new long-range jet, is entering service now. It is more fuel efficient and quieter than previous models. The price tag, with parts, is over $40 million each, based on around $500 million to be paid for the 12 planes ordered by Pan American.

Still in the civil air fleet are older Boeings, Lockheeds, and Douglas aircraft, and even a few Ford tri-motor aircraft. Reliable and durable, American-built airplanes persist in service around the world. Other widely-used air carrier aircraft are: Convair, Hawker-Siddeley, Tupolev, Ilyushin, and Vickers.[17]

Airlines and Their Suppliers: Product Liability

There is today a considerable potential for product liability cases against airlines and their suppliers. A recent case heard in a federal court of the eastern district of New York makes it easier to bring suit for damages on international flights, reversing thirty years of liability protection given international carriers by the Warsaw Convention. The public is increasingly claims oriented.

Cases are getting more complex as the dominance of the idea of strict liability in tort, in which it is necessary only for the plaintiff to prove there was a defect but not necessarily negligence, shifts much of the liability from airlines to aircraft and component manufacturers.

If one passenger survives a crash, according to a National Transportation Safety Board definition, then it is a survivable crash. Attorneys for heirs of those not surviving may then choose to sue makers of upholsterey, for example, claiming that the materials generated toxic gases and were not adequately fire-resistant. Suppliers to airlines, therefore, need considerable liability protection.[18]

Safety in the Air

U.S. air carriers in 1978 in all operations, carried more than 286 million passengers, about a 13 percent increase over 1977. There were 25 total accidents in 1978, of these 6 were fatal accidents involving 163 fatalities. (The mid-air collision in San Diego, California accounted for 144 of these air carrier deaths.)

Comparing the 1978 figures we find that over all, there were less than 1.7 fatalities per million passengers flown in 1978. The passenger fatality rate for carriers in scheduled domestic and international service was 0.006 per million passenger miles flown in 1978 with thirteen passenger fatalities. This is the second lowest rate per passenger mile ever recorded. (1970 with only two fatalities, and 0.001 rate was better.)

As the figures above show, the U.S. air carriers have a remarkably good safety record.[19]

The achievement of the nation's air carrier operation, assisted by U.S. manufacturers and by federal aviation agencies, is a great one. The work performed is economically vital and tremendously complex. As one can see by the above mention of some of the legal considerations involved, an awareness of legal rights and responsibilities is an essential one to those working in the air carrier field.

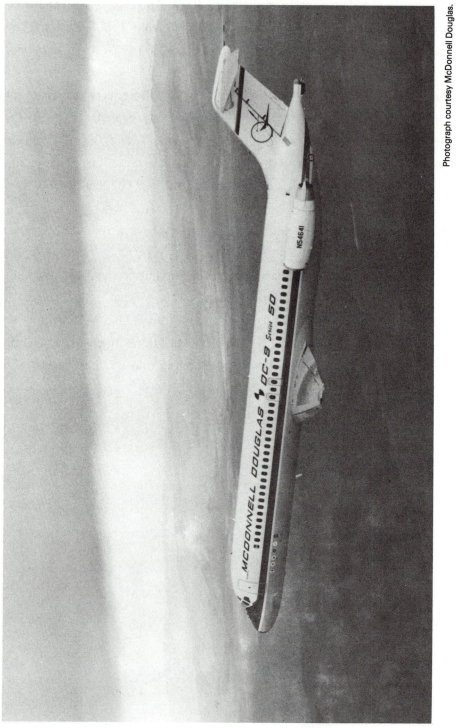

The McDonnell Douglas DC — 9 in flight.

INDEX OF JET-EQUIPPED CARRIERS

OPERATION	CARRIER GROUP	CARRIER NAME
Domestic Operations	Domestic Trunks	American Airlines, Inc. Braniff Airways, Inc. Capital Airlines, Inc. 1 Continental Air Lines, Inc. Delta Air Lines, Inc. 7 Eastern Air Lines, Inc. National Airlines, Inc. Northeast Airlines, Inc. 7 Northwest Airlines, Inc. Pan American World Airways, Inc. 2 Trans World Airlines, Inc. United Air Lines, Inc. Western Air Lines, Inc.
	Local Service Carriers	Allegheny Airlines, Inc. 8 Bonanza Air Lines, Inc. 3 Central Airlines, Inc. 4 Frontier Airlines, Inc. Hughes Air Corporation d/b/e Air West 3 Lake Central Airlines, Inc. 5 Mohawk Airlines, Inc. 8 North Central Airlines, Inc. Ozark Air Lines, Inc. Pacific Air Lines, Inc. 3 Piedmont Aviation, Inc. Southern Airways, Inc. Texas International Airlines, Inc. 6 West Coast Airlines, Inc.

1 Capital Airlines merged with United Air Lines effective June 1, 1961.
2 Pan American World Airways began reporting domestic entity operations as of July 1, 1970.
3 Bonanza Air Lines and West Coast Airlines merged with Pacific Air Lines effective April 17, 1968. On that date, following the merger, Pacific Air Lines changed its name to Air West, Inc. The transfer of certificate from Air West, Inc. to Hughes Air Corporation d/b/a Air West became effective on April 3, 1970.
4 Central Airlines merged with Frontier Airlines effective October 1, 1967.
5 Lake Central Airlines merged with Allegheny Airlines effective July 1, 1968.
6 Trans-Texas Airways changed its name to Texas International Airlines, Inc. effective December 4, 1968.
7 Northeast Airlines merged with Delta Air Lines effective August 1, 1972.
8 Mohawk Airlines merged with Allegheny Airlines effective April 14, 1972.

INDEX OF JET EQUIPMENT

EQUIPMENT GROUP	ENGINE TRUST CATEGORY	EQUIPMENT TYPE	
		MODEL	MANUFACTURER
Turbofan, 4 Engine (Wide-bodies)	Over 30,000 lbs. per engine	B-747	Boeing
Turbofan, 4 Engine (Regular-bodied)	30,000 lbs. per engine and under	B-707-100B	Boeing
		B-707-300B	Boeing
		B-707-300C	Boeing
		B-720B	Boeing
		CV-990	Convair
		DC-8-50	Douglas
		DC-8-50F	Douglas
		DC-8-61	Douglas
		DC-8-62	Douglas
		DC-8-63	Douglas
		DC-8-63F	Douglas
Turbofan, 3 Engine (Wide-bodied)	Over 30,000 lbs. per engine	DC-10	Douglas
		L-1011	Lockheed
Turbofan, 3 Engine (Regular-bodied)	30,000 lbs. per engine and under	B-727-100	Boeing
		B-727-100C/QC	Boeing
		B-727-200	Boeing
Turbofan, 2 Engine	30,000 lbs. per engine and under	BAC-1-11-200	British Aircraft Corp.
		BAC-1-11-400	British Aircraft Corp.
		B-737-200	Boeing
		B-737-200C/QC	Boeing

264

INDEX OF JET EQUIPMENT (Continued)

EQUIPMENT GROUP	ENGINE THRUST CATEGORY	EQUIPMENT TYPE	
		MODEL	MANUFACTURER
Turbofan, 2 Engine (Continued)	30,000 lbs. per engine and under	DC-9-10 DC-9-30 DC-9-50	Douglas Douglas Douglas
Turbojet, 4 Engine	30,000 lbs. per engine and under	B-707-100 B-707-200 B-707-300 B-720 CV-880 DC-8-10 DC-8-20 DC-8-30	Boeing Boeing Boeing Boeing Convair Douglas Douglas Douglas
Turbojet, 2 Engine	30,000 lbs. per engine and under	SE-210 (Caravelle)	Sud-Aviation

NOTES

[1] Robert M. Kane and Allen D. Vose, *Air Transportation* (Dubuque, Iowa: Kendall/Hunt Publishing Co., 1975), ch. 1, p. 5.

[2] Gerald Pucci, *Aviation Law*, (Dubuque, Iowa: Kendall/Hunt Publishing Co., 1977), ch. 19, p. 1; Kane and Vose, ch. 9, pp. 1-18; Stuart M. Speiser and Charles F. Krause, *Aviation Tort Law* (San Francisco: Bancroft-Whitney Co., 1978), I, pp. 49-57.

[3] F. Lee Bailey, *Cleared for the Approach* (Englewood Cliffs, N.J.: Prentice-Hall, 1977), pp. 39-47.

[4] Speiser and Krause, I, pp. 129-33.

[5] Fred Biehler, *Aviation Maintenance Law* (Basin, Wyo.: Aviation Maintenance Foundation, Inc., 1975), pp. 114-15; Speiser and Krause, I, pp. 9-13, 394.

[6] F. Lee Bailey, p. 71; Speiser and Krause, I, pp. 255-59.

[7] Speiser and Krause, I, pp. 274-76.

[8] Speiser and Krause, I, pp. 338-42; Biehler, p. 72.

[9] Rowland W. Fixel, *The Law of Aviation*, 4th ed. (Charlottesville, Va.: Michie Co., 1967), pp. 452, 456-69.

[10] Fixel p. 38; Speiser and Krause, I, pp. 497-500 and Cumulative Supplement for Volume I, page 40, February 1979.

[11] Speiser and Krause, I, 338-39.

[12] CAB Economic Regulation Part 221 of 14 CFR applies to the rules of posting and filing tariffs of air carriers.

[13] Michael J. Hart, *Outline of International Aviation Law* (St. Louis: Parks College of St. Louis University, 1975), pp. 112-13; Speiser and Krause, I, pp. 760-69.

[14] CAB Economic Regulation 212, Amendment No. 26.

[15] Fixel, pp. 82-83; Hart, pp. 172-80; Death on the High Seas Act of 1920, 46 U.S.C. 761.

[16] Discussion of these policies may be found in the chapters on federal regulation of aviation and on the CAB and deregulation.

[17] Civil Aeronautics Board, *Jet Aircraft Trends*, (Washington, D.C.: CAB, 1978).

[18] Biehler, pp. 88, 105; Speiser and Krause, *Aviation Tort Law* (San Francisco: Bancroft-Whitney Co., 1979), II, 473-76.

[19] CAB Annual Report to Congress, 1978; NTSB Press Release with attached 1978 analysis of aviation accident statistics, June 1979.

PART VI

INTERNATIONAL AVIATION LAW

Artist's conception of a Lockheed design for a proposed extreme range aircraft. The plane could be powered by nuclear power.

CHAPTER 16

THE DEVELOPMENT OF INTERNATIONAL LAW

There is no actual international law, some scholars assert, for there is no means of enforcing such laws short of war.[1] Yet, today there is a great body of agreements, custom, and moral guidelines existing among nations which serves as international law. This consensus, agreement, and consent among nations, is, in effect, international law.[2] The enforcement is generally accomplished by the pressures of world public opinion, by mutual benefits, by trade sanctions, and by the threat of the withdrawal of transportation services.[3] In aviation, this is a particularly effective sanction because airlines are vital transport links, and are essential to national prosperity and well being.

Kinds of International Law

Municipal Law. Governing the internal affairs of a nation is municipal law. It treats with individuals and groups and is directly enforceable.

International Law. Among world states there is a body of international law which depends upon good will to function. There is no way of enforcing this law short of armed conflict. International law treats with sovereign states.

Public International Law. The state in public international law is viewed as a corporate person. This body of law deals with negotiations between nations and generally accepted national rights. There is no tribunal or court.

Private International Law. This category of law depends on the courts of the various nations involved. It has to do with agreements between private individuals.

Rules of War

Oddly enough, one can see that the ancient practices between warring nations and groups evolved into some of the peacetime customs upon which today's international law is based. In times of peace there are accepted rules between most nations that facilitate trade and travel between countries.

Permission to travel through a country or in nearby waters was a concession

269

made by neutral governments or allies. The exchange of prisoners involved negotiations under flags of truce. The recognition of neutral nations gradually emerged in the eighteenth and nineteenth centuries.

The rules of war took a legalistic turn in the nineteenth century and multi-national agreements and theories were worked out. These, in turn, made a pattern for meetings for peacetime negotiations regarding the right of innocent passage and mutually beneficial rules of trade.[4]

Defining a State (Nation)

Men have thought about the question "What is a state, a nation?" for centuries. Plato wrote his treatise, *The Republic*, which described a theoretical state in which men and women had certain duties and roles all of which worked toward the benefit of the state and its future. Aristotle saw a nation as directing society for the public good, a view which the thirteenth century philosopher Saint Thomas Acquinas shared.[5]

By the seventeenth century Thomas Hobbs in England theorized that societies (states) arose by means of mutual agreement of the members. He saw a state as originating as a social compact. The rulers' role was to rule wisely and justly while the people had the duty to carry out the work and plans given them by their governors.[6]

Later in the seventeenth century John Locke proposed the idea that the people of a state comprised its power. Locke suggested that legislative power should rule over executive power, that representatives of the people should govern. This view is in general agreement with the theorist mentioned later in this chapter, Hugo Grotius, who held that a state should be a body of free men united to enjoy common rights and advantages.[7]

The modern definition of a state has come to be something of a pragmatic rather than a theoretical one. Justice John Marshall of the U.S. Supreme Court defined states as distinct political societies separated from others; a state as a unit capable of managing its own affairs and governing itself.[8]

We might then hazard a general definition of a state (nation) as: a permanently organized political society, occupying a fixed territory, and enjoying within the borders of that territory freedom from control by any other state.

The Sovereignty of Independent States

What control does a state (nation) exercise over the land, water and air space inside its boundaries? (In this discussion of international law the term "state" means a sovereign, independent nation.) Each such state in theory exercises complete control and has the right to impose such laws as seem desirable. We use the term sovereignty to describe such control. Another term which might have the same meaning is "territorial jurisdiction." This does not necessarily imply land ownership; for citizens, organizations, and public groups may own land within the state.[9]

Such sovereignty extends to vessels and aircraft registered in the states.

Control, jurisdiction, and sovereignty is obtained by states via discovery, conquest and occupation. Territory can be forfeited by lack of occupation, use or control. Territory is sometimes held because its geographical barriers have acted to offer residents control of the area. Territory can be annexed by agreement, and often in world history without agreement of its residents. Long occupation of a territory also gives a group of people certain rights to an area.[10]

Sovereignty Defined

The "accepted states" are those recognized as sovereign (independent) states by most other nations. The term "sovereignty," in turn, is understood to mean an independent political power uncontrolled, and uncontrollable, by other powers. A sovereign state has unlimited authority over the persons and property inside its boundaries. Said another way, the sovereign state has jurisdiction over persons within its borders.

The "incidents of sovereignty" include the powers of a state to:

1. negotiate and conclude treaties with other states.

2. be considered equal before the law with other states.

3. hold the power of eminent domain (power of appropriation of land or other property within the state).

4. refuse to be sued without the consent of the state itself.

5. exercise the right of domain (jurisdiction) over territory, water, persons and air within the borders of the state, and generally over its citizens wherever they are.

The "recognition" of a state as being a nation, as being a sovereign entity, is a voluntary act of other states. In recognizing a government, world states admit that the state and its government are entitled to the rights and privileges (listed above) generally held by sovereign states.[11]

The term "domain" indicates in a narrower sense the ownership of territory. "Jurisdiction" also can be said to indicate the right to exercise some power or authority. A government has jurisdiction over its persons and properties within its boundaries as noted above. Also, a court may have jurisdiction over only maritime matters, or over juvenile cases, for example, these are courts of limited jurisdiction.[12]

Sovereign nations have jurisdiction of their air space, as confirmed at the Paris Convention in 1919 and also later by the Havana Convention. The U.S. Air Commerce Act of 1926 endorsed sovereignty of airspace. With the advent of the Soviet "Sputnik I" and space flight technology, this began to change.[13]

Early Theories

The idea of creating a body of law which would prevail over the governments of nations was written about in the sixteenth century. In Europe nationalism had arisen. The princes of the various states had set up courts to deal with maritime disputes. National control extended out three miles or so from coast-lines since early defenses could reach out that far. Some nations had claimed whole seas prior to this, but the problem of control of such vast areas existed. Also, legal theorists began to contend that no one could exercise jurisdiction over the high seas (waters beyond the three mile limit).

Albericus Gentilis (1552-1608).   Gentilis, born in Italy then removed to Austria and later England, may well be called the father of international law. His innovative analysis and proposals freed international law from the bonds of past, predominantly religious approaches.

Gentilis became a noted lawyer in England. He greatly admired Roman law but did not agree that either Roman or Canon (church) law should always prevail in the law of nations. In his books Genetilis used a common sense approach to legal matters between nations. Circumstances, existing conditions, should be important in determining international rules he contended.

Aviation law has benefitted from his theory that the high seas should be open to the ships of all nations. Laying the groundwork for international treaties concerned with aviation, he wrote proposals for rules to be used in writing peace treaties. Treaties, he said, were much like contracts.[14]

Hugo Grotius (1583-1645). Grotius overshadowed the reputation of Gentilis for centuries and indeed has good reason to be acclaimed as a most important theorist in developing international law. Groitus was Dutch and very early in his life showed great intellectual powers. He studied in Holland and France, returning to practice law in his native land. He left Holland for religious reasons and took refuge in France and Sweden.

His great book, the *De Jure Belli et Pacis* published in 1626, became a standard reference on international alw for three hundred years. Grotius observed with horror the inhuman and curel practices of nations at ware. Surely, he wrote, nations should abide by some standards of morality and decency. He held that there existed among nations a customary and voluntary body of law. Grotius wished these laws reformed by reason and justice to a higher degree of humanity during times of international conflict.

Grotius expressed important ideas regarding navigation upon waterways and upon the high seas. He contended that the rivers of Europe should be open to the citizens of all nations. The principle of free navigation by all nations of many European rivers was set forth in general terms by the members of the Congress of Vienna in 1815. These matters today are regulated by treaty.

In 1609 Grotius stated that in spite of the claims of some nations to whole oceans, the seas were free to all. And the same, he noted, may be said of the air. Air should be viewed as the common property of all mankind he asserted.[15] Still, nations continued to claim control of large areas of the high seas. Finally, to some extent, nations agreed that a nation's jurisdiction extended outward from its coast line a cannon shot, or about three miles. There is still argument about this, however, with many nations claiming more area. The U.S., for example, claims an "economic zone" of two hundred miles depth along our coasts.

In 1958 the United Nations drew up a Convention on Territorial Waters and Contiguous Zones. This convention includes the principle of sovereignty over territorial sea and the air above it and confirms the right of innocent passage near a nation's coastline.[16] Coastal states, the U.N. document contends, should provide international warnings of new hazards existing in these waters.

Other Early Theorists. Among the names of those who helped to develop a framework of international law are Richard Zouche (1590-1660); Samuel von Pufendorf (1632-1694); Cornelis van Bynkershoek (1673-1743); Johann Jakob Moser (1701-1785); Emmerich de Vattel (1714-1767); Lord Stowell (1745-1836); and James Kent, late eighteenth-century American jurist.[17]

Treaties and Agreements. The Declaration of Paris of 1856 dealt with much of the law of war at sea and was one of the first of a series of agreements between naval powers. These declarations have greatly humanized the treatment of prisoners of war and, despite violations, have proved of great value.[18] Nations have found it only sensible to agree with one another.

Over the past one hundred and fifty years we have seen the signing of a great many treaties which, in effect, have become sources of international law. Some treaties, though signed by only a few nations, become the model of behavior for most of the states of the world, bringing new principles of law into being. Other treaties tend simply to codify, put into writing, certain practices agreed upon between nations.

Maritime Precedents

As noted earlier, traders moving goods by ship worked out certain international customs allowing them transit across kingdoms and through various coastal waters. Maritime precedent is important to the development of aviation law.[19]

Naturally, nations claimed jurisdiction over rivers and other waterways within the nation. Also, naturally, the question arose as to who held jurisdiction over a river or bay bounding two nations. At first the nations split the waterway down the middle, later via the principle known as the Doctrine of Thalweg, a common division was to the center of the main channel. This allowed both bordering nations the right to effectively use the waterway.[20]

Within a nation, for example in England, the law stated that the federal government had jurisdiction over bays and rivers as far up river as the tides penetrated. In the United States this law was altered by the mid-nineteenth century, so that in the United States the federal government has jurisdiction as far inland as waters are navigable. Since America was so immense, this control over United States inland waterways was needed. This concept was to affect the writing of aviation law in the twentieth century.

Aviation, arising in the late nineteenth century, threatened concepts of guarded boundaries, of fortified centers of population, and the sovereignty of national airspace. Balloons, dirigibles, and planes can easily cross geographic barriers or manmade borders. Aircraft can enter, depart or overfly a state. To aircraft, the international laws applicable to maritime trade were applied with additions.

Of interest to us in discussing maritime international law are the definitions which have emerged. In general nations agree that:[21]

1. Contiguous zones are those areas of waters near coastlines and ranging in width from three to twelve miles.

2. The archipelago theory is that all waters inside a circle of islands belong under the jurisdiction of the government of the islands. Examples of this are the Philippines and Indonesia.

3. Continental shelf ownership has evolved into the domain of the United States and about twenty other states which claim the continental shelves adjacent to those nations. The location of oil and gas in these areas makes such claims an important economic consideration.

4. Nations agree that the free seas are those beyond the territorial sea claimed as described above.

5. Hot pursuit is a term describing an internationally accepted practice that allows officers of a nation to chase and capture a ship or aircraft that has committed an offense in territorial waters, even though the chase and capture proceed into the open seas.

Vessels and Aircraft

International law in times of peace considers each nation as a person and all nations theoretically equal. Vessels (ships) are treated to a great extent as though they were movable portions of their nation of registry.

Gerhard von Glahn, however, in his book *Law Among Nations* notes that today this is no longer taken to mean that a ship is literally a territory of a

275

state, yet most rules of the state of registry do apply aboard the vessel.[22] The state of a ship is not that of its ownership but of its state of registry. The rules applicable to ships naturally came to apply to aircraft as well.

A ship is treated legally in itself as a person and may be sued. This rule evolved since owners could be foreign and hence unreachable whereas a ship could be seized, sued, and perhaps sold to pay damages. A crew member may also be sued in a foreign port.

Customarily, port authorities do not interfere with the internal discipline of a ship, but they can intervene upon request or if the peace is disturbed.

Every state (nation) has the right to sail its vessels (those registered under its flag) on the high seas. Even Switzerland registers vessels. Each state sets the conditions under which it will register vessels and grant the right to fly the state's flag. Easy conditions have caused a high number of ships to be registered under a "flag of convenience" in such states as Liberia or Panama.

While in foreign waters a ship owes a certain adherence to the navigation and other regulations of the host nation.

Right of Innocent Passage

A foreign vessel, passing through the waters of a nation, has the right to do so unmolested. This is known as the "right of innocent passage." The ship may even stop or anchor but must not engage in activities forbidden in that zone. Nations may reserve certain coastal areas for reasons of national security, to restrain fishing and other commercial activities, or to enforce public health regulations. Vessels passing through are generally less susceptible to interference aboard than are those in port or those leaving a nation's port.

A ship may be taken (to pay for damages incurred via collision) but a *person* is not to be removed from a ship passing through.[23]

The Individual

States (nations) have jurisdiction over their citizens. The definition of a citizen varies according to nation. Two general principles govern: (1) that of *jus soli* which indicates that a person is a citizen of the state in which he was born regardless of the citizenship of his parents; and (2) that of *jus sanguinis* which rules that a person is a citizen of the state of which his parents are citizens. The laws defining citizenship are too varied to allow further generalization. A person may indeed be a citizen of two or more states.

The definition of a citizen in the United States, according to the Fourteenth Amendment to the Constitution, notes that all persons born or naturalized in the United States are citizens. Also, persons born to U.S. citizens, even though born outside the U.S., are citizens if either parent has ever lived in the U.S.

Some nations, including Great Britain and the United States, allow naturalization. Naturalization is the voluntary act of becoming a citizen. This demonstrates the United States philosophy that citizenship is "alienable," that is, that it can be transferred. Some governments hold that only the place of birth is a person's homeland, that citizenship is something inalienable, not buyable, salable, nor transferable.

A sovereign state has the power to insist that one obey its laws while within its borders and can punish one if the law is broken. True, a person may escape into another state. Then, only should that other nation agree to return him (extradite him) can he be seized and punished. The United States has a policy against extradition unless a treaty exists between the U.S. and the foreign state requesting extradition. Extradition treaties are generally bilateral (both nations agreeing to and limited by the treaty). Extradition is approved as a rule only for certain crimes that civilized nations recognize plus acceptable proof of the crime.

Diplomats are generally immune from prosecution by other than their home state. Diplomatic agents also have immunity. Employees of embassies and legations and other foreign offices have certain immunities but not to the extent of the immunities possessed by diplomats or agents.

One of the individuals considered an enemy of all maritime states is the "pirate." A pirate may be defined as one who seizes vessels, goods, and/or persons in transit on the seas. Aircraft introduced a new element into the consideration of piracy. The question is whether the hijacker is a pirate or a political escapee. Since hijacking is so often tied in with a request for political asylum (sanctuary of a sort) it is not simple to extradite them for punishment. This problem and its solutions are discussed in the chapter on hijacking and other crimes aboard aircraft. Again, treaties in effect will affect the hijacker's chances of being extradited or punished.

Are corporations treated as individuals under international law and custom? Yes. Corporations have the nationality of the state (nation) in which they are incorporated. Unincorporated associations have the nationality of the state in which their headquarters or controlling body is located.[24]

Sources of International Law

International Institutes. Nations may join forces and create international organizations to set rules for a particular sphere of operations. An example is the International Civil Aviation Organization (ICAO) which was set up for the purpose of standardizing international aviation procedures and documents, and setting rules for taxation and operation of air carrier aircraft. Nations submit themselves to the rules of these organizations voluntarily.

International Commissions. Nations meet in international conferences and set up commissions for the purpose of codifying, restating, and agreeing upon customary international law. This is an increasingly important source of international agreement and is of much interest to the United Nations in their efforts to build international accord.

The United Nations has begun important work of adopting legal principles in several areas to govern international relations. One of these is the U.N. resolution dealing with the exploration and development of outer space.

Diplomatic Papers of State. In diplomatic papers states can communicate interpretations and usage of a particular state in its relations with others.

Multilateral and Bilateral Treaties. Treaties are proliferating between nations and promise to be a most important factor in the development of international law. These will be discussed in the following chapter as they pertain to international aviation law.

General Principles of Law. There are general principles which might be termed simply as "justice" in which obvious fairness necessitates that certain rules be followed. Here again, there is a lack of exactness due to the varying ways that nations view rightness and justice. A few international rules of law do exist, however, such as the one requiring that all local remedies be tried by an individual in the country that person is in at the time of the violation, before his own nation can request justice.

Rules of Comity. Simple courtesy binds nations to a number of customary practices.

Judicial Decisions. Decisions of a court in one nation do not, of course, bind other nations; yet, foreign decisions are cited when appropriate and have an impact (of choice) in international law.[25]

Public Opinion. The pressures of world opinion are becoming more and more an effective force in forming international agreements. Commentaries, books, and news media accounts and comments by world leaders play a part in this process. Improved world communication has made this impact possible.

Resolutions, Declarations. Unratified declarations and resolutions are become a force in international law. Further, the declarations and resolutions of the General Assembly of the United Nations are coming to have legal import, albeit a quasilegal one.

Overall, we see that a consensus among nations is coming to have more and more legal significance in international law, placing binding obligations upon the nations of the world.

Custom. As we have noted, custom is a source of international law. Rules of privileges and immunities of states, freedom of the high seas, and territorial jurisdictions all evolved from custom. No certain rule exists as to the exact definition of a custom, yet fairly frequent usage seems to cause a practice to be viewed as a custom. However, a vagueness exists that can result in quarreling between states. Treaties can be written to spell out practices more exactly.

Practical International Law

Since international law has been worked out at meetings of nations, built upon the work of prominent theorists and upon custom, we can see that treaties are used as the vehicles of international law. International aviation law in particular rests upon multilateral treaties.

We have seen international law evolving with respect to the rules of warfare. Essentially our present international legal system started with the Peace of Westphalia treaty of 1648 which ended the Thirty Year War. This set up the idea of a balance of power between nations, the concept of fixed national boundaries, and set forth certain duties and rights of nations.[26]

Early international law had a definite religious cast, but by the eighteenth century a more pragmatic turn occurred. Conditions that exist, whether right or wrong, are acknowledged in law today.

International law exists, then, derived from a background of practical considerations of peace and trade. It has benefitted from the theories of eminent men. Treaties have proven themselves useful statements which can be agreed upon by participating states.

The following chapter shows how international aviation law continued this development with certain new rules made necessary by the new and remarkable capabilities of aircraft.

NOTES

[1] Michael J. Hart, *Outline of International Aviation Law* (St. Louis: Parks College of St. Louis University, 1975), p. 1-3.

[2] T. W. Wallbank, A. M. Taylor, and N. M. Bailkey, *Civilization* (Chicago: Scott, Foresman and Co., 1965), I, pp. 358-59.

[3] Alexis de Tocqueville, *Democracy in America*, preface by Richard D. Heffner, (New York: Mentor Books, 1956), p. 265.

[4] Gerhard von Glahn, *Law Among Nations* (New York: Macmillan Publishing Co., Inc., 1976), 557-58.

[5] Rene David and John E. C. Brierley, *Major Legal Systems in the World Today* (New York: Macmillan Publishing Co., Inc., 1978), p. 1; Joseph R. Strayer, Hans W. Gatzke, and E. H. Harbison, *The Course of Civilization* (New York: Harcourt, Brace and World, Inc., 1961), pp. 357-59, 399.

[6] Strayer, Gatzke, Harbison, pp. 574, 598.

[7] *Ibid.*, p. 591; Hart, p. 15.

[8] Hart, p. 16.

[9] von Glahn, pp. 65-66; Hart, p. 28.

[10] von Glahn, pp. 70-71.

[11] Hart, p. 18; von Glahn, pp. 90-95; David and Brierley, pp. 520-21.

[12] von Glahn, pp. 350-51.

[13]*Ibid.*, pp. 317, 360-66; David and Brierley, p. 82.

[14]von Glahn, pp. 21, 39, 42.

[15]Hart, pp. 26-27; von Glahn, pp. 39-43, 568, 573, 625, 648; David and Brierley, p. 35.

[16]Hart, pp. 28-30. All but Russia conceded the right of innocent passage of warships.

[17]Rene A. Wormser, *The Story of the Law* (New York: Simon and Schuster, 1962), pp. 388-91.

[18]von Glahn, p. 124.

[19]*Ibid.*, pp. 309-17, 361.

[20]Hart, p. 25.

[21]von Glahn, pp. 325-26, 333; Hart, pp. 32-34; Gerard Pucci, *Aviation Law* (Dubuque, Iowa: Kendall/Hunt Publishing Co., 1977), pp. 13-19 sec. 5.

[22]von Glahn, p. 346.

[23]*Ibid.*, pp. 350-56, 361-66.

[24]Hart, pp. 37-42; David and Brierley, pp. 333-34.

[25]von Glahn, pp. 11-14, 421; Hart, pp. 43-45; David and Brierley, pp. 429, 432, 515.

[26]Paul MacKendrick, and others, *Western Civilization* (New York: Harper and Row, Publishers, Inc., 1968), pp. 280, 489.

CHAPTER 17

INTERNATIONAL AIR LAW: TREATY NEGOTIATION

Jurisdiction Over National Airspace

As balloons and aircraft took to the air, it became necessary to determine who owned the air above national territory. Was the air free to all as were the high seas? Some debated this but reserved only the first thousand feet above a nation's surface to the state. Aircraft at this time were flimsy and appealing, remember. It was soon obvious, however, that allowing foreign aircraft to fly above one's nation had its risks. Even the right to cross over, claiming the right of innocent passage, was eventually denied.[1]

As World War I began, the European states involved hurried to declare complete sovereignty over their airspace with no upper limit. Legally, matters rested here until the advent of satellites and space vehicles altered this lack of an upper limit to national airspace sovereignty. National sovereignty includes, incidentally, the airspace over the territorial seas of a nation.[2]

Right of Innocent Passage

There is no actual right of innocent passage today; but, rather, nations generally have granted certain rights of innocent passage. Foreign aircraft, it is acknowledged by the world aviation community, can be required to land only at designated port-of-entry airports, keep to assigned air corridors, and notify the host nation of their movements by means of a flight plan.

In the interests of national defense, a state may require a plane to land and show its registration. Further, certain areas may be set aside as being definitely off-limits to foreign aircraft. Even penetration of airspace adjacent to a nation may require notification, a filed notice, as for example, penetration of the U.S. Air Defense Identification Zones (ADIZ).

Aircraft in distress may land at any point, just as vessels in distress may seek refuge at the nearest port. This is a long recognized right. Customs regulations may still apply, however, for any landing on national territory by a foreign aircraft, even though an emergency caused the landing. Even military planes can seek refuge due to bad weather or mechanical malfunction. They must obey an order to land, however, or risk being forced down. Many international disagreements have arisen from such intrusions.

No one can contest the legal right of a nation to defend itself.[3]

The High Seas

No nation controls the airspace above the high seas. Most nations recognize as territorial waters those within three miles of the coast. Recently the United States has extended her marine influence to a 200 mile wide belt known as "an economic zone." Other nations have varying zones near their coastlines over which they claim jurisdiction.[4]

International Law Today

In spite of media attention to violations of treaties and some international disagreement, hundreds of treaties are operating smoothly. Air service is so valuable that those treaties dealing with aircraft are honored across the world. World law is affecting national law since certain principles are so universally recognized.

Disputes relating to air carriage are arbitrated in several world tribunals and via negotiations between states. True, some are not resolved, yet procedures for reaching agreement have been established. So long as each nation claims complete sovereignty, however, so long will international disputes occur as each vies for advantage.

The Hague Conferences

By the end of the nineteenth century in Europe there arose serious consideration of the possible uses of aerial vehicles during wartime. By this time balloons had been employed during the Franco-Prussia War to carry newspapers and mail from Paris while that city was surrounded by Prussian forces. The Hague Conference of 1899[5] resulted, among other things, in a declaration that prohibited at that time "the discharge of projectiles and explosives from balloons and by other new methods of a similar nature."

283

Aircraft, with the exception of kites and balloons, had not yet been successfully flown but many inventors were working on the problems of manned flight. Still, in 1906 the Institute of International Air Law, made up of legal experts from several nations, adopted a convention stating plainly that states overflown had definite air rights.

At the Second Hague Conference in 1907 the declaration was renewed to prohibit the use of aircraft in times of war between the contracting nations until the end of a Third Peace Conference. Few states (nations) had signed the first instrument. The second one also had little success in being signed, due to the breakthroughs in the science of flying then taking place in the United States and Europe. The major powers now wished to await developments in order to hold possible military advantage.[6]

The failure of the Hague Rules of Air Warfare to be ratified by participating nations again left international aerial law, with respect to the use of aircraft during wartime, quite unresolved.[7]

During the Italo-Turkish War of 1911-12 Italian military balloonists dropped explosive bombs on Turkish military targets. Balloons were also used for aerial reconnaissance.

An Early International Legal Code

A committee made up of lawyers, jurists, and students of international law was organized in 1909 in Paris. Committee members came from most of the European countries, the United States, and South American countries. An executive committee in Paris acted for committees in each country to make a general study of the points of law involved in air commerce between nations. The goal of the Paris committee was to obtain agreement upon an outline of rules of the air.

Annual congresses of the International Judiric Committee passed on the text of a legal code for aviation in Paris in 1911, at Geneva in 1912, and at Frankfurt in 1913.[8]

The Aero Club of America

The Aero Club of America, affiliated with the Federation Aeronautique Nationale, in unofficial action licensed pilots in the early days of flying in the

284

United States. The Aero Club also drew up an early set of rules of flight in order to promote air safety.[9]

Institute of International Air Law

In 1911 the Institute of International Air Law meeting in Madrid proposed that aircraft bear identifying markings, that they be privately or publicly owned and be of the nationality of their registry. The Institute had been at work on the legal problems of international air commerce since 1902.[10]

By 1914, with the outbreak of World War II in Europe, primitive aircraft and quite sophisticated dirigibles began to be used. Again, troops were located and troop movements plotted from the air. Limited bombing began. There were orders given aviators on both sides to limit bombing to strategic military targets but early aircraft and equipment lacked precision; therefore civilians often suffered.

Jurisdiction of National Airspace

Since planes could cross national boundaries so easily and were nearly impossible to stop, legal questions arose as to accidental penetrations and innocent passage as well as aerial, military spy, and attack penetration. Each country's national airspace belongs to that nation. Every nation, therefore, has a perfect right to prohibit passage and to seize or even destroy unauthorized aircraft penetrating national airspace.

In the Western hemisphere in 1916 the Pan American Aeronautic Federation met at Santiago, Chile. It was decided that airspace belonged to the nation below it but was free to aircraft of American states. The Federation noted that aircraft had a nationality and might bear identification markings.[11]

Again, as with the work of the Institutes of International Air Law, there was no formal acceptance (ratification) but a foundation of theory had at least been achieved.

Attempts to Write Rules for Air Warfare

Since bombing of other than military targets was difficult to define or to

285

prevent, the rules governing land warfare proved to be inadequate to govern air warfare. After World War I there were planners who sought to write a separate code to cover air warfare.

Military commanders, however, saw the potential uses of the airplane in wartime and effectively blocked treaties and agreements that would hamper their development of this new weapon. The Aerial Navigation Convention of 1919 (Article 38) left the use of aircraft in wartime quite open. Nor did the Washington Conference of 1921-22 succeed in writing an effective agreement. Still, representatives were conferring and agreements were at least drafted. Further, commissions of legal experts were set up to study the matter further.[12]

The Paris Convention

At the Versailles meeting, 1919, a convention was adopted on 13 October which would rule air commerce in Europe for the next twenty years.[13] The "Paris Convention," whose formal name was the International Convention for the Regulation of Air Navigation, agreed that:

1. nations own the air above their land and water,

2. the privilege of innocent passage may be granted by nations (with exceptions as to place and cargo).

3. airworthiness certification is required from the country of aircraft registry.

4. crew certification of competency is needed from the country of aircraft registry.

5. aircraft must carry documents such as airworthiness and registration certificates.

6. the cabotage rights of nations to favor their own aircraft are valid.

7. a deposit of funds (security) might be made to host nations to prevent the seizure of an aircraft due to a claim for design or mechanical patent infringement. (Early plane manufacturers jealously guarded their prototypes, for the science of aeronautics was so very new that each improvement in design gave a manufacturer a great advantage.)

Aerial Application of the Right of Angary

Modern rules of warfare, based on medieval wartime custom, allow warring nations the right to seize a neutral's goods or vehicles whether on the high seas, on their own territory, or on the territory of another belligerent. Compensation is eventually paid to the neutral for the use of this property. This seizure is known as the "right to angary."

Aircraft flown into areas of political conflict run this risk. The crews cannot legally be put into the belligerent's service, but such personnel can be interned. Further, flight into war zones is obviously a high-risk venture. Flights of Red Cross planes are less apt to be involved in the conflicts but still run major risks.

Following the takeover of the government of Cuba by Dr. Fidel Castro, some United States pilots flew to Cuba to bomb that country. These were primarily "larks," but were hazardous to relations between the United States and Cuba. The United States government stopped the flights by stating that crews of these planes could lose their United States citizenship by such unauthorized actions and might suffer penalties and fines.

The Hague Rules of Air Warfare (1923)

A group of jurists, representing nations of Europe, gathered at The Hague in 1922 to draft a convention covering the use of aircraft during times of war. Rules governing this matter were proposed and were known as the "Hague Rules of 1923."

As was so often the case, excellent legal ideas were worked out, yet the nations concerned failed to ratify the convention. Still, some basic rules of custom had been established.[14] A number of nations voluntarily announced that they would abide by the Hague Rules of Air Warfare. It was only practical, for example, to:

1. give neutral nations the right to refuse the aircraft of warring nations admittance to the neutral's airspace.

2. allow, if force were required to protect one's airspace, after a clear statement of this possibility, the neutral to use force to prevent planes from penetrating its airspace.

3. permit a neutral nation to move goods, including aircraft, through its jurisdiction at will. This does not mean launching aircraft or missiles for one warring nation, of course, to attack another belligerent. Nor should a neutral openly move aircraft to aid one belligerent against another.

4. obligate neutral nations to intern the crews and the aircraft of warring nations, if these aircraft enter the neutral's airspace.

5. deny the right to mount an aerial blockage. (This last recommendation proved to be difficult to enforce.)

CITEJA

The role of the Comite International Technique d'Experts Juridiques Aeriens (CITEJA) was to decide on matters dealing with private air law. Representatives from countries concerned with air commerce formed CITEJA and began to meet in 1925.

CITEJA, as a committee of the Conference Internationales de Droit Prive Aeriens (CIDPA), submitted its work to CIDPA for approval. If the approval was granted, CIDPA then referred the proposed conventions to the governments involved for ratification. CITEJA prepared very important conventions. These included the Warsaw Convention of 1929 on the air carriage of property and persons; conventions regarding damage by aircraft to persons or property on the ground and precautionary arrest dictums; the convention on the salvage of aircraft at sea; and the Convention of Rome insurance protocol.

In 1936 at Paris CITEJA worked out basic understandings regarding air commerce that provided a legal foundation for future international air law. At the 1936 conference seven matters were considered:

1. The interpretation of conventions as to whether matters properly belonged to the committee or to the judiciary.

2. The hiring and chartering of aircraft.

3. The overall limitations of liability for aircraft.

4. Matters to do with the land salvage of aircraft and saving lives in wilderness areas.

5. The insurance of aircraft engaged in international flight.

6. Aviation salvage at sea questions.

7. The legal status and documentation of air crew personnel engaged in international flight.

CITEJA continued its invaluable work through its plenary session in 1936 at Berne, Switzerland, where liability and salvage questions were considered. At Bucharest, Romania, in September 1937, CITEJA worked on the legal status of air crew members. In May 1938 in Paris, CITEJA again took up the subject of air crew members and their rights and responsibilities.[15]

The work of CITEJA was carried on by the Provisional International Civil Aviation Organization (PICAO), established by the International Civil Aviation Convention of 1944. From PICAO a permanent organization emerged, the International Civil Aviation Organization (ICAO). (ICAO will be discussed in some detail in a later chapter.)[16]

The Madrid Convention

The Ibero-American Convention, known as the "Madrid Convention," met in Madrid in 1926. The agreements worked out have since been superseded. Still, groundwork was laid for later meetings of representatives from Latin-American countries.[17]

The Havana Convention of 1931

Representatives of civil aviation in the Americas met in Havana in 1928 to work out a uniform international air law for the Americas. The conference was termed the "Havana Convention." The formal title was The Pan-American Convention, Havana, 1928.

The Havana Convention contained provisions similar to those of the Paris Agreement. An exception was that a nation might refuse to recognize another nation's airworthiness certificate. Also, the Havana Convention allowed foreign carriers to discharge cargo and passengers and then proceed on into a country for a landing at another airport.

The Havana Convention was signed in 1928 and ratified by most American nations. The rules of this agreement prevailed from 1928 to 1944.[18]

Treaty Terminology

With the ratification by the United States of the Havana Convention in 1931, the United States began a long series of agreements which also were in effect international treaties. These documents were to bear several names, that is, "convention," "concordat," "treaty" and "protocol." All of these terms generally have the same meaning.

There are differences on occasion, however, as in the use of the term "protocol" to show that a convention has been amended to some extent. In 1955, for instance, the Hague Protocol revised the Warsaw Convention of 1929.

United States law rules that all American international treaties are considered "the law of the land." The states, for instance Virginia, cannot negotiate an international treaty. The Constitution of the United States (Article I, Section 10) decrees that only the Federal government may treat with foreign powers.

The President of the United States is directed by the Constitution to make treaties with the advice and consent of the Senate. (This is the formal and exact term denoting an actual "treaty".) In practice the President alone often negotiates the treaty, giving Congress only the information he wishes to give. President Franklin D. Roosevelt at several times during World War II made such international agreements.

Formal treaties between nations, however, are not self activating but need the assent of a legislature. This is especially true in cases in which U.S. funds must be appropriated, a power reserved to the Congress. Should the United States Senate wish to amend a treaty presented to it, then all parties must assent to the changes. This may well involve renegotiation of the points affected.

A principle has emerged based on James Madison's theory that Congress might annul a treaty. Scholars generally agree that a Congressional Act is always paramount over a treaty. There is argument against this however, and the only way to resolve the argument would be to obtain a Supreme Court decision.

Executive Agreements. Until the administration of Franklin D. Roosevelt, executive agreements were only used for rather minor matters. FDR's executive agreements changed all this. His agreements virtually changed us from a neutral to a belligerent in World War II. Also, in agreements between heads of state during that war, at Tehran, Yalta and Potsdam the right to make executive agreements was exercised. With or without the authorization of Congress these are recognized by courts as binding on the United States. Is this a modern, streamlined approach to international negotiation? Or is it an evidence of the development of an "Imperial Presidency?"

In 1967, only 13 of 288 agreements required Senate action and were actually treaties. However, many of these agreements were so important in foreign policy that they really should have been ratified by Congress. The only difference between a treaty and an executive agreement is the decision of the President! He may submit it to the Senate or not. Obviously this gives a president great power.

Treaties in Effect. A nation may choose to ratify a treaty "with reservations," that is conditionally. If the treaty is to be in effect, the other state or states concerned in the treaty must accept this reservation.

The "abrogation" of a treaty is the revocation of an agreement by one of the nations involved. Whether justified or not, this is a right of world states. A treaty may also terminate due to mutual agreement, due to an original time limit set for its expiration, or due to its conflict with a new international rule.

Ratification. International treaties are not legally considered to be in effect until the governments concerned have "ratified" them by assent of their legislatures or executives. Those ratifying the treaty may consider themselves bound by it, or it may be written into the document that it becomes effective only upon ratification by a stated number of member nations. It is not entirely clear when treaties do become effective since they may actually be in effect prior to ratification. Indeed, some nations choose to adhere to a treaty without having been one of the original signers.

Annexes. As conditions require changes, "annexes" can be attached to existing treaties. These are often of a technical nature and are worked out to solve an obvious need.

Department of State Formal Notes. To record certain agreements between nations the U.S. State Department sends formal "notes" to the nations concerned. Subjects covered range from agreements to allow civil aircraft to use a foreign airfield or postal matters. Official notes offer a means of tying down arrangements in a flexible way which is less formal than treaty negotiation.

291

Notes are also used, of course, to express protest over actions of a foreign nation. In general, formal State Department notes constitute a form of treaty and a mode of communication for expressing international agreement or disagreement.

The Warsaw Convention

The Second International Diplomatic Conference on Private Air Law, later to be known as the "Warsaw Convention," met in Warsaw, Poland, in 1929. The conference was called to establish some criteria agreeable to the nations of the world to compensate air customers for the loss of air cargo or baggage. Also, there was a need to establish airline liability limits for the injury or loss of life of airline passengers. Further, more uniformity was sought in waybill, claim check, and ticket documentation.

Prior to 1929 the rights of passengers and/or the owners of goods involved in air carriage had never been clearly defined. The 1929 conference was designed to solve this problem.

The conference drafted the Convention for the Unification of Certain Rules Relating to International Transportation by Air and a Protocol (addition) thereto. The members of the conference signed the document 12 October 1929. The United States accepted the Warsaw Convention (with reservations as to government-owned or operated aircraft). Upon its ratification 15 June 1934 the Warsaw Convention and its provisions became binding on U.S. airplane owners and operators. Over one hundred governments accepted the Warsaw Convention.[19]

The five chapters of the Warsaw Convention applied to the international carriage of persons, baggage, or property, by an air carrier for compensation. They are:

1. Scope — Definition (Articles 1 and 2)

2. Transportation Documents

    Passenger Ticket (Article 3)

    Baggage Check (Article 4)

    Air Waybill (Articles 5 through 16)

3. Liability of the Carrier (Articles 17 through 30)

4. Provisions Relating to Combined Transportation (Article 31)

5. General and Final Provisions (Articles 32 through 41)

The provisions of the convention set forth the rights of passengers, shippers and consignees in the field of air transportation and provide for the enforcement of those rights.

The most difficult parts of the convention to write dealt with the liabilities that air carriers should assume. In the Warsaw Convention there are provisions which place limited liability on the air carrier in cases of accident or delay and note conditions in which the carrier is open to unlimited liabilities.

The limit of liability for the injury or death of a person was set at 125,000 gold francs or around $8,300. Only if the claimant could prove willful misconduct on the part of the carrier could unlimited liability be asked.

The airline responsibility for the loss of air freight was set at about $10 per kilogram of weight. The liability of the carrier for the loss or damage to baggage was set at approximately $330, at the time of the signing of the convention.

To effect recovery of damages, the plaintiff must file actions where the carrier has its home headquarters or has a principal place of business, or at the place of destination. The plaintiff has the option to choose between these.

According to the provisions of the Warsaw Convention, the carrier is liable for the death or injury of a passenger *prima face* (on the face of it, at first sight). This applies to loss or damage to goods or luggage. Further, the carrier is liable for delays of passengers, luggage, or goods. The carrier's liability is limited, however, unless its willful misconduct can be proved.

Several defenses were available to the carriers such as not being negligent, that there was contributory negligence by the claimant, or that the claim was not filed under the time limits set by the Warsaw Convention.

In the convention the ticket, baggage claim check, and the freight waybill assumed the form and force of a contract. Unless these documents were issued by the carrier, the carrier was not responsible for the transport of the passenger, luggage, or goods involved.

There are instances, however, by which claimants have been successful in claiming unlimited liability, one being cases in which it is asserted that a ticket was not "properly delivered" according to the terms of the Warsaw Convention.

By properly delivered, it is meant that the ticket is mailed or presented to the passenger. Also, on another occasion, a claimant contested on the grounds that the ticket or waybill did not carry legible mention of the Warsaw Convention. Each ticket is required to carry the name of the carrier, state that it is a member of the Warsaw Convention and so subject to the rules of the convention.

A factor overriding the Warsaw Convention is the recognized law of venue, or place. The laws of the nation at the accident location prevail. If, for example, the site of an accident is in Spain, the laws of Spain prevail.

Plagued by the unfairness of limited liability, the United States in November 1965 denounced the Warsaw Convention and planned to withdraw from the treaty effective May 1966 unless revisions were made.[20] In 1966 the Montreal Agreement, modifying the Warsaw Convention was drawn up and met the U.S. requirements more fully. This enabled the U.S. to continue as a member of the Warsaw Convention under the new provisions of the Montreal Agreement.

The Montreal Agreement

Among other things, the Montreal Agreement increases airline liability to $75,000 in cases in which a ticket is sold in the United States or when a scheduled point of departure, arrival, or stop is in the United States.

The Montreal Agreement provides for a readable notice to be given to each passenger citing the limits of the airline's liability. This is, as noted above, in the United States limited to $75,000 per person and approximately $8,300 during flights of an international nature outside the United States.[21]

The carrier is absolutely liable in most cases under the terms of the Montreal Agreement. Most international carriers and members of the worldwide International Air Transport Association (IATA) have signed the agreement. The IATA is an association of international air carriers. It is not a governmental association albeit some member airlines are government controlled carriers.

The Rome Conventions, 1933 and 1952

The Warsaw Convention provided passengers and shippers a measure of protection, yet it soon became apparent that there was a need for some code of regulation agreeable to the nations of the world to offer reimbursement to

294

third parties on the ground or water, if harmed or damaged by aircraft operation. A conference of concerned national representatives met at Rome in 1933 to work out an acceptable set of rules covering such liability incurred by air carriers. Formally named the Rome Convention for the Unification of Certain Rules Relating to Damages Caused by Aircraft to Third Parties on the Surface, it was dated 29 May 1933, and was signed in Rome by the United States, but declared to apply only within the continental limits of the United States, not including the (then) Territory of Alaska.[22] A maximum liability was set for damage to third parties on the ground caused by aircraft and exonerated the aircraft operator from liability under certain circumstances. Customs, military, or police aircraft are excluded from the provisions of the convention.

The convention was not ratified by the United States and so had no legal effect in the U.S. Another attempt to get agreement on this problem of compensation to third parties on the ground was made by writing the Rome Surface Damage Convention. This was signed at Rome 7 October 1952, but the U.S. did not sign nor ratify this convention. The Rome conventions are discussed here to illustrate the manner in which legal experts attempted to work out the problems of international air commerce in the 1930s and later.

The United States line of reasoning is that each nation should make the decision as to whether or not to allow an airline to come into the country without insurance against third party injury or loss. If permitted to enter without such insurance a carrier risks unlimited liability should such a third party loss occur. Obviously United States air carriers are well insured and accept certain liabilities as a matter of course.

Eventually nineteen states agreed to the Rome Convetion[23]

A Public Health Agreement

The International Sanitary Convention for Aerial Navigation was adopted by the permanent committee of the International Public Health Office on 29 April 1933. The United States ratified the treaty with reservations on 13 June 1935 and the President of the United States proclaimed it 25 October 1935.

The goal of this convention was to prescribe sanitary standards for airports, to expedite air travel through epidemic-stricken areas, and to meet the need for public health documents carried by passengers and air crew members on international flights.[24]

The Lima Conference

In 1937 the United States and ten Latin-American countries met in Lima, Peru, to establish a Permanent American Aeronautical Commission (CAPA) to work out a code of international public and private air law.

The CAPA was designed to help the member nations to coordinate and develop technical matters pertaining to aircraft, pilots, air navigational aids, airways, airports, weather services, and radio communication equipment and procedures.

The U.S., Argentina, Brazil, Chile, Colombia, Ecuador, Mexico, Panama, Peru, Uruguay, and Venezuela participated. The commission proved to be a useful one in working out the above-mentioned and other matters pertaining to aviation in the Americas.[25]

Wartime Rules Needed

Cruel bombing of civilian populations during the Japan-China conflict and during the Civil War in Spain pointed to the urgency of the development of some international code of conduct for aerial warfare. The League of Nations spoke out adopting three proposals made in 1938 by Great Britain's Prime Minister which urged belligerents not to deliberately bomb civilians nor civil property but to restrict aerial attack to strictly military targets.

Yet only two years later this principle of protecting civilians lay in ruins. Germany's deliberate use of aircraft to panic civilians and hamper military movements, and to destroy civil cities began. Great Britain retaliated. In the 1940's strategic bombing without warning was an accepted form of warfare. In the case of the United States atomic attacks upon Japan, however, leaflet warnings were dropped. Vestiges or responsibility did persist on all sides, but limited the use of aircraft, bombs and missiles very little.

Chicago Convention 1944

The U.S. near the conclusion of World War II, decided to aggressively promote international air commerce. It was recognized that the Paris and Havana Conventions were not going to be adequate for postwar commercial aviation.

Following a U.N. conference in 1944, non-Axis states were invited to convene at Chicago to consider new procedures to establish greater cooperation in international air commerce. Delegates from fifty-two states met for seven weeks and adopted an agreement called the "Chicago Convention," known formally as the Convention on International Civil Aviation. Since that time it has been ratified or adhered to by over one hundred nations and is the foundation for all international air commerce as it exists today.

The Chicago Convention's 96 articles establish the privileges and restrictions of all contracting states, provide for the adoption of international standards, recommend practices regulating air navigation, the installation of navigation facilities by member states, and further recommend the facilitation of air transportation by the reduction of customs and immigration formalities.[26]

Article I restates the sovereignty concept: "The contracting states recognize that every state has complete and exclusive sovereignty over the airspace above its territory." The Convention is applicable to civil aircraft only, not state aircraft (military, etc.). It provides for the passage of non-scheduled aircraft (subject to certain terms) but it expressly states that scheduled aircraft may not be operated for or into a territory of another state without the special permission or authorization of that state.

Article VI includes: "No scheduled international air service may be operated over or into the territory of a contracting state, except with the special permission or other authorization of that state, and in accordance with the terms of such permission or authorization."

Article VII sets out the cabotage rights of the states: "Each contracting State shall have the right to refuse permission to the aircraft of other contracting states to take on in its territory passengers, mail and cargo carried for remuneration or hire and destined for another point within its territory. Each contracting State undertakes not to enter into any arrangements which specially grant any such privilege on an exclusive basis to any other state or an airline of any other state, and not to obtain any such exclusive privilege from any other state." That is, a nation may favor its own planes but may not favor those from any other state.

Members of the Convention on International Civil Aviation, the Chicago Convention, agreed that:

1. States may have prohibited areas, may forbid aerial entry into these.

297

2. Airports of entry should be set up in each member nation.

3. Member states are to open their airspace to all nations equally.

4. Fees charged shall be standard for all foreign air carriers.

5. Fees charged shall be published and given to ICAO for publication.

6. All aircraft shall be registered and marked with identification codes.

The Chicago Convention also included the provision that rules were to be set regarding air navigation procedures and equipment; to standardize procedures for assisting aircraft in distress; and to govern the investigation of accidents.

The convention recommended the standardization of airports, radio service, weather services, air navigational facilities, communications procedures, operational rules of flight, and maps and charts.

Further, standardization was to extend to the appropriate papers to be carried in aircraft including the passenger listing. Planes belonging to the countries represented by members of the convention, it was agreed, are to carry cargo manifests and declarations.[27]

The members of the Chicago Convention envisioned a worldwide air transportation system in which pilots, ticket agents, baggage handlers, controllers, and many others could work smoothly together using carefully standardized procedures. The obvious need for such a system was helpful in reaching decisions. The work of the representatives to the Chicago Convention, however, deserves great credit for working out procedures and rules agreeable to so many nations.[28]

International Air Services Transit Agreement

Drawn up at Chicago on 7 December 1944 were two agreements which were separate from the Chicago Convention. One of these was the International Air Services Transit Agreement which states that:[29]

ARTICLE I

Section 1

Each contracting State grants to the other contracting States the following freedoms of the air in respect of scheduled international air services:

(1) The privilege to fly across its territory without landing;

298

(2)   The privilege to land for non-traffic purposes.

The privileges of this section shall not be applicable with respect to airports utilized for military purposes to the exclusion of any scheduled international air services. In areas of active hostilities or of military occupation, and in time of war along the supply routes leading to such areas, the exercise of such privileges shall be subject to the approval of the competent military authorities.

This agreement is known as the Two Freedoms Agreement. The delegates to the International Civil Aviation Conference, which convened in Chicago on 1 November 1944, signed the document on 7 December 1944. By 28 February 1945 the agreement had been signed by thirty-three countries including the United States.[30]

The International Air Transport Agreement

The second of the two agreements drawn up at Chicago, which are separate from the Chicago Convention, is known as the "Five Freedoms Agreement." Members of the International Civil Aviation Organization (ICAO) opened this agreement for signature on 7 December 1944. By 28 February 1945 twenty-one countries, including the United States had signed the document.

As Article I of the agreement states, the five freedoms granted to those nations accepting it are:

ARTICLE I

Section 1

Each contracting State grants to the other contracting States the following freedoms of the air in respect to scheduled international air services:

(1)   The privilege to fly across its territory without landing;

(2)   The privilege to land for non-traffic purposes;

(3)   The privilege to put down passengers, mail and cargo taken on in the territory of the State whose nationality the aircraft possesses;

(4)   The privilege to take on passengers, mail and cargo destined for the territory of the State whose nationality the aircraft possesses;

(5)   The privilege to take on passengers, mail and cargo destined for the territory of any other contracting State and the privilege to put down passengers, mail and cargo coming from any such territory.
. . . .

The agreement spells out in detail the procedures for carrying out the five privileges of transit and allows the country being entered the right to refuse entry under certain conditions.[31]

The Geneva Convention, 1948

In 1948 representatives of many countries interested in air transport met at Geneva to discuss the problems associated with mortgages and liens on aircraft. The Geneva Convention on the Recognition of Rights in Aircraft, has therefore often been called the "Mortgage Convention."

Unless lenders are able to claim aircraft in default of payment, the needed financing of aircraft to be used on international routes would be difficult to obtain. The members of the convention met to devise ways of protecting the rights of those purchasing aircraft or lending money with the aircraft as security.

Under the terms of the convention, properly recorded mortgages or a *hypotheque* (a French term for the right to secure property for debt) are both recognized. The aircraft need not be in the possession of the mortgage holder to offer that holder a valid claim to whole or partial ownership of the aircraft. The possession of the aircraft together with a lease made in good faith, or a purchase agreement, creates a strong legal position for the operator of the aircraft. Liens placed on the aircraft to serve as security for debts are recognized by the Geneva Convention.

The methods of legally recording claims to ownership, liens, and mortgages are carefully outlined in the convention.

According to the convention, an aircraft may be seized and sold under the laws of the nation involved. A month's notice of sale of an aircraft so seized is required at the place of registry, and the registered owner must be notified by mail prior to the sale. After the sale of the aircraft, the holder of the first recorded lien has first claim on the proceeds. There are certain exceptions to this sequence. For example, the judgement creditor for damage suffered on the surface due to aircraft operation has a claim that has high precedence. Due to the possible exceptions, mortgagors should insure the plane to cover such possible claims. Interestingly enough, the aircraft spare parts that are with the plane or kept for it, are considered a part of the aircraft. Since aircraft spares can include large subcomponents and engines, this is an important consideration.

The Geneva Convention was signed at Geneva on 19 June 1948. It went into force for the United States on 17 September 1953. The more nations that become members of this convention, naturally, the more effective it will be. At this time thirty-eight nations are currently parties to this multilateral convention.[32]

Rome Convention of 1952

There was a long-standing need among nations to agree upon some uniform mode of settling claims for damage caused by aircraft to third parties on the surface. Work on such an agreement began in 1933 in Rome and continued periodically. In 1952 a conference of interested parties met again in Rome and wrote a proposed convention. This was important work in that it laid out certain possible provisions for settling claims.

For example, the carrier was made absolutely liable with few exceptions; a limit was set to the carrier's liabilities; and carriers were required to carry insurance against possible claims by third parties on the ground. No limit to a carrier's liability was set in the event that the aircraft caused damage to third parties on the ground through a deliberate omission or act of the carrier. The aircraft is defined as being covered by the Rome Convention from the onset of takeoff power to the end of the landing roll.

The policies and limits of compensation were not satisfactory to the U.S. representatives. The United States did not become a member of the Rome Convention.[33]

The Hague Protocol of 1955 and the
Guatemala City Protocol of 1971

The Hague Protocol was written by members of a group of representatives from interested governments who met at the Hague in September 1955. The Hague Protocol amended the Warsaw Convention by doubling the liability limit for personal injury or death to be borne by the air carrier from $8,300 to $16,600 per person. Further, the protocol extended to the agents of the air carrier the limitation of liability now provided to the carrier. On 1 December 1964 the United States signed the protocol despite some controversy over what many considered still inadequate liability borne by carriers.

The Guatemala City Protocol of 1971 was designed to solve some of the problems of air carrier liability that the nations of the world had not been able to agree upon. The protocol proposed that the basic Warsaw Convention and the Hague Protocol be regarded as one instrument: the Warsaw Convention as amended at the Hague in 1955, and at Guatemala City in 1971.

To date the Guatemala City Protocol has not been ratified by the United States.[34]

The Montreal Agreement of 1966

The 1966 Montreal Agreement amended the Warsaw Convention to the extent that the United States, dissatisfied with the Warsaw Convention's low limits to liability, could remain a member of the Warsaw Convention.[35]

The liability of a carrier was raised to a $75,000 per person limit in the United States and left as agreed upon in the Warsaw Convention and the 1955 Hague Protocol for other international travel. It is stated in the 1966 Montreal Agreement that the ticket is in effect a contract between the passenger and the carrier and that clear terms must be set forth in a legible manner.

Willful misconduct still remains a possible grounds for suit with unlimited liability. The carrier still must shoulder strict liability for the safety of its passengers and cargo. Even contributory negligence may not be entered as a defense by the carrier to this liability.

Most member nations of the Warsaw Convention have signed the Montreal Agreement.

Bermuda-Type Agreements

Since it was difficult to get agreement among several nations at once in multilateral conferences, representatives of the United States and Great Britain met in Bermuda to discuss their civil aviation problems.

These representatives did their work so well that "Bermuda-type" agreements are now standard types of U.S. bilateral civil air agreements. For one thing, the Bermuda Agreement worked out between Great Britain and the

United States proved to be fairly easy to amend. This gave it a flexibility that could respond to changing national and aeronautical needs.

Routes are subject to yearly renegotiation. The agreement can be ended upon one year's notice.

Talks on the Bermuda 2 Agreement began 9 September 1976 and resulted, after eight rounds of meetings during 1976 and 1977, in a final agreement signed 23 July 1977 in Bermuda.

In a joint statement, the leaders of the United Kingdom and United States delegations explained the new agreement. They noted that Bermuda 2 replaces the first Bermuda Agreement signed in Bermuda. Thirty-one years before and expiring 21 June 1977. The old agreement was continued temporarily until Bermuda 2 could come into force. As the joint statement noted:

> More American cities are being opened to nonstop flights to and from Great Britain. In the first three years of the agreement, United States airlines will be authorized to serve Atlanta and Dallas/Fort Worth nonstop to London; a British airline will be authorized to serve Houston nonstop. After this three year period, airlines of both nations will be authorized nonstop service on these routes; one-stop services may be operated immediately. In addition, after three years the United States will be free to select a new gateway point for nonstop air services to London. British competition to the present United States flag service from Seattle to London will be permitted in the new agreement. In addition, the United States receives the rights to fly between Anchorage and London, a route that British Airways today operate en route to Tokyo. The present requirement that London-San Francisco flights by a United Kingdom airline operate via New York will be dropped. As a result, British Airways intend to inaugurate London-San Francisco nonstop flights on 1 April 1978.

> As soon as appropriate designations have been made and operating permits issued, services between the relevant points may begin. In the case of Houston the selected British carrier, British Caledonia Airways Ltd., plans to start operations on October 23. In the case of new U.S. airline nonstop services, authorization must be first obtained from the U.S. Civil Aeronautics Board (CAB).

> In addition to the new nonstop services, British airlines will be free to combine their U.S. points on each route as they choose. U.S. airlines will be permitted, subject to U.S. CAB approval, to operate direct flights to London from any U.S. city with an intermediate stop at one of the fourteen designated U.S. gateway cities. Moreover, U.S. flights may continue beyond London to any other city with transit and on-line connecting traffic rights; U.K. airlines will be permitted to operate flights from Europe through London to the United States and points beyond.

> On the North Atlantic the problem of "excess capacity" will be of continuing concern to the two nations. The Agreement provides a consultative process to deal with cases of excess provision of capacity, while ensuring that the designated airlines retain adequate scope for managerial initiative in establishing schedules and that the overall market share achieved by each designated airline

will depend upon passenger choice rather than the operation of any formula or limitation mechanism. It is also the objective of the two nations to avoid unduly frequent invocation of this consultative mechanism in order to avoid an undue burden of detailed supervision of airline scheduling by governments. The hope of the two nations is that these provisions will lead to the better use of resources and help to keep fares down.

New machinery has also been instituted to cope with problems of fares and rates on services between the territories of the two nations. A Tariff Working Group is being set up to review standards for ratesetting and make recommendations on pricing policy. The two governments hope these recommendations will lead to air fares that are more competitive and better attuned to the requirements of the public.

The United States and the United Kingdom will each have two passenger airlines authorized to operate the Transatlantic route between London and New York — British Airways, Laker Airways, Pan American and TWA. The new Laker Airways Skytrain service is due to start on or about 26 September; competitive services by the other airlines on the New York-London route are proposed. Each side is permitted one other Transatlantic route of its choice on which it may designate two airlines for passenger services. On other transatlantic routes, each nation may designate only one airline for passenger services. For routes and services in other market areas there is no general limitation on the number of designated airlines.

In the Pacific a United Kingdom airline has received additional rights between Hong Kong and the American West Coast via Japan. United States airlines have obtained certain new operating rights between Hong Kong and Singapore and between Osaka and Hong Kong.

All existing U.S. routes to Bermuda have been renewed. Atlanta, Miami and Philadelphia have been added as new U.S. gateways to Bermuda. U.K. airlines, should any wish to serve the U.S.-Bermuda market, will have their choice of three U.S. gateways. In addition, the United States gains rights from Atlanta, Baltimore, Miami and Washington through Bermuda to two points on the European Continent to be determined later.

New routes have also been granted between U.K. points in the Caribbean and the United States. U.K. airlines operating in this area will in the future have the choice of serving any two of the following U.S. mainland gateways — Baltimore, Houston, Miami, New Orleans, Tampa, Washington.

All-cargo routes have been specified separately from passenger routes. There will be new and expanded opportunities in this field which should be of advantage to airlines and shippers alike.

Charter Services. For the first time in a bilateral air services agreement charter services have been covered. The two countries have agreed that it is desirable to work towards a multilateral arrangement for charter air services. They have also agreed as soon as possible and, in any event, before the end of the year to enter into negotiations towards a bilateral agreement covering all aspects of charter services. In the absence of agreement by 31 March 1978; the two countries agreed to consult further with a view to a continuation of liberal arrangements for charter air services.

There is no change in the status of the Concorde supersonic transport as a result of the Agreement. Each side retains the rights of the previous Agreement.

Britain wished new Concorde landing rights but present rights remained in force at the time of signing of the Bermuda 2 Agreement.

The United States sees the Bermuda 2 Agreement as offering cheaper and more convenient air travel to Americans. More United States cities can now offer non-stop service to London.

The United States stood firm on the principle of competition in the international market place. The British relented on this factor to allow somewhat more competition under the new agreement than had been permitted under the previous Bermuda Agreement. Fares are to be monitored to allow airlines the lowest fares "consistent with the economic health of the airlines."

The United States insisted on liberal charter provisions in the Bermuda 2 Agreement. This offers charter flight as a dependable option for air travellers. Bermuda 2 recognizes for the first time the legal status of charter operations. On 31 March 1978 the current memorandum on charter operation expired.

Air freight shippers are granted more flexibility in taking cargo where and when they wish.

The CAB and airlines, under Bermuda 2, will decide the best type of service for gateway cities to Great Britain and beyond. The United States retains important long-haul rights to New Delhi, Tehran, and now Singapore.

From the start, the American side negotiated for airlines to retain responsibility to establish schedules they wish to fly. The United States position is that passenger choice, not government formula, should determine the share of the market each airline obtains. When the issue of excess capacity arises more consultations will take place. Meanwhile, the specter of government control will have been avoided.

The Bermuda 2 Agreement also provides that as markets grow, United States airlines can serve them. This is done by agreeing that a second United States flag airline may be added to any route where more than 600,000 passengers travel each year.

Passenger Charter Agreement (A part of the Bermuda 2 Agreement). Entering into force on 25 April 1978 was the anticipated bilateral agreement between Great Britain and the United States pertaining to charter services. The agreement recognizes that there is a market from a "section of the travelling public which is price rather than time sensitive for air service . . . . ."

An efficient air charter system is proposed in which each party to the agreement grants charter take off and landing rights to the other. The country of origin selects appropriate charter airlines requesting North Atlantic charter routes. Both parties agree to allow the charters fair competition and no limitations on the volume, frequency, or regularity of charter flights.

Certain general agreement is reached that, should charter competition threaten scheduled airlines, meetings will be held to work out this problem. Each country may regulate fares of air charters originating in that country. Enforcement of safety regulations is made a cooperative effort. The originating nation regulates its air carrier, yet, while in the other's territory, the laws of that nation prevail.[36]

Cargo Charters. Liberal provisions for cargo charters were included in the Agreement. More negotiations were scheduled to reach further agreements on cargo shorter flights.

The Agreement is to remain in effect until March 31, 1980. Prior to its expiration, Great Britain and United States negotiators are to meet to review and revise the agreement.

Bilateral Agreements (Bermuda type): Bilateral agreements were signed with Australia, Germany, the Netherlands and Great Britain among others in 1978.[37]

The country-of-origin pricing regime described in Bermuda 2 was sought and largely obtained by the United States in these agreements. This means that rates are set in the country of origin, and prevail both one-way and on round trip tickets. For example: German airlines set rates on flights to the United States and on round trip fares to the United States and return to Germany. The United States has the same privilege.

Montreal Convention, 1971

During the late 1960s and early 1970s a wave of terrorist acts of sabotage and bombings threatened the civil aviation system of the world. To meet this threat, nations sent aviation representatives to Montreal in the fall of 1971 to work out a multilateral agreement. The agreement would help to prevent incidents or to punish offenders, thereby serving as a deterrant to acts of sabotage.

The United States in signing and ratifying this agreement, (23 September 1971 and 1 November 1972 respectively) made it the law of the land in the United States. The convention entered into force 26 January 1973. (All treaties

306

to which the United States is a party become law in the United States.) Seventy-six nations are parties to the convention.

"Unlawful acts" are defined in the Montreal Convention to cover violence aboard aircraft to persons, the placement of explosive devices, damage to an aircraft to render it unsafe, interference with air navigation facilities, and false threats to endanger aircraft in flight. The convention covers accomplices as well as primary offenders.

Offenders are to be taken into custody by member nations with each contracting state agreeing to make such offenses punishable by severe penalties. Both domestic and international flights are covered by the convention. Military, customs, and police aircraft are exempted from the agreement. Extradition is urged. If a member state decides not to allow extradition of the offender, then that state shall prosecute the accused.

Overall, the convention is intended to prevent sabotage, and if delay is encountered, to smooth the way for the continuation of the air traveller or cargo, and to punish saboteurs.

The Four Montreal Protocols of 1975

After extensive prepatory work by the International Civil Aviation Organization (ICAO) from 1972 through most of 1975, delegates from sixty-six nations met in Montreal to consider the Montreal Protocols to Amend the Warsaw Convention Regime Governing International Carriage by Air. At the Montreal meeting in September 1975 the delegates, including those from the United States and Great Britain, wished to simply revise cargo provisions of the Warsaw Convention. Something more extensive emerged from their deliberations.

A major change was made in replacing the Poincare gold franc as a unit of account with a "Special Drawing Right," more in tune with world monetary valuation. The franc had been used to specify exactly the liability assumed by air carriers engaged in international air commerce.

The entire cargo system underwent considerable changes with electronic data processing being allowed in recording the movement of air cargo. This will save great amounts of time, labor, and paperwork.

A strict liability regime replaces the former presumed liability of the carrier for cargo. This is expected to greatly reduce litigation.[38] In turn, insurance costs will be reduced.

The Montreal meeting allowed the venting of annoying problems and brought the handling of air cargo forward into the electronic age of computerization.

Bermuda 2 Agreement, 1977

The Bermuda 2 Agreement is formally titled the Air Services Agreement between the government of the United States of America and the government of the United Kingdom of Great Britain and Northern Ireland.

A July 1977 White House statement on "Bermuda 2," signed by President Jimmy Carter notes:[39]

> The Agreement governing civil air services between the United States and the United Kingdom was negotiated over a period of several months and signed in Bermuda on July 23, 1977. It replaces and updates the prececessor agreement reached in 1946 and last amended in 1966.
>
> The new agreement provides for continuing the basic principle of a fair and equal opportunity for the airlines of both countries to compete, and dedicates both Governments to the provision of safe, adequate, and efficient international air transportation responsive to the present and future needs of the public and to the continued development of international air commerce. It emphasizes that both scheduled and charter air transportation are important to the consumer interest and are essential elements of a healthy international air transport system.
>
> The United States seeks an international economic environment and air transportation structure founded on healthy economic competition among all air carriers. The new agreement is consistent with this objective. We shall continue to rely on competitive market forces as much as possible in our international air transportation agreements so that the public may receive the improved service at costs that reflect efficient operations.
>
> The Agreement is one that reflects well on our two great nations. Its quality, its fairness, and its benefits to the consumer and to airlines should make it last as long as the original 1946 Bermuda Agreement. It continues our long and historic relationship with the United Kingdom.

Treaties in Force

A list of official treaties in force, as of 1 January 1978, which deal with aviation includes:[40]

The Warsaw Convention of 1929 which entered into force in the United States 29 October 1934.

The Convention on International Civil Aviation, Chicago, 1944, entered into force for the United States 4 April 1947.

International Air Services Transit Agreement, Chicago, December 1944. Entered into force for the United States 8 February 1945.

Protocol amending the Convention on International Civil Aviation of 1944, done at Montreal, 1954. Entered into force for the United States 12 December 1956.

Protocol amended the Convention on International Civil Aviation of 1944, amending Article 48(a) to increase the number of parties which may request holding an extraordinary meeting of the Assembly. Done at Rome, September 1962. Entered into force for the United States 11 September 1975.

Protocol to the Convention on International Civil Aviation to increase membership of the council to 30 members. Done at New York, 1971; entered into force for the United States 16 January 1973.

Protocol to amend the International Civil Aviation Organization Article 56, to enlarge membership of the Air Naviation Commission. Done at Vienna, 1971; entered into force for the United States 19 December 1974.

Protocol regarding the trilingual test of the Convention on International Civil Aviation (Chicago) 1944. Done at Buenos Aires 1968; entered into force for the United States 24 October 1968.

Agreement on Joint Financing of Certain Air Navigation Services with Greenland and the Faroe Islands. Done in Geneva, 1956; entered into force for the United States 6 June 1958.

Convention on Offenses and Certain Other Acts Committed on Board Aircraft, done at Tokyo, September 1963; entered into force for the United States 4 December 1969.

Convention for the Suppression of Unlawful Seizure of Aircraft (Hijacking), done at the Hague, December 1970. Entered into force for the United States 14 October 1971.

Convention for the Suppression of Unlawful Acts Against the Safety of Civil Aviation (Sabotage), done at Montreal, September 1971; entered into force for the United States 26 January 1973.

NOTES

[1]Gerhard von Glahn, *Law Among Nations* (New York: Macmillan Publishing Co., Inc., 1976), pp. 360-61.

[2]*Ibid.*, p. 367.

[3]*Ibid.*, p. 366; Michael J. Hart, *Outline of International Aviation Law*, (St. Louis: Parks College of St. Louis University, 1975), pp. 26-27.

[4]*Ibid*, Also, under the "archipelago theory," islands comprising, or belonging to, a nation claim the water inside a sweep or circle of islands as well as the waters contiguous to their shores.

[5]Rowland W. Fixel, *The Law of Aviation*, (Charlottesville, Va.: The Mitchie, 1967), pp. 27-28; Hart, pp. 56-57; von Glahn, pp. 543-44.

[6]Fixel, p. 27; 2 Scott Documents 152; "The Hague Peace Conferences of 1899 and 1907," Proceedings of The Hague Tribunal, 1899, pp. 152, 154.

[7]Fixel, pp. 27-28; Hart, p. 56.

[8]Fixel, p. 28; Hart, p. 56.

[9]Fixel, pp. 28-29.

[10]Hart, 56-57; von Glahn, pp. 465, 547, 582.

[11]Fixel, p. 31; Hart, p. 57.

[12]Fixel, pp. 29-33; Hart, p. 58; von Glahn, p. 595.

[13]3 UST, Treaties, Conventions, International Acts, Protocols and Agreements Between the United States and Other Powers, Dept. of State publication 3768; Fixel, p. 32; Hart, p. 57.

[14]Fixel, pp. 27-28; Hart, pp. 56-57; von Glahn, pp. 543-44.

[15]Fixel, pp. 33-37; Hart, pp. 62-63.

[16]Hart, pp. 61-62.

[17]Fixel, p. 37.

[18]Fixel, pp. 37-38; Hart, pp. 59-61.

[19]U.S. Treaty Series 876; 49 Stat. (Pt. 2) 3000; 4 JAC Bulletin no. 3, p. 93; Fixel, p. 38; Hart, pp. 110-152.

[20]The unfairness of limited liability was vividly demonstrated by the case of Miss Jane Froman (Ross). The very popular singer was seriously injured in 1943 in a crash in Portugal as a passenger aboard a Pan American aircraft. She was traveling to Europe for the United Service Organization (USO) to entertain service men there during World War II. Her career was ruined, her loss of earnings was enormous, and her medical costs soared over $150,000. Yet, she was able to recover only a little over $8,000 when she sued Pan American claiming negligence. This was due to the limitations on air carrier liability imposed by the Warsaw Convention. She next filed against Pan American claiming that her ticket was not properly issued to her. It had been arranged for by an agent. She lost this plea also, via a very strict interpretation of the law. The court ruled that the ticket was correctly issued by the carrier whether or not actually handed to a passenger. (Ross v. Pan American Airways, 85 N.E. 2d 880.)

[21]Done at Montreal, 14 June 1954, entered into force for the United States 12 December 1956. It is in effect today.

[22]Dept. of State Treaty Information Bulletin no. 47 (August 1933).

[23]Fixel, 39-40; Hart, pp. 160-66.

[24]U.S. Treaty Series no. 876; Fixel, p. 39.

[25]Dept. of State Treaty Information Bulletin no. 109, p. 328 (October 1938); Dept. of State Treaty Information Bulleting no. 111 (December 1938).

[26]Convention on International Civil Aviation, Chicago, 7 December 1944, entered into force for the U.S. 4 April 1947; 61 Stat. 1180; TIAS 1591; 3 Berans 944, 15 UNTS 295; see also Hart, pp. 93-109.

[27]*Ibid.*

[28]*Ibid.*

[29]International Air Services Transit Agreement, 7 December 1944, U.S. Department of State.

[30]Fixel, pp. 772-77.

[31]Fixel, pp. 778-85.

[32]4 UST 1830; TIAS 2847; 310 UNTS 151.

[33]Department of State, *Treaties in Force . . . January 1, 1978* (Washington: Superintendent of Documents, GPO, for Office of Treaty Affairs), pp. 269-70.

[34]*Ibid.*

[35]8 UST 179; TIAS 3756; 320 UNTS 217.

[36]United Kingdom of Great Britain and Northern Ireland, Air Transport Services Agreement amends agreement of 23 July 1977, as modified. Signed at Washington and London, 15 and 25 April 1978. A new Article 14, and an Annex 4, replace former ones.

[37]Press releases, early 1978, CAB, Office of Information.

[38]Gerald F. Fitzgerald, "The Four Montreal Protocols to Amend the Warsaw Convention Regime Governing International Carriage by Air," *The Journal of Air Law and Commerce*, vol. 42, no. 2, 1976, pp. 273-350.

[39]U.S. Department of Transportation, *Air Services Agreement Between the Government of the United States of America and the Government of the United Kingdom of Great Britain and Northern Ireland: Bermuda 2* (Washington: U.S. DOT, July 23, 1977), p. i.

[40]U.S. Department of State, *Treaties in Force . . . January 1, 1978*, pp. 269-76.

CHAPTER 18

INTERNATIONAL AVIATION ORGANIZATIONS

In the early years of aviation, as we have seen, simple bilateral agreements were made between nations relating to overflight and landing rights. As international flights increased these negotiations became too slow and inflexible to react to the needs of international air commerce. To meet these new needs, two major international aviation organizations were established.

The International Civil Aviation Organization (ICAO)

Under the terms of the Convention on International Civil Aviation signed at Chicago on 7 December 1944 by the United States, the International Civil Aviation Organization (ICAO) was set up. Once the Convention came into force in April 1947, ICAO came into being that same month.[1]

The ICAO is a permanent International Civil Aviation Organization created to facilitate cooperation among nations in matters of civil aviation. Its goals are, according to Article 44 of the Chicago Convention, to:

(a)   Insure the safe and orderly growth of international civil aviation throughout the world;

(b)   Encourage the arts of aircraft design and operation for peaceful purposes;

(c)   Encourage the development of airways, airports, and air-navigation facilities for international civil aviation;

(d)   Meet the needs of the peoples of the world for safe, regular, efficient, and economical air transport.

(e)   Prevent economic waste caused by unreasonable competition;

(f)   Insure that the rights of contracting states are fully respected and that every contracting state has a fair opportunity to operate international air lines;

(g)   Avoid discrimination between contracting states;

(h)   Promote safety of flight in international air navigation;

(i)   Promote generally the development of all aspects of international civil aeronautics.

The ICAO works out needed radio navigational standards to meet the changing equipment being installed by the airlines. In 1978, for example, ICAO selected the U.S./Australian-developed Microwave Landing System (MLS) as the international standard approach and landing guidance system for the future. In the next twenty years it will replace the Instrument Landing System (ILS) which has been in use at airports for nearly forty years.[2]

The ICAO has worked since its inception to standardize world aviation procedures. For example, English is accepted as the language used by air traffic controllers across the world to speak to international flights. Standards of every kind are set forth and published by the ICAO in order that pilots may have fewer elements to contend with in their complex duties. Radio navigational aids are standardized so far as possible. Units of measurement are used in agreed upon ways.

The ICAO is appointed by the member nations to the Chicago Convention to do the technical work involved in world air commerce. If this were left to bilateral and multilateral agreements alone, world standardization of air commerce would be impossible.

The permanent headquarters of the ICAO are located in Montreal, Quebec, Canada.[3]

The International Air Transport Association (IATA)

Since the member nations to the Chicago Convention did not wish to assign rate-setting to the ICAO, a voluntary association of air carriers was created to deal with that and other operational details of international air transport. Named the International Air Transport Association (IATA), it initially included the world's major airlines. To be eligible for membership an air carrier must be certificated for schelduled airline operation by governments eligible for membership in the International Civil Aviation Organization. Airlines, to be active members, must also be involved in international air services. If certificated airlines operate only within a country, they qualify only for associate memberships.[4]

The rate-setting function of the IATA was accepted in the world community of air carriers for many years following the incorporation of the association in 1945. From the Montreal, Canada, headquarters decisions regarding rates are

formulated by agreement between airline members. If ICAO member nations do not object, the rates are then accepted.[5]

The United States granted antitrust immunity to the IATA. The Civil Aeronautics Board managed to indirectly retain considerable control over international rates by exercising its right to approve U.S. inter-carrier agreements. The CAB, until recently, controlled domestic U.S. air carrier rates rather rigidly but was not granted by Congress the right to set international rates since this would impinge on the rights of other nations. CAB influence on international rates was felt, however, and later increased when CAB was given the right to approve or reject international air carrier fares by Section 1002-J of the Federal Aviation Act.[6]

The rate-making role of the IATA is the center of much attention. Another important function of the organization, however, also deserves study. One of the prime reasons for such an airline organization after World War II was to work out ways of making interline passenger ticketing and baggage checking possible. Standard forms and procedures have been perfected to date so that one may use one ticket to fly across the world using a number of airlines.

The standardization of techniques for interline cargo waybilling is also an IATA achievement. With standardized waybilling, cargo is moved worldwide by airlines belonging to many nations. Also, methods of ascertaining the compensation of the airlines concerned have been developed.[7]

Health standards for passengers and crews have been evolved to insure compliance with health rules. With the passage of years, fewer nations require immunizaton to diseases. This shared pool of diseases has spread across the world and immunities with it, as a result of the rapid transport by air.

The formal IATA goals, as listed in its Articles of Confederation are:

(a) To promote safe, regular and economical air transport for the benefit of the peoples of the world, to foster air commerce, and to study the problems connected therewith;

(b) To provide means for collaboration among the air transport enterprises engaged directly or indirectly in international air transport service;

(c) To cooperate with the International Civil Aviation Organization and other international organizations.

At each IATA Annual General Meeting, the central body of IATA, each active airline member has one vote. A twelve-member Executive Committee functions for the Annual General Meeting during the year. The IATA acts via four standing committees; financial, legal, technical, and traffic.[8]

Changes are ahead for the IATA. Two of the world's largest air carriers, Pan American World Airways and Aeroflot, left IATA in early 1979. Two large U.S. air carriers, Delta Airlines and Northwest Airlines are not IATA members. Even the governments of the foreign airlines who now belong to IATA are no longer satisfied with the fare-setting activities of the organization.

A major factor in the lessening of the IATA's effectiveness as an arbiter of prices to be charged for air carriage is the change in United States aviation policy in recent years. With the deregulation of U.S. air carriers, which is following the instructions contained in the Air Carrier Deregulation Act of 1978, open competition is resulting. Further, present U.S. policy tends to follow a pattern of bilateral, Bermuda-style agreements. Some carriers are complaining of the IATA's cumbersome traffic conference procedures and are considering dropping out. To maintain its leadership of world air carriers, IATA probably will make changes.[9] It now represents 100 airlines of 85 nations.

The Civil Aeronautics Board has made tentative findings that the IATA agreements are anticompetitive and has with CAB Order 78-6-78, asked interested parties to justify continued CAB approval of the IATA agreements on prices worked out in IATA "traffic conferences." In CAB Order 79-5-113, CAB has asked that the IATA show why the organization should continue to be exempt from U.S. antitrust laws. It is this last, the threat to IATA antitrust immunity, that may spell the end to IATA's fare-setting activities.[10]

NOTES

[1]U.S. Department of State, Treaty Affairs Office, *Treaties in Force . . . on January 1, 1978*, (Washington: Government Printing Office, 1978), Publication 8934, Department of State, 271-72.

[2]Ibid; also Michael J. Hart, *Outline of International Aviation Law* (St. Louis: Parks College of St. Louis University, 1975), pp. 205-15.

[3]See the chapter in this text, "International Air Law: Treaty Negotiation," subhead CITEJA for a discussion of ICAO's predecessor organization the Comite International Technique d'Experts Juridiques Aeriens. See also Gerhard von Glahn, *Law Among Nations* (New York: Macmillan Publishing Co., Inc., 1976), p. 329.

[4]Robert M. Kane and Allen D. Vose, *Air Transportation* (Dubuque, Iowa: Kendall/Hunt Publishing Company, 1975), Chap. 12, pp. 13-15; Hart, pp. 190-204; von Glahn, p. 329.

[5]IATA is incorporated by Act of the Canadian Parliament, 1945. (20th Parliament, 9 George VI).

[6]Statement by Dr. Alfred E. Kahn, (then) Chairman Civil Aeronautics Board, before the Aviation Subcommittee of the House Public Works and Transportation Committee, on H. R. 11145, 6 March 1978 with reference to IATA's future role in international aviation. See this same discussion in the chapter on the Civil Aeronautic Board under the the subheading "Need for Legislation."

[7]Kane and Vose, Chap. 12, pp. 13-15.

[8]Ibid; Hart, pp. 194-95.

[9]Kahn statement of 6 March 1978. See also CAB chapter "Need for Legislation."

[10]Ibid; also CAB Order 79-5-113.

PART VII

OUR EVOLVING AIR LAW

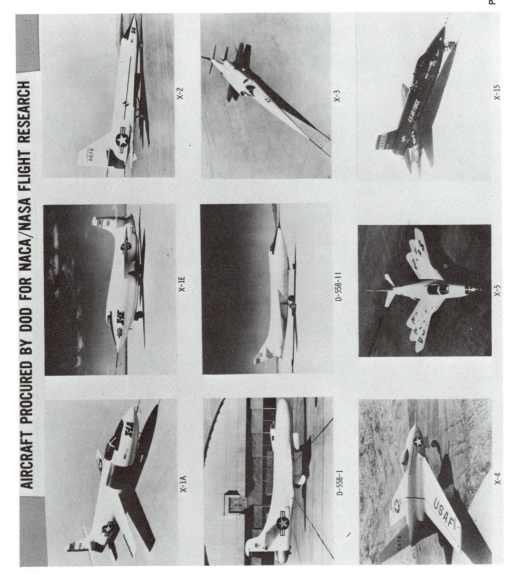

AIRCRAFT PROCURED BY DOD FOR NACA/NASA FLIGHT RESEARCH

X-2

X-3

X-15

X-1E

D-558-II

X-5

X-1A

D-558-I

X-4

Photograph courtesy NASA.

320

CHAPTER 19

SUPERSONIC FLIGHT

During the Volta Conference on High-Speed Flight at Rome in 1935 the first theoretical proposals on the advantages of the swept-back wing plan for high speed aircraft was presented by Dr. Adolf Busemann, a German aerodynamicist. Dr. Busemann suggested that a swept-back wing might prevent the formation of shock waves that would form as air flowed over a wing nearing the speed of sound. No aircraft yet existed which would reach the "sound barrier," at which air begins to form these shock waves, but scientists realized that this would be a problem. Busemann's idea was strictly theoretical.

Dr. Woldemar Voigt, chief of preliminary design for the Messerschmitt aircraft manufacturing company, was intrigued by the Busemann theory. Voigt ran wind tunnel tests which verified the Busemann hypothesis. Another Messerschmitt design scientist working on a delta wing for high speed flight, Dr. Alexander Lippisch, saw that the swept-wing design was good for high speed flight but not as desirable for low speed flying. Lippisch worked out a design for a variable-geometry wing — one which would be swept back for high speeds, and could be moved forward for good flight characteristics at lower speeds. He applied for a patent and work began on a prototype aircraft in September 1944. Americans found details of the wing-sweep research project at the end of the war when intelligence teams searched a devastated Germany for valuable German technology and data.[1]

An American, R. T. Jones, of the National Advisory Committee for Aeronautics (NACA) had been independently working on swept-wing designs. By 1947 NACA scientists suggested the swept-back wing idea to industry. During the late 1940s designers now began to evolve research aircraft that could near the speed of sound but aircraft which also suffered serious control difficulties at high speeds. (These aircraft had straight wing plans.)

Inadvertently, fighter aircraft during the 1940s were experiencing difficulties as they neared, sometimes achieved, the speed of sound in dives. The Lockheed P-38, a sleek twin engined U.S. fighter, encountered severe control difficulties at near sonic speeds. It was necessary to design a dive-stop, a flap projecting into the airstream, to slow the plane and prevent the dangerous buffeting, control "freezing," and tuck under pilots experienced near the speed of sound.

Terms came into use to fit high speed flight situations. As planes approached the speed of sound, parts of the aircraft structure began to form shock waves; this came to be called "going supersonic." The transition from subsonic to supersonic speeds was termed "transonic." As planes entered this transonic area it was found that some planes experienced shock wave formation, "compressibility effects," sooner than others. Each plane then is said to have a "critical Mach number," a speed at which portions of the aircraft go supersonic.

Improved wind tunnels in the late 1930s in Europe and the U.S. had demonstrated the desirability of thin airfoils for high speed flight. Thick wings created more drag (higher air resistance) and poor patterns of air flow at high speeds (shock waves on upper surfaces). It was found, too, that needle-like noses reduced the area of "standing waves" that formed ahead of the aircraft.

Combining the wind tunnel research with the work done by NACA, American aircraft manufacturers developed a plane with a thin, straight wing and a sharply pointed nose, and next looked about for the huge powerplants needed to propel such an advanced high speed aircraft.

Rocket-powered research aircraft were used to test the new designs intended to give the U.S. supersonic capability.[2]

The first man to cross the sound barrier in level flight was Captain Charles Yeager, USAF. Captain Yeager made the flight 14 October 1947 in a Bell X-1 rocket plane at high altitude, flying at over 670 miles per hour. The Bell X-1A in a flight on 12 December 1953 achieved a speed of 1,650 miles per hour and was later to climb to an altitude of ninety-thousand feet.

Progress continued. On 9 November 1961 the North American Aviation (now Rockwell International) X-15 aircraft was flown by Major Robert M. White to a speed of 4,093 miles per hour, a little over Mach 6. Later, a Mach 6.7 speed was attained. The "X" experimental ships flew from the Muroc Dry Lake in California. This location became the NACA Flight Research Center at Edwards Air Force Base.

It was believed for a time in the United States that the Mach-3, North American B-70 "Valkyrie" military aircraft might be a possible forerunner of a U.S. supersonic airliner. The United States has, however, tended to develop "dash oriented" military aircraft, most lacking a capability for sustained cruise at supersonic speeds required for a true supersonic transport (SST). The lack of a military aircraft design as a prototype for the development of a civil supersonic transport was to greatly hamper U.S. efforts to develop such a plane.

At the same time that the United States worked on the problems of supersonic flight, European nations carried on similar programs supported by their governments and in some countries with additional investment from the private sector.

The Terminology

Sonic Boom. In supersonic flight the plane no longer meets air slowly enough for the air it strikes to compress, squeeze aside. Rather, the plane moves so fast that it collides with the air particles, which in turn cannot compress but pile up into a conical shock wave. This is often likened to the bow-wave of a ship moving through the water. It is when this shock wave meets the ground that one feels and hears the sonic boom. The higher the plane, the softer the "boom".

Mach Numbers. Ernst Mach, an Austrian physicist, worked out the relationship between the speed of sound at a particular altitude and temperature, and the speed of an object moving through the air. He called this ratio a "Mach number." If moving through the air at twice the speed of sound, for example, we say that we are flying at Mach 2.

At low altitude levels the speed of sound is around 760 miles per hour. The speed of sound varies with variations in temperature, air density, and humidity. At high altitude flight levels the air is colder, less dense, and much less humid; hence the speed of sound is less than at the lower leves and can range at about 640 to 660 miles per hour. Commercial SSTs attain speeds of between Mach 2 and Mach 3. Military aircraft can reach still higher speeds.

Flight Regimes. This term denotes flight in certain speed ranges as listed below.

Hypersonic speeds: Over Mach 5.00.

Supersonic speeds: Mach 1.20 to Mach 5.00.

Transonic speeds: Mach 0.95 to 1.20.

Subsonic speeds: Speeds at or below Mach 0.95.

Shock Waves. As a plane goes through transonic and into supersonic speeds, shock waves may be minimized if the transition of air flow is smooth and the air passes over a smooth surface.

Canard. In aviation, a "canard" is a set of flight controls or stabilizer located ahead of the wing. The horizontal stabilizers of the U.S. XB-70s, for example, are canards.

NASA's Super Critical Wing. The top of this new wing design is flattened to delay the formation of shock waves along the front portions of the wing. There is a downturn near the trailing edge of the wing to develop lift. By causing shock wave, or compressibility effects to occur at the rear of the wing, control is enhanced and drag is reduced.

Thermal Considerations. Once the speed of sound was successfully passed, another "barrier" to high speed flight arose. It was known that supersonic aircraft with increasing speed met increasing aircraft skin temperatures. Air friction raised aircraft skin temperatures. It is necessary to use a metal that will withstand these high temperatures if SSTs are to fly much above a Mach 3 speed. At Mach 8, it is estimated that skin temperatures could reach 2,400°F. Titanium, stainless steel, and "Inconel X" (a nickel alloy), all promise increased temperature tolerance in supersonic aircraft.

The SST Race

In 1956 English aeronautical interests began to consider a bold leap into the development of supersonic transport aircraft (SST). Aircraft Designers Dietrich Kuchemann and E.C. Maskell advocated a lean delta-wing aircraft design.

Development costs were estimated at between 135 million and 175 million British pounds for two aircraft, a short-range and a long-range prototype. (The total ten years later proved to be nearer 1,000 million pounds, or $3.2 billion.) France, meanwhile, had successfully built and sold a medium-range jet airliner, the Caravelle. Staggered, finally, by the ruinous cost of SST research and manufacture, Britain joined forces with France to complete the development of the SSTs. The Anglo-French Supersonic Aircraft Agreement was signed 29 November 1962. Britain agreed to invest another 75-85 million British pounds toward the project over the next eight years.

In Russia, the aeronautical engineers proposed an SST to gain world prestige, conquer the vast distances of the USSR, and show their air potential adaptable to a civil air use.

Meanwhile, in the U.S. supersonic aircraft proliferated on paper. The proposed Boeing 733 was designed to fly at Mach 2.7 with 227 passengers. Lockheed proposed a sleek Mach 3 delta-wing airliner to carry 218 passengers; and North American sketched out another very possible airplane, a Mach 3, NAC 60, which was based on the supersonic military aircraft B-70 "Valkyrie."

The early 1960s saw Britain, France, the USSR and the United States engaged in a race to design a successful SST. Such a plane would be a great achievement, for the problems involved were massive.

Many control and design problems were still unresolved. Aircraft skin temperatures of high Mach number flight proved to be too high for aluminum alloys. Fabrication of titanium was needed. British and French designers decided to use special aluminum and accept the limitations this imposed on the speed of the aircraft. The airplane had to be sealed against the near vacuum of the stratospheric levels at which it would operate, and noise levels inside the plane had to be brought to acceptable levels.

The plane had to fly at great speeds enroute, yet approach and land at "slow" conventional speeds. This entailed a speed range of perhaps 2,000 to 200 miles per hour. Engines with the enormous thrust needed to go supersonic and fly at Mach 2 or Mach 3 were another problem. To be used to best advantage the SSTs needed long range, yet the great engines required for supersonic speed devoured quantities of fuel. There were ecological problems of noise levels at take off, sonic boom, ozone layer destruction, and radiation hazards.

All governments concerned in the SST race faced huge expenditures. National prestige was "up front and on the line." Also, there was a definite possibility of failure; expensive and politically unpopular delays and the danger of possible crashes faced SST developers.[3]

The NASA Role. Earlier, the National Aeronautics and Space Act of 1958 had been signed into law by President Dwight D. Eisenhower on 29 July 1958. The act made the National Advisory Committee for Aeronautics (NACA) the nucleus for the new National Aeronautics and Space Administration (NASA. By 1 October 1958 NACA had become a part of NASA. A portion of NASA's responsibility was to continue the development and research work on problems of high speed flight begun by NACA and to initiate new programs of basic research. These programs were designed to offer U.S. aeronautical engineers a sound foundation of basic scientific data upon which they could build designs for U.S. supersonic transports.

At NASA's Langley Research Center in Virginia, scientists used computers, wind tunnels, and experience gained in research planes to help solve the problems of building a supersonic aircraft. The variable sweep wing, one which would move to a swept back configuration for supersonic speeds and then forward for subsonic operations, was chosen.

President John F. Kennedy announced in June 1963 that the United States was to develop a supersonic transport. Early in 1964 Lockheed publicly showed its A-11, a Mach-3 aircraft design. The military supersonic XB-70 was flown.

By January 1967 contracts for the development and construction of a U.S. SST airframe were awarded to the Boeing Company. Powerplants were to be designed and built by the General Electric Company. The Boeing SST was to be a Mach-3 aircraft with wings which could be moved, swept back for supersonic speed regimes.

The SCAT Program. The Supersonic Commercial Air Transport (SCAT) program started at Langley during 1962. The goal was to develop an aircraft configuration to meet the need for a civil transport aircraft which would be safe and economically feasible at both subsonic and supersonic speeds.

Several approaches to the problems of control and stability during transonic and supersonic flight were studied at Langley and at NASA's Ames Research Center. The variable-sweep configuration was one possible answer, a fixed delta wing with a forward canard was another. This last has been most used in SST design.

Theory and experiment in NASA research helped solve a wide range of problems. The use of computers was a breakthrough in predicting and investigating the capability of designs.

Computer technology is also used to simulate air traffic situations and to learn ways to work SSTs into existing air traffic. Materials and structures testing at expected supersonic stresses and temperatures, too, is a part of the SCAT program.

The supercritical airfoil, developed at Langley, delays the formation of shock waves to higher Mach numbers. Another airfoil approach, which gives good control at very low speeds is boundary-layer control, that is air injected over the leading edge of a flap or parallel to the surface of the wing.

Much basic research has been done by NASA into control and construction problems associated with aircraft, and with spacecraft reentry, at high Mach numbers. The most efficient shape for a Mach 7 vehicle, for example, has been studied. As skin temperatures mount, how can fuel be safely housed, and how do materials alter? These and other questions have been subjects of NASA research since 1958.[4]

The First SSTs Fly

In Russia, the designer Andrei Tupolev's TU-144 made a maiden flight over Moscow on 31 December 1968, an impressive first flight of a civil airliner with supersonic capability. In France on 2 March 1969 the British-French Concorde 001 made its first flight. On 9 April 1969 the Concorde 002 was flown. Pan American planned to order several Concordes. For some years military aircraft had achieved supersonic speeds. The TU-144 and the Concorde, however, were the first supersonic planes designed for civilian use.

The Anglo-French Concorde went into service in January 1976, used by British Airways and Air France. Pan American decided, however, as early as 1973 not to order Concordes.

Russia brought to the Paris Air Show of 1973 its supersonic transport, the TU-144. The plane broke up and crashed before thousands of spectators, a bitter blow to SST prestige. By December 1975, however, the Russians were flying test routes with the TU-144.[5]

The U.S. SST Battle

The sleek Lockheed delta wing aircraft proposal lost out in the U.S. when government planners chose to develop Boeing's swing-wing design, the Boeing 2707. The idea behind the swing-wing was to provide a swept-back configuration for supersonic speeds and a more conventional platform for approach, landing, and take off at subsonic speeds.

Contracts were awarded Boeing and General Electric in April 1967 for the development and construction of a U.S. SST. The problems in building such a plane mounted, along with the costs. The possible impact on the environment, the problem of sonic boom, and the noise levels of available powerplants made the program an unpopular one. There were problems, too, in fuel economy and costs of operation.

In Britain and the U.S. groups concerned about the ecological impact of the SSTs grew in numbers, press coverage, and influence. Some obvious problems had been brought all too vividly to public attention. The shock wave that attends low level supersonic flight struck the earth on 5 August 1959 at Ottowa, Canada. There a new control tower and terminal were badly damaged as a jet fighter turned and went supersonic very close to the ground. No one was hurt but the need for more care was demonstrated.

In Britain and the U.S. in the 1960s complaints came in about sonic boom noise and some damage to glass. It was feared that historic buildings in England and France might be damaged. (Truck traffic seems a more real threat but trucks are not as dramatic to the press as are aircraft). By 1967 anti-SST organizations were engaging in a front-page battle with pro-SST interests. U.S. Senator William Proxmire joined the fight against SST development.

Development Halted. Due to the outcry of environmental groups in the U.S., anti-Nixon political forces, and the tremendous amount of money being spent on SST development, the value of the American SST program was questioned. The Boeing swing-wing design proved to be impracticable and had to be scrapped. A swept-back wing was substituted at great cost. Congressional hearings in 1970 were followed by a decisive anti-SST vote in the U.S. Senate on 24 March 1971.

In the U.S., even with the halting of production of a supersonic transport, Congress knew that technology would advance and that such a plane ultimately would evolve. To salvage knowledge gained, in July 1972 funds were allotted NASA to continue research on supersonic transport.

SSTs in Operation

The Concorde. British and French hopes for regaining a substantial part of the massive amounts of money spent on the development of the Concorde, by sales to Pan Am and TWA, were dashed by the 1973 decision of U.S. airlines not to exercise their options to buy Concordes.

By 1975 Air France, British Airways, and Iran Air planned to use the Concorde, yet American air carriers believed the price of the Concorde, $60 million each, would be hard to recoup. The U.S. tariffs on imported aircraft add another 50 percent to the cost. American air carriers chose to risk losing a share of the lucrative first-class North Atlantic passenger market. Concorde production lines at Bristol, England, were now set up to turn out only an initial sixteen aircraft.

After a campaign of publicity, record-breaking flights, and a demonstration tour of the U.S., the SST Concorde won permission to make daily flights from Paris to Dulles Airport near Washington, D.C. There was to be a test of SST operational feasibility.

The Russian TU-144. The Russian TU-144 SST was the first civil aircraft to break the "sound barrier." The Tupolev-designed aircraft was dubbed the "Concordski." Early in November 1973 the TU-144 completed a 1,931-mile inaugurative flight between Moscow and Alma-Ata, a point near the Chinese border. Once a week service was planned with a one-way ticket price set at $113.00.

The TU-144 carries 140 passengers compared with the Concorde which seats around 100 persons. After a very steep initial climb the TU-144 cruises at twice the speed of sound, flying at over fifty-two thousand feet. It is noisy inside, passengers report, because of the powerful air conditioning system needed to combat the heat generated by aircraft skin friction. To prevent the aircraft's sonic boom, or sonic "footprint," from damaging structures or alarming citizens, the Russian plane was scheduled to fly over sparsely settled areas.

The last flight of the Tupolev-144 left Moscow in June 1978 and service was officially discontinued in September 1978. No explanation was given and service has not been resumed to date.[6] The reason for withdrawing the TU-144 from service is said to be a crash, according to a *Washington Post* report, 24 June 1979.[7]

A new version of the TU-144 had made a successful supersonic flight to the Soviet Far East according to a June 1979 Moscow Radio broadcast. Mass production of the new Russian SST would start right away Moscow Radio announced.[8]

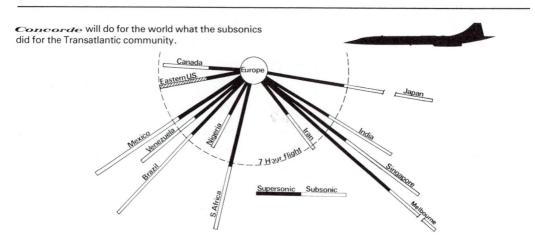

Concorde will do for the world what the subsonics did for the Transatlantic community.

Illustration courtesy British Aircraft Corporation.

A comparison of supersonic and subsonic air travel speeds.

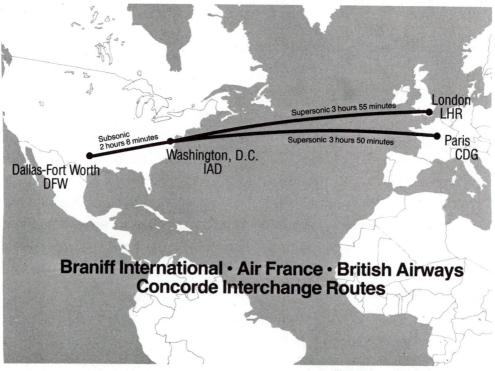

Illustration courtesy Braniff International.

Concorde Interchange Routes.

Braniff Concorde Service. Early in 1979 Braniff, a U.S. airline, began scheduled Concorde service from Dulles International Airport in Virginia to Dallas, Texas. In interchange agreements with the British Airways Corporation (BAC) and Air France, Braniff crews take over from British or French crews at the international port of entry airport (at present Dulles) and continue the Concorde flights across the U.S. at subsonic speeds to Texas.

To do this, Braniff filed a request in 1977 with the CAB for approval and worked with the FAA to find an acceptable means of providing this direct service between London and Dallas; Paris and Dallas.

Why would one wish to use an SST for subsonic flight? One reason given by Braniff is that first class passengers may now board a Concorde in Paris or London and deplane in Dallas after only one stop for fuel at Dulles International Airport in Washington, D.C. The publicity the Concorde generates is, of course, welcome to Braniff. Finally, Braniff hopes that future routes will open up to Concorde service to South America. On these routes the Concorde's supersonic speeds will be most useful over the water portion of the flights.[9]

SST Injury and Damage Problems

It was difficult for the designers and pilots of supersonic aricraft to realize the very real impact of shock waves on property and persons below aircraft flying at supersonic speeds. The evidence is accumulating, however, and is convincing both pilots and the public that there are real hazards involved.

Medical evidence shows "startle" and fear dangers possible in humans. At FAA's Oklahoma City, Oklahoma, test center ten thousand chickens were exposed every day to repeated sonic boom to determine the effects of the noise on their health. Many of the unfortunate chickens died and many of the remaining subjects were rendered sterile and exhibited symptoms of shock.[10] The supersonic boom tests in 1964 near Oklahoma City also resulted in scores of broken windows in buildings. Eventually the citizens of the area rebelled and took the matter to the courts asking that FAA and others be restrained from generating sonic booms over and near the city.

Other possible hazards that may be triggered by supersonic aircraft shock waves are earth and mud slides, mine cave-ins, and avalanches. Structural damage to buildings, in particular the old cathedrals and houses of Europe, is a possibility.

The first case in the U.S. in which damage from sonic boom was clearly exhibited was in May 1958 in Montgomery, Alabama, when a plane created a shock wave and sonic boom which demolished a new control tower nearing completion.[11]

In midafternoon on 5 August 1959, dedication ceremonies were in progress at Ottawa's nearly completed Air Terminal Building. The air traffic controllers gave permission for an F-104 Starfighter aircraft to make two low-level passes above the runway in a fly-by which was a part of the program. The pilot, however, went into a climbing turn at about five hundred feet and roared across the tower and the glass-and-steel terminal building. The four controllers in the tower dived under their desks as the plane passed overhead and a heavy sonic boom hit the area.

The control tower glass disintegrated into thousands of pieces, the terminal roof was ripped open, a curtain wall inside the terminal was distorted, and huge glass panels shattered. Observers reported that the building looked as if it had been struck by an earthquake. Amazingly enough no one was hurt. The building suffered about $300,000 worth of damage.[12]

We can see from the preceding examples that the hazards from sonic boom are real. There seems no method of preventing sonic boom though procedures for minimizing the impact of the noise and pressure exist. Planes near the ground exert the greatest air pressures, and abrupt changes of direction can focus the impact of noise and pressure. It has been found that the larger the aircraft, the larger the boom area. An "average" path of the sonic boom trailing a plane flying at supersonic speeds is around fifty miles wide. A plane flying from Los Angeles to New York could "boom" ten million people. A plane can be twenty miles away when the boom hits the surface below it. So far the only certain way to prevent sonic boom and its unacceptable results is to stay at subsonic speeds. This still leaves an immense area for SSTs to operate in — over oceans, deserts, polar regions — nearly 70 percent of the earth's surface SST advocates point out.

Legally, individuals, corporations, and groups may petition for relief according to the Constitution. To date no court has yet upheld this right. The need to promote military missions and civil air commerce have so far prevailed. As we have seen in the preceding discussion, however, the Congress did halt the U.S. development of the SST.[13]

International SST Law

The International Civil Aviation Organization is at work formulating international rules for the operation of SSTs. New international agreement is needed with the development of this new generation of aircraft because the Chicago Convention has no provisions for member nations to reject such an aircraft for safety reasons. The SST is a new phenomenon with new hazards and new requirements to be regulated. The controversy over whether or not to admit the Concorde to U.S. airspace, discussed below, demonstrates the many factors that regulatory agencies must consider.

There are national laws in many countries that prevent hazardous flights to be made, flights possibly detrimental to society. If international standards are not written, nations may be forced to write their own codes.

The SST — Legal Considerations

We have seen the efforts of governments and manufacturers to cope with the new technological problems involved in supersonic flight. New legal problems, too, have arisen with the development of supersonic flight capability.

Possible cases involving SST aircraft operation might be:

1. Claims for damages to structures due to sonic boom impact and deep-toned engine vibration.

2. Claims against unlawful taking of property, and all or part of the use of a property, due to overflight causing vibration and noise beyond acceptable limits. (Supersonic flight is prohibited).

3. Damages claimed for injury to persons due to noise and sonic boom.

4. Suits filed against airlines and/or manufacturers for damage to the environment.

5. Claims might be filed against governments for takings or injury, since military aircraft are numerous and many have supersonic capability.

333

Plaintiffs filing for remedy or damages will find it difficult to prove that an injury or loss was due to a particular aircraft overflying them. The exact flight path, time, fact of supersonic speed, and positive identification of the aircraft must be established. Further, negligence of operation must be brought out by the plaintiff, another difficult task.

Pilots can minimize the effect of sonic boom to some extent. The acceleration of an aircraft performing a pushover or a turn intensifies and focuses shock waves. Pilots must be aware of this and be responsible for avoiding such maneuvers when possible. Later in this discussion, we will see that other operating prohibitions must be observed.

As mentioned earlier, owners of real estate have property rights only to the air which lies above their property, but which is below navigable airspace as defined by the FAA. The laws of trespass, therefore, do not seem to fit cases involving SST operation. The public owns most of the airspace in the United States. Yet some trespass does take place when an owner's use and enjoyment of the property in question is interfered with, or when its market value is affected.

Flights which are not directly over a person's property can be held liable. The courts have established that flights even to one side of a property can be a taking since noise may constitute the taking factor. When a taking occurs, the owner is entitled to sue for recompense.

Suit on the grounds that the overflight is a nuisance is possible yet less tenable than the claim of an unlawful taking. If nuisance could be claimed, the suits could hamper the development of civil air commerce and military flying.[14]

There is an old legal principle that one conducting an activity which is unusual and hazardous is liable for damages caused by such actions. This might be construed as grounds for suit against supersonic boom or other damage. Concussion damage to buildings and injury to persons while engaged in blasting activities, for example, is held to be a hazardous activity and grounds for suit.[15]

Does insurance cover damages to one's property caused by supersonic aircraft? The answer seems to be that in general it does not, only in the event that one carries an all-risks policy.

Persons can file against the U.S. military for damages caused by military aircraft via the Military Claims Act. Only about $5,000 is recoverable, however, under the non-war duty clause of the act.

Should a federal employee be negligent in some way that results in damages from the flight of a supersonic aircraft, a plaintiff may file suit under the Federal Tort Claims Act. Both the Military Claims Act and the Federal Tort Claims Act require definite proof of damage and negligence to be furnished by the plaintiff, however, and it is not easy to recover full damages.

Aerial Speed Limits. Since a pilot's most urgent need is to maintain enough airspeed to keep an aircraft flying, it comes as something of a surprise to note that there are maximum speed limits today as well. To keep all aircraft within speeds that are roughly similar and therefore conforming to a traffic flow is an air traffic control need. While flying within an airport traffic area (at airports with operating control towers this encompasses a five-mile radius and extends from the surface to an altitude of three thousand feet) pilots should fly no faster than 156 knots in propeller-driven aircraft and 200 knots if flying a jet.

Further, all civil aircraft operating within the U.S. are legally required to fly at subsonic speeds.

Pro-SST Arguments

The British Aircraft Corporation (BAC) stoutly defends the Concorde. Noise levels are not markedly different from long range subsonic jets, BAC contends, and the pollution levels of as many as thirty Concordes would be slight compared with those of thousands of existing jet aircraft.

Responsible routing, the manufacturer's spokemen note, will eliminate damage or injury from sonic boom. Also, about 80 percent of the world's long range air routes lie across maritime or unpopulated areas where the Concorde can operate at supersonic speeds. The tremendous speed of the Concorde can halve travel times and so generate world trade and travel. The BAC shrugs off damage to structures or to health if SSTs are responsibly operated at high flight levels and go subsonic over populated areas.

Fuel costs, BAC argues, are efficient due to the 80 percent load factors that the Concorde flies in its all-first-class service. Further, the Concorde burns less fuel than a Boeing 747 in flying the Atlantic. The BAC disregards the fact that the Boeing 747 can, however, carry nearly five times as many passengers as the Concorde. The BAC's argument for fuel efficiency is further weakened by recent developments. Air France in the summer of 1979 announced a monthly loss of over two million dollars in its Concorde operations.

Ozone contamination, the BAC states, is slight and radiation dangers to passengers in the Concorde are reduced by the short exposure of Concorde's fast flights. The BAC admits that during periods of solar flare, flight levels will have to be reduced. Exhaustive testing and flight trials have made the Concorde a very safe airplane, the BAC insists. BAC claims prosperity for non-SST-passengers will result from the SST service because of improved air commerce and employment. This statement was made to counter accusations that only the "mink and diamond set" enjoy the benefits of the Concorde service.

Concorde development costs to Britain and France have totaled over $2.6 billion. This investment the two countries now hope will generate Anglo-French prosperity with SST use by their airlines and via manufacturing the planes for export.[16]

Concorde Facts. Presently the Concorde accommodates 108 first class passengers. The plane lands at about 180 mph. It is built of an aluminum alloy. (Faster SSTs will have to made with titanium or stainless steel exterior skins.) The supersonic "footprint" or "boom carpet" of the Concorde is estimated to be about fifty miles wide with the most intense "boom" experienced directly below the flight path.

The plane is jointly produced by the British Aircraft Corporation and Aero-spatiale-France. The total planned production at present numbers sixteen SSTs, developed and produced at an overall cost of about $3.2 billion.[17]

Present Concordes cruise at over Mach 2, or about 1,350 mph at cruise altitude (50,000 to 60,000 feet). The plane can carry a 25,000 pound payload 4,000 miles, non-stop. The Concorde cuts transoceanic air travel time in half.

Since each nation has sovereignty over its skies and landing places, each nation must weigh the values and the problems associated with permitting SST service.

The U.S. Decision on SST Service

Air France and British Airways began negotiations with U.S. authorities in 1975 requesting permission to land the Concorde at U.S. Atlantic coast airports. The (then) Secretary of Transportation, William T. Coleman, Jr., wrote the following memorandum to the FAA:

Form DOT F 1320.1 (1-67)

UNITED STATES GOVERNMENT

Memorandum

DEPARTMENT OF TRANSPORTATION
OFFICE OF THE SECRETARY

DATE: January 7, 1976

In reply
refer to:

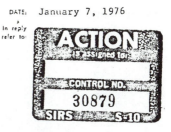

CONTROL NO.
30879

SUBJECT: Safety Recommendations

FROM : The Secretary

TO : Federal Aviation Administrator

I am requesting you, pursuant to your authority under Title VI of the Federal Aviation Act of 1958, as amended, to submit to me a memorandum providing your conclusions concerning the safety of the Concorde SST.

I would appreciate your review of all the information relating to safety that was presented at the public hearing on January 5th and of all of the submissions filed with this office and the FAA by the January 13th deadline.

This document should include an analysis of the safety issues that have been raised and evaluated within the FAA and have been raised through the public hearing process. It would be helpful if you would distinguish between those issues which are our responsibility under the FAA Act and under Article 5 of the U.K.-U.S.A. Bilateral Agreement and Article 5 of the U.S.-France Bilateral Agreement and those issues which are covered by the British and French airworthiness certificates that we are obligated to recognize under the fourth article of each agreement.

May I have your findings by January 16.

William T. Coleman, Jr.

The FAA had been studying the problems associated with SST flight and now began to look specifically at the possible use of the Concorde in the United States.

Air traffic control considerations included the fact that the Concorde is exceptionally fuel critical. That is, it arrives at its destination after an Atlantic crossing with limited fuel aboard, hence limited time left before it must land. The FAA determined that air traffic control must give the plane clearance to land or an alternate airport must be used if any delay of over thirty minutes is expected at its destination.

Also, the FAA was not entirely satisfied with the safety of fuel tanks in which the fuel is heated by transfer of the aircraft's skin friction heat to the fuel. Many hours of flight testing, however, reassured the FAA. The U.S. agency would have preferred some system which would lessen this possibility. Eventually, the FAA determined that the Concorde seemed to be a safe airplane if radiation and ozone levels were carefully monitored.

The FAA Administrator replied to Secretary Coleman on 14 January 1976 with the following communication.

Braniff International's supersonic jet transport, the Concorde.

Photograph courtesy Braniff International.

DEPARTMENT OF TRANSPORTATION
FEDERAL AVIATION ADMINISTRATION

URGENT

DATE: JAN 1 4 1976

IN REPLY
REFER TO:

WASHINGTON, D.C. 20591

SUBJECT: Concorde Safety Issues

CONTROL NO.
31134
SIRS S-10

OFFICE OF
THE ADMINISTRATOR

FROM: Administrator

TO: The Secretary

As requested in your memorandum of January 7, enclosed is FAA's analysis of Concorde safety issues which have been raised, including those discussed at your public hearing on January 5.

There are two separate FAA actions that affect the Concorde. The most immediate is the amendment of British Airways and Air France's operations specifications to allow limited operations of the Concorde in the United States. A second prospective action is the issuance of a U.S. type certificate to the manufacturers (British Aircraft Corporation and Aerospatiale) of the Concorde. To clarify the respective actions and distinguish between them, I would like to offer a brief summary of some terminology and its application.

A type certificate covers the design, construction, performance, and stability of an aircraft. This certificate assures that an aircraft meets the minimum airworthiness standards of the issuing authority. In the United States, that is the role of the Federal Aviation Administration (FAA). Our respective counterparts are the British Civil Aviation Authority (CAA) and the French Secretary General for Civil Aviation (SGAC). Only one type certificate is issued for a given aircraft type design.

An airworthiness certificate is issued for each aircraft produced under a type certificate, and it basically ensures that the aircraft is a copy of the one evaluated in issuing the type certificate. It is important to note two points:

1. Our International Agreements with England and France apply only to aircraft type and airworthiness certificates.

2. Type or airworthiness certificates do not authorize aircraft operation in the United States.

Operations specifications, the basic applicable regulations which govern foreign air carrier operation to the United States, are contained in FAR 129 which require any foreign air carrier operating any aircraft within the United States to carry current registration and airworthiness certificates issued or validated by the country of registry and to obey the air traffic rules and operating procedures when operating in the United States.

A certificate of airworthiness has been issued to the Concorde by the responsible aviation authorities of the Republic of France and the United Kingdom. By issuance of the airworthiness certificate, the aviation authorities of France and England have certified that the Concorde meets or exceeds the minimum international airworthiness standards established by Annex 8 of the International Civil Aviation Organization (ICAO). Article 33 of the Convention on International Civil Aviation (Chicago Convention) provides that:

> Certificates of airworthiness...issued or rendered valid by the contractual state in which the aircraft is registered, shall be recognized as valid by the other contracting states, provided that the requirements under which such certificates... were issued or rendered valid are equal to or above the minimum standards which may be established from time to time pursuant to this Convention.

The United States, France and England are contracting States to the Chicago Convention. The proposed operation of the Concorde would be by British Airways and Air France, the flag carriers of their respective countries where the Concorde will be registered.

There exist Bilateral Air Transport Agreements between the United States and the Republic of France and the United States and the United Kingdom. Article 4 of the Bilateral Agreements provides:

> Certificates of airworthiness...issued or rendered valid by one Contracting Party and still in force shall be recognized as valid by the other Contracting Party for the purpose of operation of the agreed services.

Article 11 of the Chicago Convention and Article 5 of the Bilateral Air Transport Agreements between the United States on the one hand and England and France on the other basically provide that the laws and regulations related to the operation and navigation of aircraft engaged in international air navigation shall be applied in a nondiscriminatory manner in each country.

These provisions do not establish or grant a right to conduct commercial transportation. The provisions of Article 11 of the Chicago Convention and Article 5 of the Bilateral Transport Agreements provide that each nation shall have the right to control such operations and navigation within its own territory provided that it does so in a nondiscriminatory manner. This right to control the operational and navigation activities that occur within the territory of a nation is independent of and distinct from the recognition of the validity of certificates of airworthiness.

The purpose of the foregoing is to distinguish between those safety issues which are our responsibility to evaluate and those which are covered by existing international agreements with the British and French. Basically, the international agreements establish that safety issues related to airworthiness are the responsibility of the British and French. As to the issuance of amended operations specifications to British Airways and Air France, given the issuance of an airworthiness certificate to the Concorde by the civil aviation authorities of England and France, safety findings are the responsibility of the British and French Governments.

In conclusion, the Concorde has been determined by the British and French certification authorities to be a safe airplane design in accordance with ICAO standards. It has also been determined to be safe by the states of manufacture through their issuance of type and airworthiness certificates. Therefore, as a foreign designed and built aircraft, it has satisfied all airworthiness requirements under existing agreements to permit its operation into the United States. Since the aircraft meets international standards and those of the states of manufacture, it can be categorized as a safe aircraft.

The FAA has not completed action upon the request for the issuance of a U.S. type certificate to the manufacturers of the Concorde. There are areas where FAA safety standards may be higher than international standards or the states of manufacture. Before a U.S. type certificate is issued it will meet all applicable FAA safety standards.

Enclosed hereto are separate analyses of the various safety issues which have been identified:

1. Fuel Reserves
2. Safety of the Departure Turn From Runway 31 Left at JFK
3. Cosmic Radiation
4. Air Traffic Procedures and Response to Eastern Region Comments
5. Explosive Decompression
6. Installation of a Fuel Tank Nitrogen Inerting System
7. Temperature Shear
8. Wind Shear

John L. McLucas
Administrator

Enclosures

A British Airways Concorde in flight.

A Concorde flown by Air France.

After public hearings, a study of the FAA material, consultation with U.S., British and French officials, Secretary of Transportation Coleman made his decision to allow limited SST operation in the United States. It was a difficult one, as the portions of the decision quoted below reveal:

342

THE SECRETARY OF TRANSPORTATION
WASHINGTON, D.C. 20590

February 4, 1976

DECISION ON THE APPLICATIONS OF AIR FRANCE AND BRITISH
AIRWAYS TO OPERATE CONCORDE AIRCRAFT TO THE UNITED STATES

The issue before me is whether to permit Concorde
supersonic transport aircraft, manufactured jointly by the
British and French, to operate in limited scheduled com-
mercial service to and from the United States as follows:
not more than four flights per day into John F. Kennedy
International Airport (JFK) located on Long Island, New
York, and not more than two flights per day into Dulles
International Airport located in Fairfax and Loudoun
Counties, Virginia.

The procedural background is as follows: On August 29,
1975, and September 21, 1975, respectively, British Airways
and Air France applied to the Federal Aviation Administration (FAA) for amendment of their respective operations
specifications. 1/ In the past, approvals of requested amendments to the operations specifications of foreign air carriers
have been almost automatic. Past applications for amendments have typically involved aircraft that were produced in
the United States and certificated by the FAA, or aircraft
that were produced in a foreign country and certificated by
such country's counterpart to the FAA and were quite similar
to aircraft already in service in this country. This decision
on the Concorde, however, raises several unprecedented
issues of public policy. The Concorde is the first commercial transportation application of the new supersonic
technology, a technology used for military aircraft for over
20 years. It is of European rather than American design and
manufacture, unlike the vast majority of the aircraft in
use worldwide today. And its environmental impact is
alleged to be significantly different from that of any civil
aircraft now in commercial operation within or to the United
States.

1/ "Operations specifications" include a list of the type
of aircraft to be flown, the airports to be served, and
the routes and flight procedures to be followed. An
application for operations specifications or for amendments thereto must be approved and issued by the FAA
before a foreign air carrier may begin commercial
service to and from the United States. See 14 C.F.R.
§129.

Because a decision to admit the Concorde could constitute a "major Federal action significantly affecting the quality of the human environment" within the meaning of the National Environmental Policy Act of 1969 (NEPA), 2/ the FAA prepared and released on March 3, 1975, a draft environmental impact statement analyzing the likely environmental consequences of permitting the aircraft to land in this country. The FAA circulated the draft for public comment. 3/ On the basis of voluminous comments and continuing research, it then prepared the environmental impact statement that was released to the public on November 13, 1975.

On that date, I also called a public hearing, to be held in Washington, D.C. on January 5, 1976. At that hearing, I listened to over seven hours of argument by proponents and opponents of the Concorde. Representatives of citizen groups, the manufacturers of the Concorde, the two foreign airlines involved, experts in technology and the environment, and American, French and British public officials addressed a series of relevant issues set forth in my Notice of Public Hearing. 4/ These issues highlighted the environmental, technological, and international factors that would have to be evaluated in reaching a decision.

On January 13 the docket for the public hearing was closed. I have reviewed the materials submitted, and a summary of new information and comment thereon has been incorporated in an Addendum to the Final Environmental Impact Statement (EIS), which I am filing today with the Council on Environmental Quality (CEQ).

Today's decision is based entirely on my review of the EIS, on the January 5 hearing, and on my subsequent review of the transcript and other written materials submitted for the record. At the public hearings, the United Kingdom's Minister of State for the Department of Industry and France's Director of Air Transport, Civil Aviation Department, each testified that there was no expressed or implied commitment that the United States was obliged to permit the Concorde to land in the United States, and no one has brought to my attention any such expressed or implied agreement.

2/ NEPA, §102(2)(C), 42 U.S.C. 4332(2)(C) (1970).

3/ The FAA held public hearings in Washington, D.C., on April 14 and 15, in New York City on April 18, 19 and 24, and in Sterling Park, Virginia, on April 21, 1975.

4/ 40 Fed. Reg. 53612 (1975).

THE DECISION

After careful deliberation, I have decided for the reasons set forth below to permit British Airways and Air France to conduct limited scheduled commercial flights into the United States for a trial period not to exceed 16 months 5/ under limitations and restrictions set forth below. I am thus directing the Federal Aviation Administrator, subject to any additional requirements he would impose for safety reasons or other concerns within his jurisdiction, to order provisional amendment of the operations specifications of British Airways and Air France to permit those carriers, for a period of no longer than 16 months from the commencement of commercial service, to conduct up to two Concorde flights per day into JFK by each carrier, and one Concorde flight per day into Dulles by each carrier. 6/ These amendments may be revoked at any time upon four months' notice, or immediately in the event of an emergency deemed harmful to the health, welfare or safety of the American people. The following additional terms and conditions shall also apply:

1. No flight may be scheduled for landing or take-off in the United States before 7 A.M. local time or after 10 P.M. local time.

2. Except where weather or other temporary emergency conditions dictate otherwise, the flights of British

---

5/ The 16 months will enable 12 months of data collection (during all four seasons) and four months of analysis.

6/ The FAA is the proprietor of Dulles and it is therefore part of my decision today to direct the Federal Aviation Administrator to permit one Concorde flight per day at Dulles by each carrier under the conditions noted. The situation with respect to JFK may be complicated by the fact that under federal policy that has hitherto prevailed a local airport proprietor has had authority under certain circumstances to refuse landing rights. If for any legitimate and legally binding reason it should turn out that the JFK part of the demonstration could not go forward--and no one has indicated to me any such final disposition by JFK's proprietor--that would obviously be extremely unfortunate and would greatly diminish, but in my opinion it would not destroy, the validity of the demonstration.

Airways must originate from Heathrow Airport and those of Air France must originate from Charles de Gaulle Airport. 7/

3. Authorization of any commercial flights in addition to those specifically permitted by this action shall constitute a new major federal action within the terms of NEPA and therefore require a new Environmental Impact Statement. 8/

4. In accordance with FAA regulations (14 C.F.R. §91.55), the Concorde may not fly at supersonic speed over the United States or any of its territories.

5. The FAA is authorized to impose such additional noise abatement procedures as are safe, technologically feasible, economically justified, and necessary to minimize the noise impact, including, but not limited to, the thrust cut-back on departure.

I am also directing the FAA, subject to Office of Management and Budget clearance and Congressional authorization, to proceed with a proposed High Altitude Pollution Program (HAPP), to produce the data base necessary for the development of national and international regulation of aircraft operations in the stratosphere.

I herewith order the FAA to set up monitoring systems at JFK and Dulles to measure noise and emission levels and to report the result thereof to the Secretary of Transportation on a monthly basis. These reports will be made public within 10 days of receipt.

7/ As will appear, one reason this demonstration is being permitted despite the environmental problems discussed herein is to avoid discrimination against foreign manufacturers and carriers. I surely see no reason why we should treat the Concorde better than it is treated at home. Thus, I am not about to subject those who live near JFK and Dulles to noise, however slight the increment, that the British and French governments regard as too great for the neighbors of Heathrow and Charles de Gaulle.

8/ It is not contemplated that another EIS would be required to permit continuation beyond 16 months

I shall also request the President to instruct the Secretary of State to enter into immediate negotiations with France and Great Britain so that an agreement that will establish a monitoring system for measuring ozone levels in the stratosphere can be concluded among the three countries within three months. The data obtained from such monitoring shall be made public at least every six months. I shall also request the Secretary of State to initiate discussions through ICAO and the World Meteorological Organization on the development of international stratospheric standards for the SST.

8/   (Cont'd) of the six flights for which provisional permission is now being granted. It is most definitely contemplated--indeed, this is the whole point of today's decision--that the Secretary of Transportation, in deciding whether to permit continuation of the six flights, will give serious attention to the various data collected during the first twelve months, and assembled and analyzed during the demonstration's final four months, and approach the question of continuation of permission for the six flights beyond the 16th month without any presumption either way being created by today's decision. The data and analysis will be made public.

REASONS FOR THE DECISION

    This decision involves environmental, technological, and international considerations that are as complex as they are controversial, and do not lend themselves to easy or graceful evaluation, let alone comparison. I shall nonetheless attempt in some detail to explain my evaluation of the most significant issues--those raised in the EIS, by the proponents and opponents of the Concorde at the January 5 public hearing, and in the submissions to the docket--and the reasons I have decided as I have. For I firmly believe that public servants have the duty to express in writing their reasons for taking major actions, so that the public can judge the fairness and objectivity of such action. Moreover, explaining our reasons in writing may help us avoid unreasonable actions. A decision that "cannot be explained" is very likely to be an arbitrary decision.

    Among the issues I perceive as relevant are:

1.   Am I compelled by either international or domestic law to permit or prohibit the landing of the Concorde in the United States? If I am not compelled by law to make a particular decision, what policy guidance does the law, including treaties, provide?

2.   To what extent is the United States bound under international law to accept the safety determinations of France and the United Kingdom? In those areas properly within its jurisdiction, has the FAA determined that the Concorde is safe?

3.   Should I consider only the impact of the proposed six flights per day in reaching my decision, or should I assume that, no matter how strictly limited my decision is today, its ultimate effect will be a major expansion of SST operations?

4.   What are the environmental impacts of the Concorde in the following four categories: air quality, energy impact, climatic impact and ozone reduction, and noise and vibration?

5.   What benefits will accrue from Concorde operations with respect to improved international travel and communication, technological advances in aviation, and improved international relations?

6. What accommodation will best minimize the more serious costs of Concorde operations while preserving its significant benefits, or to the extent such costs and benefits cannot now be confidently assessed, put us, without significant risk to the American people, in a position to assess them?

I. THE LEGAL FRAMEWORK

A. International Obligations

The rapid development of the aviation industry made necessary a system of agreements to facilitate international travel. A primary concern was that each nation be provided assurances of the safety of aircraft utilizing its airspace without having to conduct an extensive safety certification process for aircraft manufactured in other countries and owned by foreign airlines. In addition, a structure was needed to ensure a policy of nondiscrimination among nations and to promote fairness in granting particular routes. As a result, the United States and many other countries developed an international aviation structure designed to meet these and other objectives.

For purposes of the Concorde decision, the three most important international agreements are the Convention on International Civil Aviation (Chicago Convention) 9/ which was negotiated in 1944, and the two relevant bilateral air transport agreements. 10/ The Chicago Convention is concerned with ensuring the safety of international travel, through both the safety of the aircraft itself and the safety of the ground navigational and air traffic control systems. The Chicago Convention also established the International Civil Aviation Organization (ICAO), with multiple functions relating to the facilitation of international air travel.

Under the Chicago Convention, the aircraft of each contracting state which have been certified by such state as being airworthy are permitted to conduct non-scheduled, non-revenue flights into the territory of any other contracting state without obtaining prior permission. 11/   Thus the United Kingdom and France have treaty rights to conduct such non-scheduled Concorde flights into the United States. However, no scheduled commercial services by a foreign carrier may be operated into any nation unless with the express permission of that nation. 12/

9/ 61 Stat. 1180, T.I.A.S. No. 1591 (August 9, 1946).

10/ United States-France Air Transport Services Agreement, 61 Stat. 3445, T.I.A.S. No. 1679 (March 27, 1946); Bermuda Agreement, 60 Stat. 1499, T.I.A.S. No. 1507 (February 11, 1946).

11/ Chicago Convention, art. 5.

12/ Id., art. 6.

Routes for scheduled international travel are fixed by agreement between individual nations rather than through a multilateral structure. The United States has negotiated bilateral air transport agreements with both the United Kingdom and France which precisely specify routes and the method of apportioning service on those routes among the flag carriers of the two nations. The bilaterals do not specify the type of equipment that may be used.

Article 2 of the Bermuda Agreement, the bilateral agreement between the United States and the United Kingdom, provides that:

> "[t]he designated air carrier or carriers may be required to satisfy the aeronautical authorities of the Contracting Party granting the rights that it or they is or are qualified to fulfill the conditions prescribed by or under the laws and regulations normally applied by those authorities to the operations of commercial air carriers."

Article II(b) of the bilateral agreement between the United States and France contains an identical provision. In addition, the Bermuda Agreement, in language similar to that found in the bilateral with France and the Chicago Convention, provides that:

> "[t]he laws and regulations of one Contracting Party relating to entry into or departure from its territory of aircraft engaged in international air navigation or to the operation and navigation of such aircraft while within its territory shall apply to aircraft of the designated air carrier or carriers of the other Contracting Party." 13/

Pursuant to these reservations of authority, the Civil Aeronautics Board has certain authority to regulate foreign air carriers and in appropriate circumstances to suspend, reject or cancel unreasonable or discriminatory fares in foreign air transportation, and the FAA has authority to

---

13/ Bermuda Agreement, art. 5(1). See also United States-France Agreement, art. V(a); Chicago Convention, art. 11.

regulate aspects of aircraft operations that relate to
safety. It is these provisions of the international
agreements that also reserve to the United States the
authority to deny the Concorde permission to land altogether, or to place restrictions on Concorde operations,
if unrestricted permission to operate would be inconsistent with the policies expressed in the environmental
laws of the United States. 14/

These provisions, and a sense of justice as well,
demand that the laws of this country be applied fairly and
without discrimination. 15/ There are, as shall appear
later, respects in which a total ban of the Concorde at

14/ The United States could conceivably be bound by
international standards relating to environmental
characteristics under certain circumstances, but
those circumstances do not prevail here. Under
article 37 of the Chicago Convention, ICAO may
promulgate international standards on a wide variety
of subjects, including the airworthiness of aircraft.
Nations which agree to be bound by those standards
must then accept them as definitive regulations with
respect to aircraft in international service. Contracting nations may, however, under article 38,
notify ICAO that they will refuse to be bound by
particular international standards or that they will
require observance of more stringent standards,
and those standards will then not be binding on
aircraft operating in that country. If, under these
provisions, ICAO promulgated noise and pollution
standards for supersonic transport aircraft, and if
the United States did not except itself from those
standards, then this nation would not be able to
impose more stringent standards on foreign aircraft
operating into this country. ICAO has not promulgated
international noise or pollution standards for SSTs,
however, and the United States is therefore free to
regulate unilaterally the operations of the Concorde
in this country, or to ban it altogether, for
environmental reasons.

15/ Article 11 of the Chicago Convention provides that
"the laws and regulations of a contracting State...
shall be applied to the aircraft of all contracting

this time, without giving it any chance to prove itself, could conceivably be attacked as discriminatory. However, I do not feel that the provisional and restricted order I issue today can justly be so attacked. It is true that this is the first time that NEPA has been applied to requests by foreign air carriers to conduct operations into this country, but this is the first such request to operate with equipment that was not already in operation before the enactment of that statute. The Concorde is sufficiently different from subsonic jet aircraft in its environmental characteristics that admission on a trial basis and the imposition of different operating requirements are amply justified.

B.   Domestic Law

The requirement that foreign air carriers operate in accordance with operations specifications was devised, in

---

15/   (Cont'd)   States, without distinction as to nationality...." In the history of the proceedings from which article 11 evolved, some further guidance on what constitutes nondiscrimination is found. "[N]o Contracting State shall require any aircraft of another Contracting State to obey regulations relating to flight procedures, traffic control, safety requirements, and the like, or relating to public safety and order, which are more restrictive than those imposed on its own aircraft engaged in international navigation." (Emphasis added.) Proceedings of the International Civil Aviation Conference, pp. 558-559 (Department of State Pub. 2820; 1948, 1949). In addition, article 15 of the Convention requires that "every airport in a contracting State which is open to public use by its national aircraft shall likewise...be open under uniform conditions to the aircraft of all other contracting States." (Emphasis added.)

The bilateral agreements also evidence an intent to prohibit discrimination between aircraft of the United States and those of France and the United Kingdom. Article II of both agreements provides that the air carriers of one State may be required to show that they can comply with "laws and regulations normally applied" by the aeronautical authorities of the other State. Article III of both agreements prohibits discriminatory treatment in assessing charges for the use of airports.

part, as a mechanism for implementing section 601 of the
Federal Aviation Act, which empowers the Administrator "to
promote safety of flight of civil aircraft in air commerce
by prescribing...reasonable rules and regulations, or
minimum standards...as the Administrator may find necessary
to provide adequately for national security and safety in
air commerce." 16/ A requested amendment of operations
specifications can also serve other statutory ends, however.
In this case, since the amendment proposed (to permit Concorde operations) could constitute a "major Federal action
significantly affecting the quality of the human environment," 17/ NEPA applies to the decision. Thus, here, the
operations specifications decision is the mechanism by
which both safety and environmental mandates are brought
to bear. The authority to administer the Federal Aviation
Act was vested in the Secretary of Transportation by the
Department of Transportation Act of 1966 (DOT Act), but
the duties relating to aircraft safety were transferred
by the DOT Act back to the Administrator, in order to
ensure the continuity of the FAA's safety programs. 18/

   Pursuant to this statutory framework, I am relying
on the Administrator's determination that the Concorde
meets the FAA's applicable safety requirements, though I
would add that my review of the record has indicated that
the Administrator's safety determination is amply supported.
The overall decision whether to permit Concorde operations
into this country is much more than a safety decision,
however. It involves substantial questions of environmental
and aviation policy and international relations. As the
Secretary of Transportation, I am charged by the DOT Act
with "the development of national transportation policies
and programs conducive to the provision of fast, safe,
efficient, and convenient transportation...." 19/ I am
directed "to stimulate technological advances in transportation...(and) provide general leadership in the

---

16/   49 U.S.C. §1421 (1970); See also FA Act §313(a), 49 U.S.C.
      §1354(a) (1970).

17/   NEPA §102(2)(C), 42 U.S.C. §4332(2)(C) (1970).

18/   DOT Act §6(c)(1), 49 U.S.C. §1655(c)(1) (1970).

19/   Id. §2(a), 49 U.S.C. §1651(a) (1970).

identification and solution of transportation problems...." 20/
Under the Federal Aviation Act, as amended by the DOT Act,
I am also instructed to "encourage and foster the development of civil aeronautics and air commerce in the United
States and abroad." 21/ I have therefore decided to make
the policy decision myself, pursuant to my authority under
the DOT Act and to my authority under those sections of the
Federal Aviation Act whose authorities remain vested in
the Secretary of Transportation. 22/

Two environmental statutes are of particular relevance
to my decision in this case--the Noise Control Act of 1972 23/
and the National Environmental Policy Act of 1969. Under
the Noise Control Act, which is relevant insofar as it
provides policy guidance for the decision, the Federal
Aviation Administrator, after consultation with the Secretary
of Transportation, is required to promulgate such regulations
governing aircraft noise as he may find necessary. 24/ Among
the facts the Noise Control Act requires the Administrator
to consider is whether a proposed standard is "economically

20/ Id. §2(b)(1), 49 U.S.C. §1651(b)(1) (1970).

21/ FA Act §305, 49 U.S.C. §1346 (1970).

22/ See §103 of the FA Act, 49 U.S.C. §1303 (1970): "In
     the exercise and performance of his powers and duties
     under this Act the Secretary of Transportation shall
     consider the following, among other things, as being in
     the public interest: (a) The regulation of air commerce
     in such manner as to best promote its development and
     safety and fulfill the requirements of national defense;
     (b) the promotion, encouragement, and development of
     civil aeronautics; and (c) the control of the use of
     the navigable airspace of the United States and the
     regulation of both civil and military operations in
     such airspace in the interest of the safety and effi-
     ciency of both...."

23/ 86 Stat. 1234.

24/ Noise Control Act of 1972, §7(b), amending the FA Act
     §611, 49 U.S.C. §1431 (Supp. III, 1973). Under the
     Noise Control Act, the Environmental Protection Agency
     (EPA) proposes rules to the FAA, which must publish the

reasonable, technologically practicable, and appropriate
for particular type of aircraft [or] aircraft engine...." 25/

The Administrator has exercised this authority with
respect to subsonic aircraft, 26/ but he has not promulgated
a noise rule applicable to supersonic aircraft, although the
EPA has proposed several alternatives. 27/ It is significant
that with respect to subsonic aircraft the Administrator did
not impose noise standards on aircraft already built
prior to the promulgation of the standard. Moreover, the
decision not to act precipitously on supersonic aircraft
should not be surprising in light of the history of the
development of the supersonic transport. During the early
developmental stages of this type of aircraft, both in the
United States and Europe, the technological capacity to

24/ (Cont'd) proposed rule in 30 days and commence hearings
in 60 days. Within a reasonable time the FAA must
promulgate the rule, either as proposed or with modifications, or must publish a notice declining to promulgate
the rule and explaining the reasons for the action.

25/ FA Act §611(d)(4), 49 U.S.C. §1431(d)(4) (Supp. III,
1973).

26/ See 14 C.F.R. §36. The FAA promulgated this rule,
Federal Aviation Regulation, Part 36 (FAR 36) after
more than a decade of experience with jet aircraft in
commercial operation. The FAR 36 standards were originally applicable to aircraft certificated by the FAA
after 1969. In 1974, however, the standards were
applied to aircraft which had been issued a type
certificate before 1969 but which had not been flown
before 1974. This change was made largely to bring
within the regulation's coverage the newly produced
versions of older jets for which technology had been
developed to enable them to meet FAR 36. The federal
government has since developed the technology to retrofit
older jets such as the Boeing 707 and the DC-8, which
heretofore have not been covered by the noise regulations. Adoption of a retrofit rule and legislation,
if necessary, are now under consideration. The history
of aircraft noise regulations thus indicates that noise
requirements have been derived from the development of
adequate noise suppression technology.

27/ On February 27, 1975, EPA submitted to the FAA recommended noise standards for the SST that would have made

minimize the noise levels generated by an engine sufficiently powerful to drive a supersonic transport was
uncertain. Promulgation of a feasible noise rule at that
time would therefore have been highly speculative. By
the time scientists had gained a sense of the limits on
the ability to control supersonic aircraft noise levels,
the design of the Concorde was fixed and, for all practical
purposes, immutable. 28/

27/ (Cont'd) FAR 36 standards applicable to future produc-
     tion SSTs, those upon which substantive production
     effort was commenced after March 28, 1975. Current
     SSTs were not included in this proposal, but EPA
     suggested eight possible options for consideration
     ranging from exemption of the original 16 Concordes
     from any noise requirements to prohibition of their
     operation in the United States. EPA recommended option
     3, which would have allowed SST operations at U.S.
     airports designated by the FAA as suitable, if accepted
     by the local airport operator, and subject to certain
     specified operating restrictions. EPA did not elabor-
     ate on what airports would be appropriate, although
     in his testimony on December 9, 1975, before the House
     Government Operations Subcommittee on Government
     Activities and Transportation, EPA Administrator
     Russell Train stated that JFK would not be suitable
     and Dulles was questionable. At my January 5 hearing,
     EPA Assistant Administrator Roger Strelow recommended
     that Concorde be banned from both JFK and Dulles. He
     was not able to suggest any United States airport where
     such landings should be permitted. On January 14,
     EPA transmitted to FAA a new SST noise proposal that
     would apply the FAR 36 standards to any aircraft,
     including supersonics, that did not have flight time
     before December 31, 1974, the cutoff date now appli-
     cable to United States subsonic planes. FAA will
     publish this notice in the Federal Register. A copy
     of this proposal was submitted on January 13 to the
     docket in this proceeding. On January 8, 1976,
     Russell Peterson, Chairman of the Council on Envir-
     onmental Quality, recommended that all commercial
     Concorde flights into the United States be banned.

28/ In order to design the aircraft, the British and
     French had to choose an engine and then design the
     aircraft around that engine's capabilities. Thus the

I must therefore conclude that the absence of a noise rule promulgated under the Federal Aviation Act does not compel a decision either way on whether the Concorde should be permitted to land. I do believe, however, that I have a statutory obligation to consider in the present context those factors the Federal Aviation Act lists as important in a decision to promulgate a noise rule. Thus, I have concluded that the impossibility of reducing the noise level of the Concorde is a relevant factor in my decision--that as I weigh the various competing considerations I should remain aware that the British and French would not be able to modify this first generation of Concordes to reduce the noise impact.

My obligation to consider whether the environmental impact of the Concorde compels me to restrict or ban Concorde operations in the United States also arises from the National Environmental Policy Act of 1969. NEPA "makes environmental protection a part of the mandate of every Federal agency and department." 29/ The reach of NEPA extends beyond the procedural requirements of preparing an EIS and the specific legislative prescriptions of other environmental laws and compels me to undertake "a rather finely tuned and 'systematic' balancing analysis," 30/ weighing any adverse effect on the environment against the benefits to be derived from technological progress and international cooperation. If I should find that the benefits that would accrue from

---

28/ (Cont'd) engine itself was a fixed quantity very early in the design process and attempts to reduce the engine's noise levels without unacceptable reductions in thrust were unsuccessful. The manufacturers of the Concorde would be unable to modify the engine or redesign the Concorde to meet restrictive noise levels. Since the Concorde is the only aircraft for which application to land has been made, and therefore to which a noise regulation might currently apply, the promulgation of such a rule, insofar as it had present applicability, would have been nothing more than a decision to grant or deny the Concorde the right to operate into the United States.

29/ Calvert Cliffs' Coordinating Committee v. AEC, 449 F.2d 1109, 1112 (D.C. Cir. 1971).

30/ Id. at 1113.

an unlimited approval do not justify the environmental consequences, I have the authority to deny the application or to approve it conditionally or temporarily.

Compliance with NEPA requires not only that I heed the policy prescribed by that Act, but that I comply with its procedural requirements as well. I have carefully examined the final EIS, filed today, and I have concluded that it fully and accurately assesses the environmental consequences of the proposed operations. 31/

31/ During the course of public comment on the draft impact statement, there were numerous assertions that the impact statement was deficient for one reason or another. Partly as a result, the final impact statement was far more detailed. Nonetheless, I continued to hear frequent suggestions that the draft statement was so deficient that the proposed EIS should be republished as a draft. Although I understand the desire of the public to comment on a draft that resembles the final as closely as possible, I have found the vehement criticism of the draft, particularly by comparing it to the final EIS, inconsistent with an important objective of responsible government. Massive effort went into the production of the draft and final impact statements, and assertions that alterations in substance between the draft and the final should require the publication of a second draft undoubtedly discourage civil servants from admitting and correcting their mistakes. The substantially more complete final EIS illustrates the process of government working at its best, not the need to prolong the NEPA process by the requirement of an additional draft.

In order to ensure full public discussion on the EIS and to satisfy myself of its completeness and objectivity, I took several additional steps not commonly part of the process of preparing an EIS. Specifically, I released a proposed EIS in advance of the decision, heard testimony at a public hearing, extended the

As I have indicated before, I have accepted the Federal Aviation Administration's determination that the Concorde meets all United States safety requirements applicable to the aircraft of foreign air carriers operating in United States airspace. Because of the substantial public interest in safety issues, however, I invited comments on this subject at the January 5 public hearing. At the conclusion of that hearing, I directed the Federal Aviation Administrator, who was present throughout, to review the testimony and the material submitted for the record prior to January 13, and

---

31/ (Cont'd) comment period to January 13, and asked the FAA to prepare an Addendum to the EIS on the basis of comments received on the docket during that time. I am now quite satisfied that the process of comment and revision are fully adequate to support a decision in this matter. In a letter to me dated January 8, 1976, which is in the public docket, CEQ Chairman Russell Peterson evidently concurred in this conclusion on the EIS. He wrote "We believe it is a thorough and thoughtful analysis of the impacts of permitting such operations; your Department is to be complimented for having produced it. In addition, your personal efforts to encourage full and meaningful public dialogue on the Concorde are most commendable."

One participant at the public hearing suggested that the EIS is inadequate for failing to discuss safety issues. I must disagree that NEPA requires the FAA to prepare impact statements in connection with every safety decision. The Federal Aviation Act establishes a specific procedure for the regulation of aviation safety; NEPA does not append to that process a requirement that impact statements on each decision be prepared unless, as here, the decision will have a substantial environmental impact aside from safety questions of a technological nature. Moreover, the EIS does in fact consider those safety aspects that could be deemed to have environmental effect.

20

to advise me of his findings. I have reviewed those conclusions and find them amply justified, for reasons I have
outlined in Appendix I. The Federal Aviation Administrator's
conclusions are set forth in Appendix II. 32/

32/ The FAA's authority to make a safety determination is
somewhat circumscribed by the Chicago Convention, in
the interest of facilitating entry of our aircraft into
foreign airports, and of foreign aircraft into our airports. The United States is required by article 33 of
the Chicago Convention and by the Bilaterals to recognize as valid the certificates of airworthiness issued
by any other member state, "provided that the requirements under which such certificates or licenses were
issued or rendered valid are equal to or above the
minimum standards which may be established from time to
time pursuant to this Convention." The ICAO has in
Annex 8 established extensive minimum safety requirements; to the extent that any member country, in
certifying its aircraft, imposes requirements as
stringent as those in Annex 8 or more so, the United
States is required by treaty to accept that airworthiness determination, unless we have notified ICAO of our
intention to take exception under article 38.

On October 10, 1975, and December 5, 1975, the French
and British aviation authorities, respectively, certified
the Concorde as airworthy, and to the extent that the
FAA does not specifically regulate to the contrary, the
FAA is bound by treaty to accept these determinations.
Issues upon which the FAA has made an independent safety
determination include the Concorde's ability to operate
in the United States air traffic system, and its ability
to comply with United States fuel reserve requirements.
The safety of the 26 degree bank turn which the airlines
propose to execute off the end of Runway 31 Left at JFK
to comply with the Port Authority's noise regulations
has also been thoroughly tested. The FAA has accepted
the British and French airworthiness determinations
respecting range, explosive decompression, exposure to
cosmic radiation, and temperature shear.

If a United States carrier purchases or leases a
Concorde, it must receive a United States type certificate, and before issuing such a certificate the FAA
will conduct a complete safety examination, and will
require full compliance with all applicable regulations.

II. POLICY FRAMEWORK

Having concluded that I am not compelled by treaty or domestic law to admit the Concorde, and having accepted the Federal Aviation Administrator's conclusion that the Concorde complies with all applicable United States safety requirements, I now must address, as an imperative of sound public policy, whether authorization of the proposed commercial flights of the Concorde is contrary to the national interest or inconsistent with any federal statute.

This obligation requires that I evaluate the benefits to the American people of the proposed Concorde flights, the advantages of introducing commercial supersonic technology to the United States at this time, and the international implications of this decision. It requires further that I accept the mantle of responsibility proffered by NEPA to serve "as trustee of the environment for succeeding generations" assuring "for all Americans safe, healthful, productive, and esthetically and culturally pleasing surroundings." 33

These considerations cannot be completely reconciled in reaching a decision--if by reconciliation one means a decision that will receive universal acclaim--but their significance for today's generation and their consequences for tomorrow's must be articulated, weighed, and evaluated. Unfortunately, there exists no common denominator by which we may compare the values we assign to each. There is not any general consensus from which there will miraculously spring a controlling standard. It is also undeniable that one's perspective is inescapably shaped by his profession, his experience and his concept of the public interest. Government agencies are no exception: the Environmental Protection Agency, the Council on Environmental Quality and the Federal Energy Administration are opposed to the Concorde for environmental and energy reasons, while the Department of State and the National Aeronautics and Space Administration are in favor for reasons of international cooperation, technological progress, and aviation policy. This does not mean that I have not accorded great respect to the advice of these federal agencies; I have evaluated their recommendations--to the best of my ability--objectively and on the merits.

33/ NEPA §101(b)(2), 42 U.S.C. §4331(b)(2) (1970).

Our task is further complicated by the fact that some
of the values involved can be described and quantified with
precision, while others, equally important to their advocates, are more hypothetical, speculative and subjective.
It would be plain error, however, to ignore or discount a
value simply because it cannot be reduced to numbers. And
it would be error still plainer to imagine we can escape
decision because decision is difficult.

As we have benefitted from the advances of science
and technology, so must we welcome technological innovation,
recognizing that what is new is unknown and that progress
is possible only with some tolerance and assumption of risk.
But as we have established our commitment to environmental
enhancement, so must we recognize that transportation
improvements must meet environmental standards.

As we have promoted our aviation and commerce abroad,
so must we deal fairly with the technology of other nations
at home. But as we envision a world shrunk to half its
present size by the speed of supersonic travel, so must
we search for knowledge about the stratosphere and the
delicate ecological balance that sustains our health and
agricultural productivity.

Thus, sound public policy compels me to consider the
immediate and long-term advantages that would accrue to the
American people from these limited flights and then to
decide whether "the public benefits flowing from the
actions [outweigh] their environmental costs...." 34/

The benefits of admitting the Concorde include the
significantly greater speed of this aircraft, enabling
transatlantic flights in half the time needed for subsonic
passage, thereby facilitating international trade, commerce
and cultural exchange; the knowledge that will be gained
from testing the environmental consequences and commercial
viability of the Concorde in order to determine whether
private capital should be committed to the development of a
cleaner, quieter, more efficient SST; the advantages of
securing United States participation in the international
SST structure, thus putting ourselves in a position to influence international environmental, safety and atmospheric
standards; and the enhancement of international cooperation
and economic reciprocity. The benefits should also include

34/   Jones v. District of Columbia Redevelopment Land Agency,
499 F.2d 502, 512 (D.C. Cir. 1974).

the prevention or alleviation of potential harms, such as economic disruption in Britain and France, the threat of economic retaliation, the perception of unfairness or discrimination in the international community, and the charge that, by banning Concorde, the United States--as a possibly essential transatlantic terminus--would assure the demise of the program and preclude the development of a more environmentally acceptable second-generation SST. An important component of our calculation of benefits must also be fairness and equity, for there may have been probable cause for the British and French to rely upon a United States market when they made the resource commitment, now almost $3 billion, for the development of the Concorde.

In evaluating the costs of admitting the Concorde--noise, air pollution, fuel consumption, and stratospheric impact--we have the advantage of an established process mandated by NEPA, a thorough EIS prepared by the FAA, and the existence of reliable methods of measuring at least the objective impact of noise and air pollution. There are, however, subjective judgments that must be made as well, at present necessarily on the basis of insufficient information, about the impact of emissions on the stratosphere, the community's response to Concorde noise, and fuel efficiency in commercial service. These judgments would be aided by actual operating experience under controlled circumstances.

In assessing the environmental cost of Concorde flights, the analysis of the EIS is not limited to the proposed six daily flights. But in that regard I cannot emphasize too strongly that my decision today is firmly and unequivocally limited to not more than six flights per day, and that the authority I grant is provisional for 16 months from the commencement of operations, if not revoked earlier. During the last four months of this period and before any approval may become permanent for the six daily flights involved, an environmental reassessment will be made. 35/ Any additional flights beyond the six would require a new EIS.

I would nevertheless be blind to ignore, in my consideration of the application for these six daily flights, the possibility of a future expansion of operations if supersonic transports become commercially successful and environmentally acceptable. Under NEPA, when any decision may have consequences in the long run of a magnitude

---

35/ See notes 5 and 8 supra.

greater than those of the project at hand, a thorough
impact statement should reflect the potential long-term
consequences of an expanded program, even if additional
federal action and environmental analysis would be required
to approve any new increment. This enables the decision-
maker to be fully informed of the potential long term
environmental effects of an otherwise segmented program.

Although the existing evidence about the environmental
consequences of the Concorde and the substantial doubts about
its commercial viability make expansion highly questionable,
the EIS nevertheless thoroughly analyzes the effect of 25
flights a day to JFK and five to Dulles, based on this
Department's projection of the likely maximum number of
Concordes that would be needed, assuming commercial viability, to service these markets for supersonic transatlantic travel in 1987. I have reviewed this information,
and have been fully cognizant of it in reaching a decision.
But I wish to make absolutely clear to the manufacturers
of the Concorde that I would not hesitate to bar an expansion of the number of flights, or indeed even an extension
beyond 16 months of the six flights per day, if the information obtained during the 16-month demonstration shows that
the noise or emissions have a significant adverse impact
on the environment.

For these reasons, I believe the appropriate measure of
the total costs is the adverse environmental effect of the
six daily flights plus the possibility, however unlikely,
that additional flights may one day be authorized.

There is, however, one possible "cost" of Concorde
operations that I have not considered as part of my assessment of the disadvantages of permitting Concorde operations.
It was suggested at the January 5 hearing that the Concorde
will "skim the cream" off the transatlantic market, with
disastrous consequences for the already troubled American
flag carriers, Pan American and TWA. It has also been suggested that a relevant consideration should be the possibility
that the admission of the Concorde to the United States
would spell the end of the dominance of the world aviation
industry by United States manufacturers, who also deserve
protection by their government.

Without regard to whether those economic arguments
might be true, I have refused to consider either possibility
as an element of the decision I make today. I am, of course,

concerned for the welfare of the United States aviation
industry, but I also believe that competition to the
maximum extent possible is the best way to preserve a
healthy industry. Moreover, the rules of fair competition
between United States flag carriers and carriers operating
the Concorde, as they affect fares, are the direct concern
of the Civil Aeronautics Board. That agency is empowered to
review fares and to ensure that they are compensatory, and I
must therefore leave such considerations to that agency.

*

[Note added by author of *Aviation Law: An Introduction*. Parts III and IV of the Secretary's decision not quoted. Quotation of the decision continues with "Conclusion," at the end of the document.]

CONCLUSIONS

In reviewing the environmental costs of six daily
Concorde flights, I have concluded, on the basis of currently available information, that the impact on air quality,
the effect of low frequency noise vibrations and the climatic
impact of stratospheric emissions are not significant
reasons for denying limited operations.

Although we cannot predict accurately the relative fuel
efficiency of the Concorde in commercial service, I am
troubled by the probability that it will be significantly
less efficient than the subsonics. This is a factor I have
considered under NEPA, but it is not grounds for denying
United States operations. To do so would be inconsistent
with United States energy policy which seeks to improve fuel
efficiency where technologically feasible, but does not bar
the operation of transportation modes because there are
relatively more efficient alternatives available. Nor would
it be appropriate to initiate such a policy by dictating to
other countries how they should allocate their fuel resources.
In any event, the total fuel consumption of six flights a
day is not substantial when measured against total fuel
consumption for transportation. 66/

The theory of ozone reduction and the associated
increase in nonmelanomic skin cancer are, of course, of
concern. But there is genuine dissent at each point in the
causal chain--the chemical reaction, the relative ozone reduction, and the inducement of skin cancer. I have accepted the
theory nonetheless, even though it is not conclusively
established and there is not any accepted way of measuring
the impact of a few flights. Proper caution requires that I
heed the conclusions of the CIAP and NAS studies, albeit with
due recognition of the reservations and qualifications
expressed therein. I have concluded, however, that although
there might be some slight risk of additional non-fatal skin

66/ In addition, most of the fuel will be British or
     French. If it becomes necessary for the United
     States to allocate aviation fuel in the future,
     the allocation for the British and French carriers
     could be discounted by the difference between the
     Concorde's requirements and those of subsonic
     jets.

cancer from a limited number of flights over a period of 30
years, that risk is not sufficient to warrant preventing a
16 month demonstration, the stratospheric impact of which
would be miniscule. During this period there will be the
opportunity to undertake additional tests and measurements,
to seek additional scientific consensus at international
conferences already scheduled or proposed, and to conduct
the FAA-sponsored High Altitude Pollution Program. If additional knowledge makes it advisable to discontinue stratospheric flights, there will be time to make that decision.
In the interim, we must face the fact that there are other
United States-manufactured releases into the stratosphere
that unquestionably have a substantially greater adverse
impact than the limited Concorde flights. To take action
against the Concorde while failing to halt these other
releases might well be perceived as unfair.

The most serious immediate consequence of limited
Concorde operations is noise. The Concorde is noisier than
the subsonic jets, particularly on takeoff, although the
limited flights under consideration will have a negligible
impact on total aircraft noise exposure at Dulles and only a
marginally incremental impact at JFK. But at a time of
heightened environmental consciousness, any additional noise
is a serious adverse consequence. The unique characteristics
of Concorde noise and the publicity that has surrounded its
advent may well aggravate the community's response to this
source of noise. This subjective characteristic of noise
response may best be evaluated through a controlled demonstration period of sufficient length to enable an assessment,
after the initial publicity has subsided, of community
reaction to Concorde noise. A demonstration will also
enable additional testing at various measuring points to
supplement the data contained in the EIS. The information
from this demonstration will enable us to determine whether
these original Concordes should be permitted to operate into
designated United States airports in accordance with specified
operating procedures and restrictions. It will also provide
useful information in the review and evaluation of the EPA's
latest proposal for an SST noise standard, although consideration of that standard will not be delayed until the
completion of this demonstration but will proceed with
deliberate speed. Although I am deeply concerned about the
additional irritation that these few demonstration flights
may cause for some individuals within the NEF 30 and 40
contours surrounding JFK and Dulles Airports, I believe that
this environmental cost is outweighed by the benefits that
will accrue to the American people from the demonstration.

59

Although, with the exception of noise, I do not consider
the environmental consequences of these limited Concorde
flights to be substantial, I nevertheless consider this a
difficult and close decision. It is difficult because the
benefits cannot be easily quantified and depend in such
large measure upon speculation and my obviously limited
ability to predict the future. There are, of course, some
tangible benefits. The Concorde will significantly increase
the speed with which travellers can cross the Atlantic.
This will facilitate international commerce and trade and
cultural exchange. In addition, extension to the Concorde
of the opportunity to prove itself will be an expression of
international cooperation and good will between the United
States and two of our closest allies with whom we share a
substantial cultural heritage. It will help assure our
allies that we seek to act without discrimination and fairly
and equitably in our economic relations with them. It will
be an important reaffirmation of the mutual reciprocity that
has enabled the United States to benefit so substantially
from the export of its aeronautical products for the past
30 years.

I am fully cognizant of the fact that a complete bar of
the Concorde would be a popular and widely acclaimed course
of action, particularly by environmentalists and by the
citizens in many of the areas surrounding the airports.
Perhaps I would even be depicted by the press, however
mistakenly, as the man who stood up to some undefined but
sinister pressure to let the Concorde in--however absent
such "pressure" has in fact been. But I have struggled to
discount such considerations and searched instead for a
better sense of historical perspective from which to resolve
my dilemma. I have also recognized that my absolute denial
of the British and French applications would likely be the
final chapter in the saga of United States involvement with
the Concorde. Limited approval would, in all probability,
not be so conclusive, leaving the opportunity not simply for
further executive assessment--and I have structured my
decision so as to make that mandatory within 16 months--but
also for the scrutiny by the people in the United States and
other agencies of the Government.

These and several other considerations have helped
impel me toward the conclusion that a demonstration period
is appropriate. One is history, which teaches that the

benefits of new technologies are not always readily apparent at the time they are introduced. At various points in our history, if we had not acted with foresight we would never have seen the development of the steamboat, the railroad, or the automobile. The advent of the jets was accompanied by substantial debate and public apprehension. Any new technology brings with it a certain degree of risk and a substantial amount of public concern. But the technological innovation that requires tolerance at its inception also enables control of its environmental consequences. I have enough confidence in this nation's environmental commitment and in the objective judgment of the market place to be sure that if the SST does in fact become the aircraft of the future, it will only be because man will have developed the technology to meet environmental standards and to enable the SST to compete in the market place effectively. But if we bar the Concorde completely, we may well be condemning for all time or delaying for decades what might be a very significant technological advance for mankind.

The adverse consequences of a limited and controlled demonstration are worth the benefit that would accrue to the American people from observing first hand the commercial application of this technology. It will enable us to evaluate whether the SST is commercially viable, whether the consumer is willing to pay the additional cost for the reduced travel time, the extent to which fatigue and jet lag are reduced and the advantages for international commerce.

It will also permit further assessment of the environmental impact, measuring noise levels during actual commercial operations, evaluating subjective community response to the Concorde's unique noise characteristics, determining relative fuel efficiency per passenger mile, monitoring air pollution, and enabling stratospheric testing. The information derived from this demonstration will be invaluable in determining how the technology might be developed to control adverse environmental effects and what United States and international environmental standards are appropriate for the SST. Participation in the international SST route structure will also give the United States a more meaningful role in the international standard development process, particularly concerning the stratosphere.

A 16 month demonstration period will be sufficiently long to evaluate the variables of seasonality, to help justify the initial commercial investment, to test consumer and community response, and to provide both the European governments and United States private industry the opportunity to consider whether the development of cleaner, quieter, more fuel-efficient SST technology is a sound capital investment.

It may well be that further development of this technology is not economically sensible in the energy and environmentally conscious period in which we live. If so, then the Concorde will fail because it is an anachronism, and its failure will be recognized as such rather than attributed to an arbitrary and protectionist attitude of the United States out of fear that our dominance of the world aeronautical manufacturing market is threatened.

Thus, I have concluded that the benefits of an environmentally sound, commercially viable SST would be substantial. I am also convinced that we do not yet have sufficient information upon which to make a judgment about whether such an aircraft could be developed. Given the substantial effort by the French and British to initiate this technology, and the fact that United States participation may well be essential to the commercial success of the SST, I believe this demonstration is needed to determine whether a commitment to this new technology should be embraced.

Accordingly, I hereby order the Federal Aviation Administrator to issue on March 4, 1976, 67/ an order provisionally amending the operations specifications of British Airways and Air France, as described and subject to the terms and conditions set forth on pages 3 and 4 above.

February 4, 1976   William T. Coleman, Jr.
                                    Secretary of Transportation
                                    Washington, D.C.

67/ A 30-day delay in taking a proposed action from the date a final environmental impact statement is filed with the Council on Environmental Quality and distributed to commenters is required by paragraph 9.g of Department of Transportation Order 5610.1B, Procedures for Considering Environmental Impacts, which implements NEPA and follows the CEQ Guidelines, 40 C.F.R. §1500.11(b).

Possible Damage to the Ozone Layer. One of the factors which stopped U.S. SST development was the fear that SST flights might damage the ozone layer of the earth's atmosphere. Today, an FAA-funded Climatic Impact Assessment Program and NASA research has revealed a negligible impact on ozone.[18]

5. *Impact on Stratospheric Ozone*

The stratosphere contains about 90 percent of the ozone found in the atmosphere. Ozone absorbs light in the ultraviolet wavelengths (wavelengths less than about 450 nm*) and thus, has the property of screening out a portion of the solar ultraviolet radiation which would otherwise reach the earth's surface. The thickness of the ozone layer is highly variable in space and time — variations of 10 percent from day to day and of 25 percent over a year are common. There is about twice as much ozone in the polar regions as in the tropics.

The CIAP and other contemporary studies concluded that the nitrogen oxides (nitric oxide and nitrogen dioxide) emitted by Concorde engines *could* lead to reduction of stratospheric ozone through a set of chemical reactions in which ozone molecules are destroyed while the molecules of nitrogen oxides are regenerated. (The nitrogen oxides are formed from the nitrogen and oxygen in air due to combustion at high temperatures, greater than about 1800 K.) Reduced stratosphere ozone would permit more solar ultraviolet radiation, including a biologically-harmful part (280-320 nm), to reach the earth's surface.

There is a considerable body of evidence to show that exposure to the biologically-harmful part of the solar ultraviolet radiation could cause at least one type of skin cancer. Skin cancer is of two types: melanoma which is usually fatal and non-melanoma which is rarely fatal. Epidemiological and laboratory investigations indicate that increases in the biologically-harmful ultraviolet radiation would give rise to increased incidence of non-melanoma. The connection is less certain with respect to melanoma and is under intense scientific scrutiny. Thus, a decrease of ozone in the stratosphere could lead to greater incidence of at least the non-melanoma type of skin cancer. A rough rule of thumb developed by CIAP is that the percentage increase in skin cancer would be about twice the percentage decrease in ozone thickness. (The current annual rate of incidence for non-melanoma in the United States is about 240 per 100,000, while that for melanoma is about one per 100,000 population.)

Any change in solar ultraviolet radiation at the earth's surface may also have impacts on plants, animals, etc. This issue is a very active area of investigation at present and, as yet, no general conclusions can be drawn on such impacts.

Following the CIAP study, it was estimated that a fleet of 40 "Concorde-like" first-generation SSTs, operating 7.5 hours per day throughout the year, could result in a 0.29 percent decrease in Northern Hemispheric** ozone. At the same time, it was realized that further investigations were needed to reduce the scientific uncertainties associated with the CIAP estimates (estimated by the authors of the CIAP *Report of Findings* to be a factor of about 2). Since then, a number of refinements in the calculations of ozone reduction have been introduced by FAA, in the light of new laboratory data on chemical reaction rates, especially the data on the rate constant for the $HO_2 + NO$ reaction. These refinements indicate that the CIAP calculations of ozone reduction appear to have been substantial overestimates. It is questionable whether NO_x emissions from "Concorde-like" SSTs (flying at about 17 km) reduce ozone at all.*** Present results of one dimensional models considering both tropospheric and stratospheric chemistry, indicate that they do not reduce ozone, though these new data need verification before we can completely accept this important finding. Consequently, it is equally doubtful that Concorde-like SSTs would impact skin cancer rates. The National Academy of Sciences, in its recent report**** to the U.S. Congress, has concurred with these recent, though preliminary FAA findings, as is evident from its statement, "The estimated impact of NO_x (nitrogen oxides) from the exhausts of SSTs and other high-flying aircraft on stratospheric ozone is now quite small, almost certainly not a matter of immediate concern." Thus, there is ample time to undertake additional tests and measurements and to continue the FAA-sponsored High Altitude Pollution Program to reduce the remaining uncertainties and verify these new findings. If additional knowledge makes it advisable to discontinue stratospheric flights, or seek regulations to limit the impact of high altitude flight, there is sufficient time to make that decision.

6. *Climatic Impact*

The quantitative relationship between climatic changes (both on short and long time scales) and their causes is just beginning to be understood. As yet, there are no generally accepted methods to predict these changes. It is known, however, that the sun's radiation, in its passage through the atmosphere to the earth's surface, is attenuated by reflection and absorption both in the atmosphere (by air molecules, suspended particles and clouds) and in the ground (which also includes ocean surfaces). The solar energy contained in the part of the sun's spectrum below about 290 nm is almost completely absorbed in the atmosphere, mostly by molecular oxygen and ozone. The bulk of the sun's energy is in the visible part of the spectrum, that part which can be seen by the human eye. The portion of this visible energy, which is not reflected back to space, is large and reaches the ground intact. The solar energy reaching the ground is partly used for photosynthesis and partly for evaporating water from the surface, with the rest used in heating the ground. The ground, in turn, radiates energy at wavelengths far longer than the visible wavelengths. The atmosphere (along with the clouds) is opaque to much of this longer wavelength radiation and this part can be thought of as being "trapped" near the ground. This trapping phenomenon is also known as the "greenhouse effect," from the analogy with the glass roof of a greenhouse, which serves to keep heat inside it. The greenhouse effect is brought about by the presence largely of water vapor and carbon dioxide, and to a lesser extent, of ozone, in the atmosphere. It may be seen, then, that the mean temperature of the earth's surface is determined by the balance of the solar radiation used in heating the ground, radiation lost by the ground, and that part of the earth's radiation trapped near the ground. With this introduction, one can begin to see the likely trends (warming or cooling) in the mean surface temperature that might be caused, for example, by Concorde effluents.

There are three components in the Concorde exhaust which could affect the mean surface temperature:

a. The sulfur dioxide resulting from burning the sulfur in the aviation fuel can lead to particle formation at the cruise altitudes. Such particles persist for some time because of the stagnant nature of the stratosphere and they can increase the portion of the sun's radiation which is reflected back to space or is absorbed by the atmosphere. These particles, in a manner somewhat analogous to the clouds in the atmosphere, may also participate in the trapping of part of the earth's radiation (i.e., render the greenhouse effect more effective). The net impact on the mean temperature would be dependent on the relative effectiveness of the changes in the attenuating and trapping actions. Calculations carried out by CIAP, based on mathematical models of the atmosphere which did not include the greenhouse effect, indicate that there may be a slight cooling at the ground due to the emission of sulfur dioxide.

b. The water vapor present in exhaust as a natural result of fossil fuel combustion could increase the greenhouse effect, thereby leading to a warming at the ground.

c. The nitrogen oxides emitted by the Concorde may have two effects:

   i. They *may*, through the chemical cycle described earlier, destroy ozone molecules in the stratosphere. A reduction in stratospheric ozone would result in less absorption of some of the solar radiation in the stratosphere. To the extent that this stratospheric absorption is reduced, slightly more solar radiation would reach the levels below the ozone layer. A part of *this* solar radiation would be reflected back by clouds, etc., and the rest would reach the ground, giving a slight warming effect there.

   Less ozone in the stratosphere also implies a smaller trapping of the earth's radiation (i.e., diminished greenhouse effect) which would lead to a slight cooling at the Earth's surface. The nature of the net effect is still being investigated at the present time.

   ii. Nitrogen dioxide emitted in the stratosphere, can absorb a small part of the solar radiation. This could lead to a slight cooling at the ground.

The overall effect on the mean surface temperature of the simultaneous injection of sulfur dioxide, water vapor and nitrogen oxides from Concorde aircraft is hard to determine, with large uncertainties even in the direction (i.e., warming or cooling) of the likely change, but it is expected to be almost undetectable. In order to give an idea of the probable magnitude of temperature change, theoretical predictions were made following the CIAP method for a fleet of 40 Concordes operating 7.5 hours a day throughout the year.

The net impact could range from a maximum warming of about 0.003 degrees, Celsius — in neither case more than three one-thousandths of a degree. The CIAP report is qualified by an uncertainty factor of three to ten, and even taking the worst case, the change would only be on the order of three one-hundredths of a degree. It is, therefore, concluded that the possible effect of the Concorde on the mean surface temperature is insignificant. Estimates of the likely changes in associated climatic variables such as rainfall are not possible at the present time, but these correlative effects would also be clearly insignificant.

*1 nm = 1 nanometer = 10^{-9} m

**Conventionally, the ozone change due to SSTs is expressed as a percentage change of the ozone amount in the Northern Hemisphere. This is due to the fact that the flights in the Northern Hemisphere account for a very large fraction of global flights. The change in ozone is estimated by CIAP to be one-half of the Northern Hemisphere change.

***"Stratospheric Effects From Aviation," A. J. Broderick (1978), Journal of Aircraft (in press), AIAA Paper No. 77-799.

****"Response to the Ozone Protection Sections of the Clean Air Act Amendments of 1977: An Interim Report," The National Research Council, Committee on the Impacts of Stratospheric Change, 2101 Constitution Avenue, Washington, D.C. 20418, 1977.

. . . .

FAA's Environmental Assessment. The FAA's assessment of SST operation and its possible impact on the environment is given in the following quotation from FAA's *Final Environmental Impact Statement . . . SST Aircraft,* June 1978:[19]

. . . .

E. *Other Possible Environmental Impacts*

While not generally affecting the environment in terms of impact, certain features of supersonic aircraft, particularly their speed and high cruising altitude, warrant an examination of three factors which may affect passengers: Circadian Rhythm, Health Precaution, and Radiation.

1. *Circadian Rhythm*

The problem of circadian rhythm of jet lag refers to the effect upon individuals who cross multiple time zones at a high rate of speed. A generally recognized formula to calculate the rest period necessary to recover from the effects of crossing time zones at high speed has been developed. This formula identifies the following six elements in the jet lag problem: travel time in hours, the departure time, the arrival time, the number of time zones crossed, the direction of flight (west to east or east to west), and age of the traveler. Applying the formula concepts, since twice as many times zones can be traversed by SSTs in the same time period as by a subsonic aircraft, the jet lag effect may be increased. However, this effect is offset by the fact that the total travel time to traverse a given distance is reduced significantly. The circadian rhythm or jet lag effect is related to travel fatigue.

Travel fatigue is characterized by the fatigue resulting from the length of the flight time. Since supersonic aircraft reduce flight times by approximately 50 percent, the travel fatigue will be diminished for passengers on these flights.

2. *Health Precaution*

Disinfection rules to prevent the transmission of disease by aircraft have been developed which are applicable to international air transportation. These rules have been developed by the World Health Organization and implemented by ICAO.

The reduced flight time related to SSTs will not create a problem for health authorities in the detection of passenger-borne diseases. Flight time is not related to disease incubation time. Discovery of passenger-borne diseases because of reduced flight time can only be a problem if the incubation period is greater than supersonic flight time but less than subsonic flight time. This has not been a problem on present subsonic international flights of less than three hours flying time (e.g., New York or Washington to Toronto; Miami or Dallas to Mexico City) nor is it known to be a problem on Concorde flights to date.

3. *Cosmic Radiation*

Radiation affects the body by causing excitation or ionization of the atoms and molecules. These events can lead to physical and chemical changes which may affect cellular, metabolic or organ structures and functions. The effects of radiation may be classified either as somatic (long-term or short term effect on the individual himself), or as genetic (the effect on future generations). In the past, radiation protection criteria and guidelines for individuals and the general public were primarily based on possible genetic effects. As our knowledge of radiation effects has grown, it has become evident that protection of individuals and the general public from somatic effects is also important.

Radiation is a natural phenomenon that has always existed. The unit used to measure radiation dose is the rem or mrem (1/1000 of a rem). The average exposure of a person in the United States to background radiation from cosmic rays and natural radioactive materials in the earth is about 100 mrem per year. Other radiation exposures result from man's activities. It is estimated that the average annual exposure from the use of radiation in medical diagnosis and treatment is about 73 mrem per person. The average per capita nonbackground, nonmedical dose to the general public is currently about 6.6 mrem per year. Thus the average annual dose to individuals in the United States is currently about 180 mrem.

The National Council on Radiation Protection and Measurement recommend that the average whole body radiation dose (excluding medical and background exposures) to the population of the United States not exceed 170 mrem annually. However, since it cannot be demonstrated that exposure to any level of radiation does not constitute a risk, it is recommended that exposure be kept "as low as reasonably achievable."

The Federal Radiation Council had recommended upper limit of 500 mrem per year (excluding medical and background exposures) as the nonoccupational dose to an individual. This is also the limit adopted by NRC for exposure in unrestricted areas. Since it is assumed that any exposure to ionizing radiation constitutes a risk, which is assumed to increase linearly with the amount of exposure, it is recommended that all exposures be kept "as low as reasonably achievable" within these guidelines.

The risk of radiation induced cancer is considered to be the only somatic risk that needs to be taken into account in evaluating radiation protection. It has been estimated by conservative extrapolation from high dose rate experiments that the chances are about 1 in 10,000 that an individual exposed to 500 mrem will at some later date die from a radiation induced cancer. This risk is assumed herein to be directly proportional to the dose (e.g., the chances are only 1 in 50,000 that an individual exposed to 100 mrem will, at some later time, die of a radiation induced cancer). Simarily, the number of excess cancer deaths per year in a group of one million people exposed to an average radiation level of 100 mrem per year is estimated to be about 18.

Cosmic radiation is encountered in either subsonic or supersonic flight. Radiation dose-equivalent rates vary with altitude. At the cruise altitudes of supersonic aircraft, the rates were found to be approximately double those at subsonic aircraft cruise altitudes:

0.4 mrem/1 hour at 34,000 feet

1.0 mrem/1 hour at 55,000 feet

However, since SST flight times are reduced by approximately 50 percent, the total dose per flight is about the same for both SST passengers and subsonic aircraft passengers.

A potential radiation hazard at SST altitudes is caused by solar flare radiation. On rare occasions (three since 1956), the radiation at supersonic cruise altitude from a solar flare may reach levels considered sufficiently high to warrant reducing the flight

378

altitude in order to increase shielding by the atmosphere. It is expected that all SSTs will carry radiation monitoring devices, as Concordes presently do, in order to measure the radiation level and warn the pilot during a solar proton event which precedes a solar radiation increase from a solar flare. If the dose-equivalent rate exceeds the action level of 50 mrems/hour, the pilot will descent to flight levels required to maintain safety. The National Oceanic and Atmospheric Administration has developed a solar flare predicting capability and a warning network. To date there has been no incident of Concorde having to descend in altitude due to radiation exposure.

VI. *Adverse Environmental Effects Which Cannot Be Avoided*

A. *Noise*

High noise levels are an undesirable but unavoidable consequence of the jet engine for both subsonic and supersonic aircraft. Noise from both kinds of engines is present in the high and low frequency bands; with low frequency noise being more prevalent in supersonic engines, especially those with afterburning. There will be an adverse noise impact from first-generation SST aircraft allowed to operate in the United States. The extent of that impact is dependent on the volume of supersonic aircraft operations and the circumstances within which those operations occur. If future supersonic aircraft are noise certificated in accordance with FAR 36 (1969), they will generate approximately the same noise levels as the current 4-engine wide-body aircraft and have no impact on the baseline noise exposure. It is recognized that new subsonic aircraft designs will be quieter than aircraft complying with FAR Part 36 (1969) since they will be required to meet the noise levels of FAR 36 issued in March 1977. However, as stated earlier, there is no technology presently available that would allow construction and operation of an economically viable supersonic aircraft capable of meeting noise levels significantly lower than FAR Part 36 (1969).

First-generation supersonic aircraft flyovers should be readily identifiable relative to subsonic aircraft because of their distinctive noise signatures. This is a result of not only the difference in loudness, but also the spectral content in terms of low frequency noise. Specifically, between five and ten miles from brake release, the region in which the noise differences are a maximum, the Concorde's perceived loudness or noisiness under the takeoff flight path is approximately double that of B-707, four times the noisiness of a B-747, and eight times as loud as a DC-10. At the FAR 36 takeoff measurement point, 3.5 n.m. from start of roll, the Concorde's sound is approximately one-half again as loud as a 707 or DC-8, about twice as loud as a 747, and approximately four times as loud as the DC-10. The TU-144 follows the same pattern of noisiness relative to other aircraft. The perceived loudness of the first-generation supersonics will be annoying. They will interfere with communications and may cause startle. A detailed discussion of the measured noise levels of Concorde operations at Dulles is contained in the Concorde Monitoring Summary Report.

The Concorde's sound pressure level between 125 Hz to 500 Hz may be up to five times that of present subsonic jet aircraft. This low frequency aspect could induce some structural vibrations, but while perceptible, should not exceed any existing standards for structural damage.

As part of the environmental monitoring of Concorde at Dulles, the National Aeronautics and Space Administration assessed the noise-induced building vibrations associated with aircraft operations. Results show that building vibrations resulting from aircraft operations are proportional to the overall sound pressure levels and relatively insensitive to spectral differences associated with the different types of aircraft. The maximum levels of structural vibration resulting from Concorde operations were higher than those associated with conventional aircraft. However, the vibrations from nonaircraft events were observed in some cases to exceed the levels resulting from aircraft operations. Since the low frequency content of Concorde's noise signature could produce some household rattle and interference with communications, it may be annoying to residents in the immediate airport vicinity.

B. *Air Pollutant Emissions*

The emissions analysis presented in Section IV.B.3 indicates that aircraft operations have a limited impact on air quality. A worst case analysis indicates that though addition of a large number of Concorde flights into an airport could produce an increase in CO and HC, the changes are projected to be small relative to total emissions in the air quality control region. By requiring all SST engines manufactured after January 1, 1980, to meet EPA standards, the rate of increase of emissions from the SST fleet will be reduced.

C. *Stratospheric Pollution*

Sections V.B.4, 5, and 6 discuss the probable impact of Concorde's operations on the stratosphere. Concern over such operations centers on two issues: a change in stratospheric ozone and a change in earth's climate. The exhaust products responsible for the former would be the nitrogen oxides (NO and NO_2), and for the latter they would be H_2O, SO2, and NO_2.

A reduction in stratospheric ozone, should it occur, would permit increased solar radiation, in the biologically-harmful part of the ultraviolet spectrum, to reach the earth's surface. There is considerable evidence to indicate that increases in such radiation would increase the incidence of nonfatal skin cancer. There may be other biospheric impacts, which are not clearly understood at the present time.

Further studies undertaken by the FAA since the conclusion of CIAP lead to the *preliminary* conclusion that the Concorde operations may not change stratospheric ozone at all. Investigations are underway to confirm or modify this conclusion.

Insofar as the consequences on climate are concerned, all studies to date indicate only insignificant impact due to the Concorde operations.

VII. *The Relationship Between the Short-Term Use of Man's Environment and the Maintenance and Enhancement of Long-Term Productivity*

Productivity refers to the ability to do work efficiently. Greater air carrier productivity can be achieved by the development and operation of more fuel efficient and/or larger aircraft. Increased air carrier productivity provides the basis for airlines to:

● accommodate normal travel growth requirements coincident with attractive service in terms of departure and arrival schedules;

● maintain a reasonable financial return;

● provide the traveling public with reasonable service at reasonable fares; and

● maintain reasonable worldwide civil air transport fleet sizes.

The introduction of supersonic aircraft into passenger service is accompanied by a variety of uncertainties with regard to the possible impact on long-term productivity. Despite the increased speed, the limited 100-125 passenger seating capacity of the first-generation SST aircraft limits their productivity to a level significantly below that of current wide-bodies subsonic jet aircraft. A Concorde flying one round trip a day between New York and London would produce about 75,000 seats per year in the market. Concorde has the capability of flying two round trips daily which produces 150,000 seats per year. A 747 in the same market would produce about 270,000 seats per year. Also, labor cost which had dominated commercial aviation cost is no longer the sole major cost factor in view of the sharp rise in the cost of fuel. This latter consideration favors the more fuel-efficient aircraft; and appears to be a permanent change in airline economics. Finally, the relatively limited range of the present SSTs (approximately 4000 statute miles) precludes them from many nonstop international routes. Because of these various uncertainties, the SSTs are in much the same position as the early, range-limited Boeing 707 in terms of testing the demand for the type of service it offers. In the event a demand is generated, production of a fleet of SSTs could result. At present, however, it appears that economic and environmental constraints may limit the Concorde fleet to the 16 or so aircraft contemplated for production and the scope of their operations will be limited. Moreover, any SSTs beyond the 16 Concordes would be obliged to meet FAR Stage 2 noise standards in order to operate into the United States and would therefore be indistinguishable from subsonic aircraft.

VIII. *Irreversible Commitment of Resources*

A. *Fuel*

Petroleum is the only fuel which will be used in aviation for the foreseeable future. The drastically increased price of petroleum in recent years significantly affects aviation economics. The recent fuel crisis emphasized both the increase in petroleum usage over the past fifty years and the limitations on its availability. Except for one period in 1974, the aviation industry has been supplied with all the petroleum it required; and at that time 95 percent of demand was available.

The allocation of petroleum among all users, not merely transportation, is controlled by regulatory action taken by the Federal Energy Administration (10 CFR Part 211). These regulations specifically address and provide for the quantity of fuel allocated to all aviation and make provision for the allocation of bonded fuel for use in international flight operations. All fuel used for supersonic as well as subsonic aricraft are subject to those allocation rules.

All transportation modes use approximately 60 percent of the total petroleum consumed in the United States. This is approximately 25 percent of the total energy consumed in the United States. Of the total petroleum consumed by transportation in the United States, approximately 10 percent of that is consumed by all aviation use. The percentage of petroleum used in and by international flight operations is relatively small. However, if the assumed Concorde fleet size of 16 is achieved and operated an average of 8 hours per day, 288,000,000 gallons of fuel would be consumed each year or nearly 3 billion gallons over a ten year period.

In comparing supersonic fuel consumption to present subsonic airplanes, the Concorde uses approximately 146,000 pounds (20,857 to 22,462 gallons) of fuel for a 3,000 nautical mile trip (3,450 statute miles), while for a trip of the same distance, the 707-300 would use approximately 91,500 pounds of fuel, the 747 would use approximately 170,000 pounds of fuel, the DC-8-61 would use approximately 94,500 pounds of fuel and the DC-10 would use approximately 98,000 pounds of fuel. Depending on the seating configuration of the specific airplane, the Concorde would use approximately two to three times as much fuel per seat mile as the subsonic airplanes. Based on Civil Aeronautic Board figures for 1976, it is calculated that the B-747 in international operations consumed .225 pounds of fuel per passenger mile flown. (CAB Aircraft Operating Cost and Performance Report Volume XI, July 1972, page 32.) In the high density North Atlantic market, the B-747 would be more efficient than its worldwide average. Based on FAA calculations, the Concorde has used, in actual operation, .75 pounds of fuel per passenger mile over the 3300 nautical mile North Atlantic route. This is approximately three times as much as the 747 average for 1976. It is expected that future design SSTs will be more fuel efficient than current SSTs, however, the power required to travel at supersonic speeds is such that SSTs will continue to consume more fuel per passenger mile than subsonic long-haul aircraft.

B. *Material/Labor*

The materials used for the construction of the first-generation supersonic aircraft are similar to those used in subsonic aircraft.

Second-generation SSTs will probably use the same materials with an increased percentage of titanium. The following types and quantities of material are used in the Manufacture of the Concorde SST:

Type	Metric Tons Per Aircraft
Aluminum	35.2
Steel	15.6
Titanium	4.7
Chromium	1.32
Nickel	3.52
Manganese	0.09
Molybdenum	0.32
Copper	2.16
Gold	0.001
Silver	0.001
Platinum	0.001

It is expected that similar proportions of most of these materials would be required to manufacture second-generation SSTs. It is probable that a greater percentage of titanium would be used for future generation SSTs.

U.S. Regulation of SST Aircraft

The *Federal Register* of 13 October 1977 discussed proposed changes in FAR Parts 21, 36, and 91 to encompass the use of SST aircraft. The Department of Transportation's FAA submitted information as did the U.S. Environmental Protection Agency (EPA). Authority for action lay in the Noise Control Act of 1972 and the Federal Aviation Act of 1958 as amended.

Rule changes were proposed which would:

1. Exempt 16 Concorde's flown before 1 January 1980 from compliance with FAR Part 36, stage 2, noise requirements.

2. Prohibit modifications in SST's which would increase noise levels. (Larger engines, other design changes.)

3. Place operational restrictions on those SSTs which are not in compliance with Part 36.

383

4. Provide for flight tests to provide proof of noise levels not over Part 36 requirements.

Further, regulations to protect U.S. territories and land areas from sonic boom were proposed. An environmental impact statement was advocated. Public hearings were to be set after all comments were in. The deadline for comments on the proposed legislation was set for 31 December 1977.

As of 29 June 1978 FAA entered the rule changes adopted in the *Federal Register*.[20] The rules in general, restricted the number of flights, set rules of operation to deny supersonic speeds over the U.S. and its territories, and set curfews on SST operation. Other rules, designed to limit noise and emissions, were given. Concessions to the limited fuel reserves of the present generation of SST (in actuality the Concorde) were made.

No direct acknowledgment was made to the EPA's broad noise level recommendations for subsonic and SST aircraft. These, however, are not a dead issue but are still pending.

The federal government (DOT, FAA, EPA) has passed the politically sensitive issue of admitting SSTs over to local airport proprietors. These local authorities, in turn, acknowledged political pressures in their response. Passing the decisions on whether or not to allow SST operation, also passes on to local proprietorship the liabilities and possible lawsuits involved.

Dulles International Airport, for example, which is federally owned and FAA-operated, admitted SSTs under the conditions set by FAA. Management of the John F. Kennedy Airport in New York faced a public outcry against the SST. The JFK airport authorities decided not to decide. Companies seeking permission to land Concordes at that airport brought suit to force a decision and authorities then admitted SST operation. The public received the impression that this decision had been forced upon the airport's proprietors. At Dullas International, on the other hand, the SST was welcomed.

The FAA has the legal responsibility not only to act in the interests of public safety but to encourage and promote aviation. The careful demonstrations program of SST operation, with safeguards written in, comply with the safety requirement. The FAA's duty to promote aviation and realistic assessment of national economic and business interests are met by allowing SST operation. operation.

There is a current trend to bypass regulatory agencies and regulate by Congressional action. This is, of course, a response to political, public, and special interest pressures. This is seen by some as being too dogmatic and inflexible an approach. FAA's response to the SST is an example of flexible, yet responsible, action by a regulatory agency.

The following exerpt from the *Federal Register* gives rule changes adopted by FAA after a study of SST operation and public hearings:[21]

28406 [4910-13] Title 14—Aeronautics and Space

CHAPTER 1—FEDERAL AVIATION ADMINISTRATION, DEPARTMENT OF TRANSPORTATION

[Docket Nos. 10494 and 15376; Amdt. 21-47, 36-10, and 91-153]

CIVIL SUPERSONIC AIRPLANES

Noise and Sonic Boom Requirements

AGENCY: Federal Aviation Administration (FAA), Department of Transportation.

ACTION: Final rule.

SUMMARY: These final rules (1) require all civil supersonic airplanes (SSTs), except Concordes with flight time before January 1, 1980 (presently expected to include 16 Concordes), to comply with the noise limits of Part 36 of Title 14 of the Code of Federal Regulations ("part 36") that were originally applied to subsonic airplanes, in order to operate in the United States; (2) prohibit the issuance of U.S. standard airworthiness certificates to Concordes that do not have flight time before January 1, 1980, and that do not comply with part 36; (3) prohibit the operation in the United States of the excepted Concorde airplanes if they have been modified in a manner that increases their noise; (4) prohibit scheduled operations of the excepted Concorde airplanes at U.S. airports between 10 p.m. and 7 a.m., and (5) prohibit SSTs that are outside the United States from causing sonic booms in the United States when flying to or from U.S. airports. These provisions respond to the public need for the control of sonic boom and SST noise in accordance with 611 of the Federal Aviation Act of 1958, as amended by the Noise Control Act of 1972. The rules do not establish certification noise limits for future design SST's, since the technological feasibility of such standards is at present unknown. The FAA's goal is not to certificate, or permit to operate in the United States, any future design SST that does not meet standards then applicable to subsonic airplanes. This rule is issued following close coordination with the U.S. Environmental Protection Agency (EPA). A detailed discussion of FAA's disposition of EPA's proposals concerning SST noise is contained in a separate notice of decision published in this issue of the Federal Register.

EFFECTIVE DATE: July 31, 1978.

FOR FURTHER INFORMATION CONTACT:

Mr. Richard Tedrick, Program Management Branch (AEQ-220), Environmental Technical and Regulatory Division. Office of Environmental Quality, Federal Aviation Administration, 800 Independent Avenue, SW., Washington, D.C. 20591, telephone 202 755-9027.

SUPPLEMENTARY INFORMATION:

I. Synopsis

A detailed section-by-section analysis of these rules is furnished at the conclusion of this preamble. Briefly, these rules are substantively the same as those proposed in notice No. 77-23 on October 13, 1977, and have the following effects:

A. SST OPERATIONS IN THE UNITED STATES

Except for the 16 Concordes which are expected to have flight time before January 1, 1980, all SSTs are required by these rules to comply with the noise limits of part 36 in effect on January 1, 1977 ("stage 2 noise limits"), in order to operate in the United States. These are the same noise limits that were originally applicable to subsonic airplanes by part 36. It is the FAA's goal not to certificate or permit to operate in the United States any future design SST that does not meet standards then applicable to new design subsonic airplanes. Accordingly, consistent with technological developments, the noise limits in this rule are expected to be made more stringent before a future design SST is either type certificated or permitted to operate in the U.S.

B. THE FIRST 16 CONCORDES

The first 16 Concordes, which is the maximum number that Britain and France are expected to manufacture before January 1, 1980, are excepted from compliance with the stage 2 noise limits of part 36. There is presently no expiration date on this exception. However, under these rules, the excepted Concordes may not be operated on flights scheduled, or otherwise planned, for takeoff or landing at U.S. airports after 10 p.m. and before 7 a.m. local time. Moveover, these rules subject the expected Concordes that operate in the United States to an "acoustical change" requirement identical to that applied to U.S. type-certificated subsonic airplanes that have not been shown to comply with stage 2 noise limits. Like those subsonic airplanes (which are called "stage 1 airplanes" in part 36), the noncomplying Concordes may not be operated in the United States if their design is changed in a way that increases their noise levels.

C. LATER CONCORDES: "NEW PRODUCTION" RULE

Although it is expected that Concordes will not be produced beyond January 1, 1980, such production is possible. Accordingly, for any Concorde that does not have flight time before January 1, 1980, this rule prohibits the issuance of a U.S. standard airworthiness certificate unless the airplane complies with at least the stage 2 noise limits of part 36.

386

D. CONCORDE TYPE CERTIFICATION NOISE LIMITS

The British-French Concorde is the only SST for which application has been made for a U.S. type certificate. A U.S. type certificate constitutes FAA approval of the safety and environmental aspects of an airplane type and is necessary for American air carriers to operate the airplane. Because there is no presently known technology which would reduce Concorde noise levels, the maximum noise limits (for approach, takeoff, and sideline) authorized at this time by these rules for the purposes of a U.S. type certificate are the current noise levels of that airplane.

E. CONCORDE TYPE CERTIFICATION: TEST PROCEDURES

These rules broaden the detailed noise measurement and evaluation procedures of part 36 to cover supersonic (as well as subsonic) civil airplanes. In addition, various flight test provisions unique to the Concorde are included because of the special takeoff and approach testing considerations posed by the delta wing of that air plane.

F. AIRPORT PROPRIETORS' "LOCAL OPTION": NO CHANGE

These rules do not in any affect the existing legal authority of airport proprietors, acting as proprietors, to exercise their "local option" to limit the use of their airports in a manner that is not unjustly discriminatory and does not unduly burden interstate and foreign commerce. As stated in 36.5 of part 36, an FAA determination of compliance or noncompliance with part 36 does not bind an airport proprietor in its determination whether an airplane is acceptable or unacceptable for operation at its airport.

G. SONIC BOOM

These rules prohibit SST's from producing sonic booms in the United States while they are going to or from U.S. airports, even if the airplane is outside the United States at the time. Prior to these rules, supersonic flight was prohibited only while the airplane itself was in U.S. airspace.

H. CONTINUED OPERATIONS OF CONCORDE

Consistent with the provisions of these rules, FAA amendments to operations specifications of air carriers that operate Concorde may be issued without additional environmental analysis up to the numbers of total Concorde operations specified for each airport analyzed in the final environmental impact statement (EIS) for these rules. Federal issuance or amendment of operations specifications has no bearing on local airport proprietor approval of Concorde operations.

By the terms of the FAA operations specifications issued to the British Airways and Air France in April 1976, the 16-month demonstration period at Dulles Airport ended September 24, 1977. After Secretary of Transportation Brock Adams announced his decision on September 23, 1977, to issure notice No. 77-23, the two carriers were issued amendments to their operations specifications to permit the number of Concorde operations that were originally approved on February 4, 1976 (one flight per day per carrier), to continue until the issuance of these rules. After the effective date of these rules, upon application by an air carrier, Concorde operations will be authorized at Dulles International Airport up to the number specified in the EIS for these rules.

The 16-month demonstration period at John F. Kennedy International Airport ("J.F.K."), for which two Concorde flights per day for each carrier were authorized, began on November 22, 1977. However, the issuance of these rules supersedes that authorization. Authorization of Concorde operations up to the number studied in the EIS will not require further environmental analysis.

I. CONSISTENCY WITH SAFETY

These rules regulate only the noise of SST's. They do not dispose of airworthiness issues concerning the Concorde that are currently being evaluated under applicable airworthiness regulations. These rules are consistent with the highest degree of safety in air commerce.

J. FUTURE SST'S: PROGRESSIVE NOISE REDUCTION

With the issuance of these rules, the FAA takes the first step toward ensuring that future SST's are subject to the same noise levels as subsonic aircraft, and are made as fully compatible with future airport environments as possible. It is anticipated that no future SST design will be type certificated without the issuance by the FAA, after full public participation, of noise regulations that are environmentally effective and consistent with the economic and technological considerations in 611 of the Federal Aviation Act of 1958.

II. PRIOR HISTORY

These rules conclude a process that began formally with an advance notice of proposed rulemaking in 1970, and has since involved three notices of proposed rulemaking ("NPRM"), numerous public hearings, demonstration of the Concorde at Dulles and J.F.K. Airports, the preparation of two comprehensive environmental impact statements, and the consideration of over 11,300 comments from airport neighbors and other concerned citizens, airport proprietors aircraft operators, aircraft manufacturers, and Federal, State, and local governmental agencies. These comments have greatly assisted the effort to develop requirements that are balanced in their responsiveness to divergent public concerns, and are effective in terms of public relief from the noise of civil supersonic air transportation. These rules were developed over the course of 1 year in close consultation between Secretary of Transportation Brock Adams and FAA Administrator Langhorne Bond. The rules reflect the Secretary's responsibility for overall national transportation policy and his concern that these final rules properly take into account all aspects of that policy—including environmental, economic, and international aviation considerations. The history of this regulatory action is described more fully in notice 77-23, which is the most recent NPRM preceding these rules, 42 FR 55176 (October 13, 1977).

A Future U.S. SST?

Judging by the huge costs involved in its development and manufacture, the present SST engine noise levels, the problems with sonic boom, the limited number of passengers carried by present SSTs, and the fuel-hungry engines that power SSTs — it would seem that the SST might not be suited to today's world. Scientists' persistent curiosity and determination, however, have developed new theories and new manufacturing processes and have improved other high-speed flight technology. Today the SST research programs continue and are now showing signs of revival.[22]

For example, program options for advanced supersonic transport technology readiness were requested in September 1977 by the House of Representatives Subcommittee on Transportation, Aviation and Weather. A NASA spokesman reported on industry views regarding technology readiness and on NASA's summary of technology and possible SST research options.

NASA advocated:

1. An integration in development of SST airframes and propulsion systems.

2. Trans-Pacific range.

3. Double to triple payload of Concorde.

4. Acceptable noise levels.

5. Low emissions.

6. Payloads high enough to allow first class and other fares.

Industry views on time required for completion of research readiness and technology vary from the end of 1983 to the end of 1985. The three companies involved stated that they could then have enough basic research done to make a decision whether or not to produce the aircraft. The cost of such development, the three companies agreed, would be approximately $400 million for airframes and from $135 million to $400 million for engines. Costs would be spread over the six to nine years required for the advanced technology development phase.

U.S. aircraft and engine manufacturers could be technically ready to produce an SST with trans-Pacific range, one environmentally acceptable and

389

economically viable, by the end of 1984, if development of technology is pursued, a NASA spokesman concluded.

The reasons for the development of a U.S. technology capable of producing a second generation SST are: (a) airline needs for a long range commercial transport which will be profitable to operate and environmentally satisfactory. (b) U.S. leadership in commercial transport manufacture and export, (c) the application of research to many fields, and (d) employment of skilled American workers.

Federal funding of the research and development phase is needed because: (a) there is no military aircraft or similar design upon which to base an SST design, (b) the United States will benefit via employment and eventual export trade, and (c) development costs would strain the financial stability of U.S.

manufactuers. U.S. prestige and dollar export totential are involved.

The National Aeronautics and Space Administration program is now known as SCAR (Supersonic Cruise Aircraft Research). A supersonic cruise aircraft is one which can maintain supersonic speeds as opposed to our present military supersonic planes which are "dash oriented," that is, capable of bursts of speeds at very high Mach numbers. The NASA SCAR program was set up to develop basic technology in aircraft configuration, new engine designs, and fabrication techniques using new materials and methods. Great design concept improvements have resulted.

Other nations are well ahead of the U.S. at this time, but this need not be the case in the 1980s. Funding of NASA transport research is being urged. In September 1978 NASA reported to the House Committee on Science and Technology that a six-year program to provide a technological base for SST development would cost on the order of $300 million.[23]

Around $7 billion would be needed to develop a U.S. SST, industry and NASA spokesmen agree. In about three more years a research aircraft will be needed as an aid to further development of the American SST, according to a Boeing engineer. A Lockheed design engineer sees American manufacturers wanting to begin building an SST by 1985. Even if unlimited funds were available, however, it would be 1990 before an American SST could be ready for use.[24]

The U.S. SST development program continues today without the sizable Congressional appropriations that would provide U.S. technological readiness to produce an acceptable second generation SST by the mid-1980s. NASA's SCAR programs continue with only about a $10 million annual budget for basic airframe research data and approximately $6 million a year to accumulate data on a possible variable-cycle engine. (Other NASA programs aimed at improving subsonic aircraft and air traffic control claim NASA funds and attention.)

Three aircraft manufacturers, Boeing, Lockheed, and McDonnell Douglas, are now at work designing concepts for a new generation of supersonic transport aircraft. The companies are assisted by the NASA funding just mentioned, and have been through the 1970s. To government funds, all three companies have added millions in matching funds from their own coffers. [25]

The engine research grant funded by the five-year, $22 million NASA program is being carried out by two major U.S. engine manufacturers, Pratt and Whitney and General Electric.[26]

All five manufacturers mentioned above pool information derived from NASA-funded research.

At NASA's Langley Research Center. In NASA's Langley, Virginia, research facility extensive wind tunnel tests have been made of the McDonnell Douglas Advanced Supersonic Transport (the DC-AST). Using a thirty-foot-long, one-tenth full size scale model, tests on the DC-AST were run late in 1978 in the huge NASA wind tunnel to check the aerodynamic potentials in the design. It is a modified "blended body" aircraft. A blended body design is one in which the wings, control extensions, and engines are curved, smoothly blended into the fuselage. The DC-AST is a "modified blended body" in which the bottom of the wings blend in an unbroken line with the bottom of the fuselage. The top of the wing, however, has a more conventional joining with the fuselage. The McDonnell Douglas design includes windows in the passenger compartment as competing designs at present do not.

By using a blended body design, manufacturers can reduce drag and obtain higher speeds and obtain better fuel utilization. The windows present a great problem on several counts: possible radiation dangers to passengers at high levels; the problem of countering leaks at stratospheric flight levels; and drag increase due to protrusions on the surface. These and other considerations have eliminated passenger windows in many proposed SST designs.[27]

Technological Advances. New methods of forming titanium have been developed since the SST program in the U.S. was halted. This very hard, heat-resistant metal has long presented fabrication problems, becoming brittle at certain points in the process of being shaped and bent. It is difficult to cut because of its strength.

New techniques now involve shaping sheets of titanium placed one atop the other, by boring holes in the metal and injecting high pressure argon gas into the desired structure while the entire component is heated in an enormous oven. The titanium bubbles up, assumes a plasticity and when the process is completed an entire component is as strong as though made of one piece of metal. By this method a complex portion of an aircraft can be formed. The process is known as superplastic forming and diffusion bonding.

Studies are continuing to find an aluminum alloy with high resistance to heat and one which will retain its original shape regardless of the number of times it has been heated and cooled. Aluminum has the advantage of being a much less expensive metal than titanium and is more malleable.

New Engine Designs. To obtain the enormous power needed for supersonic flight and yet get noise levels at takeoff power down to acceptable levels, several approaches are being considered.

One promising field of research is the variable-cycle engine (VCE), which is in effect a relatively quiet and efficient turbo fan engine at low altitudes and a powerful turbo jet at stratospheric flight levels where SSTs cruise. Once this engine is perfected, SSTs should be able to cruise at the legally required subsonic speeds over land areas with good fuel economy. Over desert or ocean areas the plane could climb to high flight levels and use the VCE as a turbo jet for supersonic capability.

The VCE is being developed under a NASA program by the Pratt and Whitney and the General Electric engine manufacturers. The NASA funding is slated to end in 1980 at this writing. The outlook for the success of this engine at the present time is promising.

The two-in-one engine, the VCE, has turbine fans which can be adjusted to take varying volumes of air flow. Air flow is diverted to and from the turbines as needed by internal valves.

Coannular flow is used at lower flight levels to reduce engine noise. By mixing hot exhaust gases with (cooler) outside air, noise reduction results due to

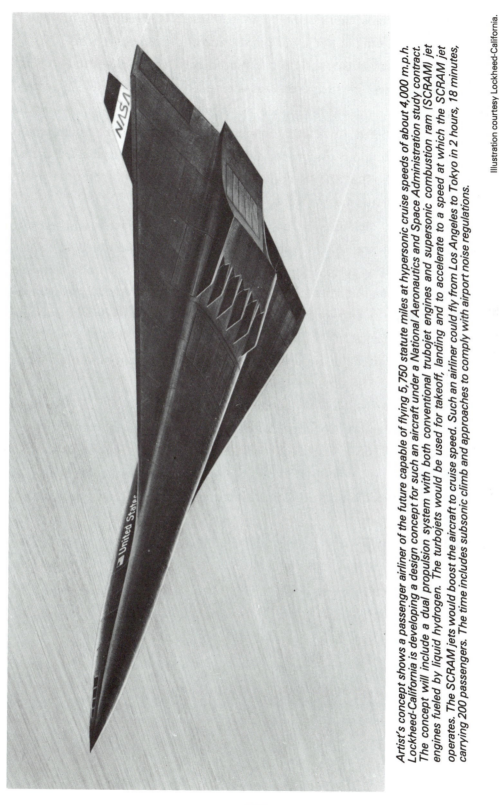

Artist's concept shows a passenger airliner of the future capable of flying 5,750 statute miles at hypersonic cruise speeds of about 4,000 m.p.h. Lockheed-California is developing a design concept for such an aircraft under a National Aeronautics and Space Administration study contract. The concept will include a dual propulsion system with both conventional trubojet engines and supersonic combustion ram (SCRAM) jet engines fueled by liquid hydrogen. The turbojets would be used for takeoff, landing and to accelerate to a speed at which the SCRAM jet operates. The SCRAM jets would boost the aircraft to cruise speed. Such an airliner could fly from Los Angeles to Tokyo in 2 hours, 18 minutes, carrying 200 passengers. The time includes subsonic climb and approaches to comply with airport noise regulations.

Illustration courtesy Lockheed-California.

the fact that cool gases move slower than hot gases. This reduction of noise is suitable for maneuvering in the lower flight levels and around airports.

A dramatic improvement has been achieved by General Electric and Pratt and Whitney designers in their proposed engine. It would use only 75 percent of the fuel now required by the Concorde engines. Also, the engine would be installed on a projected Advanced Supersonic Transport (AST) which would carry about three hundred passengers, thus reducing the fuel cost even further per passenger mile. The SST aircraft engines will, however, consume much more fuel than present subsonic transport engines.[28]

The designers at McDonnell Douglas and at Lockheed have worked out various aircraft and engine configuration plans which also will help to reduce engine noise. Mounting one engine above another deflects some noise from the surface, for example. Another plan involves the use of noise suppressing devices which can be swung into place at lower flight levels to decrease engine noise, a muffling device which would fit over the back of the engine. These are being tested with other innovations, all aimed at obtaining an advanced supersonic transport with acceptable noise levels.[29]

A Second-Generation SST. A second generation of SSTs will be developed and manufactured. Unless Congress decides to fund the development of a second generation U.S. SST, European and/or Japanese firms will build and sell them. U.S. airlines will then have to buy their SSTs from these companies. The decision must be made soon if U.S. manufacturers are to have a chance to compete on the world market.

The story of the SST is an interesting case in itself. It demonstrates the way that technology swiftly changes and "lives." It reveals legal, political and economic responses. Also, it asks us whether we are in control of our technology — or not.

NOTES

[1] Don Dwiggins, *The SST* (New York: Doubleday and Co., Inc., 1978), pp. 184-85.

[2] It is not within the scope of this volume to offer a detailed exposition of the development of supersonic flight. Excellent accounts are available which can provide the interested reader with the astonishing achievements of designers, manufacturers, and test pilots.

[3] John Costello and Terry Hughes, *The Concorde Conspiracy* (New York: Charles Scribner's Sons, 1976), pp. 47, 62-68, 114-120.

[4] Interviews with NASA Office of Public Information personnel and materials supplied by NASA, Washington, D.C., June 1979.

[5] Costello and Hughes, pp. 243-47.

[6] Jim Schefter, "New Aerodynamic Design, New Engines, Spawn a Revival of the SST," *Popular Science*, vol. 215, no. 1, p. 62.

[7] "Soviet Concord Tested," *Washington Post*, 24 June 1979, p. A18.

[8] *Ibid.*

[9] Braniff International press release, 10 February 1977; also remarks by Braniff official at Concorde press conference at Dallas-Fort Worth Airport, 10 February 1977.

[10] Michael J. Hart, *Outline of International Aviation Law* (St. Louis: Parks College of St. Louis University, 1975), p. 183.

[11] *Ibid.* p. 181.

[12] Dwiggins, pp. 64-66.

[13] Hart, pp. 181-89.

[14] Stuard M. Speiser and Charles F. Krause, *Aviation Tort Law*, ((San Francisco: Bancroft-Whitney Co., 1978), I, pp. 13-14.

[15] *Ibid.* pp. 15-18.

[16] Information supplied via Braniff International from materials published by the British Aircraft Corporation, June 1979.

[17] Schefter, p. 62.

[18] A. J. Grobecker, S. C. Coroniti and R. H. Cannon, Jr., "The Effects of Stratospheric Pollution by Aircraft," DOT-TST-75-50, December 1974. The quote is from *Final Environmental Impact Statement . . . Civil Supersonic Aricraft* (Washington: U.S. DOT, FAA, June 1978), pp. 159-66.

[19] *Ibid.* pp. 282-97.

[20] "Civil Supersonic Airplanes" Federal Register, vol. 43, no. 126, p. 28406, 29 June 1978.

[21] *Ibid.*, pp. 28406-7.

[22] Schefter, p. 62.

[23] NASA report to House Committee on Science, Technology and Transportation, September 1978.

[24] Schefter, pp. 62-65, 129-30.

[25] *Ibid.*, pp. 62-65; interview, NASA Office of Information, June 1979.

[26] *Ibid.*

[27] *Ibid.*

[28] Interview, NASA Office of Information and NASA press releases on AST research programs; Schefter, pp. 65, 129-30.

[29] *Ibid.*

CHAPTER 20

HIJACKING

Hijacking, the illegal seizure of an aircraft, was not common. Only about one a year was reported, with thirty-three incidents occurring between the calendar years 1930 and 1960. Then with the upsurge of hijacking in the 1960s the public became aware of the vulnerability of aircraft to such takeovers.[1]

Aircraft are built to take enormous changes in pressures and temperatures, and great structural stress, yet they are quite fragile in some respects. Built to be light, yet strong, they are not flying tanks. Any explosion can cause decompression when the plane's thin skin is ruptured at altitude. Control cables, instruments, and radios are all essential to safe flight and vulnerable to armed persons. The occupants of the plane are hostages.

With the Cuban crisis, a series of hijackings occurred in 1961. In all, ten occurred in that year. Media coverage brought the problem to public attention. Hijacking became a serious worldwide problem in 1968, with thirty-five incidents occurring, followed by eighty-seven in 1969, eighty-three in 1970, and fifty-nine in 1971.[2]

The Dilemma

Hijacking was a dilemma for the U.S. The United States had had a long history of offering sanctuary to those persons seeking freedom and leaving states governed by despots. This attitude is shared with many of the nations of the world. In December 1948, the General Assembly of the United Nations in their "Universal Declaration of Human Rights," noted the right of persons to seek such asylum from persecution. The statement is qualified to exclude those accused of non-political crimes who simply seek to escape justice. There is no enforcement ability in this U.N. statement, but a hope is expressed that the states of the world will respect the right to grant asylum.

Latin American countries and Spain recognize the right of asylum for political offenders in their legations or embassies, and on their public vessels. This theory might be thought to extend to include public aircraft as well.[3]

Stealing and Plundering. All states in the United States have laws against theft and plundering. Persons removing aircraft radios and other equipment, for example, fall into this category of criminal. If the thief steals in an area outside the jurisdiction of a state, U.S. federal laws cover such felonious acts. An example of federal jurisdiction is an area under U.S. maritime law.

Murder. Likewise, murder is punishable under either state or federal law, depending on where such acts are committed and other considerations. Murder, or assault, committed in national airspace falls within the federal jurisdiction if occurring on an interstate carrier.

Kidnapping. Kidnapping is defined as the taking of a person against his will, without authority, and with criminal intent to collect ransom for that person's safe return. It is a capital offense in most states. If a kidnapped person is carried across a state line, the crime then becomes a federal offense with a penalty of death.

Other Serious Crimes. Among other serious violations of U.S. state and federal law are:

Robbery, the forceful and unlawful taking of property or money by threatening life or safety or harm.

Burglary, breaking and entering a building with the intent to steal.

Theft, a term indicating that something is stolen. The penalty varies with the value of the objects taken. Criminally receiving stolen goods is a felony if the goods are received knowingly.

Arson, is the willful and malicious setting of a fire or burning.

It is a crime to attempt to commit a crime, even if the attempt fails. Carrying a concealed weapon is a crime.

Finally, to plead ignorance of the law is no defense. Citizens are expected to know the law and in any case to conduct themselves in a responsible manner.

Crime on the High Seas. On American vessels, U.S. federal authorities can reach to the miscreant and try that person in a U.S. District Court in the district where he is first apprehended, or into which he is first brought. A crime committed aboard a U.S. boat or ship and reported in a U.S. port is under the jurisdiction of federal authorities. The exception to this is that crimes committed on state waters are within the jurisdiction of the courts of that state. The state waters are not considered "the high seas." United States federal jurisdiction extends to the navigable waterways of the U.S. upon which interstate commerce moves and connecting with the high seas. The federal jurisdiction of maritime crimes is given under the provisions of federal law 18 U.S. Code 7.

Piracy. The ancient crime of piracy is with us today in the guise of hijacking of aircraft and also in the capture of small boats operating off shore. Piracy is sometimes termed a "marine felony," a robbery at sea. The crime may include burning of the vessel or aircraft, the murder and/or capture of the passengers and crew.

Piracy is a federal crime and is punishable by life imprisonment under federal law, 18 U.S. Code 1651.[4]

Jurisdiction Over the Individual

We have seen that vessels and aircraft have the nationality of their state of registry. Aboard a ship on the high seas the laws of the nation of registry prevail. In port, unless called aboard by the ship's master or an aircraft commander, or unless the peace is being disturbed, officials of the port being visited by the foreign vessel or aircraft generally do not interfere with foreign laws and customs aboard that craft.

A nation controls its own registered aircraft and the passengers aboard them when the aircraft is being operated inside its national boundaries, while over its territorial waters, and while over the high seas.[5]

Corporations hold the nationality of the nation in which they are incorporated. Groups not incorporated have the nationality of the nation in which their headquarters, controlling the operation of the group, is located.

A nation maintains jurisdiction over its citizens. We pause to note here that definitions of citizenship vary from country to country. Birth, residency, or the nationality of one's parents enters into the matter. Dual citizenship is also possible, with a person claiming citizenship in two nations.

The U.S. law claims as citizens all persons born in the U.S. or those who have been naturalized in the U.S. Also, a person born abroad to a parent who is an U.S. citizen (that parent must have resided in the U.S. at some time), is recognized as a citizen of the United States.

A nation has the right to require its citizens to obey its laws and to punish lawbreakers. This right extends to all persons within a state's national boundaries. Embassy personnel and other diplomatic personnel are customarily exempted and are generally sent to their home nation rather than being punished in the foreign state.[6]

Extradition

Foreign citizens who hold no diplomatic immunity can be fined or sentenced to prison or even executed for breaking the laws of the nation they are visiting. There are treaties between nations concerning this, yet many an American has served a sentence in a foreign prison.

Broadly speaking, nations will extradite a person accused of a crime which is recognized as such by most civilized states or a person who has attacked a head of state. Persons accused of political crimes and sought by their home government, on the other hand, may well not be extradited and can often remain in the country to which they have fled, claiming sanctuary. The U.S. has an overall policy of resistance to extradition of those seeking refuge here.

Extradition is the voluntary surrender of a person by one state to another.[7]

When hijacking changed in the 1960s from an occasional, rather romantic escapade of political refugees into a cruel and dangerous ploy of various fanatics and lunatics, the right of asylum had to be reconsidered. All nations need safe and reliable air transport of goods and passengers. It was obviously in the public interest of the nations of the world to stop hijackings.

Further, inside the United States, hijackings involved both air carriers and general aircraft. In four recent years, general aviation hijackings have equalled in number those involving air carriers. From 1961 to 1978, the record shows around 163 air carrier and 33 general aviation hijacking attempts.[8] The factor drastically reducing air carrier hijackings has been, of course, passenger and luggage screenings at enplaning points. The U.S., with thorough screening, has succeeded in almost eliminating air carrier hijacking attempts. Abroad the reduction in such attempts has been less successful.

U.S. law under the Antihijacking Act of 1974, Public Law 93-366, gives full authority to the FAA to act to prevent injury, death and property damage in hijacking incidents. The FBI can be called in, but the FAA retains authority over action to be taken.

Rockwell Commander " Executive Wing " Propjet

Rockwell Commander 700

Photographs courtesy Rockwell International.

Hijacking carries severe penalties on charges of kidnapping and hijacking. If the hijack attempt is successful, penalties given are generally heavier than in attempts foiled early in the incident. Life imprisonment, the death penalty, and 20-year sentences are provided in the Anti-hijacking Act of 1974.

As a pattern of merciless mistreatment, injury and death emerged in hijackings in the 1960s and early 1970s, worldly sympathy for hijackers with motives of greed or publicity, melted away. There remains in international law, however, sympathy for persons or groups who hijack a plane to escape persecution or religious discrimination.

Obviously, to make continued air commerce feasible, international agreement was needed. Any set of rules with enforcement and penalties written into it faced, of course, a thorny path for nations jealously guard their sovereignty. A general document that proposed certain criteria for dealing with hijacking but set no definite enforcement mode or penalties seemed more certain of ratification. Thus the International Civil Aviation Organization (ICAO) called for a convention of nations to meet in Tokyo in 1963 to discuss rules for jurisdiction over offenses aboard international flights.

Tokyo Convention on Crimes Aboard Aircraft

The Tokyo Convention was an early attempt to meet the serious threat to air commerce posed by the sudden increase in illegal seizures of aircraft. Experts from many nations had met in Rome in 1962 to write an effective draft agreement to discourage hijack attempts. The U.S. suggested that the nation in which the flight ended be required to prosecute the hijackers.

When negotiators met in Tokyo in 1963, the U.S. suggestion was omitted. Instead members of the Convention wrote an agreement to take appropriate measures to restore control over the aircraft to its commander and permit the passengers and crew to resume their journey as soon as possible. Aircraft and cargo were to be returned to their owners.

This convention put into writing what was in fact customary behavior among nations. Even so, it was 1969 before twelve nations had signed and the convention became legally operative. Thirty nations had signed by October 1970. To date, eighty-nine nations are parties to the Tokyo Convention.[9]

The International Federation of Airline Pilots (IFALPA) placed pressure on nations to adhere to the Tokyo Convention by voting to boycott any nation which refused to release aircraft, crew members, and passengers in a reasonable time. This boycott plan was later dropped by IFALPA.

The Montreal Declaration, 1970

Following a series of violent hijackings, an Extraordinary Assembly of the ICAO was called at Montreal in the summer of 1970 to get world-wide action against such crimes. Negotiators from ninety-one countries agreed unanimously to:

- Condemn acts of violence against international air carriers and civil airports.

- Urge that violence not be used against civil air transport, airports.

- Call for all nations to place hijacking deterrants into their national law and prosecute hijackers.

Six solemn resolutions followed to express regret over hijacking incidents, to condemn acts of violence, and to promise cooperation to prevent or punish hijackings. The resolutions left national sovereignty unimpaired but plainly placed world opinion and moral force against hijacking. This proved to be ineffective, however, as hijackings continued and hijackers went unpunished only weeks after the Montreal Declaration was written.[10] Therefore a diplomatic conference on unlawful seizure of aircraft was set for December, 1970, at The Hague.

The Hague Convention, 1970

The sanctions written into The Hague Convention of 1970 are requirements by participating governments to allow extradition of hijackers upon request, or to punish them according to the laws of the member nation in which the flight ended. Prosecution is not actually required but left to the judgment of authorities in the country in which the flight terminated. This allows contributory considerations to be taken into account. (The U.S. position at The Hague Conference was that *all* seizures are illegal and should be punished, but this

403

view did not prevail.)

Jurisdiction over international hijacking rests in the state of aircraft registry, the place at which the flight ends, or the country in which the lessee of the aircraft resides. To suppress hijacking the nations of the world agreed to offer no sanctuary to criminal hijackers.

The language of The Hague Convention though still weak, was more exact and stronger than that of the Tokyo Convention.[11] There are now eighty-three parties to The Hague Convention.[12]

Montreal Convention, 1971

To meet the immediate need for stopping acts of sabotage with its serious interference with world air commerce, the Convention for the Suppression of Unlawful Acts Against the Safety of Civil Aviation (Sabotage) met in Montreal. The convention signed an agreement on 23 September 1971 which entered into force for the United States on 26 January 1973.[13]

The sabotage agreement deals with acts of sabotage on the ground not covered in The Hague Convention of 1970. While not strictly "hijacking," that is, seizing and diverting an aircraft, still in the broadest sense of the term sabotage does come under the term hijacking. Both sabotage and hijacking enter into the total problem involving the deployment of force against world civil aviation.

The Future

It would seem that via the agreements just described, all facets of attack upon civil air commerce are covered. Yet, as with all international treaties, nations can enforce these agreements only if they wish to do so.

Civil air carriers can help avoid being drawn into political disputes by using care to preserve the civil nature of their cargo and passengers. To carry goods and personnel channeled into a war zone is asking for interference.[14]

A most successful deterrent to hijacking has been the careful screening of persons boarding aircraft in the United States. It may be that such screening may be the subject of a future international air safety convention.

Table I*

U.S. Scheduled Air Carrier, Hijacking Attempts

Year	Successful	Incomplete	Unsuccessful	Total Attempts
1972	8	14	5	27
1973	0	1	0	1
1974	0	1	2	3
1975	0	1	5	6
1976	1	0	1	2
1977	0	3	2	5
1978 thru June 30	0	2	1	3

General Aviation, Hijacking Attempts

Year	Successful	Incomplete	Unsuccessful	Total Attempts
1972	2	0	2	4
1973	1	0	0	1
1974	3	1	0	4
1975	4	2	0	6
1976	0	1	1	2
1977	0	1	0	1
1978 thru June 30	1	1	1	3

Comparison, United States and Foreign Hijacking Attempts

Year	U.S.	Foreign	Total
1972	31	31	62
1973	2	20	22
1974	7	19	26
1975	12	13	25
1976	4	14	18
1977	6	26	32
1978, thru June 30	6	12	18

*Source: FAA publication, *Semi-annual Report to Congress on the Effectiveness of the Civil Aviation Security Program*, 1 January — 30 June 1978.

NOTES

[1]Source of statistics, June 1979 interview with FAA security office personnel, Washington, D.C. See also table of hijacking incidents this chapter.

[2]*Ibid.*

[3]Gerhard von Glahn, *Law Among Nations*, (New York: Macmillan Publishing Co., Inc., 1976), pp. 389, 479; Edward McWhinney, "International Legal Problem-Solving and the Practical Dilemma of Hijacking," *Aerial Piracy and International Law*, (Dobbs Ferry, N.Y.: Oceana Publications, 1973), pp. 19-20; L.C. Green, "Hijacking and the Right of Asylum," *Aerial Piracy and International Law*, pp. 124-25.

[4]von Glahn, pp. 328-29; McWhinney, pp. 15-16. McWhinney notes that "aerial piracy," is a popular rather than a strictly legal term. He suggests reference to an article by Van Panhuys, on aircraft hijacking and international law, 9 *Columbia Journal of Transnational Law* 1, at 4 et see. (1970), and the provisions of the 1958 Geneva Convention on the High Seas, for comparisons between hijacking and piracy.

[5]von Glahn, pp. 328-29.

[6]Rowland W. Fixel, *The Law of Aviation*, (Charlottesville, Va.: The Michie Co., 1967), pp. 70-72; Michael J. Hart, *Outline of International Aviation Law*, (St. Louis: Parks College of the St. Louis University, 1975), pp. 37-42.

[7]Hart, pp. 38-40.

[8]FAA statistics, June 1979.

[9]The formal title of the convention is the Convention on Offenses and Certain Other Acts Committed on Board Aircraft, and the document resulting was dated 14 September 1963. The convention entered into force for the United States on 4 December 1969; 20 UST 2941; TIAS 6768; 704 UNTS 219.

[10]John R. Rhinelander, "The International Law of Aerial Piracy . . .," *Aerial Piracy and International Law*, (Dobbs Ferry, N.Y.: Oceana Publications, Inc., 1973), pp. 59-71.

[11]The formal name of The Hague Convention of 1970 is the Convention for the Suppression of Unlawful Seizure of Aircraft. It was signed at The Hague on 16 December 1970 and entered into force for the United States on 14 October 1971; 22 UST 1641; TIAS 7192.

[12]U.S. Department of State publication 8934, *Treaties in Force . . . January 1, 1978*, 9. 276

[13]Hart, 201-204; von Glahn, pp. 328-29; "Montreal Convention, 1971," 24 UST 564; TIAS 7570.

[14]*Stuart M. Speiser and Charles F.* Krause, *Aviation Tort Law*, (San Francisco: Bancroft-Whitney Co., 1978), I, pp. 585-87. Speiser and Krause note that efforts to hold the air carrier liable for hijacking injuries or damages have met with little or no success.

406

CHAPTER 21

THE FLYER AND THE FARMER

Agricultural Flying

Agricultural flying began soon after flying itself began. By 1918 attempts were being made to control insects by "dusting" forests and fields with sulphur and other chemicals.

The U.S. Forest Service also pioneered aerial application prior to World War I. By the 1920s specially equipped aircraft began to work with farmers to seed fields and to spread both insecticides and fertilizers. Men around the world worked to develop this new agricultural tool — the airplane.

Today it is estimated that over a million hours a year are flown by agricultural aircraft operators. Some of the tasks performed by agricultural aircraft include:

Insect control, crops and orchards.

Forest insect pest control.

Defoliant use.

Fertilizing of crops.

Seeding of forest, range, and crop lands.

Forest fire control.

Mosquito control.

Locust control.

Rodent control.

Regulation of Aerial Applicators

The move in the early 1960s to regulate agricultural operators, was objected to on the grounds that: state regulation sufficed, ground applicators were not so regulated, and the FAA had no authority to regulate agricultural operators. The FAA, however, proposed such regulation as a means of establishing uni-

407

form standards for air safety and for the safety of persons and property on the ground.

The FAA claims authority for the regulation of aerial applicators based on Federal Aviation Law of 1958 which directs the Administrator to regulate aircraft to protect persons and property on the ground. Authority is also given for the Administrator to certificate air agencies such as flight schools, agricultural aircraft operators, and others.

Late in 1962, the proposed rules, FAR Part 137, were offered by the FAA for comment. These, as finally written, were adopted 17 June 1965 and made effective 1 January 1966.

Prior to regulation via FAR Part 137, a system of waivers had been used. The FAA had granted these waivers to agricultural operators authorizing nonobservance of air traffic rules. There was, however, no control over dispensing various economic poisons from the aircraft.[1] Concern over the buildup of pesticides in some parts of the country prompted closer regulation. The goals the FAA also wishes to achieve are improved aircraft and personnel safety, as well as the protection of persons and property on the ground.

Part 137 provides that the applicant for an Agricultural Aircraft Operator Certificate, or the operator's chief supervisor, pass tests on aerial application techniques and on agricultural materials used. Flying skills are likewise tested. Each pilot in command must pass a similar test. The testing is designed to show that pilots and supervisors understand safe agricultural aircraft operation, and safe handling of agricultural chemicals and materials. This includes the ground storage of chemicals, their transfer and loading, as well as dispensing techniques.

Specific flight dispensing patterns or application techniques are left to the operator's discression. Part 137 does prohibit the dispensing of economic poisons for a use other than that for which it is registered with the U.S. Department of Agriculture.

State and local laws must also be complied with regarding the dispensing of chemicals and other materials.

A private agricultural operator is one who operates over property he owns or leases, or a person who has a legal interest in the crops on the property. Such operators may not conduct aerial operations for hire or over congested areas.

Commercial agricultural operators may operate for hire over property in which they have no legal interest, and may operate over congested areas. Operation over congested areas may be conducted in accordance with Part 137 rules. These allow certain exemptions pertaining to low flight over persons and property.

"Public aircraft" are those used exclusively by any government or political subdivision, which do not carry persons or property for hire. These are not required to comply with the certification rules of the Federal Aviation Regulations but may elect to do so. Public aircraft must comply with other portions of FAR Part 137 and with air traffic regulations. Public aircraft may be engaged in certain flights in the public interest such as forest fire control, mosquito control, and relief and welfare flights associated with emergency conditions or public health requirements.

Deviations from the FARs for activities to the extent necessary for relief and welfare flying, approved by an agency of the federal, state, or local government, must be reported to the FAA.(FAR Part 137 applies to these operations.)

"Grandfather provisions," are those which allow currently operating companies and individuals, by virtue of their experience and good safety records, to continue to operate. Privileges of the current holders of certificates of waiver are continued.

Also, since most agricultural operations with helicopters can be conducted within the general FAA regulations, many helicopter operators and pilots have engaged in these operations without a certificate of waiver. To give these operators the benefit of Part 137's grandfather provisions, they may automatically qualify for certification by showing that they have conducted agricultural aircraft operations in compliance with the FARs, within the preceding twelve months, without a certificate of waiver.

FAR Part 137 — Agricultural Aircraft Operations

Federal Aviation regulation Part 137 governs agricultural and other low-level flying.

Essentially, the new regulations caused little change in the way agricultural aircraft were operated. The primary difference is that instead of operating under a waiver, operators are now certificated. Applications for these certificates are submitted to the FAA district office which holds jurisdiction over the area in which the operator's home base of operations is located. Most operators with good safety records automatically qualify for certification. Knowledge and skill tests are given new entrants to agricultural flying.

In general, holders of Agricultural Aircraft Operators certificates must shape their flying to safeguard persons and property on the ground. Certain documents and records are required but FAA has decided that burdensome reports are not to be required.

Agricultural flying is a demanding operation. The actual flights require great judgment and skill. Extremely low level flight is routine. The loading and dispensing of chemicals, too, can be hazardous to ground crews and pilots unless due care is exercised.

Operators are liable for errors in performance. For example, a certain field must be located and treated. Chemicals must not drift onto adjacent fields since the defoliant or insecticide meant for one crop may make another one unmarketable. Pilots must, therefore, judge the effects of wind drift and their own prop wash on the pattern of chemicals they plan to dispense. Damage to powerlines and ground antenna is possible. Flagmen are often used to show pilots the position of the next swath to fly. Due care is needed in training these workers to avoid injuring them by collision, by exposure to the chemicals, or by propeller contact.

As one can see by these few examples, the work of an agricultural aircraft operator bristles with possible cause for liability suits. Knowledge, skill and experience, however, allow U.S. "ag pilots" to treat more than 275 million of the 326 million acres in cultivation in the United States today. Aerial application has enabled the farmer to raise more and better crops and helps keep U.S. food prices the lowest in the world.

Farmer/Operator Contracts

A clear understanding between the party hiring aerial application work and the party doing the application is, of course, essential. Conflict, ill will, and legal suits may be avoided by both parties making clear their needs for application, its timing, and the terms of compensation.

Liability generally rests on the applicator for reasonable care and safe operation. This does not mean that the person hiring an agricultural applicator has no responsibility or risk. The owner of a farm, for example, must make clear to the agricultural operator the limits of his property and the care to be exercised toward particularly vulnerable crops nearby.

The Nature of Claims. Claims for improper aerial application generally fall into four groups-

1. Claims for chemical drift onto crops, from which crop damage results.

2. Health injury due to chemicals dispensed over persons on the ground.

3. Damage to property due to contact with aircraft (power lines, telephone wires, towers, fences, buildings, livestock).

4. Injury to persons (often employees) due to propeller contact, contact with low flying aircraft, or contact with chemicals.

How Far Back? Litigation in agricultural flying cases can reach back to the aerial applicator service operator, to the person employing him, and to the manufacturer of the chemicals dispensed. Further, the manufacturers of the aircraft, engines, components and ground equipment may be involved.

Again, the law looks back through a chain of events and decisions to find the prime cause. This is the causative factor which made the damage or injury occur in spite of reasonable care all along the line as the farmer hired the agricultural work done and the operator attempted to carry on the work.

Weather Modification

Weather modification is an aerial activity often associated with agricultural needs. It is, however, much broader in application than this. Airlines and airport managements are interested in modifying the weather to prevent or dispense fog. The military also finds it essential to fly aircraft in all weather conditions and has long been interested in fog dispersal techniques. Power companies seek to enhance water resources by increasing precipitation. States, counties, and communities are often concerned with increasing rainfall for needed water, decreasing violent storm damage, or decreasing hail to lessen hail damage in the area. One can think of many other examples of non-agricultural need for weather modification.

One might ask, why tamper with the weather? Goals to be achieved include increasing rainfall or snowfall, lightening suppression, fog prevention or dispersal, hurricane strength reduction, decreasing hail damage and tornado modification.

Farmers, of course, are mightily interested in obtaining enough rainfall, reduction of hail damage, storm modification, and flood control.

Eighty percent of the weather modification activities in 1975 were carried out in the giant farming and forestry areas of the American West, west of Kansas City, Kansas. Commercial operators carried out 93 percent of this activity, federal organizations 7 percent.[2] About 5 percent of our U.S. land area was involved in all weather modification projects in that year.[3] Weather modification is quite new and still in its experimental state.

The beginning of modern aerial weather modification may well be said to be the laboratory and flight experiments of November 1946 made by Dr. Vincent Schaefer and Dr. Irving Langmuir of the General Electric Company.[4]

Techniques and Agents

In a June 1976 report the National Oceanic and Atmospheric Administration (NOAA) described activities in the calender year 1975 as follows:[5]

Techniques and Apparatus

The reported information for 1975 shows that ground-based equipment was used in 38 activities and airborne equipment in 40. The total is more than 72 because 6 projects used both ground and air techniques.

Liquid-fueled silver iodide generators or burners were the most common type of weather modification apparatus, being used in 15 ground-based projects and 14 aircraft seeding activities. Propane or acetone were normally used as fuel. The arc-type silver iodide burner was used exclusively at ground level in 17 other activities. Pyrotechnic devices including flares and rockets were employed in 21 projects. Other apparatus used in modification activities were dispensers for solids and liquids, spray nozzles, a corona discharge tower, and "cloud busters" consisting of pipes connected to a water supply.

Agents and Dispensing Rates

The active agents used for the reported activities are silver iodide, crushed frozen carbon dioxide (dry ice), polyelectrolytes, propane, charged water droplets, lithium chloride, hexadecanol, 1-5 LN (1-5-dihydroxynaphthalene), and combinations of silver iodide with other liquids or solids. A polyelectrolyte can be defined as a polymeric material having a long chain molecule and usually a cationic (positive ion) form. Chaff (metallic fibers) was dispensed from aircraft in the lightning suppression project. Compressed air was used in one cold fog modification experiment; corona discharge was the "agent" in a warm fog suppression program.

Silver iodide, by itself or in combined form, was the agent in 50 activities. Dry ice was planned for use in 12 activities, propane in 3, and polyelectrolytes in 2. In several activities, more than one agent was used.

. . .

Dispensing rates for a unit of airborne modification apparatus are considerably higher than the rates for ground-based burners or generators, although the length of dispensing time in aircraft activities is usually shorter. The dispensing rates for silver iodide range from 0.5 grams per hour in one ground-based burner to 24 kilograms per hour in a set of pyrotechnic devices on an aircraft; a flare (pyrotechnic) burns for a few minutes or less. Dispensing rates range up to 1400 kilograms per hour for dry ice, 300 for polyelectrolytes, and 38 liters per hour for propane; these dispensing rates are maintained for only a few seconds to a few minutes at a time.

Interim and Final Report Data

Table 6 is a summary of reported information on weather modification activities that were continued, initiated, or completed in CY 1975. The data were obtained from 16 interim and 61 final reports; no data were submitted on 8 projects that began late in the year (after 1 October). Although this summary table is based on incomplete data, it provides the best estimate of Federal and nonfederal weather modification activity for the year.

Table 6.--Summary of interim and final report data

		Federal	Non Federal	Total
(a)	Modification days (cumulative)	129	1,654	1,783
(b)	Modification days (stratiform clouds)	36	186	222
(c)	Modification days (isolated clouds)	17	866	883
(d)	Modification days (organized clouds)	50	510	560
(e)	Modification days (fog)	31	57	88
(f)	Modification missions	135	2,173	2,308
(g)	Airborne apparatus operation, hours	400	1,262	1,662
(h)	Ground-based apparatus operation, hours	2,499	44,527	47,026
(i)	Dry ice (kg)	0	20,662	20,662
(j)	Polyelectrolyte (kg)	0	1,265	1,265
(k)	Silver iodide dispensed by ground (kg)	63	897	960
(l)	Silver iodide dispensed by airborne means (kg)	35	592	627
(m)	Liquid propane (gal)	5,614	0	5,614
(n)	Charged H_2O (gal)	14,630	0	14,630
(o)	Lithium chloride solution (gal)	15	0	15

413

The total number of days on which weather modification activities took place is shown in table 6, item (a). In items (b) through (e), modification days are segregated by the predominant types of weather phenomena involved. The total of entries in (a) does not equal the total of (b) through (e) because the data are incomplete and because on some days more than one cloud system was involved in the operation.

Silver iodide was used as a seeding agent in 50 activities and dry ice in 11. However, the quantity of dry ice dispensed was about 13 times more than the total weight of silver iodide. The dry ice, lithium chloride, and charged water were used chiefly for fog modification; liquid propane and polyelectrolytes were also dispensed into fog, but to a lesser extent. Although fog dispersal accounted for 23 percent of the weather modification activities, the number of fog modification days is about 5 percent of the cumulative number of modification days. No modification activity was reported for four airports (74-063, 74-064, 74-065, and 74-114), an indication that fog of the type suited to the modification technique was not prevalent at these locations during the reporting period.

Further analysis of the information in table 6 shows that nonfederal efforts in modification were appreciably greater than Federal activities. There were about 13 times more nonfederal modification days than Federal, 16 times as many missions, and 18 times as many hours of ground-based operations. Nonfederal activities used 14 times as much silver iodide as Federal ground-based projects and 17 times as much as Federal airborne activities.

Safety and the Environment

The National Oceanic and Atmospheric Administration description of weather modification activities for the calendar year 1975 includes project safety and environmental factors, in the material quoted below:[6]

The previous report contained a summary of information on project safety and environmental considerations for CY 1974 (National Oceanic and Atmospheric Administration 1975). No substantial changes in the conclusions concerning these factors were found in analyzing the material reported during CY 1975.

Federal Activities

For the 14 distinct Federal projects discussed herein, 8 reported that Environmental Impact Statements (EIS) had been prepared. The remainder were engaged in projects for which prior analysis indicated that they did not significantly affect the quality of the human environment, and for which an EIS was therefore not required.

In an EIS for a weather modification project, a section is devoted to the possible effects of the seeding agent. The following paragraph from NOAA's environmental statement for Project FACE 1975 (Florida Area Cumulus Experiment) addressed this subject.

"There are no known adverse effects from the silver iodide (AgI) used for seeding. The U.S. Public Health Service Drinking Water Standards of 1962 require that the 'silver content of drinking water be less than 0.05 parts per million'; there are no standards with regard to iodide. On an average day of seeding approximately 1.5×10^4 gms of silver iodide are expended and 3.0×10^{13} gm of rain falls. If this silver iodide is evenly distributed in the rainwater, the silver content of the water would be 0.5 parts per billion---well within the U.S. Public Health Standards for drinking water. Measurements of silver in rainwater during FACE 1973 substantiated this expectation. The silver iodide that does not combine with water should stay in the atmosphere for months or years and be dispersed over a very large area with proportionately smaller concentrations. Despite the likelihood that the silver concentrations will remain well below the U.S. Public Health Standards, rainwater will be collected at several locations in the target areas as in FACE 1973 and this water will be analyzed for silver content."

The Federally sponsored projects continued to monitor current and forecast weather conditions, particularly the severe conditions. In a Florida project, seeding was restricted on days with severe weather potential, postponed during periods of abnormally high rainfall, and curtailed when crops might be damaged by rain. At a hail suppression project in Colorado, one part of the operational plan called for small rockets to dispense silver iodide. These frangible rockets weighed about a pound and their casings disintegrated before reaching the ground. However, no seeding activity was carried out in 1975.

Nonfederal Activities

Some additional information on environmental and safety aspects of nonfederal weather modification activities has been gained from a review of the initial reports of new projects in CY 1975. For example, the possible effect of silver iodide on humans is of growing concern, and part of the EIS for the South Dakota Cloud Seeding Project addresses this matter: "As was stated earlier, silver iodide is highly insoluable in water. This extreme insolubility, and the very low level of silver iodide in seeded precipitation are the primary reasons silver iodide from cloud seeding operations offers such little hazard to humans. The .0001 ppm concentration of silver iodide in seeded precipitation is well below the .05 ppm of silver allowed by the Environmental Protection Agency in drinking water, and through normal dilution even unusually higher concentrations of silver iodide in rainwater will be brought well within standards in streamflow.

"Evidence also suggests very little or no hazard to man from bioaccumulation of silver from cloud seeding. Because most land plants do not take up silver actively, there is little likelihood of silver concentrating through terrestrial food chains, nor of danger to terrestrial plants or animals if silver is used as a nucleating agent. This can be said with respect to both immediate effects and effects over a period of perhaps 20 years.

"All available evidence indicates little likelihood of adverse effects from iodine. The role of iodine in physiological processes has been well documented and incidences of toxicity from naturally occurring iodine are very rare. In fact, availability of adequate amounts of iodine in the human diet is necessary to prevent goiter, and because of the lack of naturally occuring iodine in some areas, iodine is purposely added to table salt to ensure adequate consumption. A person would have to drink 130 gallons of precipitation from a storm seeded with silver iodide to obtain as much iodine as he would from salting breakfast eggs with iodized salt."

Although the operators of major cloud seeding projects closely monitor the information provided by the National Weather Service (NWS), some require more detailed data for specific areas and purposes. In Texas, one operator installed a 3-cm weather radar at project headquarters to supply storm movement and intensity information during seeding operations. The radar data were coordinated with pilot inputs during seeding and observational flights.

Another application of radar was carried out in North Dakota. Rainfall was monitored, and when radar-estimated rainfall exceeded 2 inches, seeding was stopped in that area. On the other hand, if local residents decided that their area had too much rain, operations were suspended.

A different approach to monitoring possible damaging effects of operations was undertaken by about 700 farmers in and around a Texas project. Community officials, representing the farmers, had direct communication with the operational base and had daily contact with the radar meteorologist. Operational constraints and provisions for suspension were based on the threat of floods or excessive nucleating material, and social considerations. Thus, a human observational network was poised to furnish useful information to project decision makers.

The decision-making process in a Kansas project was lodged in a policy Board made up of representatives from each of the 11 participating counties. The Board established the following guidelines for conduct of the project:

"a. Since a high percentage of the seeding opportunities occur during frontal passage, unrestricted seeding will be allowed on a provisional basis as long as no undesirable effects result. This applies to seeding of fronts or squall lines during daylight hours, as long as flying safety is not jeopardized.

"b. Since a high percentage of hail damage occurs during severe thunderstorms, hail suppression will continue when a National Weather Service Thunderstorm Watch or Warning is in effect in all or part of the target area. Cognizance is taken of the sociological aspects of seeding during severe storm situations; however, from a scientific standpoint, there is no reason not to seed for hail suppression.

"c. Seeding activities will terminate at darkness. Since the aircraft will be based in the western portion of the target area, the aircraft may return to base after dark, at the completion of seeding operations."

The subject of seeding for hail suppression during severe storms was also noted in another program. One commercial operator in North Dakota reported that "All severe storms systems will be seeded as they penetrate the target area. The decision for modification of all systems was made by the local authority after having been advised of the possibility of criticism and/or liability should destruction be caused by those systems seeded. Decision concerning rain increase operations will be made on a weekly basis considering crop need throughout the project period."

The County Commissioners in North Dakota were authorized to suspend operations in a seeding project. The project meteorologist could also suspend operations based on information from NWA on river crest and forecast precipitation amounts. In California, one project's decision to seed was based on runoff and existing reservoir storage. Reservoirs, rainages, and streamflow stations were monitored to supply data on which to evaluate the potential for flooding by rainfall.

Federal Legislation — Weather Modification

The first specific federal legislation on weather modification was Public Law 256 enacted on 13 August 1953. Between the 1953 act and 1971, only four other laws were passed by Congress which dealt with weather modification (appropriate laws for research funds excepted).

The basic power of the federal government to regulate weather modification stems from Article I, section 8, clause 3 of the Constitution of the United States. This is known as the "commerce clause." The federal government, however, has done relatively little to regulate weather modification. (State and local laws have proliferated but lack uniformity and effectiveness.) Federal laws relating to weather modification are listed below:

Public Law 256, 13 August 1953, created an Advisory Committee on Weather Control.

Public Law 664, 9 July 1956, extended the life of the committee to 30 June 1958. The committee was directed to study and evaluate modes of weather control. It was then to advise the government regarding best future action.

Public Law 85-510, 12 July 1958, authorized the National Science Foundation to begin and support a program of study, research, and evaluation in the field of weather modification.

Public Law 92-205 was enacted on 18 December 1971, requiring all nonfederally sponsored weather modification activities in the United States to be reported to the Secretary of Commerce. Summaries of these activities were ordered published. The reporting program went into effect 1 November 1972. The National Oceanic and Atmospheric Administration (NOAA), convened by authority of Public Law 94-490, was asked by the Secretary of Commerce to do this work.

Since 1 November 1973, by virtue of amendments to Public Law 92-205 in 1972, federal agencies are also required to report their weather modification projects and activities to NOAA.

417

The Department of Commerce's NOAA now also receives reports which include safety and environmental aspects of field activities by nonfederal weather modification operators. This amendment to reporting procedures, 15 February 1974, will enable NOAA to determine if possible interference with federal research projects might occur.

Firms and agencies carrying out weather modification projects are also required to keep certain records of these activities, as well as reporting their activities to NOAA.[7]

The Beechcraft Bonanza V35B.

The National Weather Modification Act of 1978 orders an examination of weather modification processes and recommendations as to the best uses of these techniques. The act may have been prompted in part by suits filed for damages against aerial weather modification firms.

Texas is a center of such modification and some suits have resulted. There the term "cloud rustling" is used. This means that someone has "seeded" a cloud causing rain while property (downwind) may have less rainfall.

Precipitation experiments may cause rain but whether or not weather modification can alter storm intensities, or the size of hailstones falling from thunderstorms, is not completely understood. In the several suits filed, the problem for plaintiffs is proving that the weather modification company did indeed cause the weather which caused the injury or loss.[9]

The federal government has, in the view of the Department of Commerce, Weather Modification Advisory Board . . . . "an overriding responsibility for weather modification in this country . . . . To a degree, the weather has the characteristics of a commons in which the interests and welfare of all are involved . . . . the Board has identified a requirement for expanded research and development as well as an important international dimension to the field."[10]

The WMAB Report noted further, however, that a significant portion of decision-making has been remitted to the states, local communities, and the private sector. For activities (primarily operational in character) begun and funded by state and local governments, state liability rules and state law prevails.

Federal activity will be directed primarily toward the research and development of weather modification. Communication between federal and state governments is to be a prerequisite of federal program activity. Further, the public interest and safety is to be a prime consideration in these programs. Ordinarily, the National Weather Resources Management Board (NWRMB) will defer to local objections. Federal activities are to be monitored and evaluated regularly for environmental effects.[11]

Persons harmed by activities of the federal government may recover compensation under the Federal Tort Claims Act. The WMAB 1978 Report suggests that both individual claims and class action claims be allowed . . ." . . it seems appropriate to permit the claimant to apply on behalf of the class before the appropriate administrative agency, and if refused, to bring a class action in court under the Federal Tort Claims Act."[12]

The WMAB notes that the logging and reporting of weather modification activities are now required. The Board suggests in its 1978 Report that a further rule be imposed, licensing operators in the field. A number of states have this requirement. The basis of such licensing is good character and financial responsibility. The proposed federal rule would add a technical knowledge and an experience requirement. Civil penalties and stop orders are suggested to give enforcement powers to federal legislation. Further federal action is not advised by WMAB.[13]

The WMAB's position is indicated in the following quoted material.[14]

Liability Rules for Non-Federal Activities

The common law governing weather modification has been repeatedly studied by eminent legal scholars, and its main contours are well understood. In brief, weather modification operators are subject to the general rules and procedures of tort law. Under these rules, a person who has been injured by the activity of another can recover money damages to compensate for the injury if he can show (1) that the activity was carried on in a way that violated established norms of conduct; and (2) that his damage was caused by that activity.

In extraordinary cases, where he can show that irreparable harm is threatened, he may be able to move in advance of the activity to secure a court order prohibiting it. In an action for damages, the facts must be shown to the satisfaction of a jury; an injunction action is tried to the judge. These general propositions are broadly accepted, but differences in application and detail arise from State to State, and the courts in most States have not yet had occasion to address the questions in any systematic way.

To date, fewer than a dozen damage actions have been brought against weather modification operators. None of them has succeeded, although one or two are still pending.

In *Southwest Research, Inc. v. Rounsaville*, 327 S.W. 2d 417 (Tex. 1958), the court, relying on lay testimony, enjoined a hail-suppression program on the ground that it would deprive plaintiff's nearby land of moisture. Weather modification, like other time-sensitive activities, may be peculiarly vulnerable to a preliminary injuction or temporary restraining order, which may hold up operations during the favorable period, thus settling the issue without the possibility of review on appeal or sometimes even a full hearing on the merits.

The problem in every case has been proof of causation; the plaintiff has been unable to show that the harm he complains of would not have occurred but for the defendant's weather modification activities.

It does not seem likely that this perfect batting average can be maintained much longer. It seems logical that, as scientific understanding improves, proof of causation will grow progressively easier. Already, it is anomalous for the operator to sell his services by promising results, and then, when he is sued for damages, in effect to deny that he has performed.

If causation can be established, the courts will have to face the second, as yet unanswered question of what theory of liability to apply. There are essentially two choices: liability only for fault--that is, damages caused by some negligent or otherwise wrongful act of the defendant; or absolute liability--that is, for any harm caused by the defendant, no matter how careful he is. The negligence rule is less onerous for the defendant. It is sometimes said to be applicable to all forms of conduct except where the defendant's activity is especially hazardous, in which case the more stringent absolute liability rule applies. Based on this analysis, at least one State has enacted legislation declaring that weather modification is not an extrahazardous activity.

Such expedients are unlikely to be of much avail. Modern tort law, overall, is moving from a fault to a risk-spreading theory as evidenced by such developments as no-fault automobile insurance laws and absolute liability for harm caused by defective consumer products. It seems unlikely that this trend will be resisted in the weather modification field. One would expect, therefore, that most States will adopt the absolute liability standard, or some other mode of shifting a larger burden to the defendant.

In addition to this probable tightening of substantive liability rules, other developments make successful damage actions more likely as time goes on. The growing number of operations will lead to a growing number of claims. The likely increase in scale, with larger perceived damages and more solvent defendants, will make it worthwhile to commit larger litigating resources. Procedural devices, such as the class action, may permit the spreading of litigating costs among a number of claimants.

As a consequence of these developments, some operators claim that the overhanging threat of large damage judgments tends to inhibit weather modification activity. They acknowledge that liability insurance continues to be available at reasonable cost, but they argue that this situation will change after a few successful damage actions.

Weather Modification: Legal Factors

The following quoted article by Nancy L. Jones, legislative attorney, and Daniel H. Zafren, Assistant Chief, American Law Division, Congressional Research Service, summarizes the legal background and present status of the law relating to weather modification.[15]

LEGAL ASPECTS OF WEATHER MODIFICATION

(By Nancy Lee Jones, Legislative Attorney, and Daniel Hill Zafren, Assistant Chief, American Law Division, Congressional Research Service)

DOMESTIC*

The legal issues presented by weather modification are complex and unsettled. These issues can be divided generally into four broad categories: Private rights in the clouds, liability for weather modification, defenses which may be raised against such liability, and methods of controlling weather modification. Before a discussion of these issues is begun, it should be noted that the body of law concerning weather modification is slight and existing case law offers few guidelines for the determination of these issues. For this reason it is often necessary to attempt to analogize the issues which arise concerning weather modification to other, more settled, areas of law such as the general law of water distribution.

PRIVATE RIGHTS IN THE CLOUDS

Several different issues have been raised concerning private rights in the clouds: First, are there any private rights in clouds or in the water which may flow from them; second, does a landowner have any particular rights in atmospheric water; and third, does a weather modifier have rights in atmospheric water. It has been argued that there are no private rights in the clouds or their water since they are common property which belongs to everyone who would benefit from them. Analogies have been drawn to animals ferae naturae. As one commentator has stated:

> Clouds, and therefore the ability to modify weather, differ from most types of property, either real or personal, in that there is no way in which they may be captured or possessed. Man cannot force a cloud to stay over his property or keep it from passing over his property. In this respect clouds have often been compared to animals *ferae naturae*. Animals *ferae naturae* cannot be owned because they cannot be possessed. Therefore since this common law element of ownership cannot be met, they are the common property of all, not the individual property of any one person. (Citations omitted.) [1]

This theory of common ownership of the clouds and any water they might contain has also found support in one of the few cases discussing weather modification. In *Pennsylvania Natural Weather Association* v. *Blue Ridge Weather Modification Association*, 44 Pa. D. & C. 2d 749 (1968), the court stated:

> We are of the opinion that clouds and the moisture in the clouds, like air and sunshine, are part of space and are common property belonging to everyone

---

*Nancy Lee Jones, legislative attorney, American Law Division, Congressional Research Service.

[1] "Legal Aspects of Weather Modification in Texas," 25 Baylor L. Rev. 501, 502 (1973).

who will benefit from what occurs naturally in those clouds. There could be just as much injury or harm from weather modification activities as there could be from air and water pollution activities. We hold specifically that every landowner has a property right in the clouds and the water in them. No individual has the right to determine for himself what his needs are and produce these needs by artificial means to the prejudice and detriment of his neighbors.[2]

Before the issues of the rights of the landowner and the weather modifier in atmospheric water are discussed, it should be noted that some State statutes specifically reserve the ownership or right to use atmospheric water to the State.[3]

There have been a few cases which have discussed the rights of a landowner in atmospheric water. As quoted above the Pennsylvania court in *Pennsylvania Natural Weather Association* v. *Blue Ridge Weather Modification Association* did state that "* * * every landowner has a property right in the clouds and the water in them." Similarly, in *Southwest Weather Research, Inc.* v. *Duncan*, 319 S.W. 2d 910 (1958), aff'd. sub. nom. *Southwest Weather Research, Inc.* v. *Jones*, 327 S.W. 2d 417 (1959), the Texas court stated:

We believe that the landowner is entitled, therefore and thereby, to such rainfall as may come from clouds over his own property that Nature, in her caprice, may provide.

This theory enunciated in *Southwest Weather Research, Inc.* v. *Duncan* is similar to the common law doctrine of natural rights which is basically a protection of the landowner's right to use his land in its natural condition. One commentator has stated that "All forms of natural precipitation should be elements of the natural condition of the land. Precipitation, like air, oxygen, sunlight, and the soil itself, is an essential to many reasonable uses of the land * * *."[4]

However, in *Slutsky* v. *New York*, 97 N.Y.S. 2d 238 (1950), a New York court held that resort owners who were attempting to enjoin weather modification experiments "* * * clearly (had) no vested property rights in the clouds or the moisture therein." The weather modification experiments in this case were undertaken in an attempt to supply the city of New York with an adequate supply of water in the face of a drought and the court also stated that it must balance the competing interests involved.

All three of these cases have limited value in resolving the issue of a landowner's rights in atmospheric water since they involved only the narrow issue of the right of a landowner to have a temporary injunction against cloud seeding. Also both the Pennsylvania and New York decisions rested on the issue of causation; they both determined that the landowner was not entitled to relief since he had not proved that weather modification would interfere with the weather.

In the absence of a statutory determination of the ownership of atmospheric water and in the lack of a well developed body of case law, analogies may be drawn to some general common law doctrines. The doctrine of "natural rights" has already been noted above; in addition to this doctrine, the "ad coelum" doctrine may also be instructive. This concept has been attributed to Accursius of Bologna

---

[2] *Pennsylvania Natural Weather Association* v. *Blue Ridge Weather Modification Association*, 44 D. & C. 2d 749, 759–760 (1968).
[3] Colo. Rev. Stat. sec. 36–20–103; La. Rev. Stat. Ann. 37 sec. 2201; Neb. Rev. Stat. sec. 2–2401; N. Mex. Stat. Ann. sec. 75–37–3; N. Dak. Cent. Code sec. 2–07–01; and Wyo. Stat. sec. 9–267.
[4] "Who Owns the Clouds?" 1 Stan. L Rev. 43 (1948).

who stated "Cujus est solum ejus debet esse usque ad coelum." This maxim has been translated as whoever has the land ought to be possessed of all the space upward to an indefinite extent.[5] Blackstone accepted this doctrine and stated:

> Land hath also, in its legal signification, an indefinite extent, upwards as well as downwards. Cujus est solum, ejus est usque ad coelum (whoever has the land possesses all the space upwards to an indefinite extent), is the maxim of the law; upwards, therefore, no man may erect any building, or the like to overhang another's land: . . . So that the word "land" includes not only the face of the earth, but every thing under it, or over it.[6]

The coming of the airplane required some modification of this doctrine, since if a landowner owned the space above his land to an infinite extent, airplanes would have been unable to fly over land without committing a trespass. In *United States* v. *Causby*, 328 U.S. 256 (1945), the Supreme Court rejected the "ad coelum" doctrine and stated that "The air is a public highway . . ."[7] The Supreme Court also stated how much of the space above his property the landowner owns:

> The landowner owns at least as much of the space above the ground as he can occupy or use in connection with the land . . . The fact that he does not occupy it in a physical sense—by the erection of buildings and the like—is not material.[8]

It could be argued from this language that since a landowner can use the space above the ground for weather modification he also owns it.

Other analogies may be drawn to the doctrines of riparian rights and appropriation. Riparian rights have been defined as ". . . those appurtenant to land abutting a watercourse, granting the landowner the right to reasonable use of the water, subject to similar correlative rights held by owners of other lands abutting the watercourse."[9] This analogy is also not a close one since atmosphere does not flow in watercourses. It has been stated that ". . . the analogy is farfetched, if not false. . . ."[10] An analogy with the doctrine of appropriation may be considered more appropriate since it gives a priority of right based upon actual use; however, like riparian rights, appropriation rights in water are limited to water naturally flowing in the watercourses.

This doctrine of appropriation would probably be of greater help in arguing that the weather modifier has certain rights in atmospheric water.[11] The appropriation doctrine recognizes legal interests based on development and use of water, not on land ownership. It has been stated that:

> The appropriation of water consists in the taking or diversion of it from some natural stream or other source of water supply, in accordance with law, with the

[5] R. Wright, "The Law of Airspace" 13–14 (Indianapolis 1968). It has been stated that Accursius had in mind the rights of the owners of burial plots to have such land free from overhanging buildings. D. Halacy, Jr. "The Weather Changers" 205 (New York, 1968).

[6] 2 Blackstone, "Commentaries on the Laws of England" ch. 2. at 19 (p. 445 in Cooley ed. 1899) cited in R. Wright, "The Law of Airspace" 12–13 (Indianapolis, 1969).

[7] *United States* v. *Causby*, 328 U.S. 256, 260 (1945).

[8] *Id.* 264. For a detailed discussion of this case and aviation and airspace ownership generally see R. Wright, "The Law of Airspace" 101–209 (Indianapolis, 1968).

[9] 4 "Waters and Water Rights" 471 (R. Clark, ed. 1970).

[10] The Weather Modification Law Project Staff, University of Arizona, School of Law, "The Legal Implications of Atmospheric Water Resources Development and Management" 17(1968).

[11] It should be noted that the doctrine of appropriation is based on State statutory or constitutional provisions. These provisions must be examined carefully in determining rights in a specific State.

intent to apply it to some beneficial use or purpose, and consummated, within a reasonable time, by the actual application of all of the water to the use designated.[12]

It has been argued that the extension of the appropriation doctrine to weather modification would offer several advantages: This doctrine is being adopted by increasing numbers of States and is supported by a large body of statutory and case law; the administrative procedures of these statutes could be extended to cover the water obtained from weather modification; and the use of this doctrine would offer a unified approach to water law.[13] Disadvantages have also been noted with respect to the extension of the doctine: in most States which subscribe to the doctrine of appropriation, the first weather modifier to comply with the appropriation requirements could take all the moisture, and others would have no legal rights to natural rainfall; the measurement of the rain falling on the land of a rain appropriator would be difficult; other rainmaking in an area around the appropriator's land would have to be prohibited if his rights were to be protected and the questions of proof if the first appropriator claimed he did not get his share would be very difficult.[14]

Comparisons have also been made between oil and gas law and weather modification. This analogy is based upon the early theory that oil and gas, like water, were fugitive and migratory substances. This early theory evolved into two main doctrines of ownership in oil and gas: the "nonownership theory" and the "ownership-in-place theory":

The essence of the "nonownership theory" is that no person owns oil and gas until it is produced and any person may capture the oil and gas if able to do so. An interest in land is a prerequisite to the attempt to reduce the oil to possession. In "ownership-in-place" States, the nature of the interest of the landowner in oil and gas contained in his land is the same as his interest in solid minerals. [Citations omitted.] [15]

Applying either of these two theories to weather modification would appear to be of little help in establishing rights of a weather modifier to atmospheric water since both involve ownership interests in land. It should be noted that the physical differences between oil and gas and atmospheric water may render the analogy inapplicable.[16]

Analogies to the concepts of "developed water" and "imported water" may prove to be more appropriate. Developed waters are waters that "would not but for man's improvements, have become part of a stream, or waters that would otherwise have been lost by seepage or evaporation. As a general rule these waters are subject to appropriation by the parties developing or saving them." [17] One of the factors used in determining whether water is developed water is whether the water was added to the natural flow by the energy and expenditure of the claimant from a source which previously had no outlet.[18] The main difficulty faced in applying this concept to weather

---

[12] 2 Kinney, "Irrigation and Water Rights" (2d ed.) 1216 cited in W. Fischer, "Weather Modification and the Right of Capture," 8 Natural Res. Lawyer 639, 642 (1976).
[13] 4 "Waters and Water Rights" 474, (R. Clark, ed., 1970).
[14] Ibid. 473–474.
[15] The Weather Modification Law Project Staff, University of Arizona, School of Law, "The Legal Implications of Atmospheric Water Resources Development and Management.") 22 (1968).
[16] R. Davis, "State Regulation of Weather Modification," 12 Arizona L. Rev. 35 (1970).
[17] 1 "Waters and Water Rights" 341–342 (R. Clark, ed. 1970).
[18] The Weather Modification Law Project Staff, University of Arizona, School of Law, "The Legal Implications of Atmospheric Water Resources Development and Management," 25 (1968).

modifiers is establishing that the modifier actually developed the water.[19]

Imported water, which is sometimes referred to as foreign water, is "water that has been imported by a user from one watershed into another."[20] Imported water, like developed water, is not part of the natural flow of water. Persons who import water are generally given a prior right to the capture and use of such waters.[21] It has been stated that the application of the doctrine of imported water to weather modifiers would be advantageous since imported water is frequently exempted from the control of interstate river compacts.[22] Problems would also be presented by this analogy. The weather modifier must show that the water he has produced has been shifted from one watershed to another, and he must also show that the water is imported rather than contributory. In addition, the general question of proof, that is establishing that the modifier actually produced the water, would present difficulties.

LIABILITY FOR WEATHER MODIFICATION

If a drought or a severe storm occurs after weather modification attempts have occurred, issues concerning liability for damages may arise. These issues would include causation as well as the application of a number of theories of tort recovery including nuisance, strict liability, trespass, and negligence. Other bases of liability might be present depending on the particular facts and circumstances attending any specific incident. In addition, issues concerning air and water pollution could be raised. Before a general discussion of these issues is begun, it would be helpful to examine briefly State statutes which discuss liability.

Ten State statutes were found which discuss liability for weather modification. These statutes vary widely in effect and complexity. Eight of these statutes specifically provide that the State is immune from liability.[23] Five statutes were found which provide that obtaining a license for weather modification is not a defense to legal actions.[24] The statutes on weather modification are stated not to affect private contractual or legal obligations in four States.[25] Three statutes provide that weather modification is not ultrahazardous[26] while three State statutes provide that weather modification is not a trespass[27] or, in one State, not a public or a private nuisance.[28] In addition, Colo-

---

[19] For a detailed discussion of this question of proof, see W. Fischer, "Weather Modification and the Right of Capture," 8 Natural Res. Lawyer 639, 645–651 (1976).
[20] 1 "Waters and Water Rights," 339 (R. Clark, ed. 1970).
[21] Id.
[22] The Weather Modification Law Project Staff, University of Arizona, School of Law, "The Legal Implications of Atmospheric Water Resources Development and Management," 29 (1968).
[23] Colo. Rev. Stat. sec. 36–20–122; Ill. Ann. Stat. ch. 14 3/4, sec. 27; Kan. Stat. sec. 82a–1420; N. Dak. Cent. Code sec. 2–07–10; Okla. Stat. Ann. Title 2 sec. 1418; Tex. Water Code Ann. title 2 sec. 14.101; Wash. Rev. Code sec. 43.37.190 and Wyo. Stat. Ann. sec. 9–276.
[24] Col. Rev. Stat. sec. 36–20–123; Ill. Ann. Stat. ch. 14 3/4, sec. 27; Kan. Stat. sec. 82a–1420; N. Dak. Cent. Code sec. 2–07–10; Tex. Water Code Ann. title 2 sec. 14.101.
[25] Okla. Stat. Ann. title 2 sec. 1418; Tex. Water Code Ann. title 2 sec. 14.101 (with certain exceptions); Wash. Rev. Code Ann. sec. 43.37.190; Wis. Stat. Ann. sec. 195.40.
[26] Ill. Ann. Stat. ch. 14 3/4, sec. 27; N. Dak. Cent. Code sec. 2–07–10; Tex. Water Code title 2 sec. 14.101.
[27] Ill. Ann. Stat. ch. 14 3/4, sec. 27; N. Dak. Cent. Code sec. 2–07–10; Colo. Rev. Stat. sec. 36–20–123.
[28] Colo. Rev. Stat. sec. 36–20–123.

rado and Illinois statutes provide that failure to obtain a license or a permit for weather modification constitutes negligence[29] per se while Wisconsin provides that unregulated weather modification operations shall be subject to summary abatement public nuisances.[30] Illinois and North Dakota also provide that a person adversely affected by weather modification shall not be prevented by a statute on weather modification from recovering damages resulting from intentional harmful actions or negligent conduct.[31] Finally, West Virginia provides that any licensee who causes a drought or a heavy downpour or storm which causes damage to land as determined by the West Virginia Aeronautics Commission shall compensate farmers and property owners for such damage.[32]

Before any case for liability for weather modification can be made, it must first be proved that the weather modifier did in fact cause the drought, storm, or heavy rainfall which led to the damage for which compensation is sought.[33] Due to scientific uncertainties, this is a very heavy burden of proof for the plaintiff and is not often met. State statutes on weather modification provide few guidelines concerning causation. Of the 10 State statutes which discuss liability for weather modification, only the West Virginia statute discusses causation and there the statute simply recites that whether or not a weather modifier causes a drought or a storm shall be determined by the West Virginia Aeronautics Commission.

The test which is used most often in tort law to determine whether a causal relationship exists is the "but for" test. This test states that an activity is the cause in fact of a claimed consequence where the event would not have occurred but for the conduct of the actor.[34] This test has been used in some weather modification cases[35] but "judicial experience to date has shown that proof of cause in fact is a serious obstacle to recovery of damages from a weather modifier and to securing injunctive relief to bar his continued operations."[36]

Several different theories of tort liability may be argued in a weather modification case; strict liability, nuisance, negligence, and trespass. As noted above, some State statutes specifically allow or prohibit some of these types of suits. Illinois, North Dakota, and Texas all provide that weather modification is not ultrahazardous which in effect bars the use of the theory of strict liability. Strict liability results when an activity is found to be ultrahazardous, which has been defined as "necessarily involving . . . a risk of serious harm to the person, land, or chattels of others which cannot be eliminated by the

[29] Colo. Rev. Stat. sec. 36–20–123 ; Ill. Ann. Stat. ch. 14 3/4, sec. 27.
[30] Wis. Stat. Ann. sec. 195.40.
[31] Ill. Ann. Stat. ch. 14 3/4, sec. 27 ; N. Dak. Cent. Code sec. 2–07–10.
[32] W. Va. Code sec. 29–2B–13.
[33] This question of proof is very similar to that which is faced by the weather modifier in attempting to prove that certain waters are his since he caused them. See W. Fischer, "Weather Modification and the Right of Capture," 8 Natural Res. Lawyer 639, 645–651 (1976).
[34] 4 "Waters and Water Rights" 477–478 (R. Clark. ed. 1970).
[35] See, e.g. Davis and St. Amand, "Proof of Legal Causation in Weather Modification Litigation : *Reinbold* v. *Sumner Farmers, Inc., and Irving P. Krick, Inc.*" 7 J. of Weather Modification 127 (April 1975) ; 4 "Waters and Water Rights" 478–479 (R. Clark, ed. 1970).
[36] The Weather Modification Law Project Staff, University of Arizona, School of Law, "The Legal Implications of Atmospheric Water Resources Development and Management" 12 (1968) ; see also, R. Johnson, "Weather Modification Legal Study" 2–4, prepared for the Weather Modification Advisory Board, Feb. 28, 1977.

utmost care." [37] In determining whether cloud seeding is an abnormally dangerous activity, it has been stated that courts would consider the following factors:

(a) Whether the activity involves a high degree of risk of some harm to the person, land, or chattels of others;

(b) Whether the gravity of the harm which may result from it is likely to be great;

(c) Whether the risk cannot be eliminated by the exercise of reasonable care;

(d) Whether the activity is not a matter of common usage;

(e) Whether the activity is inappropriate to the place where it is carried on; and

(f) The value of the activity to the community. [38]

No case has been found where a court characterized weather modification as ultrahazardous and therefore subject to strict liability; however, this may occur in the future particularly with regard to certain types of attempted weather modification such as that involving hurricanes.

Nuisance is another liability theory which may prove useful in weather modification cases. Nuisance has been described as conduct which ". . . invades an owner's interest in the use and enjoyment of his land, and such invasion is intentional and unreasonable, negligent or reckless or regarded as an abnormally dangerous activity." [39] Controversies over nuisances are often resolved by balancing the utility of the defendant's conduct with the harm it causes. [40] Due to these characteristics of nuisance, it has been regarded by some writers ". . . as potentially the most useful in weather modification cases." [41] However, it should be noted that a Colorado statute specifically provides that weather modification is not a public or private nuisance. [42]

Negligence may also be used as a theory for recovery in weather modification cases. There are four main elements which are necessary to provide a cause of action using negligence. There must be: (1) A duty recognized by the law, which requires the actor to conform to a certain standard of conduct; (2) a failure to conform to the standard required; (3) a reasonably close causal connection between the conduct and the resulting injury; and (4) actual loss or damages suffered by the plaintiff. [43] Aside from the difficulties presented by showing a causal connection, another difficulty with the application of this theory to weather modification is that a standard for performance must be established against which the weather modifier can be measured.

Trespass as a theory of tort liability may also prove to be applicable to weather modification. Trespass may consist of an entry of a person or thing upon land which is in the possession of the plaintiff. [44] The rejection of the "ad coelum" doctrine in *United States* v. *Causby*, 328

[37] 4 Restatement of Torts sec. 319.
[38] R. Davis. "Weather Modification Litigation and Statutes," in "Weather and Climate Modification" 773 (ed. W. Hess 1974).
[39] Id.
[40] Prosser Torts. sec. 87. 4th ed. (1971).
[41] R. Davis. "Weather Modification Litigation and Statutes", in "Weather and Climate Modification" 773 (ed. W. Hess 1974).
[42] Colo. Rev. Stat. sec. 36–20–123.
[43] Prosser Torts sec. 30 (4th ed. 1971).
[44] Id. sec. 13.

428

U.S. 256 (1945), indicates that the flight of an airplane over a person's land would not necessarily be considered a trespass. However, it could be argued that the release of particles into the air by an airplane or by a weather modification station on the ground might be considered a trespass if they invaded the plaintiff's land. It could also be argued that rain, hail or other precipitation produced by weather modification would be a trespass since it did not fall there naturally but was produced artificially.[45] These arguments could be supported by citing various cases which have found a trespass even where invisible or microscopic particles have entered on the plaintiffs land they have caused harm.[46]

In addition to the various types of tort liability discussed above, weather modifiers may also be held liable for pollution or for adverse environmental impacts. Weather modification not only attempts to change the environment by producing precipitation but also adds small quantities of silver iodide or other artificial nucleants to the water or other precipitation it causes. In *Pennsylvania Natural Weather Association* v. *Blue Ridge Weather Modification*, 44 D. & C. 2d 749 (1968), the court discussed the possible environmental damage which could be done by weather modification and quoted a report of a bureau of reclamation which stated the artificial nucleants used in cloud seeding are to varying extents poisonous. However, the court held that there was no more than a possibility of harm and so did not issue an injunction. It should also be noted that the National Environmental Policy Act of 1969, 42 U.S.C. § 4321 et seq., may be relevant when weather modification is federally sponsored.[47] For example an environmental impact statement would be necessary in certain circumstances where the Federal Government was involved.

DEFENSES WHICH MAY BE RAISED AGAINST CLAIMS OF LIABILITY

In addition to the general defense that the plaintiff has failed to establish a cause of action, certain other defenses may be available to a weather modifier. These would include immunity, privilege, consent and waste.

If the weather modifier was operating under the auspices of the Federal, State, or local government, the doctrne of sovereign immunity from suit may be employed. The Federal Tort Claims Act, 28 U.S.C. § 2671 et seq., waived certain immunities of the Federal Government; specifically, its immunity from liability from the negligent or wrongful acts of its employees who are acting within the scope of their employment. This act kept immunity for the exercise of discretionary functions, however. It has been stated that the application of this doctrine to weather modification on the Federal level means that:

> Federal weather modifiers, then, may expose the United States to liability for injury careless performance of their day-to-day operations; but likely the Federal Government will be immune from liability for its decision to conduct weather modification operations and for its plans relating to the operations.[48]

---

[45] Note, "Legal Aspects of Weather Modification in Texas," 25 Baylor L. Rev. 501, 509–510 (1973).
[46] Prosser Torts. sec. 13 (4th ed. 1971).
[47] See R. Davis, "Weather Modification Law Developments." 27 Oklahoma L. Rev. 409, 436–439 (1974) : "Weather Modification." hearings before the Subcommittee on the Environment and the Atmosphere of the House Committee on Science and Technology, 94th Cong., 2d sess. 421–426 (1976). (Statement of the Natural Resources Defense Council, Inc.)
[48] 4 "Waters and Water Rights" 493–494 (R. Clark, ed. 1970).

The doctrine of sovereign immunity with regard to the States is in a somewhat uncertain condition although it may provide immunity to State employed weather modifiers in some cases. It should also be noted that eight States, Colorado, Illinois, Kansas, North Dakota, Oklahoma, Texas, Washington, and Wyoming, statutorily mandate that the State is immune from certain liability for weather modification.[49]

The application of the doctrine of sovereign immunity to local governments has resulted in a distinction between proprietary and governmental functions. It has been stated that:

> The application of this most unwieldly and unreliable test to weather modification will not be easy. For instance, a municipality's operation of a waterworks for supplying water to its inhabitants (which would seem at first glance to be a governmental operation) has been held to be a proprietary operation—subjecting the municipality to liability in tort. Thus, water supply augmentation through precipitation modification may well be a part of that proprietary function.[50]

Public necessity could also be argued as a defense to liability. This defense has actually been suggested in two cases although it was not determinative in either of them. In *Slutsky* v. *New York*, 97 N.Y.S. 2d 238 (1950), resort owners had filed for a temporary injunction to prohibit New York City from engaging in experiments which attempted to produce rain. The court held that these experiments would not interfere with the plaintiffs resort business "to any appreciable extent" and so denied the injunction. In arriving at this holding, the court emphasized that it must balance the competing interests and stated that "The relief which plaintiffs ask is opposed to the general welfare and public good. * * *" Similarly, in *Pennsylvania Natural Weather Association* v. *Blue Ridge Weather Modification Association*, 44 D. & C. 2d 749 (1968), the court refused to issue an injunction in the absence of proof that damages resulted from weather modification activities but did discuss public necessity. The court there stated:

> No individual has the right to determine for himself what his needs are and produce those needs by artificial means to the prejudice and detriment of his neighbors. However, we feel that this cannot be an unqualified right. Weather modification takes many forms and produces, or appears to produce, desirable effects. For example, there is fog suppression, lightning suppression, and hail suppression. In additon, cloud seeding has been used and will continue to be used to produce rain to relieve the water shortage in our urban areas. We feel then that weather modification activities undertaken in the public interests, and under the direction and control of governmental authority should and must be permitted.[51]

The consent of a landowner to weather modification which may affect his land may also be raised as a defense to liability. In addition, a weather modifier could also attempt to raise as a defense the public policy against waste.[52]

INTERSTATE ALLOCATION OF ATMOSPHERIC WATER

Weather modification activities and their results do not always fall neatly inside State boundaries. When they do not, substantial issues

---

[49] For citations to these statutes see footnote 23 supra.
[50] 4 "Waters and Water Rights" 494 (R. Clark, ed. 1970).
[51] *Pennsylvania Natural Weather Association* v. *Blue Ridge Weather Modification Association*, 44 D. & C. 2d 749, 760 (1968).
[52] For a discussion of these two theories of defense see 4 "Waters and Water Rights" 497–498 (R. Clark, ed. 1970).

may arise; for instance, does cloud seeding in one State take water which should have fallen in another State? No cases have arisen which directly deal with the issues raised by the interstate nature of weather modification although *Pennsylvania ex rel. Township of Ayr* v. *Fulk*, No. 53 (Court of Common Pleas, Fulton County, Pa., Feb. 28, 1968), did touch upon some of these issues. In that case a weather modifier who operated a generator in Ayr Township to suppress hail in West Virginia and Maryland was convicted of violating an ordinance which made cloud seeding an offense. The weather modifier alleged that the township ordinance was unconstitutional because it imposed an undue burden on interstate commerce but the court did not agree and stated that the ordinance was never intended to regulate commerce and that weather modification may not even be commerce.[53]

More recently, a dispute has arisen between Idaho and Washington concerning cloud seeding in Washington which allegedly takes water from clouds which would normally discharge their water over Idaho. Some Idaho officials have termed the cloud seeding "cloud rustling" and threatened to file suit.[54] No suits on this controversy have yet been filed, however.

Although no court resolution of the interstate problems involved in weather modification has been found, some States have attempted to resolve the problem by the use of legislation or interstate compacts. Twelve States have been found which have legislation discussing the interstate aspects of weather modification. Eight of these have statutes which authorize the board or commission which is responsible for weather modification to represent the State concerning interstate compacts or agreements on weather modification.[55] Two States, Colorado and New Mexico, have statutes which provide that weather modification for the benefit of other States cannot be carried on in the State with this legislation unless the State which could be benefited also allows weather modification to benefit the State with this legislation.[56]

Pennsylvania and West Virginia have statutes which provide that their weather modification law does not authorize a person to carry out a cloud seeding operation from these States for the benefit of another State which forbids weather modification.[57] Utah has a statute which prohibits cloud seeding in Utah for an adjoining target State except upon full compliance with the laws of the target State and the law of Utah.[58]

Another method of overcoming the problems presented by the interstate nature of weather modification would be to arrive at informal agreements with adjoining States. Several States provide that the board which is responsible for weather modifications has the power to enter into these agreements. However, organizations resulting from these agreements would possess little power to make binding decisions.[59]

---

[53] For a more detailed discussion and criticism of this case see R. Davis. "Weather Modification Litigation and Statutes," in "Weather and Climate Modification" 782-783 (ed. W. Hess 1974).

[54] B. Richards, "Rainmaking Effort Triggers Battle Over Cloud Rustling," the Washington Post. A-5 Mar. 1. 1977.

[55] Conn. Gen. Stat. Ann. sec. 24-7; Ill. Stat. Ann. ch. 146 3/4, sec. 9; Kan. Stat. sec. 82a-1405(f); Nev. Rev. Stat. sec. 544.080(7); N. Mex. Stat. Ann. sec. 2-07-02.5; Okla. Stat. Ann. sec. 1403(7); Tex. Water Code Ann. title 2 sec. 14.018; Wash. Rev. Code sec. 43.37.040.

[56] Colo. Rev. Stat. sec. 36-20-118, N. Mex. Stat. Ann. sec. 75-37-12.

[57] Pa. Stat. Ann. title 3 sec. 1115; W. Va. Code sec. 29-2B-14.

[58] Utah Code Ann. sec. 73-15-8.

[59] R. Davis, "State Regulation of Weather Modification," 12 Arizona L. Rev. 35, 67 (1970).

Over two-thirds of the states have laws pertaining to weather modification. A file of these is kept up-to-date at the National Oceanic and Atmospheric Administration (NOAA) in Rockville, Maryland. [16]

Most of the states with weather modification statutes require the operator to be registered or licensed. Record keeping and financial responsibility requirements must be met in over twenty of the states. Often, states begin regulation by creating a board to study weather modification inside state boundaries. Other forms of regulation at the state level include: permits for specific operations, public notice, certain possible penalties and taxation.

Some states exempt emergency operations and/or government activities from their weather modification laws.

The National Oceanic and Atmospheric Administration reviews representative legal actions involving weather modification through 1975 as follows:[17]

Legal Actions

There have been about a dozen lawsuits since the 1950's affecting planned, on-going, or completed weather modification activities (Davis 1974). Four cases arising in 1974 and 1975 are described in this section.

Davis and St. Amand (1975) reported on recent legal actions involving weather modification activities. The case, *Montana Wilderness Association v. Hodel*, challenged the issuance of a permit for seeding in the area of Hungry Horse Dam, Montana. However, the operational project was cancelled because adequate precipitation became available for the Bonneville Power Administration's needs. Later, in the summer of 1974, the court dismissed the case as moot because there was no longer any "case of controversy".

In June 1974, a hearing was held at Littlefield, Texas, on the case, *Farmers and Ranchers for Natural Weather v. Atmospherics, Inc.* The plaintiffs had filed a motion for a temporary injunction to halt seeding intended to increase rainfall and decrease hail. Their argument was that Texas courts had adopted the position in prior cases that landowners were entitled to whatever precipitation would fall naturally on their property, an implication that seeding would decrease such precipitation. However, experts testified that there had been no diminution of precipitation resulting from the seeding. In addition, lawyers for the defendants argued that more recent regulatory legislation had superseded the language in those cases. The judge ruled for the weather modifiers.

In another action, a jury trial was held in 1974, at Caro, Michigan, in the case of *Reinbold v. Sumner Farmers, Inc. and Irving P. Krick, Inc.* The plaintiff's complaint for damages, an injunction against further seeding, and an order declaring the suit to be a class action was filed in 1972. The judge ruled against the claim for an injunction; the jury did not sustain the plaintiff's claim for damages. At a prior hearing, the motion to treat the case as a class action was denied. Davis and St. Amand discuss the issue of legal causation as the crux of this trial and other weather modification litigation in which the plaintiff seeks recovery of damages for his losses. They point out that a defendant can win such a lawsuit by prevailing on that single point. Another conclusion, they make, is that the use of expert testimony is essential for the defendant as it is most persuasive to jurors as well as to judges. The authors also note that prior assertions of effectiveness by cloud seeder can and will be used against them by litigants.

A disastrous flood occurred in the area of Rapid City, South Dakota on June 9, 1972. Three years later, a class-action suit was filed against the Department of Interior (DOI) for hundreds of millions of dollars in damages. The plaintiffs claim that cloud seeding, sponsored by the DOI's Bureau of Reclamation, contributed to the flood (Hacker 1975). No further information has emerged in the press on the status of this lawsuit.

As a guide to the planning and execution of future weather modification programs, an initial attempt has been made to define what proof various States may require to grant a water right based on water developed through such programs (Jones et al. 1975). The authors developed generalized hydrologic and engineering guidelines for preparing claims, even though they recognized the difficulty, if not impossibility, at this time to provide unquestionable proof that additional water was created as a result of weather modification. As part of the study, an evaluation of a cold orographic weather modification program was made, using an atmospheric model interfaced with a runoff simulation model. Several State water resources officials were interviewed and their opinions furnished valuable input. Jones et al. concluded that the right to appropriate water arising from weather modification might properly rest with the individual States (as it does in Utah, for example) and that hydrology has seldom been used to its fullest extent in the evaluation of weather modification.

International Activities

Many countries have undertaken or have an interest in research on or the application of weather modification. Much of this activity is coordinated through the World Meteorological Organization (WMO).

An agreement between the United States and Canada is currently in force to coordinate weather modification activities and to exahange information.

The following article provides a review of weather modification activities at the state level.[18] It is quoted in part, as follows:

STATE AND LOCAL ACTIVITIES IN WEATHER MODIFICATION

(By Robert E. Morrison, Specialist in Earth Sciences, Science Policy Research Division, Congressional Research Service)

OVERVIEW OF STATE WEATHER MODIFICATION ACTIVITIES

INTRODUCTION

A majority of the States in the United States have some official interest in weather modification. Twenty-nine States have some form of law which relates to such activities, usually concerned with the various facets of regulation or control of operations within the State and sometimes pertaining to authorization for funding research and/or operations at the State or local level. The statutes dealing with weather modification for these 29 States are reproduced in appendix D. Two other States, Maryland and Massachusetts, had also enacted legislation on the subject; however, the laws in these two States have since been repealed. The general policy toward weather modification in each State is usually reflected in the weather modification law of that State; the laws of some States tend to encourage development and use of the technology, while others discourage such activities.

The current legal regime regulating weather modification has been developed by the States rather than the Federal Government, except in the areas of research support, commissioning studies, and requiring reporting of activities. The various regulatory management functions which the States perform are embodied in the collection of State laws on weather modification. These functions include such activities as (1) issuance, renewal, suspension, and revocation of licenses and permits; (2) monitoring and collection of information on activities through requirements to maintain records, the submission of periodic activity reports, and the inspection of premises and equipment; (3) funding and managing of State or locally organized operational and/or research programs; (4) evaluation and advisory services to locally organized public and private operational programs within the State; and (5) other miscellaneous administrative activities, including the organization and operation of State agencies and boards which are charged with carrying out the statutory responsibilities.

Both the kinds of weather modification functions performed and the diversity of the functions performed by the several States can be gleaned from table 1, in which are identified the chief elements of the weather modification laws for the respective States having such laws. (The information in the table was provided by Davis and reflects the content of State laws in force at the end of 1975.) [1] Hawaii's law merely mentions atmospheric waters and is not included in the table.

In order to administer the various regulatory and managerial responsibilities pertaining to weather modification within the States, an assortment of institutional structures has been established. These include State departments of water or natural resources, commissions, and special governing or advisory boards. Often there is a combination of two or more of these types of agencies or groups, separating the responsibility functions of pure administration from those of appeals, permitting, or advisory services. In the cases of particular State activities contained in the latter part of this chapter, some examples of State institutional structure for weather modification are discussed.[2]

TABLE 1.—ELEMENTS OF STATE WEATHER MODIFICATION LAWS IN FORCE AS OF THE END OF 1975[1]

State	Administrative	Funding	Licensing	Permit	Records and report	Water rights	Liability
Arizona	X			X	X		
California	X	X		X	X		
Colorado	X	X	X	X	X	X	
Connecticut	X	X					
Florida	X	X		X	X		
Idaho	X	X		X	X		
Illinois	X		X	X	X		X
Iowa		X					
Kansas	X		X	X	X		
Louisiana	X		X	X	X		
Minnesota		X					
Montana	X	X	X	X	X		
Nebraska	X	X		X	X		
Nevada	X	X	X	X	X		
New Hampshire		X					
New Mexico	X			X	X		
New York		X				X	
North Dakota	X	X		X	X	X	X
Oklahoma	X	X	X	X	X		
Oregon	X	X		X	X		
Pennsylvania	X			X	X	X	X
South Dakota	X			X	X		
Texas	X	X	X	X	X	X	X
Utah	X	X	X	X	X	X	X
Washington	X	X	X	X	X		
West Virginia	X			X	X		X
Wisconsin	X			X	X		
Wyoming	X	X		X	X		

[1] From Davis. Testimony in hearings. House Committee on Science and Technology. Subcommittee on the Environment and the Atmosphere. June 1976.

It is clear that the State weather modification laws and their attendant administration are concerned especially in a variety of ways with the regulation or control of activities within the State. This regulation often includes licensing and/or the granting of permits, and it may also include monitoring, evaluation, and reporting of operations. The various means by which weather modification is controlled are discussed in some detail in a section of the chapter of this report on legal aspects.[3] Specific laws of the States, found in full in appendix D are also summarized in table 1 of that appendix, where they are compared in terms of their being reasonably comprehensive, their providing for licensing only, or their containing some other miscellaneous provision.[4]

---

[1] Davis, Ray J., testimony in: U.S. Congress. House of Representatives. Committee on Science and Technology, Subcommittee on the Environment and the Atmosphere. "Weather Modification," hearings, 94th Cong., 2d sess., on H.R. 10039 and S. 3383, June 15–18, 1976, Washington, D.C., U.S. Government Printing Office, 1976, pp. 250–252.
[2] See p. 351 ff.
[3] See ch. 11, p. 449 ff.
[4] See p. 514 ff.

Since regulation cannot be effective without sufficient information about ongoing activities, most States which do regulate weather modification provide authority which enables officials to inspect the premises of operators and to require them to maintain daily logs and report on their activities regularly. Daily reporting is not required, however, by any State, and copies of reports filed with the Department of Commerce are also accepted in some cases as satisfactory compliance with reporting requirements. If properly analyzed by responsible State agencies, the information contained in these reports should indicate apppropriate changes or cessations to cloud-seeding operations, if any, that should be made in the public interest.[5]

The extent of involvement in research and operations varies considerably from State to State. Some States support research only, while others fund and operate both operational and research programs. In some cases funding only is provided to those localities, usually at the county level, which have established operational programs. In other States, counties and/or groups of individuals within local regions operate programs funded entirely by local citizens, but with approval and/or advisory services from State agencies. The recent 1976–77 drought conditions led some Western States to initiate emergency cloud-seeding programs as one means of augmenting dwindling water supplies. Among such measures taken on a short time basis are the emergency operations in California, Kansas, and Washington; programs in these States are discussed briefly in the sections at the end of this chapter dealing with the cases of individual States.

Within many of the States, particularly in the West, there is a broad range of weather modification research activity. Usually this research is performed by atmospheric and other scientists at the State universities or other State research agencies. Such research is frequently funded through one of the Federal agencies with major weather modification research programs, such as the National Science Foundation or the Bureau of Reclamation, or it may be supported at least in part with State funds. A few States contribute funds to a Federal research project which is conducted jointly with those States partly within their boundaries.[6]

NORTH AMERICAN INTERSTATE WEATHER MODIFICATION COUNCIL

On January 17, 1975, the North American Interstate Weather Modification Council (NAIWMC) was organized to coordinate intrastate, interstate, and possible international weather modification activities. Its main purpose was to achieve and maintain local and State control of such activities while attempting to attain a high degree on uniformity in legislation and an effective mechanism for information exchange.[7]

[5]Davis, testimony before House Committee on Science and Technology, Subcommittee on the Environment and the Atmosphere, June 1976 hearings, 94th Cong., 2d sess., p. 245.
[6]See discussion of the High Plains project (HIPLEX), under ,"Project Skywater," sponsored by the Bureau of Reclamation, ch. 5, p. 258 ff.
[7]North American Interstate Weather Modification Council: Its Purposes and Activities, Las Cruces, N. Mex., office of the NAIWMC, September 1976, Publ No. 76-2, p. 1.

The following material is quoted from the 746-page Committee Print Report submitted by the Congressional Research Service, to the Senate, 95th Congress, 2d Session:[19]

APPENDIX D

STATE STATUTES CONCERNING WEATHER MODIFICATION

Twenty-nine States were found which have some type of statute discussing weather modification. These state statutes were found by an examination of the indices to the state codes under the topics weather modification, climate control and cloud seeding. Statutes which have been repealed are not included.[1]

The following chart divides the types of weather modification statutes into three main categories: comprehensive, licensing and other. The comprehensive category would include those statutes which include provisions relating not only to licensing but also to general policy, liability, etc. State statutes put in the licensing category are entirely, or almost entirely, concerned with the licensing of weather modifiers. The "other" category would include States like Hawaii which discuss weather modification in some manner but have neither a comprehensive statute nor one concerning licensing. States for which no provisions concerning weather modification were found contain a notation of "no provisions" on the chart. The exact text of those provisions follows the chart.

It should be noted that in most cases the State codes were current through the 1976 sessions, however, in some cases the most current material available was from the 1975 sessions.

States	Types of weather modification statutes		
	Comprehensive	Licensing	Other
Alabama	No provisions		
Alaska	No provisions		
Arizona		Arizona Rev. Stat. §§ 45-2401—45-2405.	
Arkansas	No provisions		
California	California Water Code §§ 400-415; § 235. California Government Code § 53063. California Pub. Res. Code § 5093.36.		
Colorado	Colorado Rev. Stat. §§ 36-20-101—36-20-126.		
Connecticut			Connecticut Gen. Stat. Ann. § 24-5—24-8.
Delaware	No provisions		
Florida		Florida Stat. Ann. §§ 403.281-403.411.	
Georgia	No provisions		
Hawaii			Hawaii Rev. Stat. § 174-5(8).
Idaho			Idaho Code §§ 22-3201—22-3202; 22-4301—22-4302.
Illinois	Illinois Ann. Stat. ch. 146 3/4, §§ 1-32.		
Indiana	No provisions		
Iowa			Iowa Code Ann. §§ 361.1-361.7.
Kansas	Kansas Stat. §§ 19-212f; 82a-1401—82a-1425.		
Kentucky	No provisions		
Louisiana		Louisiana Rev. Stat. Ann. §§ 2201-2208.	
Maine	No provisions		
Maryland	No provisions		
Massachusetts	No provisions		
Michigan	No provisions		
Minnesota	Minnesota Stat. Ann. §§ 42.01-		

| States | Types of weather modification statutes | | |
	Comprehensive	Licensing	Other
	42.14.		
Mississippi	No provisions		
Missouri	No provisions		
Montana	Montana Rev. Codes Ann. §§ 89-310—89-331.		
Nebraska	Nevada Rev. Stat. §§ 2-2401—2-2449; 81-829.45.		
Nevada	Nevada Rev. Stat. §§ 544.010–544.240; 244.190.		
New Hampshire			New Hampshire Rev. Stat. Ann. § 432:1.
New Jersey	No provisions		
New Mexico	New Mexico Stat. Ann. §§ 75-37-1—75-31-15.		
New York			New York Gen. Mun. Law § 119–p.
North Carolina	No provisions		
North Dakota	North Dakota Cent. Code §§ 2-07-01—2-07-13; 37-17.1-15; 58-03-07.		
Ohio	No provisions		
Oklahoma	Oklahoma Stat. Ann., title 2, §§ 1401-1432.		
Oregon	Oregon Rev. Stat. §§ 558.010–558.990; 451.010; 451.420.		
Pennsylvania	Pennsylvania Stat. Ann., title 3, §§ 1101–1118.		
Rhode Island	No provisions		
South Carolina	No provisions		
South Dakota	South Dakota Compiled Laws Ann. §§ 38-9-1—38-9-22; 1-40-8; 10-12-18.		
Tennessee	No provisions		
Texas	Texas Water Code, title 2, §§ 14.001-14.112; Texas Civil Code, title 120A, § 6889-7(16).		
Utah			Utah Code Ann. §§ 73-15-3—73-15-8.
Vermont	No provisions		
Virginia	No provisions		
Washington	Washington Rev. Code Ann. §§ 43.37.010–43.37.200; 43.27A.080(6); 43.27A.180(1).		
West Virginia	West Virginia Code §§ 29-2B-1—29-2B-15.		
Wisconsin			Wisconsin Stat. Ann. § 195.40.
Wyoming		Wyoming Stat. §§ 10-4—10-6; §§ 9-267-9-276.	

---

[1] This search was completed in May 1977.

The 1979 Cessna Ag Husky at work.

Photograph courtesy Cessna Aircraft Company.

Act of God

Until weather modification techniques were evolved, flood, lightening, tornado, hail and hurricane damage, all were considered "Acts of God." Acts of God in civil law are misadventure or casualty caused by direct forces of nature, uninfluenced by human intervention, and of such a character that no amount of normal care or reasonable precaution could have prevented the damage or injury. In general, then, an irresistible force.

Possible Claims

Today, however, if a claimant can determine who to sue and how to prove responsibility, such a plaintiff might claim recompense for losses or injury resulting from weather modification activities. Damages might be claimed for:

Drought conditions and crop failures.

Floods.

Storm augmentation.

Hail size and/or intensity increase.

Typhoon or hurricane path alteration.

Class actions for air or water pollution.

Weather changes decreasing patronage of ski lodges or ocean front businesses.

Future

The licensing of all weather modification operators seems possible in the near future. Governments, both federal and state, are proceeding cautiously in regulating weather modification activities. Local opinion is of prime importance to such rule making, since local weather affects all in an area and gives them a definite right to participate in weather modification decision making.

Both public and private weather modification activities seem likely targets for suit. Yet, the difficulty of predicting weather normally is well known and often clouds the burden of proving that damage would not have occurred normally. Proof of causation is most difficult and uncertain in cases involving weather modification.

Only around one hundred weather modification projects take place in the U.S. each year. The import of such new technology is great, however, with enormous potentials for economic and social gain.

1979 PIPER BRAVE 300

1979 PIPER PAWNEE D

Photographs courtesy Piper Aircraft Corporation.

NOTES

[1]An "economic poison" is a pesticide or herbicide which is not harmful to animal life in most cases. The term is further defined in the Federal Insecticide, Fungicide, and Rodenticide Act, 7 U.S.C 135.

[2]Commercial operation comprised 93 percent of the target areas, federal operation 7 percent of target areas.

[3]Weather Modification Advisory Board, *The Management of Weather Resources*, Vol. I, Proposals for a National Policy and Program, a Report to the Secretary of Commerce from the WMAB, 30 June 1978 (Washington: Department of Commerce, 1978), pp. 17-32.

[4]Mason T. Charak and Mary T. DiGulian, "A Reveiw of Federal Legislation on Weather Modification," *Bulletin of the American Meteorological Society*, vol. 55, no. 7, July 1978, pp. 755-758.

[5]Mason T. Charak, Environmental Modification Office, NOAA, *Weather Modification Activities for Calendar Year 1975* (Rockville, Md.: U.S. Dept. of Commerce, National Oceanic and Atmospheric Administration, 1976), pp. 11-13.

[6]*Ibid*, pp. 13-16.

[7]Committee Print, 95th Cong., 2d sess., Senate Committee on Commerce, Science, and Transportation, *Weather Modification: Program, Problems, Policy and Potential* (Washington: U.S. Government Printing Office, 1978), pp. 193-202.

[8]*Ibid.* Comments are attached to the act by NOAA and included in the above committee print.

[9]Mike Edelhart, "Who'll Stop the Rain?" *Juris Doctor*, vol. 8, no. 9 (January 1979), pp. 32-34.

[10]*Management of Weather Resources*, I, pp. 147-56.

[11]*Ibid,* pp. 197-98.

[12]*Ibid,* pp. 453-55.

[13]*Ibid.*

[14]*Management of Weather Resources*, I, pp. 151-52.

[15]*Weather Modification: Program, Problems . . .*, pp. 449-58.

[16]Mary T. DiGuilan and Mason T. Charak, NOAA, "Survey of State Statutes on Weather Modification," *Bulletin of the American Meteorological Society*, vol. 55, no. 7 (July 1974).

[17]*Weather Modification Activities for Calendar Year 1975*, pp. 44-45.

[18]Robert E. Morrison, Specialist in Earth Sciences, Science Policy Research Div., Congressional Research Service, "State and Local Activities in Weather Modification," *Weather Modification: Program, Problems, Policy and Potential*, Committee Print, 95th Cong., 2d sess., Senate Committee on Commerce, Science and Transportation (Washington, U.S. Government Printing Office, 1978), pp. 331-33.

[19]*Ibid*, pp. 514-15.

[20]Suggested reading on the subject of weather modification includes: the committee print *Weather Modification, Program, Problems, Policy, and Potential*, May 1978, available from the Government Printing Office, Washington, D.C. Cite number 34-857. This 745-page book is a mine of detailed and interesting information on the subject.

CHAPTER 22

THE SPORTSMAN PILOT

General

Under certain conditions you have the legal right to risk your own life and your own property if you wish. Certainly the Wright brothers did just this. The conditions are — your are not to damage the property of others, and your are not to endanger the lives or safety of other persons.[1]

This does not mean that pilots are free to fly in a reckless and careless manner. The FAA rules that pilots shall carry out their flights in a responsible manner.[2] There is room, however, for experiment. Without such freedom, there could be no development of new types of aircraft or new flight procedures, or changes in technology.

Legally, the less maneuverable your aircraft, the more lawful right-of-way you have over other aircraft. Free balloons have the right of way over all other aircraft, with certain considerations involved which we will discuss later in this chapter. Airships come next in maneuverability, then gliders in free flight, and finally, powered aircraft.[3] All of these aircraft are regulated by the FAA.

Pleasure Flying: Airplanes

A pilot flying for pleasure is expected to use due care for his or her passengers.[4] These are considered "guests" and enter the plane voluntarily with a legal right to the same care for safety as the pilot may reasonably exercise for his own well being. The FAA forbids the careless or reckless operation of the aircraft.

Acrobatics are permitted in uncontrolled airspace. This is airspace which is not designated as an airway, airport control area, or other air traffic control use. Occupants of the aircraft must be furnished with safety equipment appropriate to the flight.[5]

Planes performing acrobatic maneuvers must observe the Federal Aviation Regulations pertaining to distances between the plane and the clouds, terrain clearance, distance from property, and those relating to legal visual flight

443

rules (VFR) flight regarding visibility and cloud ceiling minimums.[6]

The aircraft used by pilots planning to perform acrobatics must be appropriate to the maneuvers to be flown. For example, most civil aircraft are not stressed for inverted flight and are so placarded. (A placard is a sign located in the cockpit to advise the pilot of aircraft flight restrictions and operational limits.) Some aircraft are placarded against spins. Maximum limits given in the pilot's operating handbook for that aircraft as to maximum speeds, banks, and the engine and propeller limits are items to be considered by the responsible pilot.[7]

Formation flying is permitted only by prearrangement between all of the pilots involved. Passengers carried for hire may not be carried during formation flying.[8]

At air meets and airshows, some of the Federal Aviation Regulations are waived by the FAA and a written "waiver" issued to the airport operator.

Balloons

Balloons may use helium, hydrogen, natural gas, or hot air to make them literally "lighter-than-air" aircraft.

Pilots of balloons are certificated by the FAA after meeting the requirements of FAR Part 61. Other regulations pertaining to balloon operation are to be found in FAR Parts 31 and 101.

Since balloons drift with the wind, preflight weather and winds aloft information must be obtained by the pilot as a part of his legally required preflight preparations. The balloon pilot must stay clear of the clouds and advise air traffic control if the flight will be near airports, busy airways, or be in the air after dark.

Balloonists also face the legal responsibility for damage they may cause to property on the ground and, of course, injury to persons on the ground. Powerlines snagged on takeoff or landing, crops damaged by landings and/or ground recovery teams — all must be paid for by the balloon operator. Good public relations may help prevent claims. Liability protection should be carried by individuals and clubs operating balloons.

Balloons operated for hire must use an even greater degree of care for passengers carried than when carrying nonpaying, volunteer, "guest" passengers.

On 17 August 1978 three Americans completed the first successful Atlantic balloon crossing. They flew from the United States to a wheatfield in Normandy, France.

Gliders

Present-day gliding is quite a safe and delightful sport. Pilots are certificated by the FAA under the provisions of Part 61 of the Federal Air Regulations. Part 91 provides operating rules for glider (sailplane) operation.

Pilots of gliders, within the limits of their aircraft, have the same responsibilities as do pilots in other aircraft. Gliders in free flight must give way to free balloons. Pilots of gliders and sailplanes must maneuver in such a way as to reduce danger of collision with other aircraft.[9]

Parachutists

Planned parachuting operation involves advance notification to the FAA in order that appropriate Notices to Airmen (NOTAMS) may be issued.

Those persons choosing to make jumps are legally entitled to adequate instruction when paying for participation in the activity. The risks associated with parachute jumps, once the instructor and the pilot of the aircraft have carried out their duties, are assumed by the jumper.

Parachutes must be packed and inspected according to the provisions of FAR Part 149. Parachute jumping activities are further regulated by FAR Part 105 and FAR Part 91.15.[10]

Experimental and Antique Aircraft

You may build anything and, if an FAA inspector from your local FAA office agrees that the structure and powerplant seem reliable, you may then attempt to fly the device.

Antique aircraft, likewise, may be restored and flown. If these are of a certificated type acceptable to the FAA, then passengers may be carried for hire.

Due to the proven safety record of most experimental and homebuilt aircraft, the procedure of annual recertification of homebuilt aircraft is under consideration. The FAA proposes to do away with this requirement since it takes up so much of the time of FAA personnel. More than seven thousand aircraft built by amateurs for exhibition and racing would be affected. The FAA now proposes the issuance of an airworthiness certificate, after FAA inspection, for an indefinite period. Annual inspections by an A&P (Aircraft and Powerplant) mechanic would be required by the new ruling.

Muscle-powered Aircraft

Aircraft launched or propelled by foot are unregulated. Their pilots, too, need have no permits or licenses to fly these devices, at this writing. Man-powered aircraft includes: hang gliders; aircraft propelled by human strength; and the "super lights." A super-light aircraft is one launched on foot which uses a small engine to help maintain flight.

Man-propelled aircraft are those which attain flight by means of a propeller turned by pedals. One of the most successful of these is the muscle-powered plane designed by Dr. Paul McCready, and flown by Bryan Allen, the 70-pound "Condor."[11] Allen and MacCready won an $87,500 prize in Bakersfield, California, in August 1977 by flying a 1.15-mile figure eight course. The prize had been offered eighteen years earlier. Allen and MacCready were the first to build a man-powered aircraft that could qualify for it.

On Tuesday, June 12, 1979, Bryan Allen pedaled a new model titled the "Gossamer Albatross," across the English Channel. The 22-mile flight took two hours and twenty-nine minutes. Allen was often only inches above the water in the aircraft made of fine aluminum spars covered with Mylar polyester film. The aircraft has a 90-foot wingspan, weighs 55 pounds (70 pounds with safety and communications equipment needed for the Channel flight), and is powered by a man pedaling in order to turn a propeller mounted in the rear of the aircraft.

Allen, twenty-six, is a Bakersfield bio-chemist. He won a $200,000 prize for himself and the aircraft's designer Paul MacCready of Pasadena, California. The prize was put up by British industrialist Henry Kremer for the first human-powered flight across the English Channel.[12]

Hang gliding is not regulated by the FAA unless the kite or wing is towed aloft by an aircraft, a balloon or airplane. If this is the case, then FAR Part 101 applies to both the aircraft being towed and the plane doing the towing. The kite or wing, when cut loose from a surface tow, is also regulated by FAR Part 101. Any aircraft, including balloons, used to carry hang gliders aloft, are subject to FAR Part 91.18. These operations require a waiver to be issued by the FAA.

There is an Advisory Circular 60-10 published by the FAA which offers safety considerations to those persons engaging in hang gliding.

To date the sport has been the cause of numerous deaths and many serious injuries. The potential for legal suit is considerable. Such actions are hampered, however, by two considerations — the voluntary assumption of risks by participants, and the limited personal means of many of those engaged in selling hang gliding instruction.

In general, the FAA recommends that hang gliding be kept close to the ground; well below possible aircraft operations; clear of the clouds; clear of populated areas; away from controlled airspace, or buildings, and/or persons.

Lending a hang glider is legally the same as lending a plane or an automobile. If the lender does not have good reason to believe that the person borrowing the equipment is responsible, and well qualified in its operation, the lender can be held responsible for injury, death, or damage.

Dr. Paul MacCready's muscle-powered aircraft.

Photograph courtesy FAA.

NOTES

[1]FAR Part 91.9 "Careless or Reckless Operation" states that "No person may operate an aircraft in a careless or reckless manner so as to endanger the life or property of another."

[2]*Ibid.*

[3]FAR Part 91.69 governs right-of-way rules for the water operation of aircraft; for other right-of-way rules see FAR Part 91.67.

[4]FAR Part 91.9; FAR Part 91.3 which states that "the pilot in command of an aircraft is directly responsible for, and is the final authority as to, the operation of the aircraft . ."

[5]FAR Part 91.71 "Acrobatic Flight."

[6]FAR Part 91.105 "Basic VFR Weather Minimums."

[7]FAR Part 91.27.

[8]FAR Part 91.65.

[9]FAR Parts 61.69; 61.87 (c) (4); 61.105 (c); 61.115; 61.127 (d); 91.17; and other FAR Parts.

[10]FAR Part 91.15 "Parachutes and Parachuting."

[11]Associated Press, "California Man Pedals Plane Across Channel," *Los Angeles Times*, 13 June 1979, p. 1.

[12]*Ibid.*

SELECTED BIBLIOGRAPHY

Advisory Circular AC 00-2QQ, Subject: Advisory Circular Checklist. Washington: DOT, Federal Aviation Administration, 4/15/79.

Aeronautical Statues and Related Material. Washington: Civil Aeronautics Board, 1974, and supplements. (GPO).

AOPA Handbook for Pilots, 1979. Washington, DC: Aircraft Owners and Pilots Association, 1979.

Bailey, F. Lee. *Cleared for the Approach.* New York: New American Library, 1978.

Biehler, Fred A. *Aviation Maintenance Law.* Basin, Wyo.: Aviation Maintenance Foundation, Inc., 1975.

Briddon, Arnold E.; Champie, Ellmore A.; and Marraine, Peter A. *FAA Historical Fact Book: A Chronology 1926-1971.* Washington: DOT, Federal Aviation Administration, 1974.

Burnham, Frank. *Cleared to Land: The FAA Story.* Fallbrook, CA: Aero Publishers, Inc., 1977.

Charak, Mason T.; and DiGiulian, Mary T., "A Review of Federal Legislation on Weather Modification," *Bulletin American Meteorological Society,* Vol. 55, No. 7 (July 1974)

Cook, David C. *Who Really Invented the Airplane?* New York: G.P. Putnam's Sons, 1964.

Costello, John; and Hughes, Terry. *The Concorde Conspiracy: The International Race for the SST.* New York: Charles Scribner's Sons, 1976.

David, Rene; and Brierley, John E.C. *Major Legal Systems in the World Today.* London: Free Press, Collier-Macmillan Ltd., 1968.

DiGulian, Mary T.; and Charak, Mason T. "Survey of State Statutes on Weather Modification," *Bulletin American Meteorological Society,* Vol. 55, No. 7 (July 1974), pp. 751-754.

Domestic Jet Trends. Washington: Civil Aeronautics Board, 1978.

Edelhart, Mike. "Who'll Stop the Rain?" *Juris Doctor,* Vol. 8, No. 9 (January 1979), pp. 32-34.

Fixel, Rowland W., *Law of Aviation,* 4th ed. Charlottesville, Va.: Michie Company, 1967.

Fleagle, Robert G., Ed., *Weather Modification: Science and Public Policy.* London: University of Washington Press, 1969.

Flynn, Paul P. *Aviation Law.* Los Angeles: Southwestern University, School of Law, 1972.

Foster, Timothy R.V. with a foreword by Leighton Collins. *The Aircraft Owner's Handbook.* New York: Van Nostrand Reinhold, Co., 1978.

General Aviation Statistical Data: 1979 Edition. Washington: General Aviation Manufacturers Association, 1979.

Glahn, Gerhard von. *Law Among Nations.* Toronto: The Macmillan Co., 1970.

Glick, Henry Robert; and Vines, Kenneth N. *State Court Systems,* Englewood Cliffs, NJ: Prentice-Hall, Inc., 1973.

Harris, Cecil M. *Handbook of Noise Control,* 2d ed. New York: McGraw Hill, 1979.

Hart, Michael J. *Outline of International Aviation Law.* St. Louis, MO: Parks College of St. Louis University, 1975.

Heere, Wybo P. *International Bibliography of Air Law: 1900-1971.* Dobbs Ferry, NY: Oceana Publications, 1972.

Hirsch, Richard; and Trenton, Joseph John. *The National Aeronautics and Space Administration.* New York: Praeger Publisher, 1973.

Kane, Robert M.; and Vose, Allen D. *Air Transportation.* Dubuque, Iowa: Kendall/Hunt Publishing Co., 1977.

Kelly, Charles J., Jr. *The Sky's the Limit: The History of the Airlines.* New York: Arno, 1971.

Kilpatrick, James Jackson. *The Sovereign States.* Chicago: Henry Regnery Co., 1957.

Komons, Nick A. *Bonfires to Beacons: Federal Civil Aviation Policy under the Air Commerce Act 1926-1938.* Washington: U.S. DOT, Federal Aviation Administration., 1978. (GPO).

Kreindler, Lee S. *Aircraft Litigation.* New York: Practicing Law Institute, 1972.

Kreindler, Lee S. *Aviation Accident Law,* 2 volumes. New York: Matthew Bender and Company, 1963.

Langmuir, Irving. "Cloud Seeding by Means of Dry Ice, Silver Iodide, and Sodium Chloride," *Transactions of the New York Academy of Sciences,* ser.II, vol. 14, November 1951, p. 40.

Law and the Courts. Chicago: American Bar Association, 1974.

List of U.S. Air Carriers. Washington: Civil Aeronautics Board, 1979.

Lowenfeld, Andreas F. *Aviation Law: Cases and Materials.* New York: Matthew Bender, 1972.

McWhinney, Edward. *Aerial Piracy and International Law.* Dobbs Ferry, NY: Oceana Publications,Inc., 1971.

McWhinney, Edward; and Bradley, M.A. *The Freedom of the Air.* Dobbs Ferry, NY: Oceana Publications, 1968.

Misenhimer, Ted. G. *Aeroscience.* Los Angeles: Aero Products Research, Inc., 1976.

National Oceanic and Atmospheric Administration. *Weather Modification Activities for Calendar Year 1975.* Rockville, MD: U.S. Department of Commerce, NOAA, June 1976.

Padover, Saul K. *The Living U.S. Constitution.* New York: World Publilshing Co., 1968.

Phillips, C.P. "Air Warfare and Law," 21 *George Washington Law Review* (1952-1953) pp. 311-315, 395-422.

"Proposed Noise and Sonic Boom Requirements," *Federal Register.* Washington: DOT, Federal Aviation Administration, Oct. 13, 1977, pp. 55176-55184.

Pucci, Gerard. *Aviation Law: Fundamental Cases.* Dubuque, Iowa: Kendall/Hunt Publishing Company, 1977.

Ross, Martin J. *Handbook of Everyday Law.* New York: Harper & Row, Publishers, Inc., 1967.

Sixty Years of Aeronautical Research: 1917-1977. Washington, DC: National Aeronautics and Space Administration, 1978.

Spaight, J.M. *Air Power and War Rights.* London: Longmans, Green and Co.,

Speiser, Stuart M.; and Krause, Charles F. *Aviation Tort Law.* San Francisco: Bancroft-Whitney Co., Vol. I, 1978 and Vol. II, 1979.

"SST Action," Federal Register, Vol. 43. Washington: DOT Federal Aviation Administration, June 29, 1978, p. 28406.

The United States Courts: Their Jurisdiction and Work. Washington, DC: Government Printing Office, 1975.

U.S. International Air Freight Traffic. Washington: Civil Aeronautics Board, 1978.

Weather Modification Advisory Board, *The Management of Weather Resources, I.* Report to the Secretary of Commerce, 1978.

Weather Modification: Program, Problems, Policy, and Potential. Committee Print, 95th Congress, 2d Session, for Senate Committee on Commerce, Science and Transportation. Washington: U.S. GPO, 1978.

Wormser, Rene A. *The Story of the Law.* New york: Simon & Schuster, 1962.

GLOSSARY OF AERONAUTICAL TERMINOLOGY

When studying any discipline one must "learn the language." Aeronautical terminology is vivid, specialized, and interesting. The following short definitions of many aeronautical terms will aid the reader in understanding today's air commerce. Thanks are rendered to the Civil Aeronautics Board, the Federal Aviation Administration, the National Aeronautical and Space Administration, and the National Oceanic and Atmospheric Administration for lists of terms and background information used to compile this glossary.

Abandonment. A voluntary giving up of authority by the carrier to operate or serve a point or points covered in its certificate of public convenience and necessity.

Abort. To cancel or cut short a flight. To stop a takeoff roll. To stop an attempt to land.

Administrative Law Judge. A person appointed by the Civil Aeronautics Board, in accordance with Civil Service Commission regulations, to conduct hearings on behalf of the Board. The term also includes presiding officers, individual members of the Board or any other representative of the Board assigned to hold a hearing in a proceeding.

Aerodynamics. The science that deals with the movement of air and objects moving through the air.

Aeronautical Radio, Inc. (ARINC). A nonprofit radio communications facility owned by the certificated route air carriers.

Aerospace Medicine. That branch of medicine dealing with the effects of flight through the atmosphere or in space upon the human body, and with the prevention or cure of physiological or psychological malfunctions arising from these effects.

Agent, Cargo. Any person (other than the air carrier performing the direct air transportation or one of its bona fide regular employees or an indirect air carrier lawfully engaged in air transportation under authority conferred by any applicable part of the Economic Regulations of the Board) who for compensation or profit: (1) solicits, obtains, receives, or furnishes directly or indirectly property or consolidated shipments of property for transportation upon the aircraft of an air carrier, or (2) procures or arranges for air transportation of property or consolidated shipments of property upon aircraft of an air carrier by charter, lease, or any other arrangement.

Agent, Ticket. Any person (other than the air carrier performing the direct air transportation or one of its bona fide regular employees, or an air carrier which subcontracts the performance of charter air transportation which it has contracted to perform) who for compensation or profit: (1) solicits, obtains, receives, or furnishes directly or indirectly passengers or groups of passengers for transportation upon the aircraft of an air carrier, or (2) procures or arranges for air transportation of passengers or groups of passengers upon aircraft of an air carrier by charter, lease, or any other arrangement.

Agent, Travel. A person who sells air transportation services to individuals or groups on behalf of, and in the name of, air carriers.

Agreement, Bilateral. An agreement or treaty between two nations.

Agreement, Interchange (Also, Aircraft, Interchange). An agreement under which aircraft of one air carrier are utilized to provide one-plane service over its own routes and the routes of other air carriers.

Airbill (also, Air Waybill). The non-negotiable shipping document used by domestic air carriers as evidence of an air freight shipment. The document contains shipping instructions, commodity descriptions, and transportation charges applicable to the freight shipped. Sometimes used interchangeable with "air waybill" (which see) which is erroneous terminology when the domestic airbill does not meet the uniformity requirements of the air waybill.

Airbus (Aerial Bus). A jumbo jet carrying twice as many people as a 707 or DC-8 and specializing in short-and medium-length trips.

Aircraft Engine, Piston. An internal combustion engine in which the combustive explosion propels a piston(s) within a cylinder(s) and transfers the power to a crank shaft or other device to create rotational movement. Aircraft engines of this type use the rotational movement to turn a propeller.

Aircraft Engine, Turbine. An engine incorporating as its chief element a turbine rotated by expanding gases. It consists essentially in its most usual form of a rotary air compressor with an air intake, one or more combustion chambers, a turbine, and an exhaust outlet. Aircraft engines of this type have their power applied mainly either as jet thrust (turbojet or turbofan) or as shaft power to rotate a propeller (turboprop).

Aircraft Engine, Turbofan (Fan-Jet). A turbojet engine whose thrust has been increased by the addition of a low pressure compressor (fan).

Aircraft Engine, Turbojet. A turbine (gas-turbine) engine incorporating a turbine-driven compressor to take in and compress the air for the combination of fuel, with the gases of combustion (or heated air) being used to both rotate the turbine and to create a thrust producing jet.

Aircraft Engine, Turbopropeller (Prop-Jet, Turboprop). A turbine (gas-turbine) engine in which the output is taken as shaft power to drive a propeller via a reduction gear; it also has a small residual jet thrust.

Aircraft, Ground Effect Machine (GEM) (Hovercraft) Variously known as air-cushion vehicles, levapads and hovercraft which are trademark or proprietary designations. An experimental type of airborne vehicle that travels on a cushion of air over land or water, usually only a few inches to a foot or more above the surface being traversed.

Aircraft Hour, Block-To-Block (Block Hour, Ramp-To-Ramp Hour). The hours computed from the moment an aircraft first moves under its own power for purposes of flight until it comes to rest at the next point of landing.

Aircraft Piracy (Hijacking, Skyjacking). Any seizure or exercise of control, by force or violence or threat of force or violence, or by any other form of intimidation, and with wrongful intent, of an aircraft.

Aircraft, Short Takeoff and Landing (STOL). A heavier-than-air aircraft capable of taking off and landing within a relatively short horizontal distance.

Aircraft, Supersonic Transport (SST). A transport aircraft capable of a normal cruising speed greater than the speed of sound (741 mph at sea level).

Aircraft, Turbine. Includes aircraft with either tubojet, turbofan, turboprop, or turboshaft engines.

Aircraft, Vertical/Short Takeoff and Landing (V/STOL). An aircraft capable of taking off and landing vertically or in a short distance.

Aircraft, Vertical Takeoff and Landing (VTOL). A heavier-than-air aircraft that can takeoff and land vertically.

Aircraft, Wide-Body. A generic and commonly used term applied to any and all of the newest generation of jet aircraft with a fuselage diameter exceeding 200 inches and whose per engine thrust is greater than 30,000 pounds (i.e., Boeing 747, McDonnell Douglas DC-10, Lockheed L-1011).

Airframe. Framework and metal covering of an airplane body, wings and tail. The fuselage, booms, nacelles, cowlings, fairings, airfoil surfaces (including rotors but excluding propellers and rotating airfoils of engines), and landing gear of an aircraft and their accessories and controls.

Airframe Manufacturer. A company which makes or assembles the fuselage, wing, tail sections and other parts of an aircraft, but not the engines or avionics.

Air Freight Forwarder. Any indirect air carrier which, in the ordinary and usual course of its undertaking, (1) assembles and consolidates, or provides for assembling and consolidating, property for shipment by air, or performs or provides for the performance of break-bulk and distributing operations with respect to consolidated shipments, and (2) is responsible for the transportation of property from the point of receipt to the point of destination and utilizes, for the whole or any part of such transportation, the services of a direct air carrier.

Airman. Any individual who engages, as the person in command or as pilot, mechanic, or member of the crew, in the navigation of aircraft while under way; and (except to the extent the Administrator may otherwise provide with respect to individuals employed outside the United States) any individual who is directly in charge of the inspection, maintenance, overhauling, or repair of aircraft, aircraft engines, propellers, or appliances; and any individual who serves in the capacity of aircraft dispatcher or air-traffic controller.

Air Navigation Facility. Any facility used in, available for use in, or designed for use in, aid of air navigation, including landing areas, lights, any apparatus or equipment for disseminating weather information, for signaling, for radio-directional finding, or for radio or other electrical communication, and any other structure or mechanism having a similar purpose for guiding or controlling flight in the air or on the landing and takeoff of aircraft.

Airport. A landing area regularly used by aircraft for receiving or discharging passengers or cargo.

Airport Ramp (Apron). A hard-surfaced area, usually paved, adjacent to a hangar, repair shop, terminal, or the like and used to park, load, unload, service, or handle aircraft.

Airship. An engine-driven lighter-than-air aircraft that can be steered.

Air Traffic Conference of America (ATC). A division of Air Transport Association which is concerned with joint air carrier action on traffic, sales, and advertising matters. The members of ATC adopt intercarrier agreements relating to interline passenger and cargo movements, joint air carrier marketing facilities, and standards for approval, retention, and compensation of travel agents, subject to Board approval.

Air Traffic Control. A service operated by appropriate authority to promote the safe, orderly, and expeditious flow of air traffic.

Air Transport Association (ATA). The trade association of the U. S. certificated route air carriers.

Air Transportation, Intrastate. The carriage by aircraft of persons or property as a common carrier for compensation or hire wholly within the same State of the United States.

Air Transportation, Supplemental. Charter flights in the air transportation, supplementing scheduled service, performed pursuant to a certificate of public convenience and necessity issued under Section 401(d)(3) of the Act: (1) authorizing the holder to engage in charter air transportation of persons and property between any point in any state of the United States or the District of Columbia, and any other point in any State of the United States or the District of Columbia (exclusive of air transportation within the State of Alaska) or in foreign or overseas charter air transportation, or (2) authorizing the holder to engage in charter air transportation of persons and their personal baggage between any point in any State of the United States or the District of Columbia, on the one hand, and points in Central and South America, Greenland, Iceland, the Azores, Europe, Africa and Asia on the other hand.

Airway. A 10 mile wide path through the navigable airspace equipped with air navigation aids and designated by the Administrator, Federal Aviation Administration, extending from the ground upward to 27,000 feet. At and above 27,000 feet the high altitude jet route system is used.

Air Waybill, In-House. The non-negotiable shipping document issued by air freight forwarders which document or evidence a contract for carriage between the shipper and the air freight forwarder.

Albedo. A numerical indication of the percentage of incoming solar radiation that is reflected by the land, ocean, and atmosphere back into space and, attendantly, how much is absorbed by the climatic system. Another important manner for altering the Earth's heat budget, albedo can be changed by the process of urbanization, agricultural activities, changes in the character of the land surface, and by increasing or decreasing cloudiness.

Alternate Airport. An airport at which an aircraft may land if a landing at the intended airport becomes inadvisable.

Altocumulus. A principal type of cloud, 8,000 to 20,000 feet consisting of a layer where the denser parts have modified cumuliform characteristics of roundness and sharpness of outline.

Altostratus. A principal type of "middle" cloud (altitude approx. 8,900 to 20,000 feet), appearing as a fairly uniform grey layer that often covers the entire sky.

Analog Computer. A computing machine that works on the principle of measuring, as distinguished from counting.

Area Navigation High Route. An area navigation route within the airspace extending upward from, and including 18,000 feet MSL, to flight level 450.

Artificial Nucleation. Any process whereby the nucleation of cloud particles is initiated or accelerated by human intervention.

Atmosphere. The envelope of air surrounding the earth.

Avionics. Word formed from aviation electronics; the electrical and electronic devices and systems used in an aircraft.

Barnstormer. A pilot who gives exhibitions of stunt flying in country towns or rural areas.

Biannual. Occuring twice a year.

Biennial. Occuring every two years.

Blocked Space. A program under which direct air carriers offer lower rates and guaranteed space to volume shippers in return for the shipment of a predetermined minimum of freight between the same two points for a specified period of time. The rates are based and charged on the minimum space agreed upon whether utilized or not.

Cabotage. The carriage of air traffic which originates and terminates within the boundaries of a given country by an air carrier of another country. Rights to such traffic are usually entirely denied or severely restricted.

Capacity, Maximum Payload. The maximum certificated takeoff weight of an aircraft, less the empty weight, less all justifiable aircraft equipment, and less the operating load (consisting of minimum fuel load, oil, flight crew, stewards' supplies).

Carrier, Air. Any person who undertakes, whether directly or indirectly or by a lease or any other arrangement, to engage in air transportation.

Carrier, Certificated Air. One of a class of air carriers holding certificates of public convenience and necessity, issued by the Board, authorizing the holder to engage in air transportation. This group consists of certificated route carriers authorized to provide scheduled service and limited nonscheduled service, and supplemental carriers authorized to engage in nonscheduled service.

Carrier, Certificated Route Air. One of a class of air carriers holding certificates of public convenience and necessity, issued by the CAB, authorizing the performance of scheduled air transportation over specified routes and limited amount of nonscheduled operations. This general carrier grouping includes the all-purpose carriers (i.e., the so-called passenger/cargo carriers) and the all-cargo carriers. Certificated route air carriers often are referred to as "scheduled carriers," although they also perform nonscheduled service.

Carrier, Common Air. An air transportation business that holds out its services for public hire. Includes the airlines, air freight forwarders and other indirect air carriers; excludes nontransportation companies and the public at large who provide transportation services for themselves.

453

Carrier, Commuter Air. An air taxi operator which (1) performs at least five round trips per week between two or more points and publishes flight schedules which specify the times, days of the week, and places between which such flights are performed, or (2) transports mail by air pursuant to a current contract with the United States Postal Service.

Carrier, Designated Air. The carrier, a national of one country which is a party to a bilateral agreement, chosen by that country to operate service over a specific route or routes (or charter service under a charter agreement) and specifically named by diplomatic note to the other party.

Carrier, Local Service Air. A group of air carriers originally established in the late 1940's to foster and provide air service to small and medium communities on relatively low density routes to large air traffic hubs. A subsidy payment program was instituted for these carriers since their authorization by the Board was of an experimental basis and operating losses were projected for the first years of the carriers' operations. These carriers have since evolved from their "feeder" airlines origination into "regional" carriers with only certain of their operations subsidy eligible.

Carrier, Supplemental Air. An air carrier holding a certificate issued under section 401(D)(3) of the Federal Aviation Act of 1958, as amended, or a special operating authorization issued under section 417 of the Act, or operating authority issued pursuant to section 7 or 9 of Public Law 87-528. Such carrier is authorized to operate charter flights, supplementing scheduled service.

Carrier, Trunk Air. A class of certificated route air carriers (which see) receiving original certification under the "grandfather clause" of the Civil Aeronautics Act (August 22, 1938) and whose primary operations are in domestic scheduled passenger service between relatively medium and large air traffic hubs. In addition, these carriers may have certificated authority for scheduled all-cargo, scheduled international passenger and/or cargo, and nonscheduled service.

Carrier, United States Flag Air (a.k.a. American Flag). A citizen of the United States who engages in air transportation between the United States (and/or its possessions and territories) and one or more foreign countries, pursuant to a certificate of public convenience and necessity or other operating authorization issued by the Civil Aeronautics Board and approved by the President.

Category. (1) As used with respect to the certification, ratings, privileges, and limitations of airmen, means a broad classification of aircraft. Examples include: airplane; rotorcraft; glider; and lighter-than-air; and (2) as used with respect to the certification of aircraft, means a grouping of aircraft based upon intended use or operating limitations. Examples include: transport; normal; utility; acrobatic; limited; restricted; and provisional.

Ceiling. The height above the earth's surface of the lowest layer of clouds or obscuring phenomena that is reported as "broken" "overcast", or "obscuration".

Certificate of Public Convenience and Necessity. A certificate issued to an air carrier under Section 401 of the Federal Aviation Act of 1958 by the Civil Aeronautics Board authorizing the carrier to engage in air transportation. The certificate may contain certain designated routes and certain designated points or geographical areas to be served and any limitation and restrictions imposed on such service as the Board may specify.

Certificated. Holding a currently valid certificate of public convenience and necessity.

Chaff. Metallic electrical dipoles, several centimeters long, commonly made of fine wire. The original use of chaff, dropping large quantities of it from aircraft in WWII was to jam enemy radars. It is now used experimentally to alter the electrical properties of thunderstorms.

Charter, Split. A charter, in which the entire capacity of an aircraft is divided between different charterers and/or charter types.

Charterworthy. An individual or group chartering an aircraft or participating as a passenger or passengers on a charter flight who meet all the requirements for such participation as set forth by the Board in its Economic Regulations.

Cirrus. A principal cirriform cloud type, composed of ice crystals aggregated into delicate wisps or patches at high altitudes.

Civil Reserve Air Fleet (CRAF). A group of commercial aircraft with crews, which are allocated in times of emergency for exclusive military use in both international and domestic service.

Cloud. A visible aggregate of minute water and/or ice particles in the atmosphere above the earth's surface. Cloud differs from fog only in that the latter is, by definition, in contact with the earth's surface.

Cloud Seeding. Any process of injecting a substance into a cloud for the purpose of influencing the cloud's subsequent development.

Cloud Seeding Agent. Any variety of substances dispensed for the purposes of cloud seeding. In addition to the commonly used silver iodide and dry ice, a number of other materials have been experimented with for various purposes, for example, calcium chloride, urea, metaldehyde, chlorosulfonic acid, carbon black, common salt, and water spray.

454

Commission, Travel Agent. The payment by airlines to a travel agent of specified amounts of money in return for the agent's sales of air transportation. Travel agents' commissions are usually set by ATC and IATA resolutions, as approved by the Board, and are usually expressed and paid by each carrier as a percentage of the value of the air transportation sold on that air carrier.

Component. A part or section of something larger; for example, a rib section is a component of an aircraft wing.

Condensation Nucleus. A particle, either liquid or solid, upon which condensation of water vapor begins in the atmosphere.

Configuration. A particular type of a specific aircraft, rocket, etc., which differs from others of the same model by virtue of the arrangement of its components or by the addition or omission of auxiliary equipment as "long-range" configuration", "cargo configuration."

Container (Belly Pod, Cargo Pod, Igloo, see also, Pallet). An enclosed unit load device which enables small pieces of cargo or baggage to be consolidated on the ground into a larger shipping unit, to facilitate faster on — loading and off — loading of an aircraft through mechanization, enable immediate transfer to other transportation modes and to maximize the useful cubic capacity of the aircraft.

Controlled Airspace. Airspace designated as a continental control area, control area, control zone, terminal control area, or transition area, within which some or all aircraft may be subject to air traffic control.

Convection Current (or convective current). Any current of air involved in convection. In meteorology, this is usually applied to the upward moving portion of a convection circulation such as a thermal or the updraft in cumulus clouds.

Cooperative Shippers Association. A bona fide association of shippers, operating as an indirect air carrier on a nonprofit basis, that: (1) undertakes to ship property for the account of such association or its members, by air, in the name of either the association or the members, in order to secure the benefits of volume rates or improved services for the benefits of its members and (2) utilizes for the whole or any part of such transportation the services of a direct air carrier.

Cumulonimbus. (Commonly called thundercloud, thunderhead, "anvilcloud", thunderstorm.) A principal cloud type, the ultimate stage of development of cumulus or convective clouds. They are very dense and very tall, commonly 5 to 10 miles in diameter and sometimes reaching a height of 12 miles or more.

Cumulus (Cumuliform). A principal cloud type, actually a cloud "family" all of which are characterized by vertical development; a convective cloud.

Decision Height. The height at which a decision must be made, during an ILS or PAR instrument approach, to either continue the approach or to execute a missed approach.

Depreciation, Flight Equipment. Charges to expense for depreciation of airframes, aircraft engines, airframe and engine parts, and other flight equipment.

Destination, Ticket. The point of deplanement indicated on the last coupon on a whole passenger ticket (or conjunction ticket).

Digital Computer. A computer which operates on the principle of counting as opposed to measuring. See analog computer.

Dilution, Fare. The difference between the revenue which should be received for the carriage of traffic at published full fares and the revenue actually received for that carriage. The fare dilution reflects the effect of discount, promotional, and other less-than-full fares on revenues.

Dimensional Rule. A practice applicable to low density freight shipments under which transport charges are based on cubic dimensions rather than on weight.

Distance, Great-Circle. The distance on a course along a great circle of the globe, the shortest distance between two points on the earth's surface.

Docket. A record of the principal matters pertaining to a specific Board proceeding or case, including a transcript of the hearings, exhibits, and correspondence. Open to public inspection.

Drag. Forces opposed to thrust which resist movement, air friction, area being pulled through the air and thus resisting movement, friction of wheels, skis or floats against the surface during takeoff and landing.

Dry-Ice Seeding. The Dispensing of dry ice pellets into supercooled clouds for the purpose of transforming the supercooled droplets into ice crystals, which then grow and fall out. Dry ice creates a sufficiently cold environment around the droplets for them to undergo spontaneous nucleation.

Echo. In radar, a general term for the appearance, on a radar indicator, of the radio energy returned from a target. The energy reflected or scattered back from a target.

Empennage. The rear section of an airplane including the vertical and horizontal tail surfaces.

Engine Pods (Nacelle). The enclosure in which an airplane engine is housed.

Enplanements, Passenger. The total number of passengers boarding aircraft, including originating and stopover or on-line transfer passengers.

Entity. A Board established division, for reporting purposes, of a carrier's air transport operations conducted within certain geographical areas. They are as follows: (1) Domestic operations, embracing all operations within the 50 states of the United States and the District of Columbia, and shall also include Canadian transborder operations; (2) operations via the Atlantic Ocean; (3) operations via the Pacific Ocean; and (4) operations within the Latin American areas.

Escrow. A bank depositary agreement by which sums due a direct or indirect air carrier for the charter of an aircraft are deposited with and maintained in a separate account and which are paid by the bank to the direct or indirect air carrier upon the completion of the charter or upon the happening of some other event.

Estimated Time of Arrival (ETA). Estimated Time of Arrival at an airport.

Exemption. Temporary authorization pursuant to Section 416(b) of the Act permitting: (1) an air carrier to engage in air transportation in a manner otherwise prohibited by its certificate of public convenience and necessity; or (2) an air carrier or class of air carriers to engage in air transportation in a manner otherwise prohibited by the Federal Aviation Act.

Exosphere. The outermost, or topmost portion of the atmosphere.

Express. Property transported by air under published air express tariffs filed with the Civil Aeronautics Board.

Fan-Jet Engines. Inside the engine is a fan which helps to compress air entering the engine.

Fare. The amount per passenger or group of persons stated in the applicable tariff for the transportation thereof and includes baggage unless the context otherwise requires. First class fare is charged for premium quality passenger service. Coach or Tourist Fare has quality of service less than First Class.

Fare, Joint. A fare published as a single factor that applies to transportation over the joint lines or routes of two or more carriers and which is made and published by arrangements or agreement between such carriers evidenced by concurrence or power of attorney.

Fare, Standard. A fare charged for carriage in air transportation on aircraft, offering a single class of service which the carrier has designated as standard. Usually applicable to local service carriers, such fares being equal to or greater than coach fares but less than first class fares for such carriage.

Fare Structure. The particular fares charged for trips of varying distances and the relationship between coach fares and fares for the other classes of service. The manner in which the fare level should be distributed to, and recouped from, the passenger transport services operated by the air carriers. Used most often in regulatory rate-making.

Fare, Through. The total fare from point of origin to destination. It may be a local fare, a joint fare or combination of separately established fares.

Fatigue. A weakening or deterioration of metal or other material, or of a member, occurring under load, especially under repeated, cyclic, or continued loading. Also, human condition of being tired, fatigued.

Flight, Deadhead. A nonrevenue flight for the purpose of returning an aircraft from its destination.

Flight, Developmental. A flight for (a) the development of a new route either prior or subsequent to certification by the Civil Aeronautics Board; (b) the extension of an existing route; or (c) the integration of a new type of aircraft or service.

Flight Equipment (see also, Aircraft). Airframes, aircraft engines, aircraft propellers, aircraft propellers, aircraft communications and navigational equipment, miscellaneous equipment used in the operation of the aircraft, and improvements to leased flight equipment.

Flight, Extra Section. A flight conducted as an integral part of scheduled service, that has not been provided for in published schedules and is required for transportation of traffic that cannot be accommodated on a regularly scheduled flight.

Flight, Ferry. A flight for the purpose of returning an aircraft to base, for equipment equalization, or for moving an aircraft to and from a maintenance base.

Flight Level. A level of constant atmospheric pressure related to a reference datum of 29.92 inches of mercury. Each is stated in three digits that represent hundreds of feet. For example, flight level 250 represents a barometric altimeter indication of 25,000 feet; flight level 255, an indication of 25,500 feet.

Flight, Nonscheduled. A flight to, from, or between points not covered by certificates of public convenience issued by the Civil Aeronautics Board to the air carrier; flights pursuant to the charter or hiring of aircraft; or other revenue flights not constituting an integral part of the services performed pursuant to published schedules.

Flight Plan. Specified information, relating to the intended flight of an aircraft that is filed orally or in writing with air traffic control.

Flight, Scheduled. Any aircraft itinerary periodically operated between terminal points that is separately designated, by flight number or otherwise, in the published schedules of an air carrier.

Flight Visibility. The average forward horizontal distance, from the cockpit of an aircraft in flight, at which prominent unlighted objects may be seen and identified by day and prominent lighted objects may be seen and identified by night.

Foreign Air Carrier Permit. A permit issued by the Civil Aeronautics Board to a foreign air carrier authorizing it to conduct air transport operations between foreign countries and cities in the United States, either in accordance with the terms of a bilateral air transport agreement or nonscheduled air service agreement, or under conditions of comity and reciprocity.

Freezing Nucleus. Any particle which, when present within a mass of supercooled water, will initiate growth of an ice crystal about itself.

456

Freight. Property, other than express, mail, and excess passenger baggage, transported by air under published air freight tariffs filed with the Civil Aeronautics Board.

Freight Consolidation. A number of shipments traveling from one airport to another under one airline airbill or other documents serving the same purpose.

Freight, Deferred. Property received for interstate air transportation on a space available basis, after accommodation of all other revenue traffic, the carriage of which is conditioned so that such property shall not be released at the destination airport prior to a certain number of days after receipt.

Freight Express and Mail (FEM). A collective phrase used to enumerate the components of air cargo and specifically to exclude passenger baggage.

Fuel, Bonded. Aircraft fuel imported into the United States that is destined for use only in international operations and upon which federal taxes are not levied. Stored under a carrier's or supplier's bond.

Fuel, Jet. Commercial turbine-engine planes are most commonly powered by kerosene which is generally called jet fuel, in contrast to the aviation gasoline which powers piston-engine planes.

Fuel Taxes. Excise taxes paid by the airlines on the aviation gasoline and jet fuel they purchase. In addition, a number of the States levy State fuel taxes, some States on aviation gasoline, some on both avgas and jet fuel.

Fuselage. The main body of an airplane to which the wing and tail surfaces are attached.

Galley. The kitchen aboard an aircraft or ship.

General Aviation. Consists of aviation other than military and commercial common carriage and includes business flying, instructional flying, personal flying, and commercial flying such as agricultural spraying and aerial photography.

Gliding. The glide, glide angle; the ability of an aircraft to fly without a power plant, or with an inoperative power plant.

"Grandfather Rights". The automatic granting of a certificate of public convenience and necessity to those air carriers which had been in continuous operation, and in possession of an air mail contract, for a period of 90 days prior to the passage of the Civil Aeronautics Act of 1938 (Grandfather Clause, Section 401e). Automatic granting of operational authority to a common carrier which has regularly and continuously served the public prior to its subjection to regulation.

Gravity. Can also be called weight. At cruising speed in calm air, wings level, the wing supports one force of gravity "1 G". Turns and pull ups can increase this factor.

Ground Generator. In weather modification, almost invariably referring to silver iodide smoke generators that are operated on the ground (as opposed to airborne equipment).

Gyro. A device which utilizes the angular momemtum of a spinning rotor to sense angular motion of the base about one or two axes at right angles to the spin axis. Also called "gyroscope."

Hail Suppression. Any method of reducing the damaging effects of hailstorms by operating on the hail producing cloud.

Hearing. Rulemaking, licensing or adjudicatory proceeding for the taking of evidence, in the form of testimony or documents, and the presentation of arguments. Hearings may be presided over by the Civil Aeronautics Board, one or more members of the body which comprises the Board, or one or more administrative law judges.

Hub, Air Traffic. Air traffic hubs are not airports; they are the cities and Standard Metropolitan Statistical Areas requiring aviation services. Communities fall into four classes (large, medium, small, and non hubs) as determined by each community's percentage of the total enplaned passengers in scheduled and nonscheduled service of the domestic certificated route air carriers in the 50 states, the District of Columbia and other United States areas designated by the Federal Aviation Administration.

Human Engineering. The art or science of designing, building, or equipping mechanical devices or artificial environments to the anthropometric, physiological, or psychological requirements of the men who will use them.

Hygroscopic Seeding. Cloud seeding with hygroscopic material which encourages condensation and collects water vapor.

Hypersonic. 1. Pertaining to hypersonic flow. 2. Pertaining to speeds of Mach 5 or greater.

Hypersonic Flow. In aerodynamics, flow of a fluid over a body at speeds much greater than the speed of sound and in which the shock waves start at a finite distance from the surface of the body.

Hypoxia. Oxygen deficiency in the blood, cells or tissues of the body in such degree as to cause psychological and physiological disturbances. Hypoxia may result from a scarcity of oxygen in the air being breathed, or from an inability of the body tissues to absorb oxygen under conditions of low ambient pressure.

Ice Crystal Cloud. A cloud consisting entirely of ice crystals (such as cirrus); to be distinguished in this sense from water clouds and mixed clouds.

Inertial Guidance. Guidance by means of acceleration measured and integrated within the craft.

Instrument Flight Rules (IFR). Rules specified by qualified authority (FAA) for flight under weather conditions such that visual reference cannot be made to the ground and the pilot must rely on instruments to fly and navigate.

Instrument Landing Systems (ILS). Radio transmitter at certain airports. These provide radio flight path to the "instrument runway"

Interline Agreements. Involving two or more air carriers.

Interstate. Existing or occurring in, between, or across, more than one state of the United States.

Intraline. Of or relating to a single air carrier.

Intrastate. Existing or occurring within a single state. Within one state of the United States.

Jet Engines. Air enters front of engine, is compressed, pushed into combustion chamber, fuel and air mixture is burned, expands, rotates a turbine, gases rush out through exhaust nozzle and create thrust.

Latin American Civil Aviation Commission (LACAC). A regional commission of the International Civil Aviation Organization (ICAO) with the purpose of coordination and application of ICAO objectives to air transportation between the member Latin American states and to solve intra-Latin American civil aviation problems.

Lease, Dry. An aircraft lease in which the leasor provides the aircraft only. Contrasted to a wet lease.

Lease, Wet. An aircraft lease in which the leasor provides both the aircraft and the crew. Contrasted to a dry lease.

Lift. Force opposite to gravity which if powerful enough causes a plane to "lift" and fly.

Lighter-Than-Air Aircraft. Aircraft that can rise and remain suspended by using contained gas weighing less than the air that is displaced by the gas.

Load Factor, Break-Even Passenger. The revenue passenger load factor in scheduled mixed service that is required for (a) scheduled passenger revenue less passenger traffic expense to equal (b) passenger capacity expense.

Load Factor, Revenue Passenger. The percent that revenue passenger-miles are of available seat-miles in revenue passenger services, representing the proportion of aircraft seating capacity that is actually sold and utilized.

Load Factor, Revenue Ton-Mile (Overall Revenue Load Factor and Ton Load Factor). The percentage of total capacity available for passengers, freight and mail which is actually sold and utilized. Computed by dividing total revenue ton-miles actually flown by total available ton-miles.

Load Factor, Standard. A passenger load factor calculated and used by the Board as a measure for use in determining the fare level and structure (which see) for rate-making purposes. An optimizing standard used in rate-making that is intended to act as a stimulus for efficient aircraft utilization and capacity.

Mach Number. The ratio of true airspeed to the speed of sound.

Mail, Containerized. United States mail, tendered by the postal service in aircraft unit load containers to the air carrier to be transported at containerized rates.

Maintenance. Inspection, overhaul, repair, preservation, and the replacement of parts, but excludes preventive maintenance.

Major Alteration. An alteration not listed in the aircraft, aircraft engine, or propeller specifications.

Medical Certificate. Acceptable evidence of physical fitness on a form prescribed by the Administrator.

Mileage-Prorate (Proration). Division of a joint rate or fare between the carriers concerned on an agreed basis of the percentage relationship of the mileage of each carrier to the total combined mileage.

Military Airlift Command (MAC). A major command organization of the United States Air Force which provides air transportation for personnel and cargo for *all* military services on a worldwide basis. MAC is the contractor for the U.S. Air Force's Logair and the U.S. Navy's Quick-Trans.

Mockup. A full-size or scale model of an aircraft or part of an aircraft assembled for the purpose of research or testing.

Mutual Aid Pact (Mutual Aid Agreement). A voluntary agreement, subject to CAB approval, among several air carriers (originally trunk carriers only, now may include local service carriers) providing for mutual assistance in the event any party's flight operations are shut down by a strike called before exhaustion of the procedures of the Railway Labor Act, or under other special conditions.

National Air Carrier Association (NACA). The trade association of the U.S. supplemental air carriers.

National Air Transportation Association (NATA). The trade association of air taxi operators fixed-based operators.

Navigable Airspace. The airspace above the minimum altitudes of flight prescribed by regulations issued under the FAA act, and shall include airspace needed to insure safety to takeoff and landing of aircraft.

Noise. Any undesired sound.

Nonhub. A community enplaning less than 0.05 percent of the total passengers in all services and all operations for all communities within the 50 States, the District of Columbia and other U.S. areas designated by the Federal Aviation Administration.

Nonscheduled. Of or relating to air transport services or operations performed pursuant to chartering of aircraft or other activities not constituting an integral part of services performed pursuant to published schedules and related non-revenue operations.

Normal Shock Wave. A shock wave perpendicular, or substantially so, to the direction of flow in a supersonic flow field. Sometimes shortened to "normal shock."

Notice of Proposed Rulemaking. An announcement to the public that an amendment to the FAA or Civil Aeronautics Board's regulations is being considered. Interested persons are given an opportunity to comment or otherwise participate in developing the final amendments.

Nucleating Agent (or Nucleant). In cloud physics, any substance that serves to accelerate the nucleation of cloud particles. Nucleating agents may themselves be nuclei (silver iodide, salt, sulfer dioxide, dust) or they may enhance the nucleation environment (dry ice, propane spray).

Nucleation. Any process by which the phase change of a substance to a more condensed state (condensation, sublimation, freezing) is initiated at certain loci (see nucleus) within the less condensed state.

Nucleus. In physical meteorology, a particle of any nature upon which, or the locus at which, molecules of water or ice accumulate as a result of a phase change to a more condensed state; an agent of nucleation.

Official Airline Guide (OAG). A bimonthly publication of the scheduled operations and service of the air carriers. Printed in a format to show service and fares to one city from all other cities where direct or simple connecting service is available, with separate editions for North America, Worldwide, and Air-cargo services.

Omni Range. Visual Omni Range (VOR). A navigational aid; a VHF radio transmitter which sends out 360 "courses" or "bearings". Aircraft use VORs to determine their position, and use those "with voice" as radio communications stations.

On-Line. Of or relating to installations and facilities, operations, or traffic within the system of scheduled service of one air carrier.

On-Time Performance. The number and percentage of aircraft, flights arriving on time, or within 15 minutes, of the carrier's published scheduled arrival time for any specified flight or group of flights during any specified period.

Operation(s), Aircraft. The use of aircraft, for the purpose of air navigation and includes the navigation of aircraft. Any person who causes or authorizes the operation of aircraft, whether with or without the right of legal control (in the capacity of owner, lessee, or otherwise) of the aircraft, shall be deemed to be engaged in the operation of aircraft within the meaning of the Federal Aviation Act.

Operation(s), Air Freight Forwarder. The operations of the reporting forwarder conducted under its own air way bills (or other documents serving the same purpose), and not its operations as an agent of a shipper or of a direct air carrier.

Operation(s), Domestic. Flight stages within the 50 states of the United States and the District of Columbia including operation between States separated by foreign territory or major expanses of international waters.

Operator, Air Taxi. A classification of air carriers which directly engage in the air transportation of persons or property or mail in any combination of such transportation and which: (1) do not, directly or indirectly, utilize large aircraft; (2) do not hold a certificate of public convenience and necessity or other economic authority other than that provided in Part 298 of the Board's Economic Regulations; and (3) have and maintain in effect liability insurance coverage in compliance with Board requirements.

Operator, Commercial. One of a class of air carriers operating on a private for-hire basis, as distinguished from a public or common air carrier, holding a commercial operator certificate, issued by the Administrator of the Federal Aviation Administration (pursuant to Part 45 of the Civil Air Regulations) authorizing it to operate aircraft in air commerce for the transportation of goods or passengers for compensation or hire.

Operator, Fixed-Base. One who conducts a business operation at an airport or airfield, involving the selling and/or servicing of aircraft, giving flying instruction, making charter flights, etc.

Operator, In-House Tour. A division or department within the corporate framework of a direct air carrier which engages in tour wholesaling.

Operator, Tour. As used in various parts of the Board's Economic Regulations: A person which acts as an indirect air carrier by organizing, selling and operating tours by charter air transportation. Within the travel industry, TOUR OPERATOR is used interchangeably with tour wholesaler.

Origin (see also, Destination). The first point in the itinerary and the point where the passenger (or cargo) first boards a carrier at the beginning of the itinerary.

Orographic Lifting. The lifting of an air current caused by its passage up and over mountains.

Overflight. A scheduled flight which does not stop at an intermediate point in its scheduled route because: (a) the point is certified as a flag stop (which see), and there is no traffic to be deplaned or enplaned; (b) the carrier has received authority to temporarily suspend service to that point; (c) weather conditions or other safety and technical reasons do not permit landing; or (d) for any other reason. The aircraft need not fly directly over the point.

Over-The-Top. Above the layer of clouds or other obscuring phenomena forming the ceiling.

Passenger-Mile. One passenger transported one mile.

Payload. The actual or potential revenue-producing portion of an aircraft's takeoff weight, in passengers, free baggage, excess baggage, freight, express, and mail.

Pilotage. Navigation by visual reference to landmarks.

Pitch. The movement of a plane when it noses down or up. The horizontal tail sections help control pitch.

Point. "Point" when used in connection with any territory or possession of the United States, or the States of Alaska and Hawaii, means any airport or place where aircraft may be landed or taken off, including the area within fifty-mile radius of such airport or places.

Point of Origin. Where flight originates, begins.

Pooling. An agreement between two or more air carriers to share revenue in particular markets in some predetermined ratio regardless of traffic carried by each individual carrier. Unlawful without prior approval from the CAB.

Powerplant. The engine and related parts responsible for the propulsion of the plane.

Precipitation. Any or all of the forms of water particles, whether liquid or solid, that fall from the atmosphere and reach the ground.

Precipitation Echo. A type of radar echo returned by precipitation.

Precision Approach Procedure. A standard instrument approach procedure in which an electronic glide slope is provided, such as ILS and PAR.

Pressurized. Containing air, or other gas, at a pressure that is higher than the pressure outside the container.

Prohibited Area. Designated airspace within which the flight of aircraft is prohibited.

Public Aircraft. Aircraft used only in the service of a government, or a political subdivision. It does not include any government owned aircraft engaged in carrying persons or property for commercial purposes.

Pyrotechnic Generator. A type of silver iodide smoke generator in which the silver iodide forms as a part of the pryotechnic fuel mixture, capable of an extremely high output of silver-iodide nuclei.

Radiosonde. A balloon-borne instrument for the simultaneous measurement and transmission of meteorological data.

Rate. The amount per unit stated in the applicable tariff for the transportation of property (including the amount for chartering a plane) and includes "charge" unless the context otherwise requires.

Rate, Joint. A rate, published as a single factor, that applies to transportation over the lines or routes of two or more carriers and which is made and published by arrangement or agreement between such carriers, evidenced by concurrence or power of attorney.

Rate, Through. The total rate from point of origin to destination. It may be a local rate, a joint rate, or combination of separately established rates.

Rating. A statement that, as a part of a certificate, sets forth special conditions, privileges, or limitations.

Rebate. The practice of charging, demanding, collecting, or receiving less compensation for air transportation, or for any service in connection therewith, than the rates, fares, or charges specified in the air carrier's then currently effective tariffs on file with the Board.

Relative Wind. Movement of the air in relation to the whole, total, movement of the aircraft. The relative wind is opposite to the total mass movement of an aircraft.

Reporting Point. A geographical location in relation to which the position of an aircraft is reported.

Retrofit. To modify an aircraft or aircraft part, after the aircraft has come off the production line or gone into service, for the purpose of incorporating changes made in later models or to make required improvements.

Roll. Rotation around plane's longitudinal axis, rolling movement begun by lowering a wing.

Rotorcraft. A heavier-than-air aircraft that depends principally for its support in flight on the lift generated by one or more rotors.

Route. A system of points to be served by an air carrier as indicated in its certificate of public convenience and necessity. A route may include all points on a carrier's system or may represent only a systematic portion of all of the points within a carrier's total system.

Salt Seeding. Cloud seeding with salt particles, a technique that has been applied to warm (non-supercooled) clouds and fog on the principle that the hygroscopic droplets of salt solution will grow at the expense of other particles.

Service, Charter (Charter Flight). Nonscheduled air transport services whereby the party or parties receiving transportation obtains exclusive use of an aircraft at published tariff rates and the remuneration paid by the party receiving transportation accrues directly to, and the responsibility for providing transportation is that of, the accounting air carrier.

Service, Irregular. Nonscheduled inter-airport air transport services that do not constitute an integral part of scheduled services to certified points, and where each passenger or property shipment is individually documented at published tariff rates (other than charter rates) and the remuneration paid by each party receiving transportation accrues directly to, and the responsibility for providing transportation is that of, the accounting air carrier.

Service, Mixed. Transport service for the carriage in any combination of first-class, coach (tourist), and/or economy (tourist) passengers on the same aircraft. May include freight, express, and/or mail, but excludes all-first-class, all-coach and all-economy service.

Service, Nonscheduled. Includes transport service between points not covered by certificates of public convenience and necessity issued by the Civil Aeronautics Board to the air carrier; services pursuant to the charter or hiring of aircraft; other revenue services not constituting an integral part of the services performed pursuant to published schedules; and related nonrevenue flights.

Service, Scheduled. Transport service operated over an air carrier's certificated routes pursuant to published flight schedules, including extra section and related nonrevenue flights.

Service, Shuttle. A relatively low-fare, no-reservation no-frill service. The lower fare is based on the cost savings of high density seating, no reservations, and no meal or beverage service. This service is usually only offered in high traffic markets and may also require the passenger to carry his own baggage to the boarding gate.

Service, Single-Plane (Through-Plane Service). Air transport service provided between two cities so that passengers can make the trip between the two cities on the same plane, even though the flight involves one or more en-route stops.

Show Cause Order. More properly, but rather uncommon, "order to show cause". An order issued by the Civil Aeronautics Board directing the respondent to show cause why the Board should not adopt the findings and conclusions specified in the order.

Silver-Iodide Seeding. The world-wide "work-horse" method of cloud seeding, where, by any of several techniques, silver iodide crystals are introduced into the supercooled portions of clouds to induce the nucleation of ice crystals.

Simulator. A section of an aircraft built to imitate the operation of controls and avionics during flight; used in testing and training programs.

Slipping-Side Slip. Wing is lowered with nose held approximately straight. Used to lose altitude without gaining speed. Flaps perform the same function and are modern equipment.

Small Aircraft. Aircraft of 12,500 pounds or less, maximum certificated takeoff weight.

Societe Internationale De Telecommunications Aeronautiques (SITA). A reservations system for cross carrier (interline) recording of international reservations.

Solar Radiation. The total electromagnetic radiation emitted by the sun.

Sonic Boom. A noise caused by the shock wave that emanates from an aircraft or other object traveling in the atmosphere at or above the speed of sound.

Sonic Speed. The speed of sound; by extension, the speed of a body traveling at Mach 1. Sound travels at different speeds through different mediums and at different speeds through any given medium under different conditions of temperature, etc. In the standard atmosphere at sea level, sonic speed is approximately 760 miles per hour.

Space. 1. Specifically, the part of the universe lying outside the limits of the earth's atmosphere. 2. More generally, the volume in which all spatial bodies, including the earth, move.

Space Available. A term applied to passengers (cargo) who, for lack of reservations and/or for reduced-rate charges, must await the boarding of other passengers (cargo), and will not themselves be boarded unless there is additional space available on board the aircraft.

Spare Parts. Includes parts, appurtenances, and accessories of aircraft (other than aircraft engines and propellers), of aircraft engines (other than propellers), of propellers and of appliances, maintained for installation or use in an aircraft, aircraft engine, propeller, or appliance, but which at the time are not installed therein or attached thereto.

Stage Length, Average (Overall Flight Stage Length). The average distance covered per aircraft hop in revenue service, from take-off to landing. Derived by dividing the total aircraft miles flown in revenue services by the number of revenue aircraft departures performed.

Stall. Denotes loss of lift of aircraft lifting, airfoil, surfaces due to high angle of attack of the relative wind. Commonly associated with low-speed flying and/or steep bank or other abrupt change of direction.

Standard Atmosphere. A hypothetical vertical distribution of atmospheric temperature, pressure, and density which, by agreement, is taken to be representative of the atmosphere for purposes of pressure altimeter calibrations, aircraft performance calculations, aircraft and rocket design, ballistic tables, etc. Example: at sea level 29.92 inches of mercury pressure, 59° F. temperature.

Stop, Flag. A point on an air carrier's certificated route that is scheduled to be served only when traffic is to be picked up or discharged.

461

Stop, Nontraffic. An aircraft landing made for purposes other than the deplaning or enplaning of traffic. Refueling and aircraft maintenance are examples of nontraffic stops.

Stratocumulus. A principal, low-altitude, cloud type, consisting of a layer of rounded or roll-shaped elements which may or may not be merged and which usually are arranged in orderly files or a wave pattern.

Subcontractor. A business that contracts to provide service or materials necessary to the product of another contractor or manufacturer.

Sublimation. The transition of a substance from the solid phase directly to the vapor phase, or vice versa, without passing through an intermediate liquid phase.

Subsidy. Compensation paid by the Civil Aeronautics Board, pursuant to Section 406 of the Federal Aviation Act, to air carriers to enable them to maintain and continue the development of needed air services. In recent years, subsidy has been paid only to local service carriers and Alaskan carriers with the objective of assuring continued air service to small communities which do not generate sufficient traffic to support viable commercial operations. Trunkline carriers retain statutory eligibility for subsidy but no subsidy has been paid to trunklines since the 1950's.

Subsonic. In aerodynamics, dealing with speeds less than the speed of sound (see sonic speed), as in "subsonic aerodynamics."

Supercooling. The reduction of temperature of any liquid below the melting point of that substance's solid phase; that is, cooling beyond its nominal freezing point.

Supersonic. Pertaining to speeds greater than the speed of sound.

Surcharge, Fuel. A payment made by a passenger as an incremental fare charge to offset the increasing cost of aircraft fuels.

Synoptic. In general, pertaining to or affording an overall view.

Target Area. In a weather modification project, the area within which the effects of the weather modification effort are expected to be found.

Tariff. The notice of fares and rates applicable to the transportation of persons or property, and the rules relating to or affecting such fares and rates or transportation.

Tariff, Rate. A tariff containing rates and charges for the air transportation of property, other than baggage accompanying or checked by passengers.

Taxiing. Movement of aircraft on the ground under its own power.

Thermal. Pertaining to heat or temperature. Example: a column of heated air rising from a warm area on the surface, a "thermal."

Thrust. The force pushing, or pulling an aircraft or rocket forward. Also, the force exerted by burning gases in a jet engine.

Thrust Reverser. The mechanism at the rear end of a jet engine which blocks the forward thrust or power to help stop an aircraft when it lands.

Ticket. A printed document that serves as evidence of payment of the fare for air transportation. Generally, this takes the form of the standard Air Traffic Conference ticket which is composed of an auditor's coupon, agent's coupon, flight coupon(s), and passenger's coupon. It authorizes carriage between the points and via the routing indicated, and also shows the passenger's name, class of service, carrier(s), flight number(s), date of travel and all conditions of the contract of carriage.

Ticket Conjunction. Two or more tickets concurrently issued to a passenger and which, together, constitute a single contract of carriage.

Ton-Mile. One ton transported one mile. Ton-miles are computed by multiplying the aircraft miles flown on each flight stage by the number of tons transported on that stage.

Tour, Inclusive. A round-tour which combines air transportation (pursuant to an inclusive tour charter or group or individual inclusive tour tariffs in scheduled service) and land services, and which meets additional requirements of minimum days accommodations, and other land services to be included in the price of the tour.

Tour Package. A joint service that gives a traveler a significantly lower price for a combination of services than could be obtained if each had to be purchased separately by the traveler. Thus, the total price of a package tour might include a roundtrip plane ticket, hotel accommodations, meals, several sightseeing bus tours, and theater tickets.

Tour Wholesaler. A person who contracts with hotels, sightseeing and other ground components to provide ground packages, for sale to individuals, through travel agents and direct air carriers, to be used in conjunction with scheduled air transportation.

Tracer. An easily detectable substance injected into the atmosphere for the purpose of subsequent measurement and reconstruction and its history (trajectory, diffusion, etc.). Also, search for lost baggage or property.

Traffic, Blind-Sector. Revenue traffic, carried by a foreign air carrier on a flight operating in air transportation, which is enplaned at one foreign point and deplaned at another foreign point, where at least one of such points is not named as a terminal or intermediate point in the carrier's applicable foreign air carrier permit issued by the Board. No foreign air carrier may carry any such traffic unless specifically authorized in their foreign air carrier permit or by a special authorization from the Board.

Traffic, Bridge Segment. Traffic enplaned at a point preceding a service segment, flowing through the service segment and deplaning at a point beyond the service segment.

Traffic, Connecting. Passengers who deplane and/or cargo which is unloaded from one flight, at an intermediate point in the passenger's itinerary or cargo's routing, to board or be loaded on another flight, either on the same carrier or another carrier.

Traffic Density. The total amount or units of traffic traveling or carried; between two points; over a route, over a route segment; on a flight; or measured against any other unit(s) of reference.

Traffic, Down-Line Segment. Traffic enplaned at the segment origin, transported over the service segment, and destined for deplanement at a point beyond the segment destination (CAB).

Traffic, Enplaned. A count of the number of passengers boarding and tons of cargo loaded on an aircraft.

Traffic, Interline. Traffic (passengers and/or cargo) transported over the lines or routes of two or more carriers as a single movement with an interline connection.

Traffic, Intraline. Traffic (passengers and/or cargo) transported over the lines or routes of one carrier only.

Traffic, Local Segment. Traffic enplaned at the segment origin (which see) and deplaned at the segment destination.

Traffic Pattern. The traffic flow that is prescribed for aircraft landing at, taxiing on, or taking off from, an airport.

Trajectory. (Or Path). A curve in space tracing the points successively occupied by a particle in motion. At any given instant the velocity vector of the particle is tangent to the trajectory.

Transfer. An occurrence at an intermediate point in an itinerary where a passenger or shipment changes from a flight of one carrier to another flight of the same carrier or to another carrier, with or without a stopover (which see).

Transit. The movement of a passenger into and out of a point of call of the flight bearing the passenger, without transferring the passenger from one flight to another.

Transponder. A combined receiver and transmitter whose function is to transmit signals automatically when triggered by an interrogating signal.

Trip. In common speech, the term "trip" tends to include both the going and returning portions of a journey. In airline usage, it is important to distinguish between whether "trip" is used in a one-way or round-trip sense.

Turbine. A machine with which the blades of a rotor are driven by the pressure of flowing fluid, gases or air.

Turbofan. A turbojet engine which includes a special fan to increase air intake and engine thrust.

Turbojet. A jet-propulsion engine in which air is compressed and burned with fuel to turn a turbine and produce thrust.

Turboprop. A type of jet engine that uses a propeller driven by a turbine; the propeller pulls the plane and the turbine produces thrust to push the plane; also called a propjet engine.

United States (U.S.). The several States, the District of Columbia, and the several Territories and possessions of the United States, including the territorial waters and the overlying airspace thereof.

United States, Citizen of. Refers tro: (1) an individual who is a citizen of the united States or of one of its possessions; or (2) a partnership of which each member is such an individual; or (3) a corporation or association created or organized under the laws of the United States or any State, Territory, or possession of the United States, of which the president and two-thirds or more of the Board of Directors and other managing officers thereof are such individuals and in which at least 75 percent of the voting interest is owned or controlled by persons who are citizens of the United States or of one of its possessions.

United States, Continental. The 48 contiguous States, and the District of Columbia.

United States Territory. For statistical reporting purposes: areas or places under the possession and jurisdiction of the United States outside the 50 states of the United States and the District of Columbia (*e.g.*, Guam, Puerto, Rico, and the Virgin Islands).

Universal Air Travel Plan (UTAP). A credit card program operated by airlines, primarily for frequent travelers.

Upper-Air Observation. A measurement of atmospheric conditions aloft, above the effective range of a surface weather observation. Also called "sounding," "Upper-air sounding."

VFR Over the Top. The operation of an aircraft over-the-top under VFR when is not being operated on an IFR flight plan.,

Visual Flight Rules (VFR). Rules specified by qualilfied authority establishing minimum flying altitudes and limits of visibility to govern visual flight.

War Air Service Program (WASP). The program designed, pursuant to Executive Order 11490, to provide in time of national emergency for the maintenance of essential civil air routes and services, and to provide for the distribution and redistribution of air carrier aircraft among civil air transport carriers after withdrawal of aircraft allocated to the Civil Reserve Air Fleet (which see).

Water Vapor. (Also called aqueous vapor, moisture). Water substance in vapor form; one of the most important of all constituents of the atmosphere.

Weather Modification. The intentional or inadvertent alteration of weather by human agency.

Weather Radar. Generally, any radar which is suitable or can be used for the detection of precipitation or clouds.

Weight, Allowable Gross. The maximum gross weight (of the aircraft and its contents) which an aircraft is licensed to carry into the air on each flight stage.

Weight, Empty. The weight of the airframe, engines, propellers and fixed equipment of an aircraft. Empty weight excludes the weight of the crew and payload, but includes the weight of all fixed ballast, (unuseable fuel supply, undrainable oil, total quantity of engine coolant, and total quantity of hydraulic fluid).

Weight, Maximum Certificated Takeoff. The maximum takeoff weight authorized by the terms of the aircraft airworthiness certificate. (This is found in the airplane operating record or in the airplane flight manual which is incorporated by regulation into the airworthiness certificate).

Weight, Maximum Gross Takeoff. The maximum permissible weight of an aircraft and its contents at takeoff. Includes the empty weight of the aircraft, accessories, fuel, crew and payload.

Weight, Passenger. A standard weight of 200 lbs per passenger (including all baggage), used for all civil operations and classes of services.

Weight, Tare. A deduction from the gross weight of a shipment and its container made in allowance for the weight of the container. The empty weight of a container.

Wing Tip Vortices. Air movement from high pressure beneath airfoil (example, wing) to low pressure air above airfoil, above lifting surface. Vortices trail behind and below aircraft in flight.

Yaw. Turn left or right of the nose around a plane's vertical axis; a skid.

Yield. The air transport revenue per unit of traffic carried in air transportation. May be calculated and presented several ways (*e.g.*, passenger revenue per passenger-mile, per aircraft-mile, per passenger ton-mile and per passenger).

Zero G. Weightlessness.

GLOSSARY OF LEGAL TERMINOLOGY

The following are brief definitions of commonly used legal terms. For more complete definitions see law dictionaries. For example, *Black's Law Dictionary,* may be used.* (It is a comprehensive compilation of definitions of the terms and phrases of American and English jurisprudence).

Ab Initio. A Latin term meaning "from the beginning."

Action. The legal demand of one's right from another party made and insisted on in a court of justice. Form of suit for recovery of that which is one's due. — proceedings in a court by which one party prosecutes another.

Agency. Includes every relation in which one person acts for or represents another by latter's authority.

Answer. The document which the defendant in a civil lawsuit serves on the plaintiff or his attorney in answer to the summons and complaint.

Appeal. The proceeding by which a party to a lawsuit defeated in a lower court applies to a higher court (an appellate court) to determine the correctness of that decision. An APPELLATE COURT settles questions of law by reviewing cases. (Often courts of appeal have a panel of judges.)

Arbitration. A proceeding established by previous agreement in which both sides to a controversy submit their dispute to persons designated or to be chosen.

Arraignment. That part of a criminal case in which a person charged with a crime is brought before the court and advised of the charge against him.

Arrest. The legal apprehension and restraint of a person charged with a crime so that he may be brought to court to stand trial.

Assault. A threat or an attempt to do physical harm

Assignment. The transfer of a right or interest in property by one person to another.

Assignment for the Benefit of Creditors. The transfer by an insolvent debtor of all of his property to another for the purpose of arriving at an adjustment with his creditors.

Assignment of Error. The statement of the plaintiff's case on a writ of error, setting forth errors complained of.

Attachment. The proceedings by which a person or his property are restrained in accordance with a direction of a civil court to secure payment of a judgment or the presence of the person when the case is being tried.

Attorney in Fact. A person who has been appointed by another to transact business for him and in his name. He does not have to be a lawyer.

Auction. A public sale of property to the highest bidder by a person called the AUCTIONEER, who must be licensed to carry on such a business.

Award. The determination of a judicial body which grants a sum of money to the winner.

Bail. Security given to a court in exchange for the release of a person in custody to assure his presence in court later.

Bail Bond. An undertaking by which someone obligates himself to pay the amount of the bail if the person out on bail fails to appear when required.

Bailment. The relationship created when the owner of property, the BAILOR, delivers it to another, the BAILEE, for some specific purpose.

Bankruptcy. A proceeding under the federal laws, dealing with the property and debts of an insolvent debtor and his creditors.

Barratry. The act of encouraging lawsuits and inciting quarrels which ultimately end in litigation.

Battery. Actual physical beating or striking.

Bench Warrant. A process issued by a court ordering the apprehension and arrest of a person guilty of contempt of court or indicted for a crime.

Bill of Attainder. Is forbidden by the Constitution; is any law which creates a forfeiture of a person's property.

Bill of Exchange or Draft. A negotiable instrument which requires the drawee to pay a designated sum of money to the payee or subsequent holder.

Bench. A seat of judgment or a tribunal for the administration of justice. The judges taken collectively, as distinguished from attorneys, counselors or advocates, who are called "the bar."

---

*Black's Law Dictionary by Henry C. Black, 4th ed. by publisher's editorial staff, St. Paul, Minn.: West Publishing Co., 1968. 1882 pp.

Bill of Lading. An agreement between a shipper of freight and a common carrier.

Bill of Particulars. A document in a lawsuit which amplifies the information set forth in the complaint.

Binder. Used in insurance and real estate; a preliminary agreement.

Blank Endorsement. Results when an endorser of a negotiable instrument merely signs his name without specifying the person to whom he is negotiating it.

Bona Fide Purchaser for Value. Used in contracts and negotiable instruments, describes any person who acquires property or negotiable instruments in good faith and for a valuable consideration.

Bond. An undertaking; an obligation assumed by the person who executes it.

Boundary. The separation, natural or artificial, marking the confines, limits, or line of division of two contiguous states.

Breach of Contract. Failure, without legal excuse, to perform any promise which forms the whole or part of a contract.

Breach of the Peace. Any act committed by a person in a public place which disturbs the public peace and tranquility.

Brief. The "memorandum of law" prepared by each side in a suit.

Burden of Proof. The duty of a party in a lawsuit to present sufficient proof to sustain the charges that he made.

Burglary. The crime committed by a person who breaks into and enters the home of another without permission and with intent to commit a crime.

Calendar. The list of cases which is established in each court to determine their orderly disposition and trial.

Capital Crime or Offense. One which is punishable by death.

Cause of Action. The legal basis on which the plaintiff relies for his recovery against the defendant.

Certificate of Incorporation. Also called a CHARTER, is the document which creates the corporation.

Certiorari. Appellate proceeding for re-examination of action of inferior tribunal, or auxiliary process to enable appellate court to obtain further information in pending cause.

Chancery. A court of equity.

Charge. In criminal law, is the accusation made against a person that he committed a crime. In a civil action, it is the instructions on the law which the court gives the jury at the end of the trial.

Charter. Another name for the CERTIFICATE OF INCORPORATION.

Check. A negotiable instrument, a written order to a bank by its depositor requesting payment of a definite sum of money to the order of the named payee.

Civil Law. That division of municipal law occupied with the exposition and enforcement of civil rights as distinguished from criminal law. That rule of action which every nation or city has established peculiar to itself.

Coinsurance. Is a provision in fire insurance policies which requires the premises to be insured for an agreed proportion of their value.

Collusion. An agreement between two or more persons to proceed fradulently to the detriment and prejudice of an innocent and ignorant third party.

Comity Among Nations. The friendly relation existing between them so that the laws and institutions of each are recognized by the other.

Common Carrier. Any transportaiton facility which publicly undertakes to transport persons or property for a stated price and without restriction.

Common Law, is the body of law which was accumulated and collected from the decisions of the English courts and adopted as the basis of law in this country. Rests upon custom, not ethical superiority; not changeable by judgements. It is not modern civil law or canon (church) law.

Comparative Negligence. A principle of law which takes into account the negligence of both sides in an accident.

Compensatory Damages. A sum of money awarded to a plaintiff by a court or a jury as a fair and just recompense for injury sustained to person, property or reputation.

Complainant. In a criminal action the complainant is the person who, as a victim of a crime, brings the facts to the attention of the police authorities.

Complaint. The document prepared and submitted by the plaintiff in a lawsuit which sets forth his claims for recovery against the defendant. A complaint may contain several "causes of action."

Composition of Creditors. An agreement by the creditors of a person who is financially insolvent to accept a sum less than the full amount of his indebtedness.

Comprehensive Aircraft Insurance Coverage. A policy of insurance which covers the owner of an automobile for damage to his aircraft resulting from certain stated risks.

466

Condemnation. The legal machinery by which an authorized governmental agency takes private property for public use.

Condition. A provision in a contract which must be performed to make it effective.

Conditional Sale. An agreement which gives the buyer possession of personal property but not ownership until full payment is made.

Confession, (of a debt) by a debtor in a civil action under certain conditions gives the creditor the right to enter judgment for the debt. In a criminal action, it is the acknowledgment and admission of guilt to a crime with which a person is charged.

Confiscation. The act of taking private property as a penalty and a forfeit for public use.

Consent. A voluntary accord between two parties in their contractual relationship.

Consignment. The delivery of merchandise by the owner to the CONSIGNEE to be sold and the proceeds, less commission, to be returned to the CONSIGNOR.

Consolidation. The combination of two or more corporations into one, or the combination of two or more lawsuits between the same parties to be tried together.

Conspiracy. An agreement between two or more people to commit an illegal act.

Construction (of a contract or a will) is the interpretation which the court gives to its terms to arrive at the intention.

Contempt. The disobedience of the rules, orders and processes of the court or a legislative body.

Continuance. The adjournment or carry-over of a legal proceeding to another scheduled date.

Contraband. Any article which has been declared illegal for export or import.

Contract. An agreement between two or more parties enforcible in a court of law.

Conveyance. A document by which ownership in real estate is transferred.

Corporation. A form of business organization created by state authority as a legal entity.

The Corporation Incorporators are persons who form a corporation and sign the certificate of incorporation.

Corpus Delicti. The legal term for the actual tangible evidence to prove that the crime was committed.

Cost, Insurance and Freight (C.I.F.) are terms in a contract for the sale of merchandise which requires the seller to pay the insurance, cost and freight of the goods to the point of destination.

Counterclaim. The claim for relief made by the defendant in a lawsuit as part of his defense to the plaintiff's action.

Crime. A positive or negative act in violation of penal law; an offense against the State.

Criminal Law. That branch of the law which treats crimes and their punishments. Laws defining and prohibiting crimes and their punishments.

Damages. The award of money assessed to compensate for financial loss to the injured party in a lawsuit. GENERAL or COMPENSATORY damages are awarded to pay in money for the pain, suffering and injury which was sustained. SPECIAL DAMAGES are awarded for any financial loss which flows directly from the other injury sustained. This would include medical and hospital expenses and actual loss of earnings. PUNITIVE or EXEMPLARY DAMAGES are awarded in a tort action where a willful or malicious act was involved. The purpose of such damages in addition to others imposed is to punish the responsible party. This may occur in defamation where the act was particularly vicious and malicious. NOMINAL DAMAGES are imposed when the injury is negligible yet the responsibility of the party at fault must be established.

Decision. The determination of the court which deposes of the case under consideration.

Decree. A formal determination of a court, usually made in writing.

Deed. A document which transfers ownership to real estate.

Defamation. A statement made orally or in writing which injures a person's reputation in the community.

Default. A legal term meaning the failure to appear and defend a lawsuit.

Defendant. The person in a lawsuit who is charged with responsibility for creating a situation against which the plaintiff wants relief.

Defense. The justification interposed by the defendant of a lawsuit which is intended to relieve him of blame and of financial obligation.

Deliberation. The consideration given by the jury to a case so that it may arrive at its verdict.

Demurrer. The answer of a defendant to a charge made against him which denies legal responsibility though it may concede the plaintiff's contention.

Deposition. A written statement made under oath. The person making it is called the DEPONENT.

Disaffirm in law means to renege or to refuse to go through with an agreed transaction.

Dismiss. To dismiss an action or suit is to send it out of court without any further hearing or consideration.

Dissenting Opinion. The opinion (usually formal, written) in which a judge announces his dissent (lack of agreement) from the conclusions held by the majority of the court (panel of judges), and expounds his own views.

Double or Former Jeopardy. Prevents a person from being tried twice for the same offense.

Double Indemnity. A separate agreement in an insurance policy which obligates the company to pay twice the face amount of the policy if the insured dies as a result of "violent and accidental means."

Draft. A negotiable instrument, a written demand made by one person to another to pay a designated sum of money to a named third person known as the "payee."

Due Process guarantees that no person shall be deprived of his life, liberty or property without "due process of law."

Durress. Force, pressure or threats which induce a person to act in a manner contrary to his own wish.

Easement. The right of a landowner to use the land of his neighbor. A liberty, privilege, advantage without profit which the owner of one parcel of land may have in the lands of another.

- Flow as a stream
- a way over his land (for access)
- gate-way.
- Private (few)
- Public easement (all)
- something necessary for use, enjoyment of a parcel of land.

Eminent Domain. The power of the government to acquire land or property of a private individual for a necessary public purpose.

Equity. Natural right, fairness and justice. Justice between two conflicting persons. Rules, principles, and maxims of law. Equity & Chancery interchangeable terms. May indicate particular courts or areas of juris prudence. Courts of common law are outside of courts of equity. Equity grants relief to a party in cases when the mere payment of money is not adequate to help him.

Error. A mistaken judgment, incorrect belief, mistaken conception, of the facts of application of law.

Escheat. The return of land and property to the state if there is no person legally entitled to inherit.

Estate. The property belonging to a recently deceased person which must be administered and distributed in accordance with a will or the laws of intestacy.

Estoppel results when a person by his prior attitude caused someone to act in reliance upon it. A subsequent change of attitude will not be permitted or recognized by the court.

Eviction. The act which deprives a person of the use and enjoyment of property.

Ex Parte indicates that an application has been made by one litigant without notice to the other.

Exceptions. Objections which a litigant may make to the court's ruling or its charge to the jury.

Executed means that all of the terms of a contract have been fulfilled. An EXECUTORY contract still has some provisions to be complied with.

Executor (feminine: Executrix). A person named in a will to take charge of the administration of the estate subject to the supervision of the court.

Express Contract. One which has all of its provisions agreed upon by the parties. A contract is IMPLIED when it is created by the behavior of the parties.

Extended Coverage. An agreement of insurance which covers damage resulting from windstorm, hail, riot, explosion and similar stated risks.

Extortion. The offense of taking money or property from a person by threat or duress or under pretense of authority.

Extradition. The process by which fugitives from one state are returned by the authorities of another state in which they were apprehended.

Factor. Also known as a commission merchant, is a person who takes property or merchandise of another to sell for him. It is also a person (or company) who takes over the accounts receivable of a business to collect the moneys due.

Fair Preponderance of the Credible Evidence. The measure of evidence required in a civil case for the plaintiff to prevail over the defendant. This is to be distinguished from the requirement in a criminal case that the defendant be found guilty BEYOND A REASONABLE DOUBT.

Federal. Belonging to the general government or union of states. Organized under the Constitution or laws of the United States, (American law.)

Felony. A crime which is punishable by a term in a state prison. Conviction of a felony deprives a person of his civil rights. A person convicted of such a crime is known as a FELON.

Forgery. The act of making, counterfeiting or altering any writing with an intent to mislead and deceive.

Foreclosure. A proceeding in a court of law by which the right of a person against real or personal property is determined and enforced.

Fraud. A false statement of a material fact made to induce someone to rely upon it to his financial loss.

Free Alongside Ship (F.A.S.). A provision in a contract of sale which requires the seller to deliver the merchandise at a designated place for loading aboard ship.

Free on Board (F.O.B.). A provision in a contract of sale which requires the seller to deliver the merchandise at a designated place, usually to a carrier.

Garnishee (Garnishment). A notice or proceeding which requires a person who owes money to a judgment debtor to pay the judgment creditor instead.

Grand Jury. A body of citizens properly selected according to law. It examines the evidence against a person suspected of a crime and determines if he is to be held for trial (indicted, accused, charged).

Guardian. A person appointed to be a protector of the interests of a minor. A GUARDIAN AD LITEM must be appointed for a minor if he is to prosecute or defend a lawsuit.

Habeas Corpus. A legal proceeding instituted by a writ, requires the person upon whom it is served to prove that he has a legal right to the custody of the person in whose name the writ was brought.

Hearing. A formal proceeding with issues of fact or law to be tried. Parties have a right to be heard. Much the same as a trial and may end in final order being issued.

Hearsay Evidence. Evidence brought out by the testimony of a witness at a trial which is not based upon his personal knowledge but rather on information he obtained from someone else, someone not available for cross-examination. This evidence is generally not acceptable.

Holder in Due Course. A person who has obtained a negotiable instrument in a regular business transaction for a valuable consideration and without knowledge that it has any defects.

Homicide. The killing of one human being by the act of another human being.

Indemnity, in insurance, is the reimbursement for loss sustained.

Indictment. A document prepared by the district attorney and approved by the grand jury which charges a person with the commission of a crime.

Infant. Also known as a MINOR, is a person under legal age, generally 21 or 18. (State law determines).

Injunction. An order of a court which prohibits a named person from performing certain acts.

Injury. Any wrong or damage to another; either in his person, rights, reputation, or property.

Insane. The term applied to a person who is suffering from a mental disease which prevents him from knowing the consequences of his acts or that they are wrong.

Insolvent. The condition of a business when the liabilities are greater than the assets, so that the claims of the creditors cannot be paid.

Insurable Interest. The required ownership of interest a person must have to be able to take out insurance.

Intent. The design, determination, or resolve with which a person acts.

Interest. The charge made for the loan and use of money. Also, a party may have a legal ownership in whole or in part in property expressed as "legal interest," in the property (real estate or personal; aircraft, parts, or other).

Interstate. As between two or more states.

Intrastate. Wholly inside, within, the boundaries of a state. Operations inside one state.

Joint Tenants. Persons who each own an equal interest in the same property, either real or personal.

Judgment. The formal entry of the court's decision between the plaintiff and the defendant. The winner to whom money is to be paid is the JUDGMENT CREDITOR. The one who owes the money is the JUDGMENT DEBTOR.

Jurisdiction. The legal authority which a court has to try a lawsuit. It is the authority, capacity, power or right to act.

Jury (sometimes called Petit Jury). A body of citizens of the county who are selected to hear and decide a case in a civil or criminal court. The jury ascertains the facts in a case. The judge then sets the sentence or damages and settles questions of law.

Last Clear Chance. A doctrine on which recovery for injury due to negligence is based. In those states where contributory negligence by the plaintiff defeats his right to recovery, this theory may be used as an exception if the defendant, the person causing the injury, had sufficient notice of the danger to which the plaintiff was exposed and had sufficient opportunity to avoid the accident but did not do so. If these facts can be proved, the plaintiff may still recover.

Lease. An agreement by which the owner of a property rents and permits it to be used by a tenant or LESSEE on payment of a consideration.

Libel. Any statement made in writing which is defamatory and injuries the reputation of an individual in the community. If the statement is such as to hold him up to contempt or ridicule or to charge him with the commission of a crime, it is LIBEL PER SE. A libel is also a term used to indicate an unclear title, a creditor's claim upon a property.

Licensee. A person who has been given permission to enter upon the land of another for a specific purpose.

Lien. A claim which a person has against the property of another which is in his possession.

Limited Partnership. Composed of general partners and limited partners. The latter are only responsible for the amount which they actually agreed to invest in the business.

Maritime Law. A traditional body of rules, practices, and precepts. Relates to commerce, navigation, and business at sea. Relates to ships, seamen, marine affairs.

Merger. The absorption of one corporation by another, including all of its assets. Its individual existence is subsequently discontinued.

Misdemeanor. A crime which is less grave than a felony, tried before a court of special sessions and punishable in accordance with the law.

Mistake. Prevents consent and a "meeting of the minds" in the formation of a contract.

Mortgage. A contract which places real property as security for the repayment of a loan.

Motion. A formal application made to a court asking for incidental relief during the progress of a lawsuit.

Motive, influences and induces the commission of a crime.

Murder. The killing of one human being by another with a deliberate and premeditated design to cause his death.

Necessary Parties, to a litigation, must be joined as parties plaintiff or defendant in order that all issues between them may be litigated without the need for subsequent lawsuits.

Negligence. The failure of a person to use that degree of care in a certain situation which he is by law obligated to use in order to protect the rights and property of others. WILFUL NEGLIGENCE is the deliberate failure of a person to exercise due care.

Negotiable Instrument. A written document which, when properly executed and delivered can be used as a means of exchange and credit in place of money.

Nonjoinder. The failure to make necessary persons parties to a lawsuit.

Nonsuit means that a lawsuit was dismissed because it was not property proved.

Novation results when a new contract, entered into by the same parties, supersedes a previous one made by the same parties concerning the same subject matter.

Nuisance. The tort which results when a person uses his property in such a manner as to cause damage, danger and discomfort to his neighbors.

Objection. The formal protest made by a litigant at a trial to record his disapproval of a question asked by his adversary.

Offense. Not a crime but a violation of some ordinance or some local municipal regulation.

Offer. The initial step in the formation of a contract. It contains certain terms which, if accepted, may result in a contract.

Opinion of the Court. A statement by which the court sets forth the factual and legal reasons for its decision.

Opinion Evidence. Is not based on provable fact but rather upon the opinion of the witness. Generally such evidence is not admissible at a trial.

Option. A collateral agreement in a transaction which gives one of the parties, or both, the right to choose a course of action. Examples are: an option to renew a contract, or an option to keep an offer open for a specific period before the offer is terminated.

Order of a Court. A formal direction requiring that a certain act be performed or restrained.

Ordinance. A regulation established by a local government to enforce and control certain necessary activities of the members of the community.

Overrule. To make void; annul; supercede; reject by subsequent action or decision.

Parties. The persons who take part in the performance of any act, or who are directly interested in any contract, affair, or conveyance. Persons actively concerned in the prosecution or defense of any legal proceeding.

Penal Laws. Those which prohibit an act and impose a penalty for the commission of it.

Pendente Lite. A Latin phrase which means "during the period while the action is pending".

Plaintiff. The person bringing an action, party or person who sues or complains.

Pleading. The formal written document, a "plea," which states the position of a litigant in a lawsuit. It may be a complaint, an answer or, if there should be a counterclaim interposed by the defendant, a reply.

Pledge. The use of personal property as security for the payment of a loan.

Power of Attorney. A document executed by one person giving another the right and authority to act for him in certain specific situations.

Premium. The consideration paid by the insured to the insurance company in return for which the company agrees to reimburse him for the loss agreed upon in the policy.

Precedent. An adjudged case or decision of a court of justice, comprises authority and example for similar or identical cases arising afterward, or similar points of law.

Prescription. The technical term for the means by which a person may acquire a right to an easement.

Prevail. To prevail is to be accepted, adopted, commonly used. To come into force, effect, general practice.

Prima Facie. Is that amount of proof which the plaintiff must show at the trial before the defendent will be required to prove his defense to the action. Defined as, "on the face of it," at first sight."

Promissory Note. A written document by which one person promises to pay money to the proper owner at a definite time.

Proof. That evidence presented at a trial which is believed by the judge or jury.

Property. That which belongs exclusively to one; that which is proper or peculiar to any person. Right of use and disposition which one may lawfully exercise over particular things or subjects.

Prosecutor. One who prosecutes another for a crime in the name of the government.

Proxy. The authority given by a stockholder of a corporation to another to vote at the annual meeting of the corporation.

Quantum Meruit or "amount deserved". The relief in money which is awarded to a plaintiff in an action based on a contract implied by law.

Quasi-Contract. A relationship created by law with the obligations of a contract.

Quorum. The number of people which must be present at a meeting of any organization before the business of the meeting can be properly transacted.

Ratification. Approval or confirmation.

Real Estate, Real Property or Realty. Land, an interest in land or any article which is so attached to land as to become a part of it.

Rebuttal. That proof presented at a trial by the plaintiff intended to overcome the evidence introduced by the defendant.

Receiver. A person appointed by the court to gather and hold property to be disposed of by order of the court.

Recidivist. A person who reverts to criminal activity.

Referee. A person appointed by the court to take testimony and hear evidence presented by both sides.

Remedy. The means by which a violation of a right is prevented, redressed, or compensated. The means by which a right is enforced.

Replevin. The process by which personal property is recovered when it is unlawfully detained.

Reply. The document submitted by the plaintiff to a lawsuit in answering the counterclaims of the defendant.

Res Ipsa Loquitur. "The thing speaks for itself." It is a theory of recovery for personal injury which presumes that under certain conditions the injury would not have occurred if the defendant had been careful.

Res Judicata. The legal defense that the issue presented has previously been adjudicated between the same parties.

Respondeat Superior. The principle in law which transfers liability to a principal for the negligent acts of his agent.

Respondent. Party answering a bill or other proceedings in chancery.

Restrictive Endorsement. Used in negotiating a negotiable instrument to a person for a specific task such as "for collection."

Remittitur. Plaintiff remits part of the damages awarded. Applies in cases where excessive damages have been awarded.

Risk. In insurance is the specific event covered by the policy which may cause loss or damage to the property insured.

Sale by Description. Refers to a transaction in which the merchandise is described in detail and the bulk must conform to that description.

Sale by Sample. Occurs when the buyer is shown a sample of the merchandise he is buying. When the merchandise is delivered, the bulk must conform in quality to the sample.

Satisfaction of Judgment. Is a document which states that a recorded judgment has been paid and satisfied.

Seal. The stamp, mark or other formal indication used on a contract to create a presumption of consideration. By legislation, the presence of a seal on a contract now has no additional legal effect.

Sequestration. The proceeding by which property is taken and sold to satisfy a judgement.

Slander. A defamation of a person's reputation made orally. If the statement accuses him of a crime or holds him up to ridicule and it is not true, it is called "slander per se."

Special Endorsement. An endorsement of a negotiable instrument which transfers it to a named person.

471

Special Pleading. When allegations (pleadings) of contending parties are not ordinary — are of complex nature — they are called special pleadings. i.e., not just a direct denial, but one which must include special or new matter in opposition.

Specific Performance. A remedy in equity available to a person who has no adequate remedy at law.

State. A sovereign nation, a government, a country, Or, the term "state," can mean a political subdivision in a republic, or union, or federation; for example, California.

Statute. Any law passed by a legislative body.

Statute of Limitations. A series of legal provisions which limit the time when a plaintiff may bring a lawsuit.

Stay of Proceedings. A temporary delay in the proceedings of an action, usually ordered by the court to compel one of the parties to comply with its requirements.

Stipulation. An agreement between the parties of their attorneys.

Subpoena. A process issued out of a court requiring a witness to attend. If he has any books or records in his possession, he will be served with a subpoena *duces tecum* ordering him to bring them with him.

Subrogation. The substitution of the person who pays the injured party so that he may proceed to recover against the person who was responsible for the damage.

Suit. Any proceedings by one person or persons against another or others in a court of justice. Plaintiff pursues in a court legal remedy or redress for injury or enforcement of a right.

Summary Proceeding. Usually is used in dispossessing a tenant to give the landlord back his property without undue delay.

Summons. The process by which a case is brought before the court by advising the defendant that there is a claim against him.

Surety. The person who promises to make good the obligation of another.

Surrogate. A judge who presides in the court where estates of deceased persons are administered.

Taking. A "taking" is the act of gaining or receiving a possession; to deprive one of the use or possession of property; to assume ownership.

Tenant. A person who rents or leases land or real estate from the landlord.

Tenants in Common. Persons who share ownership in the same property.

Substantive Law. That part of law which creates, defines, regulates as opposed to methods of enforcement.

Testimony. The presentation of evidence by a witness under oath.

Title. Ownership in property.

Tort. A private or civil wrong committed when a person's private right is interfered with. A violation of a duty imposed by a general law.

A wrong independent of a contract. The three elements of every tort action are: (a) Existence of legal duty from defendant to plaintiff. (b) Breach of duty. (c) Damage as proximate result.

Treaty. A formal agreement between nations.

Trespass. The act of coming upon the land of another without permission.

Ultra Vires. Any act committed by a corporation through its agent which is not empowered or authorized by its charter.

Undue Influence. Any threat or persuasion which overcomes or destroys a person's consent or will to act for himself

Usury. That rate of interest charged for the loan of money which is in excess of the rate authorized within the state.

Vendee. A buyer or purchaser. A VENDOR is one who sells.

Venue. A place, a county, in which injury is declared to have been done, or fact declared to have happened. Also, county or other geographical division in which an action or prosecution is brought for trial. Place or territory within which either party may require a case to be tried.

Verdict. The determination of a jury.

Verification. A statement made under oath which confirms the contents of an accompanying document.

Void. Means, without any legal or effectual force to bind.

Voidable. Refers to an agreement that is valid and binding but in which one of the parties has the right to avoid his responsibility.

Warehouse Receipt. A statement which sets forth that certain described merchandise is being stored in the warehouse.

Waiver. The act of relinquishing a right which a person has. A government may waive compliance with a regulation for good reason or in the public interest.

Warrant. A process of a criminal court which authorized search or seizure of persons or property.

Warranty. A collateral promise related to a contract.

Willful Misconduct. Voluntary conduct intractable; intentional, not accidental.

Writ. A process of a court ordering a public officer or a private person to do a certain act.

INDEX

473

474

A Bellanca in an unusual attitude.

Photograph courtesy Bellanca Aircraft Corportation.